Law and Practice on Public Participation in Environmental Matters

Public participation has become a recurring theme and a topical issue in the field of international environmental law, with many multilateral environmental instruments calling on states to guarantee effectively the concept in their laws and practices.

This book focuses on public participation in environmental governance, in terms of public access to environmental information and public participation in environmental decision-making processes. Drawing on the body of international best practice principles in environmental law and taking a comparative stance, Uzuazo Etemire takes Nigeria as a key case, evaluating its procedural laws and practices in relation to public access to information and participation in decision-making in environmental matters. In working to clarify and deepen understanding of the current status of environmental public participation rights in Nigeria, the book addresses key issues in environmental governance for developing and transitional countries and the potential for public participation to improve the state of the environment and public wellbeing.

This book will be of great interest to undergraduate students (as further reading) and post-graduate students, academics, researchers, relevant government agencies and departments, policy-makers and NGOs in the fields of international environmental law, environmental justice, environmental/natural resource management, development studies and international finance.

Uzuazo Etemire is a Lecturer in Law at the University of Port Harcourt, Nigeria, and formerly a Law Tutor at the University of Strathclyde, Glasgaw. He is also a Barrister and Solicitor of the Supreme Court of Nigeria.

Routledge Research in International Environmental Law

Available titles in this series:

International Environmental Law and the Conservation of Coral Reefs
Edward J. Goodwin

Environmental Governance in Europe and Asia
A Comparative Study of Institutional and Legislative Frameworks
Jona Razzaque

Climate Change, Forests and REDD
Lessons for Institutional Design
Joyeeta Gupta, Nicolien van der Grijp, Onno Kuik

Common Pools of Genetic Resources
Equity and Innovation in International Biodiversity Law
Evanson Chege Kamau and Gerd Winter

International Environmental Law and Distributive Justice
The Equitable Distribution of CDM Projects Under the Kyoto Protocol
Tomilola Akanle Eni-Ibukun

The Precautionary Principle in Marine Environmental Law
With Special Reference to High Risk Vessels
Benedicte Sage-Fuller

International Climate Change Law and Policy
Cultural Legitimacy in Adaption and Mitigation
Thoko Kaime

Culture and International Economic Law
Valentia Vadi and Bruno de Witte

Law and Practice on Public Participation in Environmental Matters
The Nigerian Example in Transnational Comparative Perspective
Uzuazo Etemire

Forthcoming titles in this series:

Human Rights Approaches to Climate Change
Challenges and Opportunities
Sumudu Atapattu

International Liability Regime for Biodiversity Damage
The Nagoya-Kuala Lumpur Supplementary Protocol
Akiho Shibata

Climate Change and Forest Governance
Lessons from Indonesia
Simon Butt, Rosemary Lyster and Tim Stephens

Climate Change and Human Rights
An International Law Perspective
Ottavio Quirico and Mouloud Boumghar

Ecological Restoration in International Environmental Law
Afshin Akhtarkhavari, An Cliquet and Anastasia Telesetsky

Natural Resources Law, Investment and Sustainability
Shawkat Alam, Jahid Hossain Bhuiyan, Carmen Gonzalez and Jona Razzaque

Sustainable Development Principles in the Decisions of International Courts and Tribunals
1992–2012
Marie-Claire Cordonier Segger and Yolanda Saito

Law and Practice on Public Participation in Environmental Matters

The Nigerian Example in Transnational Comparative Perspective

Uzuazo Etemire

Routledge
Taylor & Francis Group
LONDON AND NEW YORK

First published 2016
by Routledge
2 Park Square, Milton Park, Abingdon, Oxon, OX14 4RN

and by Routledge
711 Third Avenue, New York, NY 10017

First issued in paperback 2017

Routledge is an imprint of the Taylor & Francis Group, an informa business

British Library Cataloguing in Publication Data
A catalogue record for this book is available from the British Library

Library of Congress Cataloging-in-Publication Data
Etemire, Uzuazo, author.
Law and practice on public participation in environmental matters : the Nigerian example in transnational comparative perspective / Uzuazo Etemire.
pages cm. — (Routledge research in international environmental law)
Includes index.
Based on author's thesis (doctoral) - University of Strathclyde, 2014.
Includes bibliographical references.
ISBN 978-1-138-85418-5 (hbk : alk. paper) — ISBN 978-1-315-72225-2 (ebk)
1. Environmental law—Nigeria—Citizen participation. 2. Environmental policy—Nigeria—Citizen participation. I. Title.
KTA1507.E86 2015
344.66904'6—dc23 2015000768

ISBN 13: 978-1-138-09415-4 (pbk)
ISBN 13: 978-1-138-85418-5 (hbk)

Typeset in Baskerville by
Keystroke, Station Road, Codsall, Wolverhampton

Dedication

To my parents – Mr Benson Etemire and Mrs Maria Etemire – for their unwavering commitment and extensive sacrifices towards me over the years

Contents

Table of cases

Table of statutes and policies

Table of international instruments

Acknowledgements

As this book is an outgrowth of my PhD thesis, which was undertaken at the University of Strathclyde, Glasgow, I would like to start by expressing my deepest appreciation to my principal PhD supervisor, Professor Mark Poustie, for being an excellent academic mentor. Thank you for your unflinching support, research guidance and constructive advice throughout the execution of this research. In this regard, I would also like to thank my second PhD supervisor, Dr Hakeem Yusuf, for his insightful comments on drafts of this work and for constantly providing me with much-needed motivation to continue. I am also very thankful to Professor Jana Razzaque for her very useful recommendations that served to improve this work. I must also thank the Director of the Strathclyde Centre for Environmental Law and Governance, Dr Francesco Sindico, who made invaluable contributions to this research work and strongly urged me to waste no time in transforming and publishing the PhD thesis as a book. My PhD research – which constitutes the basis of this book – was fully supported by the Campbell Burns Scholarship of the Strathclyde Law School, for which I am immeasurably grateful.

I am immensely grateful to my parents – Mr Benson Etemire and Mrs Maria Etemire – and siblings – Dr Eloho Etemire, Engr Oreva Etemire, Barr Erezi Etemire and Evi Etemire – for their unceasing encouragement and support over the years. They are the best. My profound gratitude also goes to my uncle, Professor James Asalor, for being a major source of motivation to me, and for his fatherly and professional guidance over the years. Similarly, I deeply appreciate the supportive role of my uncle, Mr Joesph Asalor. I must also thank Chioma Ogbonna for helping me obtain some materials relevant to this work and for her encouragement throughout the course of the research.

The preparation of this work for publication benefited from the rich academic environment of the Faculty of Law, University of Port Harcourt (Uniport), Nigeria. In this light, I would like to thank profusely Professor Kaniye Ebeku for the astute leadership he has provided in the Uniport Faculty of Law as Dean, and for being a major source of inspiration to me. I am also grateful to Professor Lucky Worika for being a source of motivation and encouragement, as well as Barr (Mrs) Esther Joe for the lessons of professional ethics and dedication which she ably personifies. In the same vein, my profound gratitude also goes to other members of staff of the Uniport Faculty of Law for ensuring a warm, cordial and supportive academic work environment, and they include: Dr Edward Bristol-Alagbariya, Dr Mercy Chinda, Barr Charity Kaniye-Ebeku, Barr Nelson Sobere, Barr Agent Ihua-Maduenyi, Barr Menes Muzan, Barr Ijeoma Mgbeahurike, Barr Kalada Nonju, Barr Imade Gbobo, Barr Francis Anaeme, Barr Emmanuel Owushi and Mrs Nkechi Barinua.

Finally, I thank God for the grace to complete this work. Without Him I can do nothing – John 15:5.

Foreword

It is a great pleasure to be invited to write a foreword to a book written by one's former PhD student, the more so given it is to a book which is deservedly based upon an excellent thesis.

Although Nigeria has a long and rich tradition of public participation in governance, this tradition was dealt a severe blow by the colonial regime whose stringent laws on secrecy mirroring those in the UK were largely maintained following independence. Public participation gradually re-emerged in the environmental context under the military regime with the EIA decree (now Act) in 1992 and access to information received a considerable boost more generally following the return to democracy with the Freedom of Information Act 2011. The author seeks to measure these provisions against the standard of international good practice as represented by the provisions of the Aarhus Convention which he convincingly argues is directly relevant in the Nigerian context.

The value of effective access to information and public participation measures is clear in that they can enhance a range of constitutional-type values such as legitimacy of decision-making processes and accountability of public authorities as well as arguably enhancing the quality of environmental decision-making because official or developer views can be tested and indeed because participants can bring to bear local knowledge.

The book rightly identifies that significant strides have been made in Nigeria in terms of public access to information through the Freedom of Information Act 2011 and that this compares favourably – on paper at least – with some of the best international regimes. There remain considerable exemptions but that is not uncommon in FOI regimes elsewhere not least in the UK. By way of contrast, participation in environmental decision-making falls well short of good international practice, relying on the EIA Act from the years of military dictatorship. While this focuses only on projects, there is no provision for participation in the formulation of policies, plans, programmes and legislation. However, the author indicates how such provisions could be adapted from the Aarhus Convention.

Yet it is one thing having an effective legal regime for public participation in environmental matters, it is another that it is put into practice. Putting such a regime into practice in Nigeria is challenging because of good governance and official culture issues as well as practical barriers such as the multiplicity of languages, literacy issues, access to ICT etc. So there remain considerable implementation issues in Nigeria – the successful implementation of FOI regimes requires considerable culture change on the part of officials and education of citizens as to their rights as has been seen in other states which have adopted such measures such as India with the Right to Information Act 2005. It is not yet clear whether this culture change is occurring in Nigeria to the extent needed but it is vital that it does occur. Further work on the implementation of the access to information and participation regimes in Nigeria to gauge their effectiveness would be valuable. It is clear that the development of mobile technology and the persisting pre-colonial traditions of participation appear to offer positive ways forward.

Given the severe environmental degradation in parts of Nigeria, not least areas of the Niger Delta, it is apparent that creating greater transparency would enhance accountability and might lead ultimately to better environmental decision-making and improved environmental quality. This in turn could help to improve lives and might assist in contributing to improved security in the country as well as better governance. This is clearly a major challenge but the prize is certainly worth the attempt and Etemire does chart a possible way forward here.

The work is also significant as a fine example of transnational comparative research in that it seeks to identify international best practice in the field and compares Nigerian provisions with that. It therefore has a wider value and offers a model for such a project.

My congratulations to my former PhD student on this work and I hope it is the prelude to many other significant works in what I hope will be a highly successful academic career.

Professor Mark Poustie
University of Strathclyde, Glasgow
February 2015

Abbreviations

ACHPR	African Convention on Human and Peoples' Rights
ACHR	American Convention on Human Rights
AHRLR	African Human Rights Law Reports
All NLR	All Nigeria Law Report
CD	Compact Disc
CEE	Central and Eastern Europe
CLO	Civil Liberties Organisation
CtA	Court of Appeal
Defra	Department for Environment, Food and Rural Affairs
ECHR	European Convention on Human Rights
ECJ	European Court of Justice
ECR	European Court Reports
ECtHR	European Court of Human Rights
EFCC	Economic and Financial Crimes Commission
EHRR	European Human Rights Reports
EI(S)R	Environmental Information (Scotland) Regulation
EIA	Environmental Impact Assessment
EIR	Environmental Information Regulation
EU	European Union
FEPA	Federal Environmental Protection Agency
FEPC	Federal Environmental Protection Council
FHCt	Federal High Court
FOI	Freedom of Information
FSC	Selected Judgment of the High Court of Lagos
IAIA	International Association for Impact Assessment
ICCPR	International Covenant on Civil and Political Rights
ICJ	International Court of Justice
ICT	Information and Communications Technology
ILM	International Legal Materials
Inter-Am Ct HR	Inter-American Court of Human Rights
KB	King's Bench (Law Reports)
LRC (Const)	Law Reports of the Commonwealth, Constitutional Division
MOSOP	Movement for the Survival of the Ogoni People

MRA	Media Rights Agenda
NCLR	Nigerian Constitutional Law Report
NEITI	Nigerian Extractive Industries Transparency Initiative
NESREA	National Environmental Standards and Regulations Enforcement Agency
NGO	Non-governmental Organisation
NIS	Newly Independent States
NITEL	Nigerian Telecommunications Company
NMLR	Nigerian Monthly Law Reports
NNPC	Nigerian National Petroleum Corporation
NSA	National Security Agencies
NUJ	Nigerian Union of Journalists
NWLR	Nigerian Weekly Law Report
OAS	Organization of American States
Ofwat	Water Services Regulation Authority
PCC	Public Complaints Commissions
RTIA	Right to Information Act
SEA	Strategic Environmental Assessment
SERAC	Social and Economic Rights Action Centre
TV	Television
UILR	University of Ife Law Reports
UK	United Kingdom
UN	United Nations
UNCED	United Nations Conference on Environment and Development
UNDP	United Nations Development Programme
UNECA	United Nations Economic Commission for Africa
UNECE	United Nations Economic Commission for Europe
UNECLAC	United Nations Economic Commission for Latin America and the Caribbean
UNEP	United Nations Environmental Programme
UNGA	United Nations General Assembly
UNITAR	United Nations Institute for Training and Research
UNTS	United Nations Treaty Collection
US	United States (of America)
WACA	Selected Judgments of the West African Court of Appeal
WNLR	Western Nigerian Law Reports

1 Introduction

1.1 Research statement

This book is centrally concerned with a discussion and comparative analysis that seeks to answer the question of whether, or to what extent, Nigerian laws and practices on public participation in environmental matters are in consonance with what may be considered international best practice in this field and, where it is found to be inadequate, how best the *status quo* in Nigeria can be improved to meet those standards in order to ensure better public participation. Essentially, this book aims to analyse and, where necessary, recommend reforms to Nigerian laws relating to public participation in environmental matters, as a fundamental contribution to engendering and sustaining better practices in that regard.

This analysis and law-reform exercise will uniquely be carried out on the basis of a body of international best practice principles that, as argued, is politically and legally relevant to Nigeria. This will be done in general consideration of some socio-political and economic factors in the country that are relevant to environmental public participation. To add meaning and context to this enterprise, the value of (striving for) an effective legal system on public participation in environmental governance in Nigeria will, within reasonable limits, be addressed in this book from a historical, practical and theoretical perspective.

Thematically, this book focuses on 'public participation' in environmental governance from a procedural perspective, in terms of: (1) public access to environmental information; and (2) public access or participation in environmental decision-making processes. So even though it is widely understood that 'public participation' is a 'nebulous concept', which defies general definition for several reasons,[1] there is overarching agreement in the literature that the twin aforementioned participatory elements in their diverse forms are integral parts of the 'public participation' concept.[2]

1 See NP Spyke, 'Public participation in environmental decision-making at the new millennium: structuring new spheres of public influence' *(1999)* 26 *Boston College Environmental Affairs Law Review* 263, 267.

2 See TC Beierle and J Cayford, *Democracy in Practice: Public Participation in Environmental Decisions* (Washington: Resources for the Future, 2002) 6; and DN Zillman, 'Introduction to public participation in the twenty-first century', in DN Zillman, AR Lucas and G Pring (eds),

Although the twin concepts are usually treated separately in law considering their individual value, the vital interrelationship between them is well known: public participation in environmental decision-making without environmental access to information 'would seldom advance beyond shots in the dark'[3] and, in many cases, access to environmental information is only valuable if the information can meaningfully be put to use in a decision-making context.

In addition, it is important to acknowledge the procedural concept of 'public access to justice in environmental matters' as the third major 'pillar' of the notion of 'public participation' in environmental governance. In its broad form, this theme of 'access to justice' is essentially concerned with the right of the public to access *judicial* and *administrative* review procedures in order to enforce an environmental obligation or seek a remedy for an alleged or potential breach of a substantive or procedural environment-related right, in order to ensure effective compliance with, or implementation of the relevant environment-related law. It is noteworthy that, under this broad notion of 'access to justice', there is immense opportunity for non-judicial public institutions in general (and not only courts) to play a significant role in the enforcement of environmental rights through the institution of administrative review procedures.

Such administrative procedures would usually be created as a first tier access route to justice before the opportunity to approach a court. By design, such administrative routes can help aggrieved right holders avoid traditional potential limitations to seeking remedies through a court – e.g. complex court procedures, excessive delays in disposal of cases, prohibitive costs, etc. – which are usually more pronounced in developing countries like Nigeria, as this book will later show.

However, this book will aptly explore the 'access to justice' theme only as it relates to enforcing the rights of the public to access environmental information and participate in environmental decision-making processes. This limited discussion of the 'access to justice' theme is justified on the grounds that: first, it is all that is needed to achieve the specific aim of this book; and, second, considering especially the word-limit of this particular research, the unabridged concept of 'access to justice in environmental matters' is one that will be more properly and adequately explored in a different piece of research.

Moving on, although relatively meaningful progress has been made at the international environmental law level with respect to action-based legal regimes on the twin issues of public access to environmental information and decision-making processes, action in this regard seems almost non-existent in Nigeria. The facts surrounding the popular *Ogoniland* case – *Social and Economic Rights Action Centre (SERAC) and Another v Nigeria*[4] – (discussed later) lends credence to this position. The extensive environmental degradation over the years being

Human Rights in National Resource Development: Public Participation in the Sustainable Development of Mining and Energy Resource (Oxford: Oxford University Press, 2002) 1, 2.

3 NAF Popovic, 'The right to participate in decisions that affect the environment' (1993) 10 *Pace Environmental Law Review* 683, 694.

4 (2001) AHRLR 60.

perpetuated by the Nigerian Government and private corporations in the Niger Delta and around the country, and the impact of this upon the wellbeing of the public who for many years have, in diverse ways, protested their lack of access to environmental information and decision-making processes that affects them, all raise serious questions about the value or adequacy of Nigeria's environmental procedural laws and practices, where they exist.

Considering that Nigeria has signed and ratified many international environmental law regimes that require it legally to guarantee environmental public participation rights within the country, one's curiosity is aroused as to the extent to which this expectation has been met by Nigeria. It is largely against this background, which will be elaborated on in this book, that an in-depth research relating to Nigeria's environmental procedural laws and their potential to engender and sustain effective and acceptable practices was considered a valuable exercise.

In general, in employing a unique elaborate transnational comparative methodology in the analysis and argument for reform of Nigerian laws and practices on access to environmental information and decision-making processes in an effort to unravel the research question, this book threads a novel path that represents a valuable contribution to the field of procedural environmental rights. At the very least, the discussion in this book will clarify and deepen understanding of the developmental trends and current status of environmental public participation rights in Nigeria and in the international scene as relevant to Nigeria.

It will also enable the relevant Nigerian public institutions to take the necessary actions to strengthen the legal regimes on the subject matters and their implementation, where necessary. Generally, the analysis will substantiate and improve understanding of Nigeria's status in relation to its international environmental law obligations and commitments on public participation rights, and aid public institutions in bringing the country into compliance with the latter so as better to ensure the practical realisation of the ideals of the relevant laws. Furthermore, whilst Nigeria is the national case study in this book, it is generally representative of many developing countries/countries in transition as it relates to the book's thematic focus. Thus, the general discussion, findings and recommendations in this book would be relevant to several countries across Africa, Asia, Latin America and Eastern Europe.

1.2 Setting the scene

It is not justifiably possible to pinpoint the exact time in human history when public participation, in terms of public access to environmental information and decision-making processes, started. Whilst it may well be the case that there is not much written on the history of this subject,[5] it is clear that it has been practised

5 G Pring and SY Noe, 'The emerging international law of public participation affecting global mining, energy, and resources development', in Zillman, Lucas and Pring (eds) (n 2) 11, 17.

from prehistoric times – '[w]e can trace it from the earliest humans gathering around a fire collectively planning a hunt and other communal activities'.[6] It has also being posited that its 'roots run deep in many cultures',[7] including those in Nigeria (as will be discussed in Chapter 2) and, as some argue, the drive to participate is part of human nature[8] and '[t]hrough the ages . . . [humans] have found ways to be heard'.[9]

Contemporarily, however, it is understood that, to a limited extent, international law on public access to environmental information and decision-making processes can be traced as far back as the early 1900s.[10] Nonetheless, the 1948 Universal Declaration on Human Rights,[11] in view of its Articles 19 and 20 (on access to information and right to association), has been identified as having 'provided the kernels for generalised rights' on public access to information and decision making processes;[12] seemingly a build up from the first session of the United Nations (UN) in 1946, where the UN General Assembly established in Resolution 59(1) that: '[f]reedom of information is a fundamental human right and is the touchstone of all the freedoms to which the United Nations is consecrated.'

Likewise, the 1966 International Covenant on Civil and Political Rights (ICCPR)[13] guarantees the 'freedom to seek, receive and impart information and ideas of all kinds'.[14] A similar provision is contained in various regional human rights instruments,[15] and is widely interpreted as entailing not just a negative duty which constrains governments from restricting access to information, but also imposes a positive duty on states to ensure a public right of access to information.[16]

6 Ibid, 17–18. See also A Ahmed, 'Righting public wrongs and enforcing private rights', in C Bruch (ed), *The New "Public": The Globalization of Public Participation* (Washington DC: Environmental Law Institute, 2002) 39–52.

7 Pring and Noe (n 5) 17–18.

8 See MG Kweit and RW Kweit, *Implementing Citizen Participation in a Bureaucratic Society: A Contingency Approach* (New York: Praeger, 1981) 50; and P Bachrach, *The Theory of Democratic Elitism: A Critique* (Boston: Little, Brown and Co, 1967) 99.

9 K van der Zwiep, 'Public participation as an instrument for environmental protection', in MT Nagy, M Bowman, J Dusik, J Jendroska, S Stec, Kvan der Zwiep et al. (eds), *Regional Environmental Centre for Central and Eastern Europe (REC), Manual on Public Participation in Environmental Decisionmaking: Current Practices and Future Possibilities in Central and Eastern Europe* (Budapest, 1994), available at http://archive.rec.org/REC/Publications/PPManual/FeeBased/ch12.html (last accessed 26 January 2015).

10 See the 1909 International Boundary Waters Treaty (between US and Canada), available at http://online.nwf.org/site/DocServer/Boundary_Waters_Treaty_of_1909.pdf?docID=661 (last accessed 26 January 2015).

11 10 December 1948, UNGA Resolution 217A (III), UN Doc A/810, 71.

12 C Bruch and M Filbey, 'Emerging global norms of public involvement', in Bruch (ed) (n 6) 1, 3.

13 16 December 1966, 999 UNTS 171.

14 Ibid, art 19(2).

15 See European Convention for the Protection of Human Rights and Fundamental Freedoms (ECHR), 213 UNTS 221, 4 November 1950, art 10; American Convention on Human Rights (ACHR), 22 November 1969, 1144 UNTS 123, art 13; and the African Charter on Human and Peoples' Rights (ACHPR), 27 June 1981, 1520 UNTS 217, art 9.

16 For the ACHR see *Claude Reyes v Chile*, Inter-Am Ct HR (series C) No 151, 19 September 2006, para 77, and Inter-American Declaration of Principles on Freedom of Expression, approved by the Inter-Am Ct HR at its 108th Session, 19 October 2000, Principle 4; for the ACHPR, see 'Declaration of Principles on Freedom of Expression in Africa', approved by the African Commission on Human and People's Rights at its 32nd Session, 23 October 2002, arts I and IV(1);

Furthermore, key to the development of the public right to participation in decision-making processes is the human right to political participation[17] as provided in Article 25 of the ICCPR:

> Every citizen shall have the right and the opportunity . . .:
>
> (a) To take part in the conduct of public affairs, directly or through freely chosen representatives;
> (b) To vote and to be elected at genuine periodic elections . . .[18]

The above provision clearly reflects two elements: the right to take part in 'public affairs' – a term which 'covers all aspects of public administration, and the formulation and implementation of policy' at all levels of government;[19] and the right to vote and be voted for. It is in this light that Schwartz generally asserted that Article 25(a) should be recognised as encompassing and guaranteeing the public right to participate in environmental decision-making processes and access environmental information (in order fully to realise the aim of Article 25(a)),[20] subject only to reasonable restrictions. Although the UN Human Rights Committee had, arguably, erroneously interpreted Article 25 as only relating to elected representatives and appointed officials in the case of *Marshall and Ors v Canada*,[21] thus drawing criticism,[22] commendably, a 1999 UN General Assembly Resolution rebuts the UN Human Rights Committee's narrow interpretation of Article 25, as it provides that the latter includes:

> . . . the right, individually and in association with others, to submit to governmental bodies and agencies and organizations concerned with public affairs criticism and proposals for improving their functioning and to draw attention to any aspect of their work that may hinder or impede the promotion, protection and realization of human rights and fundamental freedoms.[23]

and for a more limited but developing interpretation under the ECHR see *Sdružení Jihočeské Matky v Czech Republic*, ECtHR, Application No 19101/03, 10 July 2006, *Társaság A Szabadságjogokért v Hungary*, ECtHR, Application No 37374/05, 14 April 2009, para 35, and W Hins and D Voorhoof, 'Access to state-held information as a fundamental right under the European Convention on Human Rights' (2007) 3 *European Constitutional Law Review* 114–26.

17 J Ebbesson, 'The notion of public participation in international environmental law' (1997) 8 *Yearbook of International Environmental Law* 51, 70.
18 For a similar provision, see ACHR, art 23; and ACHPR, art 13.
19 UN Human Rights Committee, 'General Comment No 25: The Right to Participate in Public Affairs, Voting Rights and the Right of Equal Access to Public Service (Art. 25)', CCPR/C/21/Rev.1/Add.7, adopted at the Committee's 57th session, 12 July 1996, para 5.
20 ML Schwartz, 'International legal protection for victims of environmental abuse' (1993) 18 *Yale Journal of International Law* 362, 369–70.
21 Communication No 205/1986, UN Doc CCPR/C/43/D/205/1986 (1991).
22 See e.g. Ebbesson (n 4) 70–72.
23 UNGA Declaration on the right and responsibility of individuals, groups and organs of society to promote and protect universally recognised human rights and fundamental freedoms, Annex to UNGA Resolution, A/Res/53/144, 8 March 1999, art 8.

Considering the above and more, it has been strongly asserted that public access to *environmental* information and decision-making measures draw from, and are rooted in the more general and established body of human rights.[24] Hence it is not surprising to find, for example, that even though the focus of a regime such as the UN Economic Commission for Europe (UNECE) Convention on access to information, public participation in decision-making, and access to justice in environmental matters[25] (Aarhus Convention – an important source in this book) is on environmental procedural rights, it does recognise in its preamble the vital link between public access to environmental information and decision-making processes and 'the enjoyment of basic human rights'. It is in this light that a number of international and regional human rights authorities have read the public right to access *environmental* information and decision-making processes into various established human rights, albeit from the limited anthropocentric perspective.

For example, the public right to participate in environmental decision-making processes has been upheld by the UN Human Rights Committee in several cases[26] on Article 27 of the ICCPR, which provides that: '[i]n those States in which ethnic, religious or linguistic minorities exist, persons belonging to such minorities shall not be denied the right, in community with the other members of their group, to enjoy their own culture, to profess and practise their own religion.' Regarding this provision, the UN Human Rights Committee has made clear that '[t]he enjoyment of those [minorities' religious and cultural] rights . . . require [states to put in place] . . . measures to ensure the effective participation of members of minority communities in decisions which affect them.'[27]

Other existing human rights that have been mobilised and reinterpreted as guaranteeing to an extent the public right to environmental information (whether requested or not) and decision-making processes include the right to life,[28] the right to private and family life,[29] the right to health and the right to a satisfactory environment.[30]

24 See G Händl, 'Human rights and perfection of the environment', in A Eide, C Krause and A Rosas (eds), *Economic, Social and Cultural Rights: A Textbook* (2nd edn, The Hague: Kluwer Law International, 2001) 303, 318.

25 25 June 1998, 2161 UNTS 447, available at http://www.unece.org/fileadmin/DAM/env/pp/documents/cep43e.pdf (last accessed 26 January 2015).

26 See *Ilmari Lansman and Ors v Finland* (1996) ICCPR Comm No 511/1992, para 9.5, and *Apirana Mahuika and Ors v New Zealand* (2000) ICCPR Comm No 547/1993, para 9.8.

27 UN Human Rights Committee, 'General Comment No 23: The Right of Minorities (Art 27)', CCPR/C/21/Rev.1/Add.5, adopted at the Committee's 50th session, April 1994, paras 7 and 6.1.

28 See e.g. *Oneryildiz v Turkey* [2004] ECHR 657, paras 62 and 84–88 (on accessing environmental information). See also *Maya indigenous community of the Toledo District v Belize*, Case 12.053, Report No 40/04, Inter-Am Ct HR (2004), para 154–55 (on participation in environmental decision-making).

29 See e.g. *Guerra v Italy* (1998) 26 EHRR 357, paras 50–54, and *McGinley and Egan v United Kingdom* (1999) 27 EHRR 1, paras 97 and 101 (on accessing environmental information); *Taskin v Turkey* (2006) 42 EHRR 50, para 118–119 (on participation in environmental decision-making); and the *Maya* case (n 28).

30 See e.g. the *Ogoniland* case (n 4) paras 44, 53, and 70–71 (on access to environmental information and decision-making processes).

At this juncture it is important to note briefly that, although Nigeria has ratified the ICCPR, it is yet to implement it domestically in line with section 12 of the 1999 Constitution of the Federal Republic of Nigeria[31] (as amended) (Nigerian Constitution), which provides that treaties ratified by Nigeria are only enforceable in Nigeria if they are enacted into law by the National Assembly (Parliament). However, in reality, the 1999 Nigerian Constitution (as amended) contains similar human rights provisions to the ICCPR, but it is felt that domesticating the ICCPR would probably make the interpretation and application of its provisions at the international level more influential in the local jurisdiction.[32] Nonetheless, Nigeria still owes an international obligation both domestically and fully to make directly effective the rights and obligations contained in the treaties it has ratified.

Moving on, even though many international initiatives on the environment, both soft and hard laws, continued to harp on about public access to environmental information and decision-making processes,[33] it was the 1992 Rio Declaration on Environment and Development (Rio Declaration)[34] that 'crystallized the emerging norms'[35] and made them a significant topic in the international environmental law and policy arena. Particularly, Principle 10 of the Rio Declaration, which is signed by almost every nation in the world, including Nigeria, provides that:

> Environmental issues are best handled with participation of all concerned citizens, at the relevant level. At the national level, each individual shall have appropriate access to information concerning the environment that is held by public authorities, including information on hazardous materials and activities in their communities, and the opportunity to participate in decision-making processes. States shall facilitate and encourage public awareness and participation by making information widely available. Effective access to judicial and administrative proceedings, including redress and remedy, shall be provided.[36]

The significance of Principle 10 in the field of international environmental law cannot be overstated. Since the institution of Principle 10, apart from Agenda 21, which slightly elaborates on the principle,[37] a plethora of international and regional environmental law initiatives have incorporated elements of Principle 10,[38] chief of which is the popular Aarhus Convention. Even international

31 Cap C23, Laws of the Federation of Nigeria, 2004.

32 See E Egede, 'Bringing human rights home: an examination of the domestication of human rights treaties in Nigeria' (2007) 51(2) *Journal of African Law* 249, 273.

33 See Pring and Noe (n 5) 28–50.

34 Adopted by the UN Conference on Environment and Development (UNCED), 3–14 June, 1992, (1992) 31 ILM 874.

35 Bruch and Filbey (n 12).

36 See also Principle 22.

37 See Agenda 21, ch 8.

38 See e.g. Memorandum of Understanding for Cooperation on Environment Management in East Africa (for Kenya, Tanzania and Uganda), done at Nairobi, Kenya, 22 October 1998; and the

institutions such as the World Bank,[39] the World Trade Organization,[40] and the African Development Bank[41] have also had their programmes influenced and underpinned by Principle 10. Although several countries admit that more still needs to be done in this regard, it is acknowledged that Principle 10 has objectively helped to progress national legislation and practice in environmental democracy.[42] Thus, Principle 10 has been kept on the front burner of discussions in environmental law, and its status has risen far beyond that of a mere soft law.

In fact, Händl had argued as early as 1992 that, based on the human rights root of the public right to access environmental information and decision-making processes and their implementation in many countries, the twin concepts 'warrant our unreserved endorsement as internationally protected rights: their normative reach is well defined, their claim to potential universal validity believable'.[43]

In 2012, he further argued that the significance of Principle 10 has 'coalesced to the point where the normative provisions of Principle 10 must be deemed legally binding . . . today the rights of access to information, public participation, and access to justice arguably represent[s] established human rights',[44] which states must guarantee. In a similar vein, there is increasing support for the growing notion that, since Principle 10 is widespread in laws and has gained wide acceptance among states (*opinio juris*), it has or may have acquired the status of general or customary international law.[45] After all, the International Court of Justice (ICJ) recently held in the *Pulp Mills* case (*Argentina v Uruguay*)[46] that an environmental impact assessment (EIA) in a transboundary context (which as a

Organization of American States Inter-American Strategy for the Promotion of Public Participation in Decision-making for Sustainable Development (OAS Public Participation Strategy), done at Washington DC, USA, 13–14 April 2000. For more see Bruch and Filbey (n 12) 1, 5.

39 See N Bernasconi-Osterwalder and D Hunter, 'Democratizing multilateral development banks', in Bruch (ed) (n 6) 151–64.

40 See N Gertler and E Milhollin, 'Public participation and access to justice in the World Trade Organization', in Bruch (ed) (n 6) 193–202.

41 See A Fall, 'Implementing public participation in African Development Bank operations', in Bruch (ed) (n 6) 165–74.

42 J Foti, 'Rio+20 in the rear view: countries commit to improve environmental democracy', *WRI Insight*, 2 July 2012, available at http://insights.wri.org/news/2012/07/rio20-rear-view-countries-commit-improve-environmental-governance (last accessed 26 January 2015).

43 G Händl, 'Human rights and protection of the environment: a mildly "revisionist" view', in C Trindade (ed), *Human Rights, Sustainable Development and the Environment* (San José: IIDH/BID, 1992) 117, 139–40.

44 G Händl, 'Declaration of the United Nations Conference on the Human Environment (Stockholm Declaration), 1972 and the Rio Declaration on Environment and Development, 1992', UN Audiovisual Library of International Law (2012), 6, available at http://untreaty.un.org/cod/avl/pdf/ha/dunche/dunche_e.pdf (last accessed 26 January 2015).

45 A growing view highlighted in C Bruch, 'Legal frameworks for public and stakeholder involvement', a presentation at the Regional Workshop on Public Participation in International Waters Management in Latin America and the Caribbean, held in Montenegro, Uruguay, on 6–9 December 2006, available at http://iwlearn.net/abt_iwlearn/events/workshops/p2/20061207/p2lac07-bruch (last accessed 26 January 2015).

46 Judgment, ICJ Reports 2010, 14, available at http://www.icj-cij.org/docket/files/135/15877.pdf (last accessed 26 January 2015).

general principle should necessarily involve public consultation and access to related environmental information[47]) is now considered a requirement of 'general international law' (and not merely a treaty-based obligation) on the ground that the practice 'has gained so much acceptance among States'.[48]

Whilst the actual legal status of Principle 10 may be debatable as there are other scholars who hold the view that the principle does not yet reflect general or customary international law,[49] this is, however, not the place to resolve the issue. It nonetheless suffices to argue here that Principle 10 is a fast emerging rule of general or customary international law. Indeed, Cameron and Mackenzie had noted more than a decade ago that: '[w]e can already perceive a broad consensus on the validity of a right to access of information and decision-making procedures and there is something approaching an international consensus that the citizen must be given rights that can be directed at *global* environmental protection.'[50] This rising status of Principle 10, together with its human rights essence, is arguably sufficient to place a strong moral obligation (that is fast approaching a (non-treaty based) legal one) on states like Nigeria that are committed to such regimes, so as expeditiously to ensure that their laws and practices are in consonance with the objectives of those norms.

1.3 Methodological approach

Grounded in its socio-political and theoretical contexts, this research employs a mainly doctrinal and comparative approach to realising its multifaceted core objective of evaluating and suggesting improvements to Nigerian laws and practices relating to public participation in environmental governance, in view of certain international best practice principles that are relevant to Nigeria. As Emeritus Professor Esin Örücü has noted: 'comparative law research is open ended – the methodology being dictated by the strategy of the comparative lawyer – and there is no standard methodology.'[51]

Her work, together with that of Professor Ralf Michaels and others, provides huge support for the use of the 'international best practice' model, as will be employed in this book, as a basis for comparison and improvement of a national regime.[52] A fundamental question that necessarily arises at this juncture is: as it

47 A Boyle, 'Pulp Mills case: A commentary', 3, available at http://www.biicl.org/files/5167_pulp_mills_case.pdf (last accessed 26 January 2015).

48 Note 46 para 205.

49 See e.g. J Ebbesson, 'Public participation', in D Bodansky, J Brunnée and E Hey (eds), *The Oxford Handbook of International Environmental Law* (Oxford and New York: Oxford University Press, 2007) 681, 685.

50 J Cameron and R Mackenzie, 'Access to environmental justice and procedural rights in international institutions', in A Boyle and M Anderson (eds), *Human Rights Approach to Environmental Protection* (Oxford: Oxford University Press, 1996) 129, 134.

51 E Örücü, 'Developing comparative law', in E Örücü and D Nelken (eds), *Comparative Law: A Handbook* (Oxford and Oregon: Hart Publishing, 2007) 43, 48–49.

52 R Michaels, '"One size can fit all" – some heretical thoughts on the mass production of legal transplants', in G Frankenberg (ed), *Order from Transfer: Comparative Constitutional Design and Legal*

relates to public access to environmental information and decision-making processes, what reasonably constitutes 'international best practice principles', at least, as will be used in this book as a basis for comparison and improvement? The answer follows.[53]

In view of the importance of ensuring public access to environmental information and decision-making processes, it is no surprise that a copious number of international environmental regimes contain provisions on those themes as it relates to their specific focus.[54] Examples of such (binding international) regimes that have long been ratified by Nigeria, include the 1972 Convention for the Protection of World Cultural and Natural Heritage,[55] the 1989 Basel Convention on the control of transboundary movements of hazardous wastes and their disposal,[56] the 1992 UN Framework Convention on Climate Change,[57] the 1992 UN Framework Convention on Biological Diversity,[58] the 2000 Protocol on Biosafety to the Convention on Biological Diversity,[59] and the 1994 UN Convention to Combat Desertification in those countries experiencing serious drought and/or desertification, particularly in Africa (UNCCD).[60] In addition, notable international 'soft' law instruments, which prescribe and contain provisions relating to public access to environmental information and decision-making processes and were approved by Nigeria include the Rio Declaration, Agenda 21,[61] as well as the World Charter for Nature.[62]

Even though the above regimes broadly indicate international best practice as it relates to public access to environmental information and decision-making processes, their provisions on the subjects are mostly general and brief. Consequently, it is necessary to unpack these provisions in order truly to understand their import and relevance and enable a useful discussion on what could be done in a country like Nigeria to fulfil the objectives of these provisions. To a reasonable extent, the Aarhus Convention has arguably achieved this, even though the Convention is not directly applicable to Nigeria since it is not a party to it. It is argued here, however, that the Aarhus Convention has reorganised (in a single document), clarified and elaborated on legislative and practical steps that would successfully implement the more general access requirements in those international regimes referred to above and their like.

Culture – Studies in Comparative Law and Legal Culture Series (Cheltenham and Northampton: Edward Elgar Publishing, 2013) 56.

53 The following response includes a limited adaptation, expansion and update of materials from section 2.1 of the article: U Etemire, 'Public access to environmental information: a comparative analysis of Nigerian legislation with international best practice' (2014) 3(1) *Transnational Environmental Law* 149.

54 See Pring and Noe (n 5).

55 World Heritage Convention, 6 November 1972, 1037 UNTS 151, art 27.

56 Basel Convention, 22 March 1989, (1989) 28 ILM 657, arts 4(2)(h) and 10(4).

57 Climate Change Convention, 9 May 1992, (1992) 31 ILM 849, art 6.

58 Biodiversity Convention, 5 June 1992, (1992) 31 ILM 818, arts 13 and 14(1)(a).

59 Biosafety Protocol, adopted 29 January 2000, art 23.

60 Desertification Convention, 17 June 1994, (1994) 33 ILM 1328, arts 5(d), 10(2)(f) and 19.

61 14 June 1992, (1992) 31 ILM 874, eg ch 10, para 10.10 and ch 36.

62 28 October 1982, (1983) 22 ILM 455, arts 15, 18 and 23.

In other words, for a country like Nigeria, it is here argued that developing its relevant laws and practices in consideration of the Aarhus Convention is, more or less, the same as taking steps to complying with its other direct international environmental treaty and soft law commitments in the broad sense.[63] The contention here is *not* that the general provisions of the Aarhus Convention currently constitute general or customary international law, which would make them legally binding on countries that, like Nigeria, that have not acceded to the regime. Rather, the main argument for the Convention's legal and political relevance to Nigeria is that it is the most comprehensive, concrete and coherent interpretative guide available for properly implementing Principle 10 norms.

This point is partly confirmed by the broad acceptance and wide support received by the Convention for its potential at the international, regional and national levels of authority, both from governments and civil society (groups), as will be discussed below. No other regime in this field has such a reputation, or anything close to it. Thus, whilst Nigeria is *not* under a direct international legal obligation to follow specifically the provisions of the Aarhus Convention, developing its laws and practices in consideration of the Convention's provisions is currently the most widely acknowledged way for it to implement Principle 10 norms adequately, from both a normative and a practical standpoint.

The above perspective is in line with those of the former UN Secretary-General Kofi Annan and the United Nations Environmental Programme (UNEP), that lauded the Aarhus Convention as 'the most impressive elaboration'[64] and 'advanced articulation'[65] of Principle 10 of the Rio Declaration, respectively. And it is in that light that the subsequent chapters of this book that frame the international best practice principles comparator will make use of the Aarhus Convention (widely held as providing procedures which are generally 'practical, concise and action-oriented')[66] as its main element. Although central to it, the best practice framework will not only be made up of the provisions of the Aarhus Convention, but will include other provisions of international environmental treaties, soft laws and regimes that show the intention of the international community and generally and specifically overlap with, or are amplified by, the provisions of the Aarhus Convention.

Apart from the 2014 Aarhus Convention implementation guide (Aarhus Implementation Guide),[67] the decisions of the Aarhus Convention Compliance

63 See UN Institute for Training and Research (UNITAR), 'Rio Principle 10 National Profile and Action Plan Project', available at http://www.unitar.org/egp/rio-principle-10-projects (last accessed 26 January 2015).

64 S Stec and S Casey-Lefkowitz, *The Aarhus Convention: An Implementation Guide* (New York and Geneva: UN, 2002), Foreword.

65 UNEP, *Manual on Compliance With and Enforcement of Multilateral Agreements* (Nairobi: UNEP, 2006) 109.

66 RE Hallo, *Access to Environmental Information in Europe: The Implementation and Implications of Directive 90/313/EEC* (The Hague: Kluwer Law International, 1996) 434–35.

67 J Ebbesson, H Gaugitsch, J Jendroska, F Marshal and S Stec, *The Aarhus Convention: An Implementation Guide* (2nd edn, New York and Geneva: UN, 2014).

Committee will also be used to shed practical light on some provisions of the Convention. The Compliance Committee is charged with the responsibility of reviewing compliance by parties to the Aarhus Convention, in terms of their laws and practices, against the requirements of the Convention when they received communication from members of the public or other sources; its members who are mandated to act in their personal capacity (not as representative of their countries) are nominated by non-governmental organisations (NGOs) together with signatories and parties to the regime.[68]

1.3.1 International best practice principles: why the central use of the Aarhus Convention?

The need to justify the central use of the Aarhus Convention as largely embodying international best practice principles (and not only suited to the UNECE region from whence it emanated) and hence appropriate to measure the status of the Nigerian system against its requirements, and use it as a basis for improvement where necessary, is fundamental to this book. In what follows, an effort is made to rationalise the position of Jendroska – who served as the Vice Chairman of the Working Group negotiating the Aarhus Convention – which is in line with the view taken in this book, that the Convention has the potential to drive and encourage countries 'to keep up with the best "world" standards and practices' in relation to public access to information and decision-making processes in general.[69]

First, it is a fact that the Aarhus Convention is a UNECE regional convention. However, it is more than that. It is also a fruit of the wider international environmental and human rights laws considering that it was inspired by, and firmly rooted in a number of such key international initiatives.[70] Apart from recognising the link between public participation and 'the enjoyment of basic human rights', the Convention in its preamble makes reference to Principle 1 of the 1972 Stockholm Declaration of the United Nations Conference on the Human Environment,[71] Principle 10 of the Rio Declaration (which popularised

68 See Aarhus Convention, art 15; and Meeting of the Parties to the Aarhus Convention, 'Decision 1/7: Review of Compliance', ECE/MP.PP/2/Add.8, 2 April 2004, available at http://www.unece.org/fileadmin/DAM/env/pp/documents/mop1/ece.mp.pp.2.add.8.e.pdf (last accessed 26 January 2015).

69 J Jendroska, 'UNECE Convention on access to information, public participation in decision-making and access to justice in environmental matters: towards more effective public involvement in monitoring compliance and enforcement in Europe', a paper delivered at the 5th International Conference on Environmental Compliance and Enforcement, held in California, USA, on 16–20 November 1998, 153, 160, available at http://www.inece.org/5thvol1/jendroska.pdf (last accessed 26 January 2015).

70 See M Visar, *The Transposition of the Convention on Access to Information, Public Participation in Decision-Making and Access to Justice in Environmental Matters (The Aarhus Convention) with the Legislation of Kosovo* (The Regional Environmental Center (REC) for Central and Eastern Europe, March 2006) 8.

71 Adopted by the UN Conference on the Human Environment, 5–16 June 1972 (1972) 11 ILM 1416.

the three 'pillars' of public participation that were adopted in the Aarhus Convention[72]), as well as the World Charter for Nature.

It is therefore argued that the Aarhus Convention to a large extent simply serves further to articulate the norms of these international initiatives that apply widely and constitute a standard for many nations across the world, including Nigeria, which has committed itself to them. The most important case to substantiate this argument about the global significance of the Aarhus Convention is probably *Taskin v Turkey*.[73] In that case, the fact that Turkey had not signed the Aarhus Convention did not stop the European Court of Human Rights (ECtHR) from directly reading the provisions of the Convention into the European Convention on Human Rights (ECHR) (to which Turkey is a party) 'in a particularly extensive form' in deciding the matter.[74]

Also, the Aarhus Convention was arguably drafted to have an 'international outlook' and to be acceptable in many societies across the world, hence it is uniquely open for ratification by any member state of the UN subject to the approval of the Meeting of the Parties to the Convention.[75] Already, among other non-UNECE countries, Cameroon and Mongolia have formally expressed their interest in acceding to the Convention to the latter's secretariat,[76] which increasing interest has caused the Meeting of the Parties to the Convention to adopt a more detailed procedure for approving the accession of non-UNECE countries.[77]

This argument for the transnational value and potency of the Aarhus Convention is also made based on the fact that its provisions benefited from considerations that extended beyond government perspectives, a single continent, or one only relevant to developed countries with developed democracies. This point is evidenced by the fact that European and Central Asian countries (as members of the UNECE), including largely established democracies (e.g. the UK) and countries with teething democracies (e.g. Kazakhstan), as well as 'developed countries' (e.g. the UK) and 'countries in transition' or 'developing countries' (e.g. Kazakhstan), were all involved in negotiating the Aarhus Convention.

72 See C Johnson, 'Improved access regime for environmental information and the role of the Information Commissioner' (2004) 6 *Environmental Law Review* 219, 220.

73 (2006) 42 EHRR 50.

74 A Boyle, 'Human rights and the environment: where next?' (2012) 23(3) *European Journal of International Law* 613, 624.

75 Aarhus Convention, art 19(3).

76 For Cameroon, see Meeting of the Parties to the Aarhus Convention, 'Report of the Second Extraordinary Session of the Meeting of the Parties', ECE/MP.PP/2010/2, 15 October 2010, 4–5, available at http://www.unece.org/fileadmin/DAM/env/pp/prtr/docs/2011/ece_mp.pp_2010_2_eng.pdf; for Mongolia, see Meeting of the Parties to the Aarhus Convention, 'Report of the Fourth Session of the Meeting of the Parties', ECE/MP.PP/2011/2, 19 August 2011, 9, available at http://www.unece.org/fileadmin/DAM/env/pp/mop4/Documents/Post_Session/ece.mp.pp.2011.2.eng.pdf (last accessed 26 January 2015).

77 Meeting of the Parties to the Aarhus Convention, 'Decision IV/5 on Accession to the Convention by non-United Nations Economic Commission for Europe Member States', ECE/MP.PP/2011/CRP.3, 1 June 2011, available at http://www.unece.org/fileadmin/DAM/env/pp/mop4/Documents/ece_mp_pp_2011_CRP_3_Accession_e.pdf (last accessed 26 January 2015).

Furthermore, the extensive public participation in the initiation[78] and creation of the Aarhus Convention, 'arguably unprecedented in the history of international law',[79] makes the regime the most public-access-friendly environmental treaty with its provisions generally extend beyond the traditional restrictive views of government. After extensive consultation, representing the views of hundreds of non-state entities and interested individuals from diverse countries, NGO delegates, armed with a wealth of vital information on access experiences, participated in negotiating and drafting the Aarhus Convention 'on a more or less equal basis' with country representatives.[80]

Therefore, as should be expected, the Convention largely reflects principles or rights which have been broadly viewed as 'universal in nature';[81] 'a fundamental step in the process of worldwide democratisation' especially for countries 'with no traditions of citizen participation and responsible environmental law-making';[82] and having the 'potential to serve as a global framework for strengthening citizens' environmental rights' and 'the application of Principle 10 in other regions of the world', according to Kofi Annan.[83] Consequently, the Convention's principles can be applied, with relevant adaptation, in countries around the world, especially those that have chosen a democratic system of government, as Nigeria has.[84]

In light of the above, one can find that even states like Nigeria that have not signed or ratified the Convention look to it for guidance when drawing up or evaluating the status of their access laws as it relates to the environment;[85] examples include Brazil[86] and Mauritius.[87] The intercontinental relevance of the Aarhus Convention has also been acknowledged by the Organisation of American States (OAS) (made up of all 35 independent states of the Americas) in its adopted public participation strategy (PPS, formed with input from governments and civil society groups in all OAS states).[88] This public participation strategy, which

78 J Wates, 'NGOs and the Aarhus Convention', in T Treves, M Frigessi di Rattalma, A Tanzi, A Fodella, C, Pitea and C Ragni (eds), *Civil Society, International Courts and Compliance Bodies* (The Hague: TMC Asser Press, 2005) 167, 177.

79 Jendroska (n 69) 156.

80 See Wates (n 78) 178; Jendroska (n 69) 156; and R Hallo, 'Access to Environmental information: the reciprocal influences of EU law and the Aarhus Convention', in M Pallemaerts (ed), *The Aarhus Convention at Ten: Interactions and Tensions Between Conventional International Law and EU Environmental Law* (Groningen: Europa Law Publishing, 2011) 55, 60–61.

81 Stec and Casey-Lefkowitz (n 64) 6.

82 Quoting the Italian Government. A Antonelli and A Biondi, 'Implementing the Aarhus Convention: some lessons from the Italian experience' (2003) 5(3) *Environmental Law Review* 170.

83 Stec and Casey-Lefkowitz (n 64), foreword.

84 See Hallo (n 80) 62.

85 See J Wates, 'The future of the Aarhus Convention: perspectives arising from the Third Session of the Meeting of the Parties', in M Pallemaerts (ed) (n 80) 383, 395.

86 See SA Nascimento da Nóbrega, 'Access to environmental information: a comparative analysis of the Aarhus Convention with Brazilian legislation' (2011) 2 *Environmental Law Network International Review* 87–88: 'That the Brazilian legislation was inspired by the Aarhus Convention was confirmed [to the author] in email communication from 03 of August of 2010 with Fabio Feldmann who is the author of the Brazilian Law 10.650/03': ibid, 88.

87 UNEP, Fourth Programme for the Development and Review of Environmental Law, UNEP/GC.25/INF/15/Add.2, 29 October 2008, 3.

88 Note 38.

broadly aims to promote proper implementation of Principle 10 in the Americas, generally draws on the Aarhus Convention to support its recommendations, and recognises it as a 'landmark' regime and a 'good example' of formalised Principle 10 rights that 'has become a useful mechanism' for ensuring proper implementation of the latter.[89]

Similarly, with the support of the UN Economic Commission for Latin America and the Caribbean (UNECLAC), several UNECLAC countries that are currently furthering the process of realising a regional convention for the implementation of Principle 10, have explicitly indicated that such an instrument will possibly be based on the Aarhus Convention, among others that have been influenced by the Convention:[90] 'A number of other regions of the world show a strong interest in the Aarhus Convention and are discussing the development of similar obligations.'[91]

The following position of Professor Ralf Michaels sheds some light as it relates to the expansive value of the Aarhus Convention, in view of preceding and succeeding arguments: '[t]his approach is analogous to universalism [in a generally sense] in comparative law (footnote omitted). Notably, because the standard is not, ideally, drawn from one background but instead incorporates worldwide differences' it can be reasonably used for the reform and improvement of laws and practices in many countries around the world which may even have somewhat different legal and political cultures.[92] To facilitate such an objective, the Aarhus Convention provides for some 'flexibility' in deciding how some of its obligations will be implemented 'in view of the varying legal systems and governance capacities of various Parties across the UNECE region',[93] and was drawn up with the conviction that its implementation 'will contribute to strengthening democracy'.[94]

This is what has been and is still being achieved in central and eastern European (CEEs) states and newly independent states (NISs) that are parties to the Aarhus Convention, where, even though more still needs to be done, the Convention has positively impacted on 'national legislation, national practices, and national attitudes' in opening up secretive and exclusive systems of governance that used

89 See ibid, 19 and 24.

90 See J Miller, 'Implementation of Principle 10 of the Rio Declaration of the United Nations Conference on Environment and Development', a presentation at the Conference on Sustainable Development in Latin America and the Caribbean, held in Bogota, Colombia, 5–9 March 2013, available at http://www.eclac.cl/rio20/noticias/paginas/6/48936/2.-Janice_Miller.pdf (last accessed 26 January 2015); and UNECLAC, 'ECLAC's Submission to the compilation document to serve as basis for the preparation of the zero draft of the outcome document of Rio+20', para 7, available at http://www.eclac.cl/rio20/noticias/paginas/6/43766/SE111097-ECLAC_inputs_to_Zero_draft.pdf (last accessed 26 January 2015).

91 Stec and Casey-Lefkowitz (n 64) 6.

92 Michaels (n 52) 68.

93 M Mason, 'Information disclosure and environmental rights: the Aarhus Convention' (2010) 10(3) *Global Environmental Politics* 10, 21–22.

94 Aarhus Convention, preamble.

to exist in those states.[95] Sharing a similar political history with the aforementioned states, the same can be achieved in Nigeria by generally adapting and applying principles similar to those in the Aarhus Convention.

As a further testament to its expansive value and influence, the Aarhus Convention now serves as inspiration for the formulation of new international environmental instruments, for instance, the UNEP Manual on Compliance with and Enforcement of Multilateral Environmental Agreements.[96] Importantly, the same can also be said of the 2010 UNEP Guidelines for the development of national legislation on information, public participation and access to justice in environmental matters (Bali Guidelines)[97] that was developed with input from civil society groups and governments from around the world, and adopted by the UNEP Governing Council;[98] most of its guidelines are similar to the provisions of the Aarhus Convention. This fact will be demonstrated in subsequent chapters where the guidelines (and provisions from other regimes) will be combined with provisions of the Convention to reflect international best practice.

Notably, the Bali 'Aarhus-like' Guidelines were said to be primarily for developing countries (such as Nigeria), to help them implement their commitments under Principle 10 of the Rio Declaration; of which, in order to ensure proper implementation of the 'Aarhus-like' Guidelines, UNEP and the UN Institute for Training and Research (UNITAR) are executing training and capacity development projects across a number of regions (Africa, Latin America and the Caribbean, and Middle East and Asia-Pacific as a first step) and countries that have committed themselves to developing national legislation on Principle 10.[99] There is also the draft Commentary to the Bali Guidelines,[100] which, in addition, expounds on each of the main guidelines and makes explicit reference to portions of the Aarhus Convention. Although the text of the Commentary was

95 S Kravchenko, 'New laws on public participation in the newly independent states', in Zillman, Lucas and Pring (eds) (n 2) 467, 473. See also C Walek, 'The Aarhus Convention and its practical impact on NGOs: examples of CEE and NIS countries' (2000) 3(1) *The International Journal of Not-for-Profit Law*, available at http://www.icnl.org/research/journal/vol3iss1/art_5.htm (last accessed 26 January 2015).

96 See generally note 65.

97 Adopted by the Governing Council of UNEP, UNEP/GCSS.XI/11, Decision SS.XI/5, Part A, 26 February 2010.

98 The UNEP Governing Council is a political body made up of 58 Members States (with African states holding 16 seats, with the others held by states from all other continents of the world) elected by the UN General Assembly for three-year terms with the responsibility of recommending and providing environmental policies. See UNGA Resolution (XXVII), art 1, available at http://www.unep.org/PDF/UN_GA_2997.pdf (last accessed 26 January 2015).

99 See A Juras, 'The Bali Guidelines for development of national legislation on access to information, public participation and access to justice in environmental matters', a presentation at the first meeting of focal points appointed by governments of the signatory countries of the Declaration on the Implementation of Principle 10, held in Santiago de Chile, on 6–7 November 2012, available at http://www.eclac.cl/rio20/noticias/paginas/8/48588/Alexander_Juras_English.pdf (last accessed 26 January 2015).

100 Available at http://www.unep.org/civil-society/Portals/24105/documents/Guidelines/Commentary-to-the-guidelines-for-the-development-of-national-legislation.pdf (last accessed 26 January 2015).

not negotiated by governments or adopted by the UNEP Governing Council, it was developed by UNEP 'taking into account the comments received from Governments and civil society groups from around the world'.[101]

The role played by African and other governments (especially, but not only, through the UNEP Governing Council) and civil society groups in the formulation and adoption of the 'Aarhus-like' Bali Guidelines is, again, a testament to the intercontinental relevance of the principles in the Aarhus Convention. Furthermore, the fact that the Aarhus Convention could be useful in the African, and indeed the Nigerian, context and should inform environmental governance in the country is a point that has been hinted at by a number of researchers.[102]

Importantly, in a UN Economic Commission for Africa (UNECA) report on improving environmental public participation in Africa, the Aarhus Convention was embraced and recognised as 'a model of a public participation regime'.[103] Similarly, a study commissioned by the African Union to help African governments implement the Article 23 'Public Awareness and Participation' provision of the Cartagena Protocol on Biosafety, has expressed the benefit of '[d]raw[ing]-up an African convention similar to the Aarhus Convention on public participation or adopt[ing] the Aarhus Convention'.[104]

What is more, an important point to emphasise is that a straightforward and general comparison with the Aarhus Convention is arguably valuable in its own right, given its role in its field as an exemplary international instrument and law reform tool. In spite of the Aarhus Convention not being a formal source of law for Nigeria, it is again argued that it still bears political and legal relevance for the country. This is so in light of the developing notion of the transnationalisation of environmental law, especially considering that environmental law is itself 'inherently polycentric and multicultural' in nature and deals with subject matters that often extend beyond national boundaries.[105] It is argued that, as part of the

101 UNEP Guidelines for the development of national legislation on information, public participation and access to justice in environmental matters, 2010, Annex, available at http://www.unep.org/civil-society/Portals/24105/documents/Guidelines/GUIDELINES_TO_ACCESS_TO_ENV_INFO_2.pdf (last accessed 26 January 2015).

102 See C Bruch, 'Regional opportunities for improving environmental governance through access to information, public participation, and access to justice', a paper delivered at the 8th Session of the African Ministerial Conference on Environment (AMCEN), held in Abuja, Nigeria, on 3–6 April 2000, 7–8, available at http://www.eli.org/pdf/africa/csamcen00.pdf (last accessed 26 January 2015); C Bruch and R Czebiniak, 'Globalizing environmental governance: making the leap from regional initiatives to transparency, participation, and accountability in environmental matters' (2002) 32 *Environmental Law Reporter* 10428, 10443–444; R Mwebaza, 'Improving environmental procedural rights in Uganda', in MC Bonilla, EF Fernández, S Jemaiel, R Mwebaza and D Zhandayeva (eds), *Environmental Law in Developing Countries: Selected Issues* (Vol II, Cambridge: IUCN, 2004) 3, 38–39; and AA Ibrahim and B Rohan, 'The Aarhus Convention as a model for advancing citizens' rights in Africa' (1999) 6(2) *Innovation* 29.

103 UNECA, *Improving Public Participation in the Sustainable Development of Mineral Resources in Africa* (Addis Ababa: UNECA, 2004) 15–16 and 37.

104 MW Kamara, *Public Participation in African Biosafety Regulations and Policy* (African Union Commission, September 2010) 8.

105 See V Heyvaert and T Etty, 'Introducing transnational environmental law' (2012) 1(1) *Transnational Environmental Law* 1, 3–5; and E Fisher, 'The rise of transnational environmental law and the expertise of environmental lawyers' (2012) 1(1) *Transnational Environmental Law* 43–52.

notion of transnational environmental law, certain environmental legal principles and standards acquire authority not by virtue of international or domestic enactment, but by virtue of influential factors such as basic usefulness, esteem, explanatory power, and overlap and affinity with other sources of law (formally) recognised by a state.

This offers an explanation as to why states including Brazil and Mauritius have taken to improving and evaluating their laws and practices with the guidance of the provisions of the Aarhus Convention despite not being parties to it. It is arguably also the reason why the ECtHR confidently applied the requirements of the Convention to Turkey despite its not being a party to the regime. A similar trend exists as well in Nigeria where 'mere compliance with existing municipal law is no longer acceptable to environmentally concerned communities as good enough justification by government and developers for their actions'.[106] Rather, these states strive to hold the government and developers to account based on 'better laws' operational elsewhere, such as the Aarhus Convention. Also, environmental rights activists in Nigeria operate on similar standards and use the Aarhus Convention and other legal norms as guideline for their work and campaigns, in so far as they relate to environmental procedural matters.[107]

In sum, when all the issues discussed above are aggregated, two fundamental points become apparent and further highlight the legal and political relevance of the Aarhus Convention to Nigeria. First, if or when an international convention on Principle 10 materialises, it is almost certain that such a regime would be formulated along the lines of the Aarhus Convention and the Bali Guidelines, especially considering that there is currently an increasing governmental and civil society call for such progression.[108] Second, given the foundational make-up, extensive support and wide and increasing influence of the Aarhus Convention, it is arguably an authoritative reflection of a burgeoning set of general or customary rules of international (environmental) law which can be used as an effective interpretative guide in non-treaty contexts.

All these arguably make the Aarhus Convention both a reasonable and acceptable comparative basis – or to form the core thereof – on which meaningfully to assess the adequacy of Nigerian laws and practices in terms of the extent to which they fulfil the country's (Principle 10) international environmental

106 Y Omorogbe 'The power of the people: public participation and control in resource-rich states', a presentation at the 36th Annual Conference of the Nigerian Society of International Law, held in River State, Nigeria, on 14–16 September 2006.

107 See West African Insight, 'Oil exploration, environmental rights, and the future of Nigeria's Niger delta', *West African Insight*, 10 October 2010, available at http://westafricainsight.org/articles/view/61 (last accessed 14 February 2015).

108 See Article 19, 'Rio+20: incorporating Principle 10 and the right to information', 2 November 2011, available at http://www.article19.org/resources.php/resource/2808/en/rio+20:-incorporating-principle-10-and-the-right-to-information (last accessed 26 January 2015); and The Access Initiative, 'UNEP Governing Council to decide future of access principles in Nairobi', 6 February 2009, available at http://www.accessinitiative.org/blog/2009/02/unep-governing-council-decide-future-access-principles-nairobi/ (last accessed 26 January 2015).

commitments and their ability to ensure meaningful public participation in fact. And, where necessary, this assessment would enable recommendations to be made for the improvement of Nigerian laws and practices, considering surrounding local circumstances.

1.4 Structure

In terms of how materials are structured to address the research question and objectives, the next chapter – Chapter 2 – provides a vital general sketch of the relevant historical, social, political and economic context of this book. It analyses, amongst others, the status of public participation as an integral part of (environmental) governance in early traditional Nigerian societies; the suppression and overshadowing of this form of governance by one of secrecy and public exclusion and the negative effect of this on the environment and society; the initiatives taken so far to reverse this trend; and the need to assess and strengthen those initiatives, mainly from the perspectives of their origin and effectiveness.

Chapter 3 goes on to provide a theoretical foundation for the book, shedding further light, from that perspective, on issues discussed in the preceding chapter and grounding the doctrinal discussion in subsequent chapters. Largely, the chapter clarifies who 'the public' is that should participate in environmental governance; discusses the status of (environmental) public participation within a number of political traditions in order to effectively suggest that Nigeria embraces a more open and inclusive political tradition that is beneficial to the environment and human wellbeing; and evaluates the value of (environmental) public participation – in terms of its potential benefits/justifications and its potential disbenefits/criticisms – which highlights the need for an effective environmental public participation regime in Nigeria.

After the largely contextual chapters above, the others are comprised of the doctrinal and comparative elements of the book, where the issue of public access to environmental information is handled first, followed by that of public participation in environmental decision-making processes. Accordingly, Chapter 4 presents an analysis of certain participatory norms which arguably represents international best practice principles on public access to environmental information that are relevant to Nigeria and should serve as an acceptable model for related regimes in the country. Then the counterpart Chapter 5 evaluates the regime on public access to (environmental) information in Nigeria, especially against the normative requirements in Chapter 4 and local circumstances, injecting recommendations as the chapter unfolds. The format of Chapters 4 and 5 is similar to that of Chapters 6 and 7 which, as against environmental information, are concerned with regimes on public participation in environmental decision-making processes. Chapter 8 is the concluding chapter, where the various strands of the discussion in the preceding chapters will be briefly tied together; the aim here would generally be to more clearly highlight the central point of the book, especially in terms of the findings and recommendations made.

Bibliography

Access Initiative, 'UNEP Governing Council to decide future of access principles in Nairobi', 6 February 2009, available at http://www.accessinitiative.org/blog/2009/02/unep-governing-council-decide-future-access-principles-nairobi/ (last accessed 26 January 2015).

Ahmed A, 'Righting public wrongs and enforcing private rights', in Bruch C (ed), *The New "Public": The Globalization of Public Participation* (Washington DC: Environmental Law Institute, 2002) 39.

Antonelli A and Biondi A, 'Implementing the Aarhus Convention: some lessons from the Italian experience' (2003) 5(3) *Environmental Law Review* 170.

Article 19, 'Rio+20: Incorporating Principle 10 and the right to information', 2 November 2011, available at http://www.article19.org/resources.php/resource/2808/en/rio+20:-incorporating-principle-10-and-the-right-to-information (last accessed 26 January 2015).

Bachrach P, 'Interests, participation, and democratic theory', in Pennock JR and Chapman JW (eds), *Participation in Politics* (New York: Lieber-Atherton, 1975) 39.

Beierle TC and Cayford J, *Democracy in Practice: Public Participation in Environmental Decisions* (Washington DC: Resources for the Future, 2002).

Bernasconi-Osterwalder N and Hunter D, 'Democratizing multilateral development banks', in Bruch C (ed), *The New "Public": The Globalization of Public Participation* (Washington DC: Environmental Law Institute, 2002) 151.

Boyle A, 'Human rights and the environment: where next?' (2012) 23(3) *European Journal of International Law* 613.

Boyle A, 'Pulp Mills case: a commentary', available at http://www.biicl.org/files/5167_pulp_mills_case.pdf (last accessed 26 January 2015).

Bruch C, 'Regional opportunities for improving environmental governance through access to information, public participation, and access to justice', a paper delivered at the 8th Session of the African Ministerial Conference on Environment (AMCEN), held in Abuja, Nigeria, on 3–6 April 2000.

Bruch C, 'Legal frameworks for public and stakeholder involvement', a presentation at the Regional Workshop on Public Participation in International Waters Management in Latin America and the Caribbean, held in Montenegro, Uruguay, on 6–9 December 2006, available at http://iwlearn.net/abt_iwlearn/events/workshops/p2/20061207/p2lac07-bruch (last accessed 26 January 2015).

Bruch C and Czebiniak R, 'Globalizing environmental governance: making the leap from regional initiatives to transparency, participation, and accountability in environmental matters' (2002) 32 *Environmental Law Reporter* 10428.

Bruch C and Filbey M, 'Emerging global norms of public involvement', in Bruch C (ed), *The New "Public": The Globalization of Public Participation* (Washington DC: Environmental Law Institute, 2002) 1.

Cameron J and Mackenzie R, 'Access to environmental justice and procedural rights in international institutions', in Boyle A and Anderson M (eds), *Human Rights Approach to Environmental Protection* (Oxford: Oxford University Press, 1996) 129.

Draft Commentary to the UNEP Guidelines for the Development of National Legislation on Information, Public Participation and Access to Justice in Environmental Matters, available at http://www.unep.org/civil-society/Portals/24105/documents/Guidelines/Commentary-to-the-guidelines-for-the-development-of-national-legislation.pdf (last accessed 26 January 2015).

Ebbesson J, 'Public participation', in D Bodansky, J Brunnée and E Hey, *The Oxford Handbook of International Environmental Law* (Oxford and New York: Oxford University Press, 2007) 681.

Ebbesson J, Gaugitsch H, Jendroska J, Marshall F and Stec S, *The Aarhus Convention: An Implementation Guide* (2nd edn, New York and Geneva: UN, 2014).

Egede E, 'Bringing human rights home: an examination of the domestication of human rights treaties in Nigeria' (2007) 51(2) *Journal of African Law* 249.

Etemire U, 'Public access to environmental information: a comparative analysis of Nigerian legislation with international best practice' (2014) 3(1) *Transnational Environmental Law* 149.

Fall A, 'Implementing public participation in African Development Bank operations', in Bruch C (ed), *The New "Public": The Globalization of Public Participation* (Washington DC: Environmental Law Institute, 2002) 165.

Fisher E, 'The rise of transnational environmental law and the expertise of environmental lawyers' (2012) 1(1) *Transnational Environmental Law* 43.

Foti J, 'Rio+20 in the rear view: countries commit to improve environmental democracy', *WRI Insight*, 2 July 2012, available at http://insights.wri.org/news/2012/07/rio 20-rear-view-countries-commit-improve-environmental-governance (last accessed 26 January 2015).

Gertler N and Milhollin E, 'Public participation and access to justice in the World Trade Organization', in Bruch C (ed), *The New "Public": The Globalization of Public Participation* (Washington DC: Environmental Law Institute, 2002) 193.

Hallo RE, *Access to Environmental Information in Europe: The Implementation and Implications of Directive 90/313/EEC* (The Hague: Kluwer Law International, 1996).

Hallo R, 'Access to environmental information: the reciprocal influences of EU law and the Aarhus Convention', in Pallemaerts M (ed), *The Aarhus Convention at Ten: Interactions and Tensions between Conventional International Law and EU Environmental Law* (Groningen: Europa Law Publishing, 2011) 55.

Händl G, 'Declaration of the United Nations Conference on the Human Environment (Stockholm Declaration), 1972 and the Rio Declaration on Environment and Development, 1992', UN Audiovisual Library of International Law (2012).

Händl G, 'Human rights and protection of the environment: a mildly "revisionist" view', in Trindade C (ed), *Human Rights, Sustainable Development and the Environment* (San José: IIDH/BID, 1992) 117.

Händl G, 'Human rights and perfection of the environment', in Eide A, Krause C and Rosas A (eds), *Economic, Social and Cultural Rights: A Textbook* (2nd edn, The Hague: Kluwer Law International, 2001) 303.

Heyvaert V and Etty T, 'Introducing transnational environmental law' (2012) 1(1) *Transnational Environmental Law* 1.

Hins W and Voorhoof D, 'Access to state-held information as a fundamental right under the European Convention on Human Rights' (2007) 3 *European Constitutional Law Review* 114.

Ibrahim AA and Rohan B, 'The Aarhus Convention as a model for advancing citizens' rights in Africa' (1999) 6(2) *Innovation* 29.

Jendroska J, 'UNECE Convention on access to information, public participation in decision-making and access to justice in environmental matters: towards more effective public involvement in monitoring compliance and enforcement in Europe', delivered at the 5th International Conference on Environmental Compliance and Enforcement, held in California, USA, on 16–20 November 1998, available at http://www.inece.org/5thvol1/jendroska.pdf (last accessed 26 January 2015).

Johnson C, 'Improved access regime for environmental information and the role of the Information Commissioner' (2004) 6 *Environmental Law Review* 219.

Juras A, 'The Bali Guidelines for development of national legislation on access to information, public participation and access to justice in environmental matters', a presentation at the first meeting of focal points appointed by governments of the signatory countries of the Declaration on the Implementation of Principle 10, held in Santiago de Chile, on 6–7 November 2012, available at http://www.eclac.cl/rio20/noticias/paginas/8/48588/Alexander_Juras_English.pdf (last accessed 26 January 2015).

Kamara MW, *Public Participation in African Biosafety Regulations and Policy* (African Union Commission, September 2010).

Kravchenko S, 'New laws on public participation in the newly independent states', in Zillman DN, Lucas AR and Pring G (eds), *Human Rights in National Resource Development: Public Participation in the Sustainable Development of Mining and Energy Resource* (Oxford: Oxford University Press, 2002) 467.

Kweit MG and Kweit RW, *Implementing Citizen Participation in a Bureaucratic Society: A Contingency Approach* (New York: Praeger, 1981).

Mason M, *Environmental Democracy* (London: Palgrave Macmillan, 1999).

Meeting of the Parties to the Aarhus Convention, 'Decision 1/7: Review of Compliance', ECE/MP.PP/2/Add.8, 2 April 2004, available at http://www.unece.org/fileadmin/DAM/env/pp/documents/mop1/ece.mp.pp.2.add.8.e.pdf (last accessed 26 January 2015).

Meeting of the Parties to the Aarhus Convention, 'Decision IV/5 on Accession to the Convention by non-United Nations Economic Commission for Europe Member States', ECE/MP.PP/2011/CRP.3, 1 June 2011, available at http://www.unece.org/fileadmin/DAM/env/pp/mop4/Documents/ece_mp_pp_2011_CRP_3_Accession_e.pdf (last accessed 26 January 2015).

Meeting of the Parties to the Aarhus Convention, 'Report of the Fourth Session of the Meeting of the Parties', ECE/MP.PP/2011/2, 19 August 2011, available at http://www.unece.org/fileadmin/DAM/env/pp/mop4/Documents/Post_Session/ece.mp.pp.2011.2.eng.pdf (last accessed 26 January 2015).

Meeting of the Parties to the Aarhus Convention, 'Report of the Second Extraordinary Session of the Meeting of the Parties', ECE/MP.PP/2010/2, 15 October 2010, available at http://www.unece.org/fileadmin/DAM/env/pp/prtr/docs/2011/ece_mp.pp_2010_2_eng.pdf (last accessed 26 January 2015).

Michaels R, '"One size can fit all": some heretical thoughts on the mass production of legal transplants', in Frankenberg G (ed), *Order from Transfer: Comparative Constitutional Design and Legal Culture – Studies in Comparative Law and Legal Culture Series* (Cheltenham and Northampton: Edward Elgar Publishing, 2013) 56.

Miller J, 'Implementation of Principle 10 of the Rio Declaration of the United Nations Conference on Environment and Development', a presentation at the Conference on Sustainable Development in Latin America and the Caribbean, held in Bogota, Colombia, 5–9 March 2013, available at http://www.eclac.cl/rio20/noticias/paginas/6/48936/2.-Janice_Miller.pdf (last accessed 26 January 2015).

Mwebaza R, 'Improving environmental procedural rights in Uganda', in Bonilla MC, Fernández EF, Jemaiel S, Mwebaza R and Zhandayeva D (eds), *Environmental Law in Developing Countries: Selected Issues* (Vol II, Cambridge: IUCN, 2004) 3.

Nascimento da Nóbrega SA, 'Access to environmental information: a Comparative analysis of the Aarhus Convention with Brazilian legislation' (2011) 2 *Environmental Law Network International Review* 87.

Omorogbe Y, 'The power of the people: public participation and control in resource-rich states', a presentation at the 36th Annual Conference of the Nigerian Society of International Law, held in River State, Nigeria, on 14–16 September 2006.

Örücü E, 'Developing comparative law', in Örücü E and Nelken D (eds), *Comparative Law: A Handbook* (Oxford and Oregon: Hart Publishing, 2007) 43.

Popovic NAF, 'The right to participate in decisions that affect the environment' (1993) 10 *Pace Environmental Law Review* 683.

Pring G and Noe SY, 'The emerging international law of public participation affecting global mining, energy, and resources development', in Zillman DN, Lucas AR and Pring G (eds), *Human Rights in National Resource Development: Public Participation in the Sustainable Development of Mining and Energy Resource* (Oxford: Oxford University Press, 2002) 11.

Schwartz ML, 'International legal protection for victims of environmental abuse' (1993) 18 *Yale Journal of International Law* 362.

Spyke NP, 'Public participation in environmental decision-making at the new millennium: structuring new spheres of public influence' (1999) 26 *Boston College Environmental Affairs Law Review* 263.

Stec S and Casey-Lefkowitz S, *The Aarhus Convention: An Implementation Guide* (New York and Geneva: UN, 2002).

UN Human Rights Committee, 'General Comment No 23: The Right of Minorities (Art 27)', CCPR/C/21/Rev.1/Add.5, adopted at the Committee's 50th session, April 1994.

UN Human Rights Committee, 'General Comment No 25: The Right to Participate in Public Affairs, Voting Rights and the Right of Equal Access to Public Service (Art 25)', CCPR/C/21/Rev.1/Add.7, adopted at the Committee's 57th session, 12 July 1996.

UN Institute for Training and Research (UNITAR), 'Rio Principle 10 National Profile and Action Plan Project', available at http://www.unitar.org/egp/rio-principle-10-projects (last accessed 26 January 2015).

UNECA, *Improving Public Participation in the Sustainable Development of Mineral Resources in Africa* (Addis Ababa: UNECA, 2004).

UNECLAC, 'ECLAC's Submission to the compilation document to serve as basis for the preparation of the zero draft of the outcome document of Rio+20', available at http://www.eclac.cl/rio20/noticias/paginas/6/43766/SE111097-ECLAC_inputs_to_Zero_draft.pdf (last accessed 26 January 2015).

UNEP, *Manual on Compliance With and Enforcement of Multilateral Agreements* (Nairobi: UNEP, 2006) 109.

UNEP, Fourth Programme for the Development and Review of Environmental Law, UNEP/GC.25/INF/15/Add.2, 29 October 2008.

van der Zwiep K, 'Public participation as an instrument for environmental protection', in Nagy MT, Bowman M, Dusik. J, Jendroska J, Stec S, van der Zwiep K et al. and others (eds), *Regional Environmental Centre for Central and Eastern Europe (REC), Manual on Public Participation in Environmental Decisionmaking: Current Practices and Future Possibilities in Central and Eastern Europe* (Budapest, 1994), available at http://archive.rec.org/REC/Publications/PPManual/FeeBased/ch12.html (last accessed 26 January 2015).

Visar M, *The Transposition of the Convention on Access to Information, Public Participation in Decision-Making and Access to Justice in Environmental Matters (The Aarhus Convention) with the legislation of Kosovo* (The Regional Environmental Center (REC) for Central and Eastern Europe, March 2006).

Walek C, 'The Aarhus Convention and its practical impact on NGOs: examples of CEE and NIS Countries' (2000) 3(1) *The International Journal of Not-for-Profit Law*, available at http://www.icnl.org/research/journal/vol3iss1/art_5.htm (last accessed 26 January 2015).

Wates J, 'NGOs and the Aarhus Convention', in Treves T, Frigessi di Rattalma M, Tanzi A, Fodella A, Pitea C and Ragni C (eds), *Civil Society, International Courts and Compliance Bodies* (The Hague: TMC Asser Press, 2005) 167.

Wates J, 'The future of the Aarhus Convention: perspectives arising from the Third Session of the Meeting of the Parties', in Pallemaerts M (ed), *The Aarhus Convention at Ten: Interactions and Tensions between Conventional International Law and EU Environmental Law* (Groningen: Europa Law Publishing, 2011) 384.

West African Insight, 'Oil exploration, environmental rights, and the future of Nigeria's Niger delta', *West African Insight,* 10 October 2010, available at http://westafricainsight.org/articles/view/61 (last accessed 14 February 2015).

Zillman DN, 'Introduction to public participation in the twenty-first century', in Zillman DN, Lucas AR and Pring G (eds), *Human Rights in National Resource Development: Public Participation in the Sustainable Development of Mining and Energy Resource* (Oxford: Oxford University Press, 2002) 1.

2 Society, political governance and public participation in Nigeria

2.1 Introduction

The adequacy, implementation and effectiveness of public access laws on environmental information and decision-making processes are usually influenced by wider considerations related to the country, such as its political, administrative[1] and wider legal cultures as they have been moulded over the years and continue to be influenced by their history. Thus, at the base of such laws and their implementation in Nigeria is this wealth of political, administrative and legal history which calls for examination. Accordingly, the purpose of this chapter is to explain, assess and attempt to create an understanding of how the aforementioned considerations have contributed to shaping the current character and working of public access laws in Nigeria, especially as they relate to the environment. It will also serve to trace the development of the relevant environment-related public access laws and highlight the need for adequate legal mechanisms that contribute to ensuring transparency in governance, as well as affording the populace the requisite opportunities to participate in decision-making, especially in an environmental context.

2.2 'Nigeria' before 1960: government and the peoples

2.2.1 The early 'Nigerian' states

Modern-day Nigeria is a creation of the British colonialists and the point that 'the boundaries adopted to create the modern state of Nigeria never had any geophysical or social significance to the indigenous peoples of the region' before the arrival of the colonialists does not undermine the fact that, prior to their arrival, there was vital social and economic interaction between the various distinct indigenous groups of the delineated region.[2] This region currently

1 See MR Anderson, 'Human rights approach to environmental protection: an overview', in AE Boyle and MR Anderson (eds), *Human Rights Approaches to Environmental Protection* (Oxford: Clarendon Press, 1998) 1, 19.

2 T Falola and MM Heaton, *A History of Nigeria* (New York: Cambridge University Press, 2008) 17–18.

occupied by Nigeria was made up of numerous nation states and societies, each with its own linguistic, legal and political system, with varying degrees of openness and public participation opportunities in governance. Of the around 250 ethnic groups in Nigeria, three made/make up the majority of the country's population: the Hausa-Fulani in the north (about 29 per cent), the Yoruba in the south-west (about 20 per cent) and the Igbo in the south-east (about 18 per cent).[3]

Archaeological evidence suggests that a common denominator of all the early nation states and societies is that they were decentralised in nature several thousand years ago.[4] However, with the passage of time, in what has been broadly classified as the two main African political patterns,[5] some of these societies had developed more centralised political state structures, whilst others continued with their politically decentralised state structures until the arrival of the British colonialists.[6] However, it can be said that even in societies with a mostly centralised political administrative structure, the general paternalistic relationship that usually exists between the ruler and the ruled, which is broadly an element of pre-colonial traditional African societies,[7] may well have continued to persist in those societies before the British colonial era. So, whilst the ruled may pay tribute and taxes, the understanding was that the ruler had to benefit the ruled from what he/she had received.[8] In addition, 'the people were . . . partakers in benefits of the trade of the kingdom, albeit to differing extents. Also, the resources were utilised for the benefit of the community in question or for sections of that community. Benefits accrued to the areas from which resources had been taken. This changed with colonialism',[9] as will be discussed below.

The various groups in the northern part of present-day Nigeria are a good example of nation states and societies that had developed, and were generally administered by broadly centralised bureaucracies. This was largely made possible by the advent of Islam and the trans-Saharan trade, which linked many of the groups in that part of Nigeria with North Africa and the rest of the Arab world.[10] Some of the major and broadly centralised and monarchically ruled states that emerged in the Northern and parts of the Middle Belt regions of Nigeria include:

3 See T Falola and A Genova, *Historical Dictionary of Nigeria* (Maryland: Scarecrow Press, 2009) xxxi–xxxii; and Library of Congress, 'Country profile: Nigeria', July 2008, 9, available at http://lcweb2.loc.gov/frd/cs/profiles/Nigeria.pdf (last accessed 27 January 2015).

4 Ibid, 16, 18 and 21–22.

5 M Fortes and E Pritchard, 'Introduction', in M Fortes and E Pritchard (eds), *African Political Systems* (London: KPI Ltd, 1987) 1, 5.

6 Ibid.

7 Y Omorogbe, 'The legal framework for public participation in decision-making on mining and energy development in Nigeria: giving voices to the voiceless', in DN Zillman, AR Lucas and G Pring (eds), *Human Rights in National Resource Development: Public Participation in the Sustainable Development of Mining and Energy Resource* (Oxford: Oxford University Press, 2002) 549, 551.

8 See ibid; and L Mair, *African Kingdoms* (New York: Oxford University Press, 1977) 95.

9 Omorogbe (n 7) 551–52. See also W Rodney, *How Europe Underdeveloped Africa* (Washington DC: Howard University Press, 1982) 69.

10 See RH Dusgate, *The Conquest of Northern Nigeria* (London: Frank Cass, 1985); and M Adamu, *The Hausa Factor in West African History* (Zaria: Ahmadu Bello University Press and Ibadan: Oxford University Press, 1978).

the Kanem-Bornu Empire, which emerged between the 8th and the 13th centuries in the north-eastern region towards Lake Chad; the Jukun states which arose before the 14th century south of the Kanem-Bornu Empire and including parts of the Middle Belt region; as well as the, probably 14, autonomous Hausa states which emerged, with the gradual decline of the Kanem-Bornu Empire, in the 15th and 16th centuries occupying much of the North and Middle Belt regions.[11]

However, the peak of the Islamic ascendancy in the north of Nigeria was the launch of the Fulani *Jihad* in 1804, which succeeded in bringing most parts of the Northern and Middle Belt regions of Nigeria, on the face of it at least, under the 'centralised and hierarchical theocratic rule of the Sokoto Caliphate'.[12] Nonetheless, the reality was that this arrangement did not significantly restrict many communities from governing themselves in line with their extant and relatively open political structures.[13] That arrangement also did not hinder members of the relevant communities from having a voice in governance giving the allowances created by the political and administrative structure of the Sokoto Caliphate, which evolved in different ways over the century.[14]

The Caliphate, headed by the sultan resident in the capital of Sokoto, was organised around about 30 largely independent emirates, headed by emirs (who, in a council, were in charge of appointing the sultan)[15] with loose allegiance to the sultan who was mainly a spiritual head supported by taxes from the emirates.[16] Although new emirs had to be approved by the sultan, he 'almost always approved of whoever had been locally nominated' and rarely ever interfered in any significant way in the administration of the emirates.[17]

The decentralisation of authority in the Sokoto Caliphate went further than that. The ruling councils of some of the emirs were made up of various interest groups; there were sub-emirates, under major emirates, with no ties to the sultan; further, there were local village and even ward heads selected by their communities for grassroots governance; legitimate and effective pressure groups were in place; even slaves (and other commoners) held positions of public administration and authority etc.[18] In short, given the variety of state structures within the Sokoto Caliphate, even though a degree of centralised power was accepted in some emirates, 'there were definite policies to [not only] maintain competition for office at the centre . . . [but to] inhibit the growth of centralized, monocratic power' in the major emirates at least.[19]

11 See Falola and Heaton (n 2) 26–29.
12 EE Osaghae, *Crippled Giant: Nigeria Since Independence* (London: Hurst & Co Publishers Ltd, 1998) 3. See also Falola and Heaton (n 2) 70.
13 Falola and Heaton (n 2) 65.
14 See P Burnham and M Last, 'From pastoralist to politician: the problem of Fulbey "aristocracy"' (1994) 34 *Cahiers d'études Africaines* 313–57.
15 Ibid.
16 See JN Paden, 'The Sokoto Caliphate and its legacies (1804–2004)', available at http://www.dawodu.com/paden1.htm (last accessed 27 January 2015).
17 Falola and Heaton (n 2) 65–66.
18 See ibid; and Burnham and Last (n 14).
19 Burnham and Last (n 14) 325.

Moving on, the south-west is another region of modern-day Nigeria where early societies had generally metamorphosed into mostly centralised political structures ruled by monarchies. The significant entities in this region included the Benin Kingdom, which probably first emerged around the 10th century and came to dominate mainly the (former) mid-west region; and the Ile-Ife Kingdom, which clearly emerged around the 12th century as a regional power in much of the Yoruba-speaking areas of the south-west,[20] until its political might was eclipsed by the rise of the Oyo Empire, which dominated the Yorubaland from the 16th century.[21]

However, the Yoruba system of government, referred to as a 'constitutional monarchy',[22] is particularly notable for having demonstrated a clear form of participatory 'monarchical democracy', which 'involved many checks and balances – eloquent of a long, studied evolution'.[23] So even though the *Alafin* of the Oyo Empire was the king, the powerful institutions of the *Oyo Mesi* and the *Ogboni* kept his power in check.[24] Whilst the *Oyo Mesi* was a council of seven principal state counsellors in charge of heading the army and electing as well as removing the *Alafin*, and with whom the *Alafin* was required to consult for advice and legitimisation of his decisions on important state matters, the *Ogboni* fraternity was a powerful widespread institution that represented popular opinion, wielding religious authority and acting as a check on the *Oyo Mesi* (which wielded political power) by moderating their views.[25] As further noted by Elias, the political structure of the Oyo Empire was complex and very detailed, in a manner that allowed for relative openness and incorporation of public views in governance:

> In the governance of the realm, the Alafin was assisted by a council consisting of all the paramount chiefs, each of whom was in his own chiefdom similarly assisted by a local council of chiefs, each of whom was in turn assisted by a council of all the local family heads. This hierarchy of advisers was based upon the principle of representation and of mandate, so that each paramount chief or family head was required to seek or obtain the mandate of the community or group represented by him whenever important decisions were to be taken affecting the general welfare of the kingdom.[26]

More than that, as noted earlier, there existed highly politically decentralised and open state systems in many other parts of Nigeria that worked for the public good. A good example of this is the political system of the Igbo people, who were and

20 Falola and Heaton (n 2) 22–26.
21 Ibid, 24.
22 Library of Congress (n 3) 2.
23 W Ademoyega, *The Federation of Nigeria from Earliest Times to Independence* (London: George G. Harrap & Co, 1962) 41–42 and 65.
24 See GT Stride and C Ifeka, *Peoples and Empires of West Africa: West Africa History, 1000–1800* (Edinburgh: Nelson, 1971) 298–300.
25 See ibid; and Falola and Heaton (n 2) 50.
26 TO Elias, *Nigeria: The Development of its Laws and Constitution* (London: Steven & Sons, 1967) 11.

remain the dominant group in the south-eastern part of present-day Nigeria. Although the Igbo political institutions varied across the various Igbo groups – with very few even adopting some monarchical characteristics from neighbouring centralised states – the vast majority of Igbo communities were highly decentralised and open.[27] They adopted a system of governance where 'democracy was direct and real',[28] hence the popular Igbo sayings: '*Igbo enwe eze*' (i.e. 'the Igbos have no kings')[29] and *Ezebuilo* (i.e. 'a king is an enemy').[30]

Accordingly, at a level, there were generally the village-group meetings in which decisions were made through consensus by a council of elders comprised of family heads who were answerable to their villages and kinship groups.[31] There were also the consultative village assemblies that ensured transparency, where basically anyone had the right to express their views and participate in decision-making.[32] Decisions by the village-group council were not binding as any one village could legitimately choose not to abide by them and could not be forced into submission.[33] One Nicolas Peter-Okoye, in an interview, described the level of access to information and decision-making process the public in Igboland had in the pre-colonial era:

> In my village, Enugwu-Uku, whenever anything was to be done, the *ekwe* [a wooden drum] would be beaten by the designated person. When it is beaten, people know that there is something to be done, and that people should come to the village square for information. To the extent that people were to be affected by actions to be taken, they had to be involved in the decision, there was nothing like just ordering them.[34]

Similar open and disaggregated political systems existed in the societies of many other ethnic groups in the Nigerian region, such as those of the Tiv in the Middle Belt, and the Isoko, Urhobo, Ibibio, Ijaw, Efik, Annang and Kalabari in the southern region.[35] Owing to the high level of openness and fragmentation of political power in these decentralised states and their like, some early foreign scholars referred to them as 'stateless societies'.[36] Conversely, such a characterisation

27 Falola and Heaton (n 2) 22.
28 Ademoyega (n 23) 65.
29 C Azuonye, 'Igbo Enwe Eze: monarchical power versus democratic values in Igbo oral narratives', in G Furniss and L Gunner (eds), *Power, Marginality, and African Oral Literature* (Cambridge: Cambridge University Press, 1995) 65.
30 C Achebe, *There was a Country: A Personal History of Biafra* (London: Penguin Books, 2012) 246.
31 AA Gordon, *Nigeria's Diverse Peoples: A Reference Sourcebook* (California: ABC-CLIO Inc, 2003) 37.
32 Falola and Heaton (n 2) 22.
33 Ibid.
34 A Obe, 'The challenging case of Nigeria', in A Florini (ed), *The Right to Know: Transparency for an Open World* (New York: Colombia University Press, 2007) 143.
35 See ET Bristol-Alagbariya, *Participation in Petroleum Development: Towards Sustainable Community Development in Niger Delta* (Dundee: Centre for Energy, Petroleum and Mineral Law and Policy, 2009) 105–29; Falola and Heaton (n 2) 22; and Osaghae (n 12) 3.
36 See Fortes and Pritchard (n 5) 5.

has come to be termed 'misleading', especially as '[t]rue statelessness implies a lack of political authority and, therefore, the existence of anarchy, which none of these societies exhibited.'[37]

Perhaps, this unique quality of politically disaggregated states, together with the broadly effective public administration in centralised bureaucracies which embraced a level of openness and public participation,[38] formed the foundation upon which a former colonial administrator, Sir Hugh Clifford, described the diverse traditional forms of government the colonists encountered as 'the natural expression of their innate political genius', to the Nigerian Council in 1920.[39]

This discussion demonstrates that open and public participatory governance, where government had its focus on the public good was, to a reasonable extent, not alien to many of the constituent parts of Nigeria.[40] As some have argued, this was generally the case in many traditional African societies,[41] where, '[h]istorically . . . public participation was central to natural resource management'.[42] In fact, the fact that public participation was an integral part of governance in many traditional Nigerian societies is reflected in many local proverbs, which served as principles of governance; e.g. 'a herbalist that refuses to ask laymen what leaves he looks for in the bush, must have difficulties getting what he wants', and 'one finger cannot remove lice from the head'.

These elements of democracy, which are woven in varying degrees into the fabric of many cultural groups that make up Nigeria, and still persist to an extent, largely inform the expectations of the wider populace of how current governance, which may affect their environment, should be carried out; this is in terms of ensuring appropriate and adequate public access to environmental information and decision-making processes in view of current societal development and not necessarily a call for the country to return to those exact modes of traditional public participation. Thus, as one will expect, any attempt to create a different order or an unusual barrier between the government and the governed, without the relevant public support, may only be viewed and approached as an abnormality by many. This is the case of the British colonialists who arrived in the 19th century with their own method of public administration and governance.

37 Falola and Heaton (n 2) 21. See also Osaghae (n 12) 3.
38 See Osaghae (n 12) 2.
39 Debates, 29 December 1920, 20–22, cited in Elias (n 26) 13.
40 Omorogbe (n 7) 551.
41 See Ademoyega (n 23) 52–66.
42 C Odote and MO Makoloo, 'African initiatives for public participation in environmental management', in C Bruch (ed), *The New "Public": The Globalization of Public Participation* (Washington DC: Environmental Law Institute, 2002) 121.

2.2.2 Nigeria under British colonial rule

Aptly put, the governance of indigenous Nigerians by the British colonialists has been described as 'politically suppressive, economically exploitative, socially discriminating and culturally polluting'.[43]

British colonisation of the area that came to be 'Nigeria' officially began in 1861 when Britain annexed Lagos as a British colony, even though it had been interfering in the local politics of the people in the preceding years.[44] From its base in Lagos, it took the British over 40 years to colonise the entire area of contemporary Nigeria; by roughly 1903–1906 they had created and were in control of the Colony and Protectorate of Lagos, the Protectorate of Southern Nigeria, and the Protectorate of Northern Nigeria, consisting of previously independent states under indigenous leadership and governance.[45] These indigenous societies were brought together under the rule of the colonial authority with the use of violence by the British military and the willingness or threat to use violence to achieve their ends.[46] Efforts to implement colonial rule over these indigenous states continually met with widespread passive and active resistance from the locals.[47]

The role of multinational companies in the colonisation of Nigeria is also worth emphasising. In particular, the activities of the gargantuan 'chartered Royal Niger Company [RNC] were instrumental in gaining ultimate control of the Niger and the Benue for the British'.[48] Rather than proclaim a protectorate status over the Niger and Benue and shoulder the consequential cost, as was its practice in other areas, the British Government took a different approach by granting a royal charter to RNC, a British mercantile company, over those areas. Under the charter, 'the RNC came to control the [political administration and] trade on the Niger between the delta and Nupe and on the Benue as far as Yola', and the administration of these areas were to be paid for by the RNC.[49]

The RNC forced the locals to sign treaties that granted it extensive trade rights and political sovereignty over their territories, all with the backing of the British military.[50] For example, the Brass community of the delta was once destroyed and thousands killed by the Royal Navy at the behest of RNC 'to ensure that the company had a monopoly over palm-oil trade for which the town was famous'.[51] The governing authority of RNC was subsequently revoked, and the areas it

43 See PN Nwokolo, 'The Nigerian press and the law of sedition: a progressive interpretation' (2012) 23(1) *Review of Education* 201, 217.

44 Falola and Heaton (n 2) 94–95.

45 See ibid, 86; and Osaghae (n 12) 4.

46 See Falola and Heaton (n 2) 85–86 and 109; and Osaghae (n 12) 4.

47 See Falola and Heaton (n 2) 106–109.

48 Ibid, 93.

49 Ibid, 98–99.

50 Ibid, 100–102.

51 N Bassey, 'Trade and human rights in the Niger delta of Nigeria', available at http://www.worldhunger.org/articles/06/africa/bassey.htm (last accessed 27 January 2015). See also Falola and Heaton (n 2) 100–102.

administered came under the direct control of the British Government,[52] which continued to expropriate the natural resources of local communities for export to Britain, to the detriment of the locals.[53]

Moving on, in 1914, the southern and northern territories that were previously administered separately by the colonialists were amalgamated as a single country called 'Nigeria' to ensure a more effective and efficient colonial administration.[54] In consonance with the dominant method of operation of the colonialists, the general consensus or consent of the indigenous peoples of the various regions were not sought on this important move, which saw the removal of customs frontiers between the 'two countries', the adoption of a single weekly *Gazette* and currency, the unification of infrastructure, taxation and judicial systems and bureaucracy, amongst other changes.[55] In short, the amalgamation was not popular amongst the indigenous population, especially in the north.[56]

In further reorganisation, the colonialists foisted on the entire country a centralised, closed and largely non-participatory political and administrative system, even in places that ran more open and participatory systems immediately prior to colonisation.[57] This was done in ways which included the substantial extension of the traditional powers of kings (where these existed) and the appointment of warrant/paramount chiefs (where the likes of kings did not exist) to rule over the people in line with the biddings of the colonialists.[58] In addition, the character of the political and administrative structures established everywhere was one 'rooted in authoritarianism and ethnic divisions, widespread illiteracy, and extreme marginalization' of the indigenous peoples.[59]

Accordingly, the laws and policies created in this era were also mainly to aid the interests of the colonial government and were not focused on furthering the interests of the public or their inclusion, but exclusion.[60] For example, the fairly participatory traditional processes for managing and allocating land for development in most places across Nigeria were partly restricted and centralised by the colonists, particularly in the north, with a series of enactments which endowed the High Commissioner with title and control of land.[61]

52 Falola and Heaton (n 2) 101–104.

53 Omorogbe (n 7) 552.

54 See Osaghae (n 12) 11–12.

55 CM Ngou, 'The 1959 elections and formation of the Independence Government', in PP Ekeh and G Asiwaju (eds), *Nigeria Since Independence: The First 25 Years*, Vol V: *Politics and Constitutions* (Ibadan: Heinemann, 1989) 81.

56 A Adeleye, 'Amalgamation of 1914: was it a mistake?', *Vanguard*, 18 May 2012, available at http://www.vanguardngr.com/2012/05/amalgamation-of-1914-was-it-a-mistake/ (last accessed 27 January 2015).

57 See Elias (n 26) 24–50; and Osaghae (n 12) 2.

58 See Azuonye (n 29) 67; and Falola and Heaton (n 2) 117.

59 Algiers Declaration, adopted by the OAU Assembly of Heads of State and Government at its 35th Ordinary Session, 12–14 July 1999, AHG/Dec.1(XXXV), OAU Doc DOC/OS(XXVI) INF.17a (1999).

60 See Omorogbe (n 7) 552–53.

61 See CS Ola, *Town and Country Planning Law in Nigeria* (Ibadan: Oxford University Press, 1977) 15–17; C Nwalimu, *The Nigerian Legal System: Private Law* (Vol 2, New York: Peter Lang Publishing Inc, 2009) 312–15; and AN Allot, 'Nigeria: Land Use Act' (1978) 22(2) *Journal of African Law* 136.

Also, the interest of the colonialists in not making information generally available to the colonised people and in supressing the free flow of information, which might undermine the imperial government, was expressed in the introduction and enforcement of the Official Secrets Act – the legislative expression of its own tradition of secrecy which dates back to 1911.[62] Apparently, this was with the aim to deprive the public even further from having the capacity to effectively participate in governance or hold the colonial government accountable, in any way. Similarly, with the aim of gagging the public and the press and quashing criticism or disclosure of even accurate facts that were contrary to the position or interest of the colonial government, the draconian Sedition Offences Ordinance of 1909 was promulgated and strictly enforced.[63]

Similarly, even though the British colonial administration utilised the concept of 'indirect rule' (i.e. rule through traditional kings and authorities) to govern most local areas, its ideal aim of 'respect[ing] traditional political institutions and promot[ing] continuity between indigenous and colonial regimes' remained a mirage.[64] In practice, apart from the fact that the system facilitated the exclusion of (educated) members of the public from participating in governance:[65]

> indirect rule [also] alienated traditional authorities from their subject population through their association with the colonial regime. Furthermore, traditional rulers found that they maintained their power at the behest of British colonial officers, who made sure that colonial directives where enforced at all times. Insubordinate indigenous rulers soon found themselves ousted and their places taken by more malleable replacements.[66]

In summary, in the colonial era transparency and public participation in governance were generally at their lowest ebb across Nigeria as the fulfilment of the exploitative motives of the colonialists necessitated the shutting out of the public from the business of governance. Whatever open, participatory and people-focused elements that were part of governance in the traditional societies were largely washed away by the attendant negative impacts of colonialism, so much so that the politics, public administration, laws and institutions of independent Nigeria continue to be influenced, to an extent, by its colonial past with the blessing of successive Nigerian governments.[67]

62 Obe (n 34) 148.

63 See FIA Omu, *Press and Politics in Nigeria, 1880–1937* (London: Longman Group, 1978) 182–86; and Nwokolo (n 43) 201–213 and 215–16. See also *Rex v Agwuna and Ors* (1949)12 WACA 456; *The African Press v The Queen* (1952) 14 WACA'57; *Queen v The African Press and LK Jakande* (1957) WNLR 1; *Ogidi v COP* (1960) 5 FSC 251.

64 Falola and Heaton (n 2) 110.

65 Elias (n 26) 34.

66 Falola and Heaton (n 2) 110–111.

67 See Odote and Makoloo (n 42); and M Owusu, 'Comparative politics, history, and political anthropology', in M Owusu (ed), *Colonialism and Change* (The Hague: Monte Publishers, 1975) 25, 39–40.

At the end of the Second World War, there was an escalation of organised resistance to colonial rule by Nigerians, essentially agitating for 'greater respect, participation in government, and independence'.[68] When it became obvious to the British, by the late 1950s, that colonial rule could hardly be sustained, they entered into dialogue with Nigeria's anti-colonial leaders; the decolonisation process had started.[69] In December 1959, general elections were conducted and, by 1 October 1960, Nigeria had become independent.

2.3 Nigeria after independence: government and the people

2.3.1 From independent civilian government . . .

The first indigenous government upon independence was a civilian government in the style of a parliamentary democracy. Apart from widely held general elections to choose parliamentary representatives, and similar to the *status quo* in the colonial era, there was no meaningful improvement in the transparency of governance and the participatory status of the larger public. Contrary to expectations, the indigenous ruling elites generally did not seek to adopt elements of the relatively open, participatory and people-focused traditional systems of governance that existed in parts of Nigeria and were also generally in line with the democratic form of government they were meant to be running.[70] Rather, as it appeared, governance, as in the colonial era, was generally about the interests of those in government: '[o]fficial corruption, rigged elections, ethnic baiting, bullying, and thuggery dominated the conduct of politics in the First Republic, which existed from 1960 to 1966.'[71] Unfortunately, the testimony of the Second Republic,[72] which lasted from 1979 to 1983, was similar in character to that of the First.[73]

Generally, despite its political independence in 1960 and the attainment of republican status in 1963, 'the legal and political systems [of Nigeria] were [and are currently and largely] still based on the colonial tradition and standards'[74] – largely averse to the fundamental idea that 'the independence of our laws and legal institutions is seen as a necessary corollary to political

68 Falola and Genova (n 3) xxxv–xxxvi.
69 Ibid, xxxvi.
70 See Elias (n 26) 13.
71 Falola and Heaton (n 2) 159.
72 There was no continuity between the First and Second Republics as the First Republic was truncated in 1966 by military takeover and civilian government (the Second Republic) was only restored in 1979.
73 See T Forrest, 'The political economy of civil rule and the economic crisis in Nigeria (1979–1984): the struggle for spoils' (1986) 13(35) *Review of African Political Economy* 4–26; and Obe (n 34) 145.
74 C Obiagwu and CA Odinkalu, 'Nigeria: combating legacies of colonialism and militarism', in AA An-Na'im (ed), *Human Rights under African Constitutions: Realizing the Promise for Ourselves* (Pennsylvania: University of Pennsylvania Press, 2003) 211, 215.

independence'.[75] This is partly evidenced by the fact that laws introduced by the colonial government to prevent government transparency and suppress the campaign of the indigenous peoples for openness and self-rule, as well as similar post-colonial laws, were retained or enacted by the various governments of the newly independent Nigeria, especially as they found such laws useful for their own political purposes in supressing any form of public opposition or call for accountability.[76]

In that light, the Official Secrets Act of 1962[77] was enacted; it prohibited the transmission of 'classified matter', defined so nebulously[78] that any government information could fall under it. An example of this, showing government obsession with secrecy at this early stage, is the Federal Ministry of Justice deciding to stamp as 'secret' papers it was going to file in court even though, in accordance with the Evidence Act, these became public documents of which certified copies could be obtained (in theory).[79]

Fundamentally, such secrecy laws were not expressly invalidated by the various constitutions made after independence. So even though Nigeria's Independence Constitution of 1960, as well as those of 1963 and 1979, made provision for the right to 'receive and impart ideas and information without interference' – the scope of which does not clearly, but only possibly, includes the imposition of a positive duty on the state to ensure public access to information – there was the equivocal proviso which gave the government the power to impose restrictions on government workers and make or retain laws that are 'reasonably justifiable in a democratic society . . . in the interest of defence, public safety, public order, public morality, or public health'.[80] With this in place, the government continued to implement the arguably undemocratic Official Secrets Act. And of course, if there is no public access to information, talks of public participation in decision-making under this democratic setting was meaningless.

The same applies to the received law on sedition, which significantly curtailed public expression and debate. For example, on that basis, the Supreme Court of Nigeria in the case of *DPP v Chike Obi*,[81] a year after independence, held that although it was constitutional (under section 24 of the 1963 Constitution, on freedom of speech) for the government to be criticised, it could not be criticised in a 'malignant' manner; whereas, the seditious issue in the case was merely that a member of the House of Representatives had published a pamphlet entitled

75 GNK Vukor-Quarshie, 'Criminal justice administration in Nigeria: Saro-Wiwa in review' (1997) 8 *Criminal Law Forum* 87, 104.

76 Obiagwu and Odinkalu (n 74) 215.

77 Cap 335 Laws of the Federation of Nigeria, 1990.

78 Section 9(1) of the Act defines classified matter as 'any information or thing which under *any system of security classification* from time to time in use by or by any branch of the government, is not to be disclosed to the public and of which the disclosure to the public would be prejudicial to the security of Nigeria' (emphasis added).

79 Obe (n 34) 173–72.

80 See 1960 Independence Constitution of Nigeria, s 24; 1963 Constitution of the Federal Republic of Nigeria, s 25; 1979 Constitution of the Federal Republic of Nigeria, s 36.

81 (1961) 1 All NLR 186 at 194.

'The people – facts that you must know', accusing public office holders of exploiting the weak and oppressing the poor.[82]

However, the application of the law on sedition was somewhat relaxed by the courts in the Second Republic in favour of more freedom of speech based on 'the principle that debate on public issues should be uninhibited, robust and wide open and that it may well include vehement caustic and sometimes unpleasantly sharp attacks on government and public officials'.[83] Nonetheless, the sedition law remained on the books (until this day, despite being in a democratic era), available, at least, to ground the arrest and harassment of those who chose to express themselves contrary to government interest.[84]

Strangely, however, it was in the Second Republic that Nigeria ratified the 1981 African Charter on Human and People's Rights[85] in 1983, which provides for the public 'right to receive information' (like the 1979 Nigerian Constitution at the time),[86] as well as the right of every citizen 'to participate freely in the government of his country, either directly or through freely chosen representatives in accordance with the provisions of the law'.[87] Even though this Charter was domesticated in 1983 by the enactment of the African Charter on Human and People's Rights (Ratification and Enforcement) Act,[88] its provisions were hardly interpreted or implemented to enable better public access to information and/or decision-making processes. Rather, the opposite continued to be the case.

2.3.2 . . . to military rule

With the new democratic government of the First Republic still finding its feet, and at a time when public dissatisfaction with the government was high, the military overthrew the civilian administration in January 1966 through a bloody *coup d'état*. For about 28 years,[89] mostly through *coups d'état* and counter-*coups d'état*, several military dictators ruled Nigeria autocratically. Right from the first *coup d'état*, their aim, as several military dictators would usually claim, was to revive the economy, end misrule and massive corruption (financial and otherwise) that had generally become the character of government.[90] However, these aims were

82 Ibid, 189–90. See also *Attorney-General Western Nigeria v African Press and Ayo Ojewumi* (1965) 1 All NLR 12.

83 *State v Ivory Trumpet Publishing Co Ltd and Ors* (1984) 5 NCLR 736, 756 (Araka CJ, as he then was). See also *State v Arthur Nwankwo* (1985) 6 NCLR 645.

84 See e.g. Committee to Protect Journalists, 'Nigerian editor charged with sedition, jailed', *Refworld*, 29 January 2008, available at http://www.refworld.org/docid/48243c6523.html (last accessed 27 January 2015).

85 27 June 1981, 1520 UNTS 217.

86 Article 9.

87 Article 13.

88 Cap A9, Laws of the Federation of Nigeria, 2004.

89 Basically, the military ruled from 1966–1999, excluding the short-lived Second Republic of 1979–1983 and the Interim National Government of August 1993–November 1993.

90 See Falola and Heaton (n 2) 172; and Vukor-Quarshie (n 75) 104.

largely not achieved,[91] especially as the primary motivation and preoccupation of most of the military dictators was the primitive accumulation of public funds and personal gratification, and not public service.[92]

Crude oil, which was first discovered in the Niger Delta area of Nigeria in 1956 – four years before independence – began to witness massive price increases only in the late 1960s and 1970s for some external reasons.[93] With rising production, government revenue from crude oil skyrocketed: from a mere ₦200,000 in 1958, the first commercial production, revenues in 1970, 1974 and 1976 rose to ₦166 million, ₦3.7 billion and ₦5.3 billion, respectively.[94] By 1974, about 82 per cent of the Nigerian Government's revenue, as opposed to roughly 1–10 per cent during the First Republic, came from crude oil alone, even as other revenue-earning sectors (e.g. agriculture and manufacturing) necessary for a stable economy were neglected and left to dwindle significantly.[95] Once Nigerian soldiers had gained a hold on the country's oil wealth, it was difficult to relinquish.[96] Kleptocracy was generally the order of the day under military rule. In fact, as noted by Alhaji Shehu Musa, the Second Republic's Secretary to the Federal Government of Nigeria, the scary fact in Nigeria was not just that officials were corrupt, but that corruption was official.[97]

The mismanagement of the country's economy by the military led to a significant plunge in the living standards of salaried civil service workers.[98] This naturally led to an explosion in corruption in its diverse forms in the civil service, including 'extorting money from anyone whose misfortune it was to have to transact business with government', as workers tried to weather the storm caused by the rocketing inflation.[99] This was in addition to ensure their financial security, by hook or by crook, in view of the rampant sacking and retirement of numerous public officers by the military without due process or, indeed, any process at all.[100] Basically, under the military, Nigeria went from being a relatively rich country to a poor one.[101]

91 TI Ogowewo, 'Why the judicial annulment of the constitution of 1999 is imperative to the survival of Nigeria's democracy' (2000) 44 *Journal of African Law* 135, 141.
92 Foreword by the Chairman, Hon Justice Chukwudifu A Oputa, 'Synoptic overview of the Human Rights Violations Investigation Commission Report: summary, conclusions and recommendations' (2002) 2–3, available at http://www.nigerianmuse.com/nigeriawatch/oputa/ (last accessed 27 January 2015).
93 These reasons include the 1973 Arab-Israeli war and the historically remarkable fourfold price increase by the Organisation of Petroleum Exporting Countries (OPEC) in that period. See Obe (n 34) 146.
94 Falola and Heaton (n 2) 182.
95 See ibid, 182–83; and Osaghae (n 12) 20.
96 Obe (n 34) 145.
97 T David-West, 'Buhari: the politics of religion', *The Sun*, 1 December 2014, available at http://sunnewsonline.com/new/?p=93431 (last accessed 14 February 2015).
98 See Obe (n 34) 145.
99 Ibid, 145 and 149.
100 Ibid, 145.
101 See ibid, 149; and Foreword by the Chairman, Hon Justice Chukwudifu A Oputa (n 92) 2–3.

In 1998, a few months before the end of the last military regime in the country, Nigeria was ranked as the fifth most corrupt country in a survey of 85 countries undertaken by Transparency International.[102]

Away from the economic front, the military governments usually dissolved and/or ruled without the civilian legislature, having had their law-making function absorbed by the executive Supreme Military Council,[103] which was chaired by the military head of state.[104] The promulgation and enforcement of exclusive decrees that trampled on the fundamental rights of citizens was the hallmark of law-making and governance under military rule. It was in this era that the revolutionary and highly controversial Land Use Decree No 6 of 1978 was promulgated by the then military ruler, General Olusegun Obasanjo. This extant, far-reaching Land Use Decree (now an Act)[105] removed title in land from individual Nigerians, families and communities, including the management of same from family heads and chiefs, vesting these on the governor of states (for urban land) and local governments (for rural lands), to be held in trust and used for the common benefit of all Nigerians.[106]

This land law, which leaves members of the public with only a 'right of occupancy', has remained the subject of much criticism from an environmental perspective,[107] especially as it was not enacted with any public participation or even debated by representatives of the public. In fact, the military dictatorship decided not to follow 'the recommendation of the majority opinion of the Land Use Panel it had set up to study the existing customary system of land tenure and make appropriate recommendations for reform, not to nationalise land in Nigeria'.[108]

Apart from other areas of natural resource mining and exploration in the country, the effect of this Land Use Decree was probably more significantly felt by the inhabitants of the Niger Delta than other areas. The Decree contains provisions allowing the government to appropriate land for 'overriding public interests', a phrase defined by the Decree to include 'the requirement of the land for mining purposes or oil pipelines or for any purpose connected therewith'.[109] Prior to the Decree, the process of crude oil exploration and production involved

102 Transparency International, 'The Corruption Perceptions Index (1998)', available at http://archive.transparency.org/policy_research/surveys_indices/cpi/previous_cpi/1998#how-to-read (last accessed 27 January 2015).

103 Depending on the military regime, this body may be styled 'Armed Forces Ruling Council' or 'Provisional Ruling Council'; their functions were the same.

104 E Okpanachi and A Garba, 'Federalism and constitutional change in Nigeria' (2010) 7(1) *Federal Governance* 1, 5.

105 Cap L5, Laws of the Federation of Nigeria, 2004.

106 See ss 1 and 2. See also *Abiola v Yakubu* (1991) 5 NWLR (pt 190) 130, where the court finally determined the far-reaching effect of the decree.

107 See e.g. RT Ako, 'Nigeria's Land Use Act: an anti-thesis to environmental justice' (2009) 53(2) *Journal of African Law* 289–304; KSA Ebeku, 'Oil and the Niger delta people: the injustice of the Land Use Act' (2002) 35(2) *Law and Politics in Africa, Asia and Latin America* 201–31.

108 VE Kalu, 'State monopoly and indigenous participation rights in resource development in Nigeria' (2008) 26(3) *Journal of Energy and Natural Resources Law* 418, 425.

109 Land Use Decree, s 28. Under that provision, 'overriding public interest' also means: the requirement of the land by government 'for public purposes'; 'the requirement of the land for the

a tripartite agreement.[110] First, before companies could prospect for oil, they had to seek and obtain the requisite licence from the federal government, which has the power to grant such licences being the legal owner of all mineral resources, including oil, in Nigeria.[111]

If successful with the federal government, 'it was necessary to approach the relevant family or community for permission to enter into *their land* to carry out the oil exploration and/or production activity that the government had earlier permitted':[112] 'The family or community, as legal owners of the land at the time, negotiated terms of entry, rent payable for use of land and other benefits that the family or community would derive from the company.'[113] So what the Land Use Decree did was to take away people's rights to seek to manage the impact of the oil industry on them.[114]

Furthermore, section 1(1) of the first military decree – the Constitution (Suspension and Modification) Decree No 1 of 1966 (subsequent adopted by other military governments) – subordinated the 1963 Constitution to military decrees and abrogated its bill of rights aspect, amongst other parts.[115] Thus, under the military, such basic rights as to liberty, fair hearing, freedom of expression, movement and association, were largely unavailable to the public.[116] Accordingly, state secrecy was the norm and public participation in governance was generally suppressed. It was common practice for human rights activists and pro-democracy activists to be arrested and/or executed in defiance of due process, as was the case of Dele Giwa, the outspoken editor of the popular *Newwatch* magazine, who was murdered through a parcel bomb[117] and Ken Saro-Wiwa, a minority rights activist, with eight of his *Ogoni* kinsmen, who were 'judicially murdered' in order to shut them up.[118]

With the abrogation of human rights laws, the enforcement of draconian decrees and the practical violation of the public's human rights by military

extraction of building material' (only in the case of a customary right of occupancy); and the illegal alienation by the occupier of any right of occupancy.

110 RT Ako, 'Enforcing environmental rights under Nigeria's 1999 constitution: the localisation of human rights in the Niger delta region', in K De Feyter, S Parmentier, C Timmerman and G Ulrich (eds), *The Local Relevance of Human Rights* (Cambridge: Cambridge University Press, 2011) 270, 274.

111 See e.g. Petroleum Decree No 51 of 1969 (now Petroleum Act, Cap P10, Laws of the Federation of Nigeria, 2004), s 1; and the 1999 Nigerian Constitution (as amended), s 44(3).

112 Ako (n 110) 274.

113 Ibid.

114 Ibid, 274–75.

115 See Obiagwu and Odinkalu (n 74) 218.

116 O Oko, 'Seeking justice in transitional societies: an analysis of the problems and failures of the judiciary in Nigeria' (2006) 9 *Brooklyn Journal of International Law* 10, 11.

117 See Centre for Socio-Legal Studies, 'Justice sector reform and human rights in Nigeria' (Abuja: Centre for Socio-Legal Studies, 2009) 3, available at http://censolegs.org/1.pdf (last accessed 27 January 2015).

118 Amnesty International, 'Nigeria: time for justice and accountability', 2000, 1, available at http://www.amnesty.org/en/library/asset/AFR44/014/2000/en/a677253f-dc60-11dd-bce7-11be3666d687/afr440142000en.pdf (last accessed 14 February 2015). See also A Maja-Pearce, *From Khaki to Agbada: A Handbook for the February 1999 Elections in Nigeria* (Lagos: Civil Liberties Organisation, 1999) 12–17.

administrators, one may ask about the whereabouts of the judiciary – popularly termed 'the last hope of the common man'. Although not abrogated, successive military governments characteristically promulgated decrees that ousted the jurisdiction of the courts in major areas of concern. An example is the broad Federal Military Government (Supremacy and Enforcement Powers) Decree No 13 of 1984, which was a staple in several military regimes.[119] This decree ousted the jurisdiction of the court to entertain or continue any civil proceedings or adjudicate on any matter bordering on whether any human rights provision of the constitution has been or would be contravened in view of anything done or proposed to be done in pursuance of any decree or edict.[120] These measures further contributed to creating the enabling environment for the traditions of secrecy and exclusivity to thrive in government.

In essence, the hands of the courts were largely tied in cases where members of the public were not comfortable with the decisions or actions of the various agencies of government under the military. In that light, in the case of *Wang Chin-Yao & Ors v Chief of Staff, Supreme Headquarters*,[121] Justice Adenekan Ademola of the Court of Appeal held that 'on questions of civil liberties, the law courts must as of now blow muted trumpet'.[122] Similarly, Justice Alfa Belgore of the Supreme Court, in the case of *Nwosu v Imo State Environmental Sanitation Authority*,[123] also described human rights litigation under the military as a fruitless 'journey of discovery'.[124] In short, the following observation of Justice Samson Uwaifo of the Court of Appeal (as he then was), in the case of *Okeke v Attorney-General of Anambra State*,[125] aptly captured the general attitude or response of the judiciary to rights-suspending and jurisdiction-ousting provisions of military decrees:

> Once the provisions of a Decree or Constitution ousting the jurisdiction of the courts on any specific matters are clear and unambiguous, the courts are bound to observe and apply them. They are not entitled, *even when the ouster has drastic effect on the right of any person*, to approach its interpretation by a false or twisted meaning given to it by unacceptable restricted construction . . . It is not also a proper attitude for judges to read into such a statute the meaning it does not bear either in order to exercise jurisdiction or to readily abandon it.[126]

119 See e.g. Federal Military Government (Supremacy and Enforcement of Powers) Decree No 28 of 1970; and Federal Military Government (Supremacy and Enforcement of Powers) Decree No 12 of 1994.

120 See JB Dada, 'Impediments to human rights protection in Nigeria' (2012) 18(1) *Annual Survey of International and Comparative Law* 67, 78–79. See also IE Sagay, 'Recent trends in the status and practice of the rule of law in Nigeria' (1988) No 3 *ASUU Monograph Series* 5–6.

121 [1986] LRC (Const) 319.

122 Ibid, 330.

123 (1990) 2 NWLR (pt 135) 688.

124 Ibid, 727.

125 (1992) 1 NWLR (pt 215) 60 at 86, paras B–F.

126 Emphasis added. A similar view was held by the courts in *Okumagba v Egbe* (1965) 1 All NLR 62; *Kanada v Governor of Kaduna State* [1986] 4 NWLR (pt 35) 361; and *Attorney-General Lagos State v Dosunmu* (1989) 3 NWLR (pt 111) 552.

Arguably, the judiciary's general acceptance of the encroachment of their jurisdiction by the military is seemingly tied to the legitimation of military rule in Nigeria, right from the first military incursion into government.[127] Legal scholars and the public generally expected that the judiciary would at least have demonstrated better creativity in its interpretation and application of draconian laws and engaged in meaningful judicial activism to protect civil liberties and their jurisdiction.[128] Indeed, whilst some judges made reasonable efforts in that regard,[129] 'the great majority of judges' applied the decrees in line with the expectations of the military.[130]

Although the [Supreme] Court mustered some courage to insist on judicial review of the executive and legislative actions of the federal military government in the *Lakanmi* case [1970], it capitulated in *Adejumo v Johnson* (1972)' and thereafter generally maintained a literal interpretation of military decrees.[131] This was mainly so given the promulgation of the Federal Military Government (Supremacy and Enforcement Powers) Decree No 28 of 1970 barely two weeks after the decision of the *Lakanmi* case to counter the latter decision.[132] Understandably, this attitude of the military countering judicial pronouncements with decrees shows the uniquely difficult situation the judiciary was in, not to mention the barefaced disobedience to court orders[133] and possible threats to the positions, lives and families of 'rebellious' judges by the military.

Perhaps also, as it seems, the judiciary's legitimation of the militarisation of governance and its general lukewarm attitude to legislative aberrations are not unconnected with its colonial heritage of the British legal system:

> At inception, judges of the superior (and many lower) courts were trained in the British common law system, with its *minimalist* constitutional conception of the role of judges. Added to this is the colonial context in which the role

127 See *Isaac Boro v The Republic* (1967) NMLR 163; *Council of the University of Ibadan v Adamolekun* (1967) 1 All NLR 223; and *E O Lakanmi & Ors v The Attorney-General (Western State), The Secretary to the Tribunal (Investigation of Assets Tribunal) and the Counsel to the Tribunal* (1971) UILR 201, where the Supreme Court of Nigeria, amongst others, referred to the military takeover of power as a 'handover', and went on to accord recognition to the military government as one borne out of 'necessity' (that is, the civil unrest that fell out of the 1964 elections) and thus a 'constitutional government' within the contemplation of the 1963 Republican Constitution. For further discussion see HO Yusuf, 'Calling the judiciary to account for the past: transitional justice and judicial accountability' (2008) 30(2) *Law and Policy* 194, 211–214.

128 See MAA Ozekhome, 'Decrees, ouster clauses and judicial ineptitude' (1989) *Law and Practice* 7; U Osimiri, 'Nigeria: critic of the Money Laundering Decree No 3 1995' (1997) 1(1) *Journal of Money Laundering Control* 84, 91–93; and MM Akanbi and AT Shehu, 'Rule of law in Nigeria' (2012) 3 *Journal of Law, Policy and Globalization* 1, 4–5.

129 See F Viljoen, 'Application of the African Charter on Human and Peoples' Rights by domestic Courts in Africa' (1999) 43(1) *Journal of African Law* 1, 7–11, for some of such cases.

130 Centre for Socio-Legal Studies (n 117) 4.

131 See Yusuf (n 127) 211–212.

132 See ibid, 212.

133 See JN Aduba, 'The protection of human rights in Nigeria', in AO Obilade and C Nwankwo (eds), *Text for Human Rights Teaching in Schools* (Lagos: Constitutional Rights Project, 1999) 109, 129–32; and Dada (n 120) 78.

> of judges was even more linear and limited in governance ... In the pre-independence period, it was virtually unthinkable that courts would upturn colonial legislation. This attitude had a strong influence on the post-independence judiciary.[134]

Thus, under military rule, emergency legislation, exclusionism and state exceptionalism became a standard mode of law-making and governance in Nigeria.[135] After many years of moral and institutional decay under the military, the last major military dictator, General Sani Abacha, died in June 1998 in controversial circumstances. General Abdulsalami Abubakar took over power and, seeing the already heightened public pressure across the country for a transition to civilian democratic rule, he conducted elections between December 1998 and February 1999, which ushered in the current Fourth Republic.

2.3.3 The new democratic era: 1999–2012

Civilian democratic rule was restored in May 1999. It has been the longest period of civilian rule in the country's history and has witnessed several transfers of power by elections: Olusegun Obasanjo was president from 1999–2003 and 2003–2007, Umaru Musa Yar'Adua from 2007–2010, and Goodluck Jonathan from 2010 to the present. However, one cannot but note the 'militarised' foundation of this Fourth Republic and the general apprehension it birthed as to the fact that an undemocratic military regime can hardly give birth to a democratic one that will be truly open and participatory in the public's interest.[136] For instance, the presidential election which heralded the return to civilian rule in 1999 was marred with substantial allegations of electoral malpractice (which was also the case with the 2003, 2007, 2011 elections to varying degrees), with the result of the election described by a former military state governor as 'a mere military arrangement';[137] the military regime at the time was uncomfortably responsible for establishing political party certifying bodies, establishing electoral bodies and funding political parties.[138]

Furthermore, there is the extant 1999 Nigerian Constitution (as amended) which includes, amongst others, the bill of rights, and is meant to be the supreme law that forms the underlying basis for the country's political and legal system. This fundamental document is continually being frowned on and perceived as

134 Emphasis added. HO Yusuf, 'The judiciary and political change in Africa: developing transnational jurisprudence in Nigeria' (2009) 7(654) *International Journal of Constitutional Law* 654, 664.
135 See ibid, 662; and Centre for Socio-Legal Studies (n 117) 3.
136 See Obe (n 34) 145.
137 *Tribune*, 'OBJ's election was military arrangement, not zoning – Bako', *Tribune*, 14 August 2010. See Obe (n 34) 168.
138 J Amoda, 'Review of the 1999 Constitution, Nigerian democracy (1)', *Vanguard*, 6 December 2011, available at http://www.vanguardngr.com/2011/12/review-of-the-1999-constitution-nigerian-democracy-1/ (last accessed 27 January 2015).

illegitimate by wide sections of the public that argue for its annulment, it being a product of military dictatorship.[139] The military's undemocratic temperament did not allow for meaningful public participation in the constitution-making process and, arguably, the outcome generally did not reflect the true wishes of the people.[140]

In addition, unlike some other human rights systems discussed in Chapter 1, to date, none of the provisions of the 1999 Nigeria Constitution (as amended) has been officially recognised as embodying the right of the public to access (environmental) information or decision-making processes. Also, the right to 'receive and impart ideas and information without interference' in section 39(1) of the 1999 Nigeria Constitution (as amended) is made subject to a similar equivocal proviso[141] as that contained in previous constitutions discussed earlier.[142] Partly based on the proviso, the new democratic government similarly retained and implemented the Official Secrets Act[143] in a manner that has been noted as '[incompatible] with a constitutional guarantee of free expression'.[144]

Nonetheless, even though this new era has witnessed some progress in the polity, the initial apprehension has equally proved to be largely justified. Commendably, the Obasanjo-led democratic government established bodies including the Economic and Financial Crimes Commission (EFCC) that indeed recorded some successes, albeit limited, in its fight against corruption.[145] However, over the years, the effectiveness of the anti-corruption bodies has greatly waned, broadly indicating the government's half-hearted and selective approach in the fight against corruption.[146] For example, the potential of the proactive 'sunshine' freedom of information (FOI) legislation to expose the environment of secrecy in which corruption thrives, is well known. Yet, rather than combine this proactive mechanism with the potential of the mostly reactive crime-fighting agencies to reduce corruption, Obasanjo, as reported, was mainly against the idea of enacting FOI legislation when the civil society solicited his support on this.[147] Similarly, the Obasanjo-led government ratified but never implemented, in line with section

139 See Ogowewo (n 91).

140 The 25-member Constitutional Debate Collating Committee, which put together the 1999 Constitution was set up by General Abdulsalami Abubakar (the then head of state) in November 1998 with the sole purpose of organising nationwide consultations and public debates on the 1995 draft Constitution, with a time limit of only *two months* (which seems insufficient for such a task to be properly executed, despite its limited scope). It is further telling on the credibility of the constitution-making process and the legitimacy of the 1999 Constitution when one finds that, according to the Constitution of the Federal Republic of Nigeria (Promulgation) Decree No 24 of 1999, the undemocratic military leadership made 'such amendments as were deemed necessary in the public interest and for the purpose of promoting the security, welfare and good governance of the people of Nigeria'. See Okpanachi and Garba (n 104) 5–6.

141 See 1999 Nigerian Constitution (as amended), ss 39(3) and 45.

142 See note 80.

143 Cap 03 Law of the Federation of Nigeria, 2004.

144 Obiagwu and Odinkalu (n 74) 222.

145 Falola and Heaton (n 2) 239–41.

146 Ibid, 241.

147 Obe (n 34) 154–55, 158–60.

12 of the 1999 Nigerian Constitution (as amended),[148] the African Convention on Preventing and Combating Corruption,[149] which obliges states to adopt access to information legislation in order to fight corruption.[150]

Little wonder Nigeria to date has continually been ranked as one of the most corrupt countries in the world by the international watchdog Transparency International; in 2012, out of 176 countries surveyed, Nigeria was ranked the 37th most corrupt country.[151] Hence, generally, not much has changed in the country's civil service, which to an extent has remained ineffective and inefficient owing to corruption and other elements such as underfunding and excessive bureaucratic bottlenecks that, in turn, continues to feed corruption in the system.

On the economic front, the government since 1999 has done reasonably well when compared with the military rulers. In this era, the nation has witnessed growth in foreign direct investment,[152] gross domestic product[153] and the non-oil sector (although crude oil still constitutes about 95 per cent and 75 per cent of the country's export and revenue, respectively),[154,155] as well as a general reduction in the rate of inflation.[156] However, these improvements have generally not led to a significant improvement in the living standard of the majority of Nigerians, especially those in the rural areas, which have not received much attention development-wise and where around half of the population resides.[157] There are still serious issues with poverty in Nigeria: about 60.9 per cent of the population (urban: 52.0; rural: 66.1) is said to be living in 'absolute poverty',[158] up from

148 According to that provision, '[n]o treaty between the Federation and any other country shall have the force of law except to the extent to which any such treaty has been enacted into law by the National Assembly'.

149 11 July 2003 (2004) 43 ILM 3.

150 Article 9.

151 Transparency International, 'Corruption Perception Index (2012)', available at http://cpi.transparency.org/cpi2012/results/ (last accessed 27 January 2015).

152 See World Bank, 'World development indicators', April 2006, 341, available at http://data.worldbank.org/sites/default/files/wdi06.pdf (last accessed 27 January 2015); and World Bank, 'World development indicators', April 2012, 367, available at http://data.worldbank.org/sites/default/files/wdi-2012-ebook.pdf (last accessed 27 January 2015).

153 I Onuba and O Abioye, 'Nigeria now Africa's biggest economy, overtakes South Africa', *Punch*, 7 April 2014, available at http://www.punchng.com/news/nigeria-now-africas-biggest-economy-overtakes-safrica/ (last accessed 27 January 2015).

154 UNECA, 'Country case study: Nigeria', 2013, available at http://www.uneca.org/sites/default/files/uploaded-documents/era2013_casestudy_eng_nigeria.pdf (last accessed 27 January 2015).

155 See International Monetary Fund, 'Nigeria: Article IV consultation', July 2012, 4, available at http://www.imf.org/external/pubs/ft/scr/2012/cr12194.pdf (last accessed 27 January 2015).

156 Central Bank of Nigeria, 'Economic Report Fourth Quarter 2012', February 2013, 23, available at http://www.cbn.gov.ng/Out/2013/CCD/CBN%20Economic%20Report%20for%20the%20Fourth%20Quarter%20of%202012.pdf (last accessed 27 January 2015).

157 World Bank, 'Nigeria Economic Report', No 1, May 2013, available at http://www-wds.worldbank.org/external/default/WDSContentServer/WDSP/IB/2013/05/14/000333037_20130514101211/Rendered/PDF/776840WP0Niger0Box0342041B00PUBLIC0.pdf (last accessed 27 January 2015).

158 That is, those who can scarcely/only afford the bare essentials of life. National Bureau of Statistics, Nigeria, 'Nigeria poverty profile 2010', January 2012, 10 and 14, available at http://www.nigerianstat.gov.ng/pdfuploads/Nigeria%20Poverty%20Profile%202010.pdf (last accessed 14 February 2015).

54.7 per cent in 2004.[159] However, a recent empirical research has raised reasonable doubt about the availability of reliable data with which to measure correctly the decline or increase in Nigeria's wealth or poverty rate, and strongly suggests that Nigeria is richer than the records show and that poverty may not be as widespread as current records show.[160] Nonetheless, the general fact that poverty is still rife in Nigeria, and particularly in rural areas, is indisputable.

Further, necessary jobs have not been created and unemployment remains high: 23.9 per cent in 2011, up from 21.1 per cent in 2010.[161] As at 2010, 'adult literacy rate'[162] was above average and increasing: 57.9 per cent of the population (urban: 73.6; rural: 49.5) can read and write with understanding in the country's lingua franca – the English language, but about 71.6 per cent (urban: 83.0; rural: 65.5) can read and write in any language (i.e. English or any of the about 500 Nigerian native languages;[163] Hausa-Fulani, Yoruba and Igbo languages being the most widely spoken and written indigenous languages).[164] In addition, there is still widespread deficiency of basic public necessities and social services such as power supply, health care, public transportation and adequate educational facilities.[165]

Notably however, the country's information and telecommunications (ICT) industry has witnessed drastic improvements since 2001. In the 1990s, the state-owned telecommunications company – NITEL – only supplied about 450,000 telephone lines for the whole country.[166] However, with the full liberalisation and deregulation of this sector in the wake of the new democratic era, and the coming of private mobile phone companies, the number of subscribers grew from about 866,782 (mobile: 266,461; fixed telephony: 600,321) in 2001[167] to 113,195,951 *active* lines (mobile: 110,124,075; fixed telephony: 418,166) in 2012,[168] meaning that teledensity grew from about 0.73 per cent in 2001 to 80.85 per cent in 2012.[169]

159 Ibid, 15–16.
160 M Jerven, *Poor Numbers: How we are Misled by African Development Statistics and What to Do about it* (Ithaca and London: Cornell University Press, 2013).
161 African Economic Outlook, 'Nigeria', 2012, 2, available at http://www.africaneconomicoutlook.org/fileadmin/uploads/aeo/PDF/Nigeria%20Full%20PDF%20Country%20Note.pdf (last accessed 27 January 2015).
162 Defined to include persons aged 15 years and above. National Bureau of Statistics, Nigeria, 'The national literacy survey', June 2010, 12, available at http://resourcedat.com/wp-content/uploads/2012/04/National-Literacy-Survey-2010.pdf (last accessed 27 January 2015).
163 R Blench, *An Atlas of Nigerian Languages* (3rd edn, May 2011), available at http://www.rogerblench.info/Language/Africa/Nigeria/Atlas%20of%20Nigerian%20Languages-%20ed%20III.pdf (last accessed 27 January 2015).
164 National Bureau of Statistics, Nigeria, 'The national literacy survey' (n 162) 20.
165 See African Economic Outlook (n 161); and Falola and Heaton (n 2) 242.
166 Falola and Heaton (n 2) 236.
167 Nigerian Communications Commission, 'Annual subscriber data: 2001–2011', available at http://www.ncc.gov.ng/index.php?option=com_content&view=article&id=125:art-statistics-subscriber-data&catid=65:cat-web-statistics&Itemid=73 (last accessed 27 January 2015).
168 Nigerian Communications Commission, 'Annual subscriber data: 2012', available at http://www.ncc.gov.ng/index.php?option=com_content&view=article&id=125:art-statistics-subscriber-data&catid=65:cat-web-statistics&Itemid=73 (last accessed 27 January 2015).
169 See Nigerian Communications Commission, 'Annual subscriber data: 2001–2011' (n 167); and Nigerian Communications Commission, 'Annual subscriber data: 2012' (n 168).

The growth of public access to the internet has also increased from 0.6 per cent in 2000 to 28.4 per cent in 2011,[170] which will likely be higher in subsequent years, with services being mostly in the urban areas. Other relevant ICT data as at 2011 include national access to television, 44.7 per cent (urban: 78.6; rural: 35.7) and radio, 82.9 per cent (urban: 91.7; rural: 80.5).[171] These ICT developments could mean a great deal for the working of public access laws in Nigeria, as will be discussed in subsequent chapters.

All of these socio-economic and political factors or indices on official corruption, poverty, illiteracy, language diversity, ICT penetration etc. highlighted so far are important when considering the character, potential and implementation of public access laws in Nigeria.[172] According to the draft Commentary on the Bali Guidelines, there may be situations in which specific measures to facilitate adequate access to information and decision-making processes should be considered, for example when illiteracy is widespread or when minorities do not adequately understand the (official) language(s) used by the public authorities or where an applicant for information has a disability that requires information to be provided in a particular form.[173] It is in this light that some of such information will be referred to in discussions in subsequent chapters.

On the environmental front, the economic growth of the country has come at much cost to the environment. Generally, major cities face serious environmental degradation from developmental, commercial and industrial activities which are incompatible with the character of the areas in which they are sited, deforestation, noise and improper disposal of industrial wastes.[174] These issues have resulted in negative implications for public health in the cities and the general wellbeing of the inhabitants.[175]

In particular, the Niger Delta region of Nigeria, which is one of the world's largest wetlands and from which the mainstay of the country's economy – crude oil – is being extracted has become an international theme largely for the

170 International Telecommunications Union (ITU), 'Measuring the information society', 2012, 211, available at http://www.itu.int/ITU-D/ict/publications/idi/material/2012/MIS2012_without_Annex_4.pdf (last accessed 27 January 2015); and International Telecommunication Union, 'Percentage of individuals using the internet 2000–2011'.

171 National Bureau of Statistics, Nigeria, '2011 Annual socio-economic report: access to ICT', 2012, 11–12, available at www.nigerianstat.gov.ng/pages/download/35 (last accessed 27 January 2015).

172 See e.g. YTB Babalola, AD Babalola and FO Okhale, 'Awareness and accessibility of environmental information in Nigeria: evidence from delta state' (2010) *Library Philosophy and Practice (e-journal)*, available at http://digitalcommons.unl.edu/cgi/viewcontent.cgi?article=1478&context=libphilprac (last accessed 27 January 2015).

173 Commentary on Bali Guidelines 1 and 8.

174 See UJ Orji, 'An appraisal of the legal frameworks for the control of environmental pollution in Nigeria' (2012) 38(2) *Commonwealth Law Bulletin* 321, 323; and SI Omofonmwan and GI Osa-Eboh, 'The challenges of environmental problems in Nigeria' (2008) 23(1) *Journal of Human Ecology* 53, 54.

175 See JO Adelagan, 'The history of environmental policy and pollution of water sources in Nigeria (1960–2004): the way forward', 2004, available at http://userpage.fu-berlin.de/ffu/akumwelt/bc2004/download/adelegan_f.pdf (last accessed 27 January 2015); and Omofonmwan and Osa-Eboh (n 174).

negative reason of environmental pollution occasioned by oil exploration. This exploration is done mainly by multinational oil companies in which the Nigerian Government (through the Nigerian National Petroleum Corporation – the oil industry regulator) owns a majority stake.

Being conducted in an unsustainable manner, arguably with the complacency and complicity of the Nigerian Government, these activities in the region have, amongst others, resulted in extensive gas flaring and massive oil spills which have devastated water bodies (including underground water) and forests, caused serious land pollution and loss of biodiversity, as well as persistent noise and light pollution (from flaring gas), and air pollution which has resulted in high occurrences of acid rain in the region.[176] Apart from the severe health problems (e.g. respiratory and skin diseases) amongst the residents of the area, the degradation of the environment has immensely affected their livelihood as their main occupations are usually fishing, farming and hunting, thus pushing them further into poverty.[177]

In addition, development-wise, Niger Delta communities have received relatively little or no benefit from the exploration of crude oil,[178] contrary to what could have been the case in pre-colonial traditional societies as previously stated. When affected communities make efforts to protest this injustice, the protests are usually brutally quelled by the government, similar to the relations between the colonialists, RNC and the indigenous people as earlier discussed. The result of all these has being a rise in non-violent, as well as armed and violent anti-government and anti-oil-company activists amongst the ethnic minorities who live in these areas,[179] involving attacks on oil installations, kidnapping of oil company workers and gun battles with Nigerian security operatives in the Niger Delta region.[180]

This instability in the region threatened both the national and international economic stability,[181] with Nigeria, for example, losing about ₦8.7 billion (US$543,750,000) in oil revenues per day as a result of the conflict.[182] However, since 2009 the violence in the region has subsided, even though it has remained an issue.[183] This is as a result of the arguably unsustainable solution of granting

176 See KK Aaron, 'Human rights violation and environmental degradation in the Niger delta', in E Porter and B Offord (eds), *Activating Human Rights* (Oxford, Bern and New York: Peter Lang, 2006) 193–215; and Orji (n 174) 324.

177 See CO Opukri, 'Oil induced environmental degradation and internal population displacement in the Nigeria's Niger delta' (2008) 10(1) *Journal of Sustainable Development in Africa* 173.

178 K Edu, 'A review of the existing legal regime on the exploration of oil and the protection of the environment in Nigeria' (2011) 37(2) *Commonwealth Law Bulletin* 307, 308.

179 V Ojakorotu and LD Gilbert, 'Understanding the context of oil violence in the Niger delta of Nigeria', in V Ojakorotu and LD Gilbert (eds), *Checkmating the Resurgence of Oil Violence in the Niger Delta of Nigeria*, available at http://www.iags.org/Niger_Delta_book.pdf (last accessed 27 January 2015).

180 See ibid.

181 British Broadcasting Corporation, 'Nigeria attacks raise oil prices', *British Broadcasting Corporation*, 20 February 2006, available at http://news.bbc.co.uk/1/hi/business/4731366.stm (last accessed 27 January 2015).

182 Orji (n 174) 325.

183 See e.g. S Daniel, 'Why bunkering, kidnappings are back in the Niger delta: security agencies', *Vanguard*, 30 March 2013, available at http://www.vanguardngr.com/2013/03/why-bunkering-kidnappings-are-back-in-niger-delta-security-agencies/ (last accessed 27 January 2015).

amnesty (and training opportunities with financial assistance) to some members of the armed groups in the region,[184] whilst neglecting community demands such as ending pollution, providing basic amenities, and enabling better community access to environmental information and decision-making processes that affect them.[185]

On the whole, the plight of those in the Niger Delta, especially as it concerned their being kept in the dark on environmental issues affecting them and excluded from decision-making processes on those issues, came to the fore in the well-known case of *Social and Economic Rights Action Centre (SERAC) and Another v Nigeria* (the *Ogoniland* case)[186] that was decided by the African Commission on Human and Peoples' Rights. In that case, the applicants alleged, amongst others, that the Nigerian Government withholds from the Ogoni communities information on the dangers created by oil activities and that they had not been involved in the environment-related decisions seriously affecting the development of Ogoniland and its residents.[187]

On these points, the Commission recognised the procedural aspects of Articles 16[188] and 24[189] of the African Charter, holding that in order for states to comply with the 'spirit' of those provisions, of which the Nigerian Government had failed, they must, amongst others, require and publicise environmental and social impact studies prior to any major industrial development and 'provid[e] information to those communities exposed to hazardous materials and activities',[190] as well as provide 'meaningful opportunities for individuals to be heard and to participate in the development decisions affecting their communities'[191] and those 'likely to be affected' by such decisions.[192] Thus, the Commission 'appealed' to Nigeria to comply with this expectation.[193]

However, apart from the fact that the inferred obligations in the *Ogoniland* case are not detailed and arguably quite narrow, the decision is only recommendatory and so not legally binding on Nigeria, given the limited powers of the Commission.[194] Little wonder Nigeria did not comply with the generality of the

184 See D Adeyemo and L Olu-Adeyemi, 'Amnesty in a vacuum: the unending insurgency in the Niger delta of Nigeria', in Ojakorotu and Gilbert (eds) (n 179).
185 KSA Ebeku, 'Niger delta oil, development of the Niger delta and the new development initiative: some reflections from a socio-legal perspective' (2008) 43 *Journal of Asian and African Studies* 399, 402–403.
186 (2001) AHRLR 60.
187 Ibid, para 4.
188 Which provides that: '(1) Every individual shall have the right to enjoy the best attainable state of physical and mental health. (2) States Parties to the present Charter shall take the necessary measures to protect the health of their people . . .'
189 Which provides that: '[a]ll peoples shall have the right to a general satisfactory environment favourable to their development.'
190 *Ogoniland* case, paras 53 and 70–71.
191 Ibid, para 53.
192 Ibid, para 71.
193 Ibid.
194 African Charter, art 45.

Commission's decisions. Moreover, even though Articles 16 and 24 of the African Charter are part of the implementing legislation in Nigeria and this decision of the Commission could have a persuasive influence on how those provisions should be interpreted, it remains to be seen whether the largely minimalist and conservative Nigerian judiciary will adopt the Commission's non-traditional and radical interpretation of those provisions.[195] In any case, this discussion shows that express, detailed and binding provisions on those issues of environmental public access were and are still required and relevant to Nigeria.

2.4 Environment-related public access laws in Nigeria

2.4.1 Development

Despite the general official secrecy and the public exclusion from participation in governance that characterised the military era, the 'environment' is perhaps the only sector that, legally speaking, received a measure of special treatment in that regard. Ironically, therefore, in an environmental context, some credit must be given to the Nigerian military as it was mainly during their rule – particularly the military era of 1987–1992 – that the twin issues of public access to environmental information and decision-making processes were introduced into the 'legal bloodstream' of Nigeria. However, how did this come about? In 1987, toxic chemical wastes in five shipment loads, totalling 3884 metric tonnes, of Italian origin, was illegally dumped in a small village named Koko in Delta State, Nigeria.[196] The toxic waste had been dumped on the property of a farmer named Sunday Nana, who later told investigators that he had been offered ₦500 (US$250 then) a month for the use of the land by a foreigner and was not aware that the chemicals dumped thereon were toxic.[197]

As part of the decisive response by the military government of the day to this illegality, which response included the use of diplomatic pressure to force the Italian Government and company responsible to remove the waste from Nigeria,[198] perhaps the first environmental law that alluded to anything resembling public involvement – the Federal Environmental Protection Agency (FEPA)

195 See EP Amechi, 'Litigating right to healthy environment in Nigeria: an examination of the impacts of the Fundamental Rights (Enforcement Procedure) Rules 2009 in ensuring Access to justice for victims of environmental degradation' (2010) 6(3) *Law, Environment and Development Journal* 320, 324.

196 A Adegoke, 'The challenges of environmental enforcement in Africa: the Nigerian experience', paper presented at the Third International Conference on Environmental Enforcement, held in Oaxaca, Mexico, on 25–28 April 1994, 43–44, available at http://www.inece.org/3rdvol1/pdf/adegoro.pdf (last accessed 27 January 2015).

197 See J Olsen and T Princen, *Hazardous Waste Trade, North and South: The Case of Italy and Koko, Nigeria* (Washington DC: Institute for the Study of Diplomacy, School of Foreign Service, Georgetown University, 1994) 1–3.

198 SG Ogbodo, 'Environmental protection in Nigeria: two decades after the Koko incident' (2009) XV *Annual Survey of International and Comparative Law* 1, 2.

Decree No 58 of 1988[199] – was promulgated.[200] This decree *empowered* FEPA to disseminate environmental information and engage in providing public education,[201] but made no provision for the public to request any such information or even an *obligation* on FEPA to disseminate any information. Similarly, whilst the decree mentions 'public investigations on pollution',[202] it makes no reference to the wider notion of public participation in any form.[203] This was, however, a step forward by the military, considering that the FEPA Bill had earlier been placed before the democratic parliament of the Second Republic, which failed to ratify it despite the rising environmental problems at that time.[204]

However, still in reaction to the catalytic illegal dumping issue, in 1989, being a product of an international collaborative workshop with UNEP, FEPA published the National Policy on the Environment (with a revised edition published in 1998).[205] The policy's goal of achieving sustainable development includes the need to 'raise public awareness and promote understanding of the essential linkages between the environment, resources and development, and encourage individual and community participation in environmental improvement efforts'.[206] The policy also contained proposals for developers to be compelled to conduct EIA studies before commencing their activities.

Nonetheless, important as these efforts were, they did not do much to deal with the age-old issues of public exclusion from environmental decision-making processes, especially given their weaknesses and lacunae. As had always been the case, project appraisals were usually limited to feasibility studies and economic-cost-benefit analysis and did not take social and environmental impacts of projects into consideration;[207] this, despite the 1981–1985 National Development Plan providing that 'feasibility studies for all projects both private and public should be accompanied by environmental impact assessment statements'.[208] In addition, it was also normal for public opinion about the potential impact of

199 This decree has been repealed and replaced by the 2007 National Environmental Standards and Regulations Enforcement Agency (NESREA) Act, Federal Republic of Nigeria Official Gazette No 92, Vol 94 of 31 July 2007.

200 Adegoke (n 196) 44.

201 Decree No 58, s 5(b), (d) and (e).

202 Ibid, s 9(d).

203 For a review of Decree No 58, see A Adekunle, 'The Federal Environmental Protection Agency Decree 1988 No 58' (1992) 36(1) *Journal of African Law* 100–102.

204 Adegoke (n 196) 43–44.

205 Nigerian National Policy on the Environment (Revised), done under the auspices of the UN Development Programme (UNDP), 1998, para 6.6(f), available at http://www.nesrea.org/images/National%20Policy%20on%20Environment.pdf (last accessed 27 January 2015).

206 National Policy on the Environment, 1989, para 2(d).

207 O Ameyan, 'Environmental impact assessment: insight into the environmental impact regulatory process and implementation for qualifying projects', a paper presented at the seminar titled 'Preparing business in Nigeria for environmental challenges and opportunities' organised by Manufacturing Association of Nigeria, held in Lagos, Nigeria, on 4 November 2008, 2, available at http://softwaresupermart.com/mangreencourses/papers/paper6b.pdf (last accessed 27 January 2015).

208 Cited in L Atsegbua, V Akpotaire and F Dimowo, *Environmental Law in Nigeria: Theory and Practice* (2nd edn, Benin: Ambik Press, 2010) 231.

projects or activities on their environment and livelihood not to be considered,[209] especially as the communities were rarely aware of the proposed projects in the areas until work had commenced.[210]

However, in the Niger Delta area for example, as environmental pollution continued to escalate with its attendant negative impact, as noted above, community agitation for solutions to their plight intensified; first, peacefully, then violently when it became obvious that they were being ignored by the companies and the government.[211] Largely reputed as the first major rebellion by oil-bearing communities was that conducted in February 1966 by the Adaka Boro-led Niger Delta Volunteer Force against oil injustice in their territory; this rebellion was brutally crushed in 12 days by the Nigerian military with the alleged support of Shell.[212] Thereafter opposition was relatively non-violent in nature until the early 1990s.[213] It was particularly in 1990 that the non-violent Niger Delta-based Ken Saro-Wiwa-led Movement for the Survival of the Ogoni People (MOSOP), which, amongst others, has the mandate of promoting democratic awareness and protecting the Ogoni environment, was formed.[214] This marked 'a watershed in the development of protests in the Niger Delta region'.[215]

From 1990, MOSOP led massive local protests and sensitisation schemes (on the ground and in the media) about their plight and unjust exclusions from processes of governance relating to their environment and resources.[216] Also, MOSOP unprecedentedly internationalised its campaign by approaching international governmental bodies and environmental and human rights NGOs, some of which in turn began putting pressure on the relevant oil companies and supporting MOSOP.[217]

In addition, there were other scattered protests by various groups in the region that frequently involved violence in the early 1990s. The most notable of these happened in October 1990 in the town of Umuechem, Rivers State, where about 80 unarmed community youths protesting at the gates of the Shell facility in the town were killed and 497 houses were destroyed by the Nigerian security outfit.[218] This is reputed to be 'the first major documented case of military repression to draw international attention to the Delta and serve as a catalyst for subsequent

209 Ameyan (n 207).

210 R Adomokai and WR Sheate, 'Community participation and environmental decision-making in the Niger delta' (2004) 24 *Environmental Impact Assessment Review* 495, 497.

211 Ibid, 498.

212 See International Crisis Group, *The Swamp of Insurgency: Nigeria's Delta Unrest* (Dakar and Brussel: International Crisis Centre, 2006) 4; Ako (n 110) 276.

213 E Osaghae, 'The Ogoni uprising: oil politics, minority agitation and the future of the Nigerian state' (1995) 94 *African Affairs* 325, 326.

214 See http://www.mosop.org/about_us.html (last accessed 27 January 2015).

215 Ako (n 110) 277.

216 See Osaghae (n 213) 336 and 325–44 generally; Ako (n 110) 276–78; and Human Rights Watch, 'Protests and repression in the Niger delta', available at http://www.hrw.org/reports/1999/nigeria/Nigew991-08.htm (last accessed 27 January 2015).

217 Osaghae (n 12) 335.

218 Human Rights Watch (n 216).

protests'.[219] In what was to become a norm in the Niger Delta, this government brutality is shamefully reminiscent of the earlier noted manner in which the military might of the then colonial government was readily available to protect by lethal means the interest of foreign 'investors' whose activities were inimical to the wellbeing of locals in the Niger Delta.[220]

Thus, it became necessary for oil companies and the government to find ways of engaging and consulting with communities before and during projects.[221] The increasing public agitation, together with the media and international pressure and the need to crystallise the efforts of the new environmental wave, seemingly led the federal military government in 1992 to enact the Environmental Impact Assessment (EIA) Decree No 86 of 1992, which came into force in the entire country.[222] The EIA Decree aims to mainstream environment-related considerations into development projects and was a relatively major step in the fight for the right of the public to access environmental information and environmental decision-making processes, as it contains some binding provisions with respect to these twin issues,[223] as EIA regimes are generally supposed to.[224] To this day, EIA Decree No 86 (now an Act)[225] has remained the extant law mandating EIAs to be conducted on relevant projects before their commencement, and giving the public a possible opportunity to influence the final decision determining whether, and in what manner, the project should proceed.

Although there is general recognition in the EIA Decree that adequate information is needed for effective public participation in environmental assessment and decision-making processes,[226] it contains a very limited provision in this regard. As is usually the case with EIA laws, the EIA Decree provides for the establishment of a 'public registry', which is to contain and allow public access *only* to information produced or relating to a specific activity that is subject to environmental assessment.[227] However, this 'public registry' provision is laced with a number of provisos and broad exemptions that could easily undermine the content of the public register, and public access to it.[228] In fact, it has been noted that the establishment of such a public registry containing the stipulated information is hardly being implemented.[229] All these meant that

219 International Crisis Group (n 212) 6.
220 RT Ako and P Okonmah, 'Minority rights issues in Nigeria: a theoretical analysis of historical and contemporary conflicts in the oil-rich Niger delta region' (2009) 16 *International Journal on Minority and Group Rights* 53, 59.
221 Adomokai and Sheate (n 210) 498.
222 See PC Williams, 'The Environmental Impact Assessment Act and processes as an environmental and livelihood advocacy tool', in B Obayanju and M Obaseki (eds), *Defending the Environment: The Role of Environmental Impact Assessment* (Benin City: Environmental Rights Act, 2009) 7, 9.
223 Ibid.
224 P Sands, *Principles of International Environmental Law: Frameworks, Standards and Implementation* (Manchester: Manchester University Press, 1995) 579.
225 Cap E12, Laws of the Federation of Nigeria, 2004.
226 EIA Decree, s 57(4)(c).
227 Ibid, s 57.
228 Ibid, s 57(4) and (6).
229 Bristol-Alagbariya (n 35).

there was still no meaningful public right to access environmental information under the military.

Hence, the drive by the civil society for a wide public right to access information held by public institutions, which coincidentally began in 1992, the same year the EIA Decree was promulgated, was still on full course. This advocacy for FOI legislation, which 'originated as a citizen-led demand and was for the most part led by ordinary folks',[230] was spearheaded by human rights activists, mainly the Civil Liberties Organisation (CLO), that realised that the execution of their human rights objectives was being hindered by lack of access to vital information.[231] The Nigerian Union of Journalists (NUJ), facing the same problem of access, was soon in collaboration with the CLO, which led to the formation of an NGO – Media Rights Agenda (MRA). The campaign for FOI legislation spread from its human rights foundation to include issues of corruption and lack of accountability in government, all issues that adversely impacted the environmental and the wellbeing of Nigerians.[232]

After public consultations, those bodies drafted and refined the first FOI Bill, and sent it to the government of the day led by General Sani Abacha (ruled from 1993–1998) for enactment as a decree; but as expected, the Bill never became law.[233] With the death of Abacha and the transition to civil rule in 1999, the civil society relaunched ITS campaign. Upon the swearing-in of President Obasanjo in 1999, the draft FOI Bill was sent to him for onward presentation to the National Assembly as an Executive Bill, given that executive-sponsored bills stand a better chance of being enacted.[234]

As noted earlier in this chapter, Obasanjo was not interested. In opposing the Bill, he claimed, albeit wrongly, that the FOI Bill was mostly imported from foreign countries without taking account of Nigeria's 'peculiar local situations'.[235] However, he failed to come up with his own locally sensitive version of the FOI Bill. Obasanjo also complained about the Bill allowing non-citizens to access information, claiming, again wrongly, as subsequent discussion in this book will show, that this 'is not done anywhere else in the world'.[236] Again, he made no attempt to 'rectify' and support the Bill, thus suggesting that the real issues were not the 'problems' he pointed out, but that public access to information was just not 'his thing'.

Yet, upon return to civilian rule in 1999 and under the leadership of Obasanjo, one can argue that a few measures were put in place in attempt to make the government appear genuinely open. For example, the federal government started

230 CA Odinkalu, 'Nigeria's Freedom of Information Law: how friends launched a movement', *Open Society Foundations*, 3 June 2011, available at http://www.soros.org/voices/nigeria-s-freedom-information-law-how-friends-launched-movement (last accessed 27 January 2015).
231 Obe (n 34) 151–52.
232 Ibid, 151–54.
233 Ibid, 153–54.
234 Ibid, 154–55.
235 Ibid, 160.
236 Obe (n 34) 160.

publishing the monthly statutory allocation paid to state and local governments, and in 2004 the Nigerian Extractive Industries Transparency Initiative (NEITI) – with the duty of publishing auditors' reports on how much the relevant industries pay to the government – was established.[237]

However, the voluntary and/or narrow nature of these measures[238] constitute(d) a fundamental limitation on their usefulness in an environmental context, and were entirely no substitute for an FOI law, especially as the public could not request specific information under them. So, upon realising the anti-FOI attitude of Obasanjo, the Bill was transmitted directly to the National Assembly in 1999; '[t]he bill excited strong passions and strong suspicions' in the National Assembly.[239] The FOI Bill was sponsored and supported by a number of legislators, some of whose enthusiasm to see the bill enacted soon waned, whilst others joined the pack of those that were determined to prevent the Bill (which had scaled a number of enactment processes in the National Assembly) from proceeding further.[240]

Following sustained public pressure, the National Assembly passed a harmonised version of the Bill in February 2007 and forwarded the same to the president – Obasanjo – for assent so that it could become law as required by the Nigerian Constitution.[241] However, Obasanjo exercised his constitutional power to withhold consent.[242] This meant that the constitutional power of the National Assembly to override the president's veto with two-thirds majority vote was activated.[243] The National Assembly was, however, dissolved in May 2007 upon the end of its tenure without having exercised this power. Even after Obasanjo left office in May 2007, the attitude of his successor, President Yar'Adua, towards the Bill, was no different. The progress of the FOI Bill continued to experience challenges, and was subjected to continuous revision and debate in the reconstituted National Assembly, even into the regime of Jonathan, who became president upon the death of Yar'Adua.

So it is noteworthy that, for more than a decade into the new democratic dispensation, there was no public right to access information and the culture of secrecy persisted. This was made possible by the subsistence of a plethora of laws, some of which had colonial and military dictatorship origins,[244] and the fact that most public servants were/are required to swear oaths of secrecy when employed or appointed. Chiefly, the Official Secrets Act, a retained colonial law, made it a crime for civil servants to give out classified official information, and for anyone

237 Ibid, 162–63.
238 Ibid.
239 Odinkalu (n 230).
240 See ibid, and Obe (n 34) 159.
241 Section 58(1).
242 See the 1999 Nigerian Constitution, s 58(4).
243 Ibid, s 58(5).
244 See e.g. Evidence Act; Public Complaints Commission Act; Statistics Act; Criminal Code Act, National Security Agencies Act, respectively, caps E14, P37, SIO, C38 and N74, Law of the Federation of Nigeria, 2004.

to receive or reproduce such information.[245] What made this law and its implementation draconian even under the new democratic dispensation was the fact that (similar to older practices referred to above):

> Virtually all government information in Nigeria is classified as top secret . . . the level of secrecy is so ridiculous that some classified government files contain ordinary information like newspaper cuttings which are already in the public domain . . . So impenetrable is the veil of secrecy that government departments withhold information from each other . . . . There are also instances where civil servants refuse to give the National Assembly documentation after being asked to do so.[246]

However, on 24 May 2011, after about 12 years of legislative dithering and revisions, the final version of the FOI Bill was adopted by the National Assembly, and it was signed into law by the current Nigerian president on 28 May 2011. Legally speaking, the FOI Act[247] marked the end, to a large extent, of a century of legalised widespread official secrecy in Nigeria, and established the right of the public to access information held by public institutions within defined limits. Importantly, the FOI Act applies to the whole country, including all the states.[248] It also generally supersedes the Official Secrets Act and the like, as it guarantees the public's right of access to (environmental) information '[n]otwithstanding anything contained in any Act, law or regulation'.[249]

2.4.2 The need for adequacy assessment and potential strengthening

The primary public access laws that are relevant in this book and will be extensively discussed in subsequent chapters in comparative perspective with international best practice principles are the Nigerian EIA and FOI Acts. At the UNEP level, it has already been noted that a major reason why many developing countries have not fared well in the practice of ensuring public access to environmental information and decision-making processes is that they 'lack *adequate* laws'.[250]

245 Section 1.
246 S Olukoya, 'Rights-Nigeria: Freedom of Information Bill proves elusive', *Inter Press Service*, 21 June 2004, available at http://ipsnews.net/africa/interna.asp?idnews=24297 (last accessed 27 January 2015).
247 Federal Republic of Nigeria Official Gazette No 36 Vol 98 (2011).
248 CA Odinkalu, 'Myths about the FOI Act', *Right to Know*, 25 August 2011, available at http://www.r2knigeria.org/index.php/undestanding-the-foia-2011 (last accessed 27 January 2015).
249 See ss 1(1), 28 and 30(2).
250 A Juras, 'The Bali Guidelines for development of national legislation on access to information, public participation and access to justice in environmental matters', a presentation at the first meeting of focal points appointed by governments of the signatory countries of the declaration on the Implementation of Principle 10, held in Santiago de Chile, on 6–7 November 2012, available at http://www.eclac.cl/rio20/noticias/paginas/8/48588/Alexander_Juras_English.pdf (last accessed 27 January 2015).

Similarly, in newly independent states, the gaps in environmental public participation laws have been identified as resulting in practice in that area being poor or even non-existent.[251] Such laws need to be strengthened so that they can better contribute to ensuring meaningful practice in access to environmental information and decision-making processes.

In Nigeria in particular, to a large extent, the assessment of the adequacy of the above stated regimes is made necessary by the nature of the political environment under which they were formulated and the circumstances surrounding their emergence as highlighted below. Although these elements do not *necessarily* colour the adequacy of a law, they could. Certainly, they also give rise to a level of curiosity as to the adequacy of the public access rights actually granted under the above Nigerian Acts, especially when one considers the earlier discussed public complaints about the effectiveness of the laws, particularly the EIA Act, which has been around for more than two decades.

First, the EIA Act does not have a democratic foundation even though '[p]ublic participation is a fundamental component of the . . . (EIA) process'.[252] The EIA Act, as earlier noted, is a product of a ruling military dictator and neither the public nor their representatives were adequately consulted for their input during its formation. This is unlike the formation of the Aarhus Convention, for example, that, as noted in Chapter 1, involved extensive public participation in the process, which contributed to making the regime the most public-access-friendly environmental treaty. Second, the formation of the EIA Decree was mainly *reactive* and not *proactive*, as hinted at above. Arguably, it was likely not borne out of a reasoned desire adequately to guarantee public participatory rights for its potential benefits to the society or to implement properly any relevant international obligation/commitment, a fact that may have affected the quality of the EIA Act.

In addition, the late 1980s and the dawn of the 1990s was also the era in which so-called development assistance agencies including the African Development Bank[253] and the World Bank[254] began to mainstream environmental considerations into their lending or project financing decisions by requiring borrower

251 S Kravchenko, 'New laws on public participation in the newly independent states', in Zillman, Lucas and Pring (eds) (n 7) 467, 502.

252 N Hartley and C Wood, 'Public participation in environmental impact assessment: implementing the Aarhus Convention' (2005) 25 *Environmental Impact Assessment Review* 319.

253 See P Sands and J Peel, *Principles of International Environmental Law* (3rd edn, Cambridge: Cambridge University Press, 2012) 672; African Development Bank, 'Handbook on stakeholder consultation and participation in ADB operations', 2001, 7, para 3.1.7, available at http://www.afdb.org/fileadmin/uploads/afdb/Documents/Policy-Documents/Handbook%20on%20Stakeholder%20Consultaion.pdf (last accessed 27 January 2015); and African Development Bank, 'An evaluation of environmental mainstreaming in African Development Bank support to the road transport subsector: approach paper', 2010, 1, available at http://www.afdb.org/fileadmin/uploads/afdb/Documents/Evaluation-Reports-_Shared-With-OPEV_/Environmental%20Mainstreaming%20in%20Road%20transport.pdf (last accessed 14 February 2015).

254 World Bank, 'Operational Directive 4.00, Annex A: environmental assessment (1989)', available in P Sands, R Tarasofsky and M Weiss (eds), *Principles of International Environmental Law* Vol IIB, *Documents in International Environmental Law* (Manchester: Manchester University Press, 1994) 1324.

countries (such as Nigeria) to undertake some sort of formalised EIA procedure (generally including public participation) for relevant projects. In fact, the early EIAs to be carried out in developing countries were usually 'demanded' by such agencies and were 'not as a response to a widespread indigenous demand for better environmental protection'.[255] Being so pressured, and possibly not entirely out of their own volition, it may be argued that, as in many developing countries, Nigeria might have adopted the 'lowest common denominator' approach in designing the EIA regime.[256]

On the contrary, however, Ameyan (Director, Department of Environmental Assessment, Federal Ministry of Environment) has stated that: '[t]he Federal Government of Nigeria enacted the . . . [EIA Act] as a demonstration of her commitment to the Rio Declaration'.[257] This makes some sense, on a superficial level at least, given that the EIA was enacted in the same period that the Rio Declaration was produced. Conversely, there are reasonable counter-arguments to the effect that successive Nigerian leaders, especially the military, were in the habit of publicly endorsing international environmental agreements, but deliberately domesticating them, if at all, in an inappropriate and superficial manner at variance with the essence of the agreement being domesticated.[258] The result of the analysis in the subsequent chapter dealing with the EIA Act will, however, test the veracity of Ameyan's position.

What is more, years after the promulgation of the EIA regime, the extent of environmental pollution in the country continued to increase, especially in areas such as the Niger Delta. Whilst the implementation of an adequate EIA law alone may not drastically reduce pollution – especially as EIA laws only relate to *some* projects, usually do not deal with cumulative impacts and generally do not perform the functions of substantive environmental laws that have a major role to play in securing substantive environmental outcomes – the implementation of its participatory element should make a reasonable contribution to reducing environmental pollution and its effects.

Environmentally aggrieved members of the public do not feel this contribution has been made. They continue, amongst others, to protest about the lack of transparency and public participation in environment-related activities that affect them as engendered by weak and inequitable procedural laws and practices that have failed to improve their status in relation to private companies and the government.[259] Again, apart from the queries as to the practical implementation

255 C Wood, 'Environmental impact assessment in developing countries: an overview', a paper presented at the conference on *New Directions for Impact Assessment for Development: Methods and Practice*, held in Manchester on 24–25 November 2003, 5, available at http://www.sed.man.ac.uk/research/iarc/ediais/pdf/Wood.pdf (last accessed 27 January 2015).

256 Ibid, 7.

257 Ameyan (n 207) 2. See also Principles 17 and 10 of the Rio Declaration.

258 See N Agbara, 'From Rio Principle 17 to EIA Act 1992: the historical perspective to Environmental Impact Assessment Regulations: basic concepts and legal provisions', in Environmental Rights Action/Friends of the Earth, Nigeria, *Defending the Environment: The Role of Environmental Impact Assessment* (Benin: ERA/FoEN, 2009) 37, 47.

259 Bristol-Alagbariya (n 35) 6–8; see also Ebeku (n 185) 415.

of the regime which this situation raises, the matter of the adequacy of the law itself to support the required practice is also put in issue, especially as to whether its provisions are in compliance with international best practice in line with Nigeria's international obligations and commitments.

By the same token, even though the FOI Act was formulated under a democratic regime and constitutes a significant blow to official secrecy, it also raises similar questions as with the EIA Act, which necessitates an assessment of the quality of public access right it contains. The facts on the ground as discussed above with respect to the current era remain that the moral and institutional decay inflicted by past governments, especially the colonialist and the military, continue to linger on and shape governance. This raises reasonable suspicions as to the quality or adequacy of the FOI Act enacted in such an environment to turn the corner of the country's history of official secrecy that lasted for about a century.

Also, there is the fact that the FOI Bill was passed into law after undergoing an alarming 12 years of legislative dithering and fine-tuning, coupled with the general government antagonism the Bill received. Although this is not unusual for a country looking to transit from an era of legalised secrecy to one of relative openness, it nonetheless creates the suspicion that the final product may be a watered-down version of a model FOI law, especially as it relates to the environment. Generally, this is partly what the analysis in subsequent chapters will strive to test. However, considering the fact that the FOI Act is relatively new, there is little practical implementation experience to discuss as it relates to the Act.

These apart, Nigeria has ratified and signed up to many international environmental law regimes that call for relevant states to put in place legal measures that guarantee public access to environmental information and decision-making processes. Therefore, beyond any domestic need for viable legal access rights, or even arguments about the level of contribution such laws can make in changing the generally unfavourable attitude of government agencies to public access in terms of ensuring transparency and public participation in environmental governance, there exists a separate international law argument for Nigeria to guarantee these public rights to the standards dictated by the applicable international environmental initiatives to which they are bound or committed. Besides, the Nigerian Government has claimed that the FOI Act is 'consistent with international best practice'.[260] There is the urgent need to test the veracity of this position, especially from an environmental law perspective as the subsequent chapter on the FOI Act will accomplish, lest the government rests on its laurels in the belief that it has fully satisfied its international commitments in this regard if, in fact, this turns out not to be the case.

260 The Federal Ministry of Justice, Nigeria, 'Nigeria's 4th Periodic Country Report: 2008–2010 on the implementation of the African Charter on Human and People's Rights in Nigeria', August 2011, 14, available at http://www.achpr.org/files/sessions/50th/state-reports/4th-2008-2010/staterep4_nigeria_2011_eng.pdf (last accessed 27 January 2015).

Finally, the need to assess and, where necessary, strengthen the relevant access laws in Nigeria is not strictly a legal one, especially as it relates to how, and the environment in which the relevant laws were developed. It includes other pragmatic, political and sociological arguments, some of which are ingrained in earlier parts of this chapter, which issues will be further highlighted and discussed in the context of the subsequent and mostly theoretical chapter.

2.4.3 Anti-access culture of public institutions and public access laws

Public institutions are obviously important in promoting environmental democracy and ensuring the effective implementation and enforcement of environmental procedural rights in the polity, particularly when they have a culture of transparency and openness to the public. There is the argument that even though '[t]here is room for improvement in public participation laws and practices . . . laws alone are not sufficient to create a truly participatory democracy. Cultural changes are needed, especially in countries with deeply entrenched customs based on official secrecy [and public exclusion].'[261]

Although the latter part of this statement was made with reference to European countries, especially public institutions in the so-called 'countries in transition' (central and eastern European states (CEEs) and newly independent states (NISs)), the same advice or need for cultural change also applies to public institutions in Nigeria, which were also 'born and bred' in an environment of official secrecy and anti-public participation for many decades, and presently run a democracy with teething problems.

However, even though adequate laws 'alone' cannot create an effective participatory democracy and change closed age-old cultures of public institutions, it is arguably the most fundamental element in catalysing and sustaining these required changes.[262] It will also constitute a rallying point and help to ground, in a significant way, public protests/campaigns for public institutions to open up to the public, in terms of ensuring access to information and relevant decision-making processes.

Accordingly, adequate access laws, especially when privately enforceable, can, over time and in a positive way, significantly neutralise the anti-public access disposition of public institutions and make them more genuinely open and accountable to the public. Put differently, and in line with Tardi's thoughts,[263]

261 UNECE and UNEP, 'Assessment of progress in sustainable development since Rio 1992 for Member States of the United Nations Economic Commission for Europe', CEP/AC.12/3, 20 July 2001, xv, available at http://www.unece.org/fileadmin/DAM/env/documents/2001/cep/ac12/cep.ac.12.3.e.pdf (last accessed 27 January 2015).

262 See S Kravchenko, 'Strengthening implementation of MEAs: the innovative Aarhus compliance mechanism', a paper presented at the Seventh International Conference on Environmental Compliance and Enforcement, in Marrakech, Morocco, on 7–15 April 2005, 4, available at http://inece.org/conference/7/vol1/Kravchenko.pdf (last accessed 27 January 2015).

263 G Tardi, 'Law as a counterweight to politicisation in democratic public management' (2012) 38(4) *Commonwealth Law Bulletin* 591, 595–96.

adequate and privately enforceable public access laws which create rights, duties and standards can, in defining acceptable standards for political action and public administration, make a significant contribution in positively reshaping the attitude of public institutions in Nigeria.[264]

This view is also hugely supported by the comparative law expert, Professor Ralf Michaels, who, by elegant examples, sufficiently demonstrated that legal transplantations or law reform can change or transform different cultures in line with the goals of the reform.[265] This is what is being witnessed, as noted in Chapter 1, in 'countries in transition' where 'national practices, and national attitudes' to governance are being transformed from their closed and exclusive nature to an open and inclusive one by the implementation of the Aarhus Conventions principles in their national legislation.

2.5 Conclusion

Efforts have been made in this chapter to set out the general but relevant socio-political context of this book. It has showed that, whilst transparency and public participation were integral parts of governance in the many nation states and societies that now make up Nigeria (and should not be seen as a form of governance alien to Nigeria generally), the colonialists dealt a serious blow to this style of governance. Similarly, several post-colonial Nigerian governments retained colonial laws and made new ones, which helped to sustain the culture of secrecy and public exclusion from decision-making processes, but for the EIA Act and the recent FOI Act which presented a glimmer of hope in this regard, especially in an environmental context. The need for an assessment and potential strengthening of the public access regimes in Nigeria was also discussed. This discussion was executed mostly based on the practical, political and historical backgrounds of the relevant regimes. However, taking this further, the next chapter will, amongst others, also address the issue from a mostly theoretical perspective.

Bibliography

Aaron KK, 'Human rights violation and environmental degradation in the Niger delta', in Porter E and Offord B (eds), *Activating Human Rights* (Oxford, Bern and New York: Peter Lang, 2006) 139.

Achebe C, *There was a Country: A Personal History of Biafra* (London: Penguin Books, 2012).

Adamu A, *The Hausa Factor in West African History* (Zaria: Ahmadu Bello University Press and Ibadan: Oxford University Press, 1978).

Adegoke A, 'The challenges of environmental enforcement in Africa: the Nigerian experience', paper presented at the Third International Conference on Environmental

264 See Atsegbua, Akpotaire and Dimowo (n 208) 304.

265 R Michaels, '"One size can fit all": some heretical thoughts on the mass production of legal transplants', in G Frankenberg (ed), *Order from Transfer: Comparative Constitutional Design and Legal Culture – Studies in Comparative Law and Legal Culture Series* (Cheltenham and Northampton: Edward Elgar Publishing, 2013) 56, 68 ff.

Enforcement, held in Oaxaca, Mexico, on 25–28 April 1994, available at http://www.inece.org/3rdvol1/pdf/adegoro.pdf (last accessed 27 January 2015).

Adekunle A, 'The Federal Environmental Protection Agency Decree 1988 No 58' (1992) 36(1) *Journal of African Law* 100.

Adelagan JO, 'The history of environmental policy and pollution of water sources in Nigeria (1960–2004): the way forward', 2004, available at http://userpage.fuberlin.de/ffu/akumwelt/bc2004/download/adelegan_f.pdf (last accessed 27 January 2015).

Adeleye A, 'Amalgamation of 1914: was it a mistake?', *Vanguard*, 18 May 2012, available at http://www.vanguardngr.com/2012/05/amalgamation-of-1914-was-it-a-mistake/ (last accessed 27 January 2015).

Ademoyega W, *The Federation of Nigeria from Earliest Times to Independence* (London: George G. Harrap & Co, 1962).

Adeyemo D and Olu-Adeyemi L, 'Amnesty in a vacuum: the unending insurgency in the Niger delta of Nigeria', in Ojakorotu V and Gilbert LD (eds), *Checkmating the Resurgence of Oil Violence in the Niger Delta of Nigeria*, available at http://www.iags.org/Niger_Delta_book.pdf (last accessed 27 January 2015).

Adomokai R and Sheate WR, 'Community participation and environmental decision-making in the Niger delta' (2004) 24 *Environmental Impact Assessment Review* 495.

Aduba JN, 'The protection of human rights in Nigeria', in Obilade AO and Nwankwo C (eds), *Text for Human Rights Teaching in Schools* (Lagos: Constitutional Rights Project, 1999) 109.

African Development Bank, 'Handbook on stakeholder consultation and participation in ADB operations', 2001, available at http://www.afdb.org/fileadmin/uploads/afdb/Documents/Policy-Documents/Handbook%20on%20Stakeholder%20Consultaion.pdf (last accessed 27 January 2015).

African Development Bank, 'An evaluation of environmental mainstreaming in African Development Bank support to the road transport subsector: approach paper', 2010, available at http://www.afdb.org/fileadmin/uploads/afdb/Documents/Evaluation-Reports-_Shared-With-OPEV_/Environmental%20Mainstreaming%20in%20Road%20transport.pdf (last accessed 14 February 2015).

African Economic Outlook, 'Nigeria', 2012, available at http://www.africaneconomicoutlook.org/fileadmin/uploads/aeo/PDF/Nigeria%20Full%20PDF%20Country%20Note.pdf (last accessed 27 January 2015).

Agbara N, 'From Rio Principle 17 to EIA Act 1992: the historical perspective to environmental impact assessment regulations: basic concepts and legal provisions', in Environmental Rights Action/Friends of the Earth, Nigeria, *Defending the Environment: The Role of Environmental Impact Assessment* (Benin: ERA/FoEN, 2009) 37.

Akanbi MM and Shehu AT, 'Rule of law in Nigeria' (2012) 3 *Journal of Law, Policy and Globalization* 1.

Ako RT, 'Nigeria's Land Use Act: an anti-thesis to environmental justice' (2009) 53(2) *Journal of African Law* 289.

Ako RT, 'Enforcing environmental rights under Nigeria's 1999 constitution: the localisation of human rights in the Niger delta region', in De Feyter K, Parmentier S, Timmerman C and Ulrich G (eds), *The Local Relevance of Human Rights* (Cambridge: Cambridge University Press, 2011) 270.

Ako RT and Okonmah P, 'Minority rights issues in Nigeria: a theoretical analysis of historical and contemporary conflicts in the oil-rich Niger delta region' (2009) 16 *International Journal on Minority and Group Rights* 53.

Allot AN, 'Nigeria: Land Use Act' (1978) 22(2) *Journal of African Law* 136.

Amechi EP, 'Litigating right to healthy environment in Nigeria: an examination of the impacts of the Fundamental Rights (Enforcement Procedure) Rules 2009 in ensuring access to justice for victims of environmental degradation' (2010) 6(3) *Law, Environment and Development Journal* 320.
Ameyan O, 'Environmental impact assessment: insight into the environmental impact regulatory process and implementation for qualifying projects', a paper presented at the seminar titled 'Preparing business in Nigeria for environmental challenges and opportunities' organised by Manufacturing Association of Nigeria, held in Lagos, Nigeria, on 4 November 2008, available at http://softwaresupermart.com/mangreencourses/papers/paper6b.pdf (last accessed 27 January 2015).
Amnesty International, 'Nigeria: Time for justice and accountability', 2000, 1, available at http://www.amnesty.org/en/library/asset/AFR44/014/2000/en/a677253f-dc60-11dd-bce7-11be3666d687/afr440142000en.pdf (last accessed 14 February 2015).
Amoda J, 'Review of the 1999 constitution, Nigerian democracy (1)', *Vanguard*, 6 December 2011, available at http://www.vanguardngr.com/2011/12/review-of-the-1999-constitution-nigerian-democracy-1/ (last accessed 27 January 2015).
Anderson MR, 'Human rights approach to environmental protection: an overview', in Boyles AE and Anderson MR (eds), *Human Rights Approaches to Environmental Protection* (Oxford: Clarendon Press, 1998) 1.
Atsegbua L, Akpotaire V and Dimowo F, *Environmental Law in Nigeria: Theory and Practice* (2nd edn Benin: Ambik Press, 2010).
Azuonye C, 'Igbo Enwe Eze: monarchical power versus democratic values in Igbo oral Narratives', in Furniss G and Gunner L (eds), *Power, Marginality, and African Oral Literature* (Cambridge: Cambridge University Press, 1995) 65.
Babalola YTB, Babalola AD and Okhale FO, *'Awareness and Accessibility of Environmental Information in Nigeria: Evidence from Delta State'* (2010) *Library Philosophy and Practice (e-journal)*, available at http://digitalcommons.unl.edu/cgi/viewcontent.cgi?article=1478&context=libphilprac (last accessed 27 January 2015).
Bassey N, 'Trade and human rights in the Niger delta of Nigeria', available at http://www.worldhunger.org/articles/06/africa/bassey.htm (last accessed 27 January 2015).
Blench R, *An Atlas of Nigerian Languages* (3rd edn May 2011), available at http://www.rogerblench.info/Language/Africa/Nigeria/Atlas%20of%20Nigerian%20Languages-%20ed%20III.pdf (last accessed 27 January 2015).
Bristol-Alagbariya ET, *Participation in Petroleum Development: Towards Sustainable Community Development in Niger Delta* (Dundee: Centre for Energy, Petroleum and Mineral Law and Policy, 2009).
British Broadcasting Corporation, 'Nigeria attacks raise oil prices', *British Broadcasting Corporation*, 20 February 2006, available on: http://news.bbc.co.uk/1/hi/business/4731366.stm (last accessed 27 January 2015).
Burnham P and Last M, 'From pastoralist to politician: the problem of Fulbey "aristocracy"' (1994) 34 *Cahiers d'études Africaines* 313.
Central Bank of Nigeria, 'Economic Report Fourth Quarter 2012', February 2013, available at http://www.cbn.gov.ng/Out/2013/CCD/CBN%20Economic%20Report%20for%20the%20Fourth%20Quarter%20of%202012.pdf (last accessed 27 January 2015).
Centre for Socio-Legal Studies, 'Justice sector reform and human rights in Nigeria' (Abuja: Centre for Socio-Legal Studies, 2009), available at http://censolegs.org/1.pdf (last accessed 27 January 2015).

Committee to Protect Journalists, 'Nigerian editor charged with sedition, jailed', *Refworld*, 29 January 2008, available at http://www.refworld.org/docid/48243c6523.html (last accessed 27 January 2015).

Dada JB, 'Impediments to human rights protection in Nigeria' (2012) 18(1) *Annual Survey of International and Comparative Law* 67.

Daniel S, 'Why bunkering, kidnappings are back in the Niger delta: security agencies', *Vanguard*, 30 March 2013, available on: http://www.vanguardngr.com/2013/03/why-bunkering-kidnappings-are-back-in-niger-delta-security-agencies/ (last accessed 27 January 2015).

David-West T, 'Buhari: the politics of religion', *The Sun*, 1 December 2014, available at http://sunnewsonline.com/new/?p=93431 (last accessed 14 February 2015).

Draft Commentary to the UNEP Guidelines for the development of national legislation on information, public participation and access to justice in environmental matters, available at http://www.unep.org/civil-society/Portals/24105/documents/Guidelines/Commentary-to-the-guidelines-for-the-development-of-national-legislation.pdf (last accessed 27 January 2015).

Dusgate RH, *The Conquest of Northern Nigeria* (London: Frank Cass, 1985).

Ebeku KSA, 'Oil and the Niger delta people: the injustice of the Land Use Act' (2002) 35(2) *Law and Politics in Africa, Asia and Latin America* 201–31.

Ebeku KSA, 'Niger delta oil, development of the Niger delta and the new development initiative: some reflections from a socio-legal perspective' (2008) 43 *Journal of Asian and African Studies* 399.

Edu K, 'A review of the existing legal regime on the exploration of oil and the protection of the environment in Nigeria' (2011) 37(2) *Commonwealth Law Bulletin* 307.

Elias TO, *Nigeria: The Development of its Laws and Constitution* (London: Steven & Sons, 1967).

Falola T and Genova A, *Historical Dictionary of Nigeria* (Maryland: Scarecrow Press, 2009), available at http://lcweb2.loc.gov/frd/cs/profiles/Nigeria.pdf (last accessed 27 January 2015).

Falola T and Heaton MM, *A History of Nigeria* (New York: Cambridge University Press, 2008).

Federal Ministry of Justice, Nigeria, 'Nigeria's 4th Periodic Country Report: 2008 – 2010 on the Implementation of the African Charter on Human and People's Rights in Nigeria', August 2011, available at http://www.achpr.org/files/sessions/50th/state-reports/4th-2008-2010/staterep4_nigeria_2011_eng.pdf (last accessed 27 January 2015).

Foreword by the Chairman, Hon Justice Chukwudifu A Oputa, *Synoptic Overview of the Human Rights Violations Investigation Commission Report: Summary, Conclusions and Recommendations* (2002) 2–3, available at http://www.nigerianmuse.com/nigeriawatch/oputa/ (last accessed 27 January 2015).

Forrest T, 'The political economy of civil rule and the economic crisis in Nigeria (1979–1984): the struggle for spoils' (1986) 13(35) *Review of African Political Economy* 4.

Fortes M and Pritchard E, 'Introduction', in Fortes M and Pritchard E (eds), *African Political Systems* (London: KPI Ltd, 1987) 1.

Gordon AA, *Nigeria's Diverse Peoples: A Reference Sourcebook* (California: ABC-CLIO Inc, 2003).

Hartley N and Wood C, 'Public participation in environmental impact assessment – implementing the Aarhus Convention' (2005) 25 *Environmental Impact Assessment Review* 319.

Human Rights Watch, 'Protests and repression in the Niger delta', available at http://www.hrw.org/reports/1999/nigeria/Nigew991-08.htm (last accessed 27 January 2015).

International Crisis Group, *The Swamp of Insurgency: Nigeria's Delta Unrest* (Dakar and Brussel: International Crisis Centre, 2006).

International Monetary Fund, 'Nigeria: Article IV consultation', July 2012, available at http://www.imf.org/external/pubs/ft/scr/2012/cr12194.pdf (last accessed 27 January 2015).

International Telecommunication Union, 'Percentage of individuals using the internet 2000–2011'.

International Telecommunications Union (ITU), 'Measuring the information society', 2012, available at http://www.itu.int/ITU-D/ict/publications/idi/material/2012/MIS2012_without_Annex_4.pdf (last accessed 27 January 2015).

Jerven M, *Poor Numbers: How We Are Misled by African Development Statistics and What To Do About It* (Ithaca and London: Cornell University Press, 2013).

Juras A, 'The Bali Guidelines for development of national legislation on access to information, public participation and access to justice in environmental matters', a presentation at the first meeting of focal points appointed by governments of the signatory countries of the Declaration on the Implementation of Principle 10, held in Santiago de Chile, on 6–7 November 2012, available at http://www.eclac.cl/rio20/noticias/paginas/8/48588/Alexander_Juras_English.pdf (last accessed 27 January 2015).

Kalu VE, 'State monopoly and indigenous participation rights in resource development in Nigeria' (2008) 26(3) *Journal of Energy and Natural Resources Law* 418.

Kravchenko S, 'New laws on public participation in the newly independent states', in Zillman DN, Lucas AR and Pring G (eds), *Human Rights in National Resource Development: Public Participation in the Sustainable Development of Mining and Energy Resource* (Oxford: Oxford University Press, 2002) 467.

Kravchenko S, 'Strengthening implementation of MEAs: the innovative Aarhus compliance mechanism', a paper presented at the Seventh International Conference on Environmental Compliance and Enforcement, in Marrakech, Morocco, on 7–15 April 2005, available at http://inece.org/conference/7/vol1/Kravchenko.pdf (last accessed 27 January 2015).

Library of Congress, 'Country Profile: Nigeria', July 2008, 9, available at http://lcweb2.loc.gov/frd/cs/profiles/Nigeria.pdf (last accessed 27 January 2015).

Mair L, *African Kingdoms* (New York: Oxford University Press, 1977).

Maja-Pearce A, *From Khaki to Agbada: A Handbook for the February 1999 Elections in Nigeria* (Lagos: Civil Liberties Organisation, 1999).

Michaels R, '"One size can fit all": some heretical thoughts on the mass production of legal transplants', in Frankenberg G (ed), *Order from Transfer: Comparative Constitutional Design and Legal Culture – Studies in Comparative Law and Legal Culture Series* (Cheltenham and Northampton: Edward Elgar Publishing, 2013) 56.

National Bureau of Statistics, Nigeria, 'The national literacy survey', June 2010, available at http://resourcedat.com/wp-content/uploads/2012/04/National-Literacy-Survey-2010.pdf (last accessed 27 January 2015).

National Bureau of Statistics, Nigeria, 'Nigeria poverty profile 2010', January 2012, available at http://www.nigerianstat.gov.ng/pdfuploads/Nigeria%20Poverty%20Profile%202010.pdf (last accessed 14 February 2015).

National Bureau of Statistics, Nigeria, '2011 Annual Socio-Economic Report: access to ICT', 2012, available at www.nigerianstat.gov.ng/pages/download/35 (last accessed 27 January 2015).

Ngou CM, 'The 1959 elections and formation of the Independence Government', in Ekeh PP and Asiwaju, G (eds), *Nigeria Since Independence: The First 25 Years*, Vol V: *Politics and Constitutions* (Ibadan: Heinemann, 1989) 81.

Nigerian Communications Commission, 'Annual subscriber data: 2001–2011', available at http://www.ncc.gov.ng/index.php?option=com_content&view=article&id=125:art-statistics-subscriber-data&catid=65:cat-web-statistics&Itemid=73 (last accessed 27 January 2015).

Nigerian Communications Commission, 'Annual subscriber data: 2012', available at http://www.ncc.gov.ng/index.php?option=com_content&view=article&id=125:art-statistics-subscriber-data&catid=65:cat-web-statistics&Itemid=73 (last accessed 27 January 2015).

Nwalimu C, *The Nigerian Legal System: Private Law* (Vol 2, New York: Peter Lang Publishing Inc, 2009).

Nwokolo PN, 'The Nigerian press and the law of sedition: a progressive interpretation' (2012) 23(1) *Review of Education* 201.

Obe A, 'The challenging case of Nigeria', in Florini A (ed), *The Right to Know: Transparency for an Open World* (New York: Colombia University Press, 2007) 143.

Obiagwu C and Odinkalu CA, 'Nigeria: combating legacies of colonialism and militarism', in An-Na'im AA (ed), *Human Rights under African Constitutions: Realizing the Promise for Ourselves* (Pennsylvania: University of Pennsylvania Press, 2003) 211.

Odinkalu CA, 'Nigeria's Freedom of Information Law: how friends launched a movement', *Open Society Foundations*, 3 June 2011, available at http://www.soros.org/voices/nigeria-s-freedom-information-law-how-friends-launched-movement (last accessed 27 January 2015).

Odinkalu CA, 'Myths about the FOI Act', *Right to Know*, 25 August 2011, available at http://www.r2knigeria.org/index.php/undestanding-the-foia-2011 (last accessed 27 January 2015).

Odote C and Makoloo MO, 'African initiatives for public participation in environmental management', in Bruch C (ed), *The New "Public": The Globalization of Public Participation* (Washington DC: Environmental Law Institute, 2002) 121.

Ogbodo SG, 'Environmental protection in Nigeria: two decades after the Koko incident' (2009) XV *Annual Survey of International and Comparative Law* 1.

Ogowewo TI, 'Why the judicial annulment of the constitution of 1999 is imperative to the survival of Nigeria's democracy' (2000) 44 *Journal of African Law* 135.

Ojakorotu V and Gilbert LD, 'Understanding the context of oil violence in the Niger delta of Nigeria', in Ojakorotu V and Gilbert LD (eds), *Checkmating the Resurgence of Oil Violence in the Niger Delta of Nigeria*, available at http://www.iags.org/Niger_Delta_book.pdf (last accessed 27 January 2015).

Oko O, 'Seeking justice in transitional societies: an analysis of the problems and failures of the judiciary in Nigeria' (2006) 9 *Brooklyn Journal of International Law* 10.

Okpanachi E and Garba A, 'Federalism and constitutional change in Nigeria' (2010) 7(1) *Federal Governance* 1.

Ola CS, *Town and Country Planning Law in Nigeria* (Ibadan: Oxford University Press, 1977).

Olsen J and Princen T, *Hazardous Waste Trade, North and South: The Case of Italy and Koko, Nigeria* (Washington DC: Institute for the Study of Diplomacy, School of Foreign Service, Georgetown University, 1994).

Olukoya S, 'Rights-Nigeria: Freedom of Information Bill proves elusive', *Inter Press Service*, 21 June 2004, available at http://ipsnews.net/africa/interna.asp?idnews=24297 (last accessed 27 January 2015).

Omofonmwan SI and Osa-Eboh GI, 'The challenges of environmental problems in Nigeria' (2008) 23(1) *Journal of Human Ecology* 53.

Omorogbe Y, 'The legal framework for public participation in decision-making on mining and energy development in Nigeria: giving voices to the voiceless', in Zillman DN, Lucas AR and Pring G (eds), *Human Rights in National Resource Development: Public Participation in the Sustainable Development of Mining and Energy Resource* (Oxford: Oxford University Press, 2002) 549.

Omu FIA, *Press and Politics in Nigeria, 1880–1937* (London: Longman Group, 1978).

Onuba I and Abioye O, 'Nigeria now Africa's biggest economy, overtakes South Africa', *Punch,* 7 April 2014, available at http://www.punchng.com/news/nigeria-now-africas-biggest-economy-overtakes-safrica/ (last accessed 27 January 2015).

Opukri CO, 'Oil induced environmental degradation and internal population displacement in the Nigeria's Niger delta' (2008) 10(1) *Journal of Sustainable Development in Africa* 173.

Orji UJ, 'An appraisal of the legal frameworks for the control of environmental pollution in Nigeria' (2012) 38(2) *Commonwealth Law Bulletin* 321.

Osaghae E, 'The Ogoni uprising: oil politics, minority agitation and the future of the Nigerian state' (1995) 94 *African Affairs* 325.

Osaghae EE, *Crippled Giant: Nigeria Since Independence* (London: Hurst & Co Publishers Ltd, 1998).

Osimiri U, 'Nigeria: critic of the Money Laundering Decree No 3 1995' (1997) 1(1) *Journal of Money Laundering Control* 84.

Owusu M, 'Comparative politics, history, and political anthropology', in Owusu M (ed), *Colonialism and Change* (The Hague: Monte Publishers, 1975) 25.

Ozekhome MAA, 'Decrees, ouster clauses and judicial ineptitude' (1989) *Law and Practice* 7.

Paden JN, 'The Sokoto Caliphate and its legacies (1804–2004)', available at http://www.dawodu.com/paden1.htm (last accessed 27 January 2015).

Rodney W, *How Europe Underdeveloped Africa* (Washington DC: Howard University Press, 1982).

Sagay IE, 'Recent trends in the status and practice of the rule of law in Nigeria' (1988) No 3 *ASUU Monograph Series* 5.

Sands P, *Principles of International Environmental Law – Frameworks, Standards and Implementation* (Manchester: Manchester University Press, 1995).

Sands P and Peel J, *Principles of International Environmental Law* (3rd edn Cambridge: Cambridge University Press, 2012).

Sands P, Tarasofsky R and Weiss M (eds), *Principles of International Environmental Law*, Vol IIB, *Documents in International Environmental Law* (Manchester: Manchester University Press, 1994).

Stride GT and Ifeka C, *Peoples and Empires of West Africa: West Africa History, 1000–1800* (Edinburgh: Nelson, 1971).

Tardi G, 'Law as a counterweight to politicisation in democratic public management' (2012) 38(4) *Commonwealth Law Bulletin* 591.

Transparency International, 'Corruption Perceptions Index (1998)', available at http://archive.transparency.org/policy_research/surveys_indices/cpi/previous_cpi/1998#how-to-read (last accessed 27 January 2015).

Transparency International, 'Corruption Perception Index (2012)', available at http://cpi.transparency.org/cpi2012/results/ (last accessed 27 January 2015).

Tribune, 'OBJ's election was military arrangement, not zoning – Bako', *Tribune,* 14 August 2010.

UNECA, 'Country case study: Nigeria', 2013, available at http://www.uneca.org/sites/default/files/uploaded-documents/era2013_casestudy_eng_nigeria.pdf (last accessed 27 January 2015).

UNECE and UNEP, 'Assessment of progress in sustainable development since Rio 1992 for Member States of the United Nations Economic Commission for Europe', CEP/AC.12/3, 20 July 2001, available at http://www.unece.org/fileadmin/DAM/env/documents/2001/cep/ac12/cep.ac.12.3.e.pdf (last accessed 27 January 2015).

Viljoen F, 'Application of the African Charter on Human and Peoples' Rights by domestic courts in Africa' (1999) 43(1) *Journal of African Law* 1.

Vukor-Quarshie GNK, 'Criminal justice administration in Nigeria: Saro-Wiwa in review' (1997) 8 *Criminal Law Forum* 87.

Williams PC, 'The Environmental Impact Assessment Act and processes as an environmental and livelihood advocacy tool', in Obayanju B and Obaseki M (eds), *Defending the Environment: The Role of Environmental Impact Assessment* (Benin City: Environmental Rights Act, 2009) 7.

Wood C, 'Environmental impact assessment in developing countries: an overview', a paper presented at the conference on new Directions for Impact Assessment for Development: Methods and Practice, held in Manchester on 24–25 November 2003, available at http://www.sed.man.ac.uk/research/iarc/ediais/pdf/Wood.pdf (last accessed 27 January 2015).

World Bank, 'World development indicators', April 2006, 341, available at http://data.worldbank.org/sites/default/files/wdi06.pdf (last accessed 27 January 2015).

World Bank, 'World development indicators', April 2012, 367, available at http://data.worldbank.org/sites/default/files/wdi-2012-ebook.pdf (last accessed 27 January 2015).

World Bank, 'Nigeria economic report', No 1, May 2013, available at http://www-wds.worldbank.org/external/default/WDSContentServer/WDSP/IB/2013/05/14/000333037_20130514101211/Rendered/PDF/776840WP0Niger0Box0342041B00PUBLIC0.pdf (last accessed 27 January 2015).

Yusuf HO, 'Calling the judiciary to account for the past: transitional justice and judicial accountability' (2008) 30(2) *Law and Policy* 194.

Yusuf HO, 'The judiciary and political change in Africa: developing transnational jurisprudence in Nigeria' (2009) 7(654) *International Journal of Constitutional Law* 654.

3 Theoretical foundations of public participation: an environmental context

3.1 Introduction

The purpose of this chapter is to create a theoretical foundation and framework within which more legal and practical discussions will be made in subsequent chapters. To achieve this, from a general environmental perspective, there will first be a clarification of the nature of the central concept of 'the public' that should participate. Next, various public participatory and political theories and their implications in an environmental context will be explored in order to understand how they determine the extent of public space available for participation and to enable a call for, and justification of, the best political tradition suited for effective public participation. The value of public participation, mainly in an environmental context, is also discussed from the angles of justifications and criticisms of the concept. Thereafter, in a 'wrap-up' fashion, an effort is made to improve understanding of the best environment for public participation to thrive.

3.2 Who is 'the public'?

Other players in the game of environmental governance, including the government and private corporations and developers are easy to identify. However, there is the need to clarify who 'the public' is that should ordinarily be provided with opportunities to participate in environmental governance, in terms of access to environmental information and decision-making processes and access to justice as it relates to the later elements. Two erroneous assumptions continue to thrive: that of government officials generally being more inclined to equating 'activists' with the public,[1] even though they are only a fraction of the populace,[2] and the

1 TD Abel and M Stephan, 'The limits of civic environmentalism' (2000) 44(4) *American Behavioral Scientist* 614, 623.

2 BL Williams, HK Suen, S Brown, RA Bruhn, R de Blaquiere and SE Rzasa, 'Hierarchical linear models of factors associated with public participation among residents living Near the US Army's chemical weapons stockpile sites' (2001) 44(1) *Journal of Environmental Planning and Management* 41, 45.

assumption that the public is a 'single homogenous, identifiable entity', which clearly is not the case.[3]

In reality, the public is 'a collection of numerous, continually shifting interests and alliances',[4] which may be in conflict with each other. Although there are debates as to whether or not the public should be defined as a collection of individuals or a collection of groups,[5] the fact remains that when it comes to participation in environmental matters there is generally a combination of elements of the individualist and pluralist approaches, and this is arguably the most effective strategy.[6] This is the position in the Aarhus Convention in which 'the public', as distinct from the government, is defined as 'one or more natural or legal persons, and, in accordance with national legislation or practice, their associations, organizations or groups'.[7] This definition will include individuals, youths, women, NGOs, grassroots organisations and private corporations.

However, with reference to environmental decision-making at least, that may not mean that everyone is empowered to participate in every environmental decision-making process, as whoever can participate should ordinarily be 'concerned' with the relevant issue. The Aarhus Convention defines 'public concerned' as 'the public affected or likely to be affected by, or having an interest in, the environmental decision-making; for the purposes of this definition, non-governmental organizations promoting environmental protection and meeting any requirements under national law shall be deemed to have an interest'.[8] This definition is, however, adopted in this book to the extent that private corporations in certain cases may be distinguished from the 'public concerned' and be viewed as owing certain participatory duties to the latter.

Furthermore, and arguably subsumed under the Aarhus Convention's definition of 'public concerned', there are at least two categories of the public which may overlap and/or conflict: (1) public of *place* – those tied to a physical space through geography; and (2) public of *interest* – which may have commonalities in how they relate to a particular environment as beneficiaries or contributors to its condition, but are not tied to the physical space. This is an adaptation and compression of Duane's 'three types of community', of which the third category identified by Duane is 'community of *identity*' – described as those connected by social characteristics but may transcend place.[9] Arguably, however, that third category can be viewed as a sub-set of the 'community of *interest*', which is now styled 'public of *interest*' above. Similarly, McAllister

3 FW Pontius, 'Public involvement in regulation development', in BL Pontius, *Drinking Water Regulation and Health* (New Jersey: John Wiley & Sons, 2003) 251.
4 L Ortolano, *Environmental Regulation and Impact Assessment* (New York: John Wiley & Sons, 1997) 404.
5 J Glicken, 'Effective public involvement in public decisions' (1999) 20(3) *Science Communication* 298, 305–307.
6 See ibid.
7 Article 2(4).
8 Article 2(5).
9 TP Duane, 'Community participation in ecosystem management' (1997) 24 *Ecology Law Quarterly* 771, 772.

highlights the fact that the public can be thought of in terms of spatial proximity, resource dependence and level of concern for the resource, or a combination of all three.[10] Again, although a useful categorisation by McAllister, the second element can fall under the third.

What is more, in reality, relating with these categories of the public could be daunting, and their interests difficult to reconcile, within the context of environmental participation. For instance, whilst the public of *interest* may be happy to have a landfill to accommodate their wastes, the public of *place*, in whose locale the landfill is to be situated, may be unhappy or unwilling to accommodate it. Separately, who has an interest and should be involved in a decision to divert a major water course as a result of development? Clearly, those living close to it (*place*), but not them alone. The sailors and passengers who travel on the water, those who earn their livelihood from fishing in the water or utilise it as a source of irrigation, environmental NGOs etc., all have *interests* that must be given a voice and the opportunity to influence the decision. Sometimes, these interests could involve the entire nation and even citizens of neighbouring countries where there is a transboundary effect. A primary challenge, therefore, which is hinted at in Principle 10 of the Rio Declaration, is to find and engage 'the relevant level' of the public.

Finally, the scope of the term 'public' may present some complexities when used in the context of 'public participation', considering the existence of other similar terms such as 'citizen action', 'citizen rights', 'citizen participation', 'citizen involvement' and 'community involvement (or participation)' etc. In addition, according to Wengert, '"public participation" and "citizen involvement" [and indeed other listed terms] have many meanings and connotations, depending on the situation to which it is applied and the ideology, motivations, and practical orientation of the users'.[11]

However, Langton's distinction, which is widely accepted and adopted in this book, is to the effect that '*public* participation' is more encompassing than terms including '*citizen* involvement', '*citizen* participation' and '*community* involvement (or participation)', as it goes beyond the potential restrictions of the word 'citizen' (i.e. a legally recognised national of a state) to include those who are not considered citizens (e.g. mere residents, visitors or those in other states who may be affected by environmental activities in another),[12] and the word 'community', to include those who may have no community attachment (e.g. a visitor), as the word may suggest.

10 ST McAllister, 'Community-based conservation: restructuring institutions to involve local communities in a meaningful way' (1999) 10(1) *Colorado Journal of International Environmental Law and Policy* 195, 207.

11 N Wengert, 'Citizen participation: practice in search of a theory' (1976) 16 *Natural Resources Journal* 23.

12 S Langton, 'What is citizen participation?' in S Langton (ed), *Citizen Participation in America* (Massachusetts: Lexington Books, 1978) 16–17, 20–21.

3.3 Public participation and political theories

From the discussion so far, the close link between public participation and the political orientation in a society is apparent and worthy of further consideration. Indeed, the importance of considering public participation in the context of broad political theories is heightened by the fact that the extent, and as rightly submitted by Ebbesson, the impact, of public participation, are largely dependent 'on the political context . . . and substantive norms' that are prevalent in a society.[13] Positive efforts have been made to demonstrate further the close and dynamic linkage between public participation and politics.[14] With the political culture of a country being a germane factor for a thriving system of public participation, an effort will be made broadly to consider certain fundamental political theories and what they mean for public participation in any society which leans towards any of the political traditions more than it does towards others, seeing that elements of each tradition feature to some extent in every society.[15]

3.3.1 Rational elitism and public participation

The theory of rational elitism emphasises the fact that decision-making for the benefit of a society be left to experts called the 'elite' – usually a select group of people with specialised training, intellect, experience, wealth or other distinguishing factors. This group of people will usually include political leaders, government administrators, military chiefs, politically influential members of the royal family, the aristocracy, heads of powerful economic enterprises and scientific elites.[16] Whilst the doctrine generally does not accommodate general public participation as a solution to societal problems, it may allow very limited participation by members of the public when they hold information that may assist the *experts* in making 'technically superior decisions',[17] or when the public is expected to choose, by voting, the governing elite.[18]

However, in general, such an oligarchical political system subjects public participation to the lowest rung of the ladder, whilst stressing the inevitability of a select few with distinguishing capabilities or status in solving societal problems. This political disposition is usually exemplified in the types of state with an

13 J Ebbesson, 'The notion of public participation in international environmental law' (1997) 8 *Yearbook of International Environmental Law* 51, 59.

14 See MG Kweit and RW Kweit, *Implementing Citizen Participation in a Bureaucratic Society: A Contingency Approach* (New York: Praeger, 1981) 162.

15 However, a society is generally termed after its most dominant political tradition.

16 See F Bealey, 'Democratic elitism and the autonomy of elites' (1996) 17(3) *International Political Science Review* 319, 323.

17 B Barton, 'Underlying concepts and theoretical issues in public participation in resource development', in DN Zillman, AR Lucas and G Pring (eds), *Human Rights in National Resource Development: Public Participation in the Sustainable Development of Mining and Energy Resource* (Oxford: Oxford University Press, 2002) 77, 85–86.

18 See B Checkoway and JV Til, 'What do we know about citizen participation? A selective review of research', in Langton (ed) (n 12) 25, 27.

authoritarian monarchy in which power is held by a ruling family, as is the case in North Korea or one controlled by military (or even elected civilian) dictators, as was clearly the case in Nigeria as discussed in Chapter 2.

What then, for instance, would be the practical implication for public participation in environmental matters in a predominantly elitist society where governance is closed and the government is largely centralised and unaccountable to the public? According to Richardson and Razzaque, in such a setting environmental decision-making is treated as 'complex and technical, requiring primarily technical and administrative expertise'.[19] In the rational elitist view, since the public generally lacks the ability to engage meaningfully in environmental decision-making, why waste scarce resources providing the public with meaningful access to environmental information or, indeed, creating an opportunity for members of the public to overturn the decisions of 'superior minds' or hold them accountable? In other words, under such an elitist system, there would usually be undue restrictions on access to environmental information and justice. The result of such a closed and centralised system of environmental governance can be seen in the disastrous environmental record of Eastern European countries prior to1991 and China.[20]

From the above, an obvious weakness in the position of rational elitism is its tendency to over-emphasise the technical/scientific nature of environmental issues, when in fact the latter includes other non-scientific aspects (e.g. social, cultural, political and economic), which the lay public can grasp and make a substantial contribution towards. This is exactly what is indicated by the following Nigerian local adage (which may be thought of as a principle of traditional governance): 'a herbalist that refuses to ask laymen what leaves he looks for in the bush, must have difficulties getting what he wants'; whilst it is the province of the herbalist to make the medicine, getting the herbs in the first place requires the contribution of the lay public.

Furthermore, there is the likelihood that the rational elite will overlook the fact that, whilst environmental risk, its severity and manageability may be established by experts, the socially acceptable level of such environmental risk remains one that can only be rightly gleaned by seeking, understanding and considering the opinion of the relevant public.[21] In that context, this public opinion, which has its importance downplayed by rational elites, is crucial in achieving any governmental aim of making effective and acceptable environmental policies and managing environmental risks.

In addition, the justification of rational elites for not adequately involving the public in a meaningful manner on the grounds of their inability to engage

19 BJ Richardson and J Razzaque, 'Public participation in environmental decision-making', in BJ Richardson and S Wood (eds), *Environmental Law for Sustainability* (Oxford: Hart Publishing, 2006) 165, 170.

20 P Birnie, A Boyle and C Redgwell, *International Law and the Environment* (3rd edn Oxford: Oxford University Press, 2009) 289.

21 P Slovic, 'Perception of risk' (1987) 236(4799) *Science* 280–85.

meaningfully in technical matters is weak from two perspectives. First, the public is not a homogenous entity made up of 'non-technically' minded people as there are individuals and NGOs with better technical expertise than what may be available to the state – indeed, empirical evidence of ordinary members of the public collecting, analysing and deploying environmental information from industrial sites in their communities establishes clear limitations to the views of rational elitists on the public's competence.[22]

Second, even if a large section of the relevant public has certain limitations in its competence to participate, as will be elaborated on below, it is important to note the views of other theorists who, rather than view such incompetence as a hindrance to participation at certain levels, have highlighted the importance of participation in aiding personal development of individuals, including the skills needed for self-governance.[23]

Surprisingly, however, an elitist system, in rare cases, could help balance out some excesses that may result from an open public participatory system. In Nigeria, for example, some rural and poor communities, irrespective of the findings of an EIA and whether or not there are measures in place to mitigate serious (potential) environmental harm that has been revealed, will clamour for, and resist any attempt at relocating or discontinuing a project because of the developmental benefits that will come to the deprived community.[24]

This could be argued to be participation-gone-wrong in an environmental context. This also, it is submitted, is where the much criticised stance of Ophuls and Hardin, that authoritarian politics is the solution to the increasing environmental crisis, may find some relevance.[25] That is, a degree of authoritarian measure could enable such a flawed process to be discontinued and reconstituted differently, perhaps, with the participation of interested non-community entities such as NGOs. 'At worst', a measure of authoritarianism could also give effect to a different and arguably better decision of either mitigating potential harm, or relocating or discontinuing such a harmful project, against the wish of the public. However, on the whole, an elitist society is obviously not the proper environment for beneficial public participation to thrive, and Jefferson's opinion may be a more sustainable solution to the above 'participation-gone-wrong' problem. He states:

> I know of no safe repository of the ultimate power of the society but the people themselves; and if we think them not enlightened enough to exercise

22 D O'Rourke and GP Macey, 'Community environmental policing: assessing new strategies of public participation in environmental regulation' (2003) 22(3) *Journal of Policy Analysis and Management* 383.

23 See M Evans, 'Karl Marx and the concept of political participation', in G Parry (ed), *Participation in Politics* (Manchester: Manchester University Press, 1972) 127, 136–37.

24 Y Omorogbe, 'The legal framework for public participation in decision-making on mining and energy development in Nigeria: giving voices to the voiceless', in Zillman, Lucas and Pring (eds) (n 17) 549, 581.

25 See W Ophuls, 'Leviathan or oblivion?', in HE Daly (ed), *Towards a Steady-State Economy* (San Francisco: WH Freeman, 1973) 15; and G Hardin, *Exploring New Ethics for Survival: The Voyage of the Spaceship Beagle* (New York: Viking Press, 1972).

> control with a wholesome discretion, the remedy is not to take it from them, but to inform their discretion by education . . .[26]

3.3.2 Liberalism and public participation

Another political orientation that could be brought to bear on public participation is that of liberalism. Although not proposing the opposite of what rational elitism proffers, liberalism, which has several variations, generally seeks to ensure a better standing for the individual in society by stressing the need to guarantee the individual's rights to liberty and equality and for state interference in private life to be restricted. In essence:

> Liberalism took shape initially to contest the absolute powers of the monarch or the church. It asserted that the political system should protect the rights or civil liberties of the individual, and should maximize individual freedom of choice. Political power should be limited by requiring the consent of the governed, and should be limited to the public sphere. In the private aspects of an individual's life, including much of social and economic life, government has no business.[27]
>
> . . .
>
> [T]he state must be restricted in scope and restrained in practice to ensure the maximum possible freedom of every citizen.[28]

Thus, the fundamental characteristics of liberalism are wrapped in the general philosophy of individualism within which liberal thinkers including John Locke, Immanuel Kant and John Stuart Mill defended their political principles.[29] To the liberals, the divide between the public and private spheres must be realised 'because in that way political principles respect . . . the fallibilist, autonomous, or experimental attitude which we as persons should maintain at the deepest level of our self-understanding'.[30]

Whilst liberals (noted for such concepts as 'individualism', 'autonomy' and 'independence') have been viewed as 'turning a blind eye' on how people are connected to one another through complex networks of relations and institutions, they have largely succeeded in generating the belief that a proper political order is 'one in which people are able to develop their natural interests free from arbitrary use of political authority and coercive power', stopping short of proclaiming

26 HA Washington (ed), *The Writings of Thomas Jefferson* (Vol 7, New York: Riker, Thorne & Co, 1854) 177.
27 Barton (n 17) 87.
28 D Held, *Models of Democracy* (3rd edn Cambridge: Polity Press, 2006) 262.
29 C Larmore, 'The moral basis of political liberalism' (1999) 96(12) *Journal of Philosophy* 599, 603.
30 Ibid.

individual sovereignty as the means to this condition.[31] This obviously goes against the basic tenets of elitism.

The liberal theory is, however, fraught with many problems. First, it is largely unrealistic for individuals to conduct their affairs in the private sphere without public consequences.[32] Second, when viewed more narrowly within the context of public participation in environmental matters, the shortcomings of liberalism quickly appear. For instance, the theory has been criticised for 'offering a rationale against wider rules for standing in environmental litigation' as it advocates for individuals to take action in pursuance of their own interests, essentially in the private sphere.[33]

This situation is furthered by the liberal notion that if only the wellbeing of the general public is at stake, then the matter is in the public domain and only the government can deal with it. Thus, it has been noted that the liberal approach does not favour the protection of the environment in general, 'which are of a diffuse, collective, and fragmented character'.[34] Furthermore, under liberalism, one could see the access and flow of environmental information between the government and the governed greatly limited as a result of the division established between them. This could be harmful to both public and private interests as, for instance, their ability to respond to, or prevent (potential) environmental harm would have been eroded by lack of adequate and timely access to information.

Viewed from a different perspective, liberalism in some cases could help to promote the interest of the minority public in a society open to public participation. This possibility is evident in the fact that 'democratic majorities can easily decide not to respect particular rights, especially those of unpopular minorities', which tension can be diffused by arguing from a liberal perspective of 'freedom' and 'equality' for all; that there are basic rights which accrue to every individual and must be respected, such as freedom of expression.[35] These are the kinds of argument that have the potential to further the general wellbeing of the minorities in the Niger Delta area, for example, who suffer from environmental and natural resource injustice.

However, whilst the emphasis of liberalism on separation would ultimately create a society devoid of effective public participation, the elements of freedom and equality for all individuals which it advocates are necessary for effective public participation. Yet, for these conditions to be realised, even famous liberals including Locke, Montesquieu, Bentham and Mill had to accept that one must embrace democracy.[36]

31 Held (n 28) 263–64.
32 Barton (n 17) 88.
33 Ibid.
34 Ebbesson (n 13) 56.
35 JS Dryzek, *Deliberative Democracy and Beyond: Liberals, Critics, Contestations* (Oxford: Oxford University Press, 2000) 10–11.
36 Barton (n 17) 87.

3.3.3 Participatory democracy and public participation

Democracy, which, in literal Greek terms, means 'rule by the people' (*demos* means the people, and *kratein* means to rule), has become the most fashionable political tradition in today's world. From the Aristotelian view of humans being political beings who can only achieve self-fulfilment through active involvement in politics, the largely acceptable idea that '[public] participation arises from the classical theory of democracy' is not new.[37] The essence of democracy has also been captured in two words – *equality* (i.e. equal opportunity for all citizens to exert influence through political activity if they choose to do so) and *sovereignty* (which denotes a 'government that derives from and responds to the wishes of the people [and] must do no more and no less than the people desire').[38] However, Rousseau posits that this does not mean that every interest can be satisfied all the time, as the general will must in certain circumstances override the particular will.[39]

As previously alluded to, democracy embraces and furthers the fundamental liberal tenets concerning 'the centrality of an 'impersonal structure' of public power, of a constitution to help guarantee and protect rights, of a diversity of power centres within and outside the state, of mechanisms to promote competition and debate between alternative political platforms'.[40] On the other hand, it also necessarily involves a process of electing a body of individuals who will work for the interest of the electorate. Whilst this voting process may be a common denominator in elitism, liberalism and democracy, the frontiers of democratic principles have since been pushed further from the post of representative government by the urgings of some active democrats.

Although, to some, the right to vote for representatives seems satisfactory,[41] democrats such as Rousseau, who hold the more pervading view which rests on political equality, have refused to see this as the accurate picture of democracy. He essentially argues that democracy could only exist on a face-to-face basis where state power (over information and decision-making processes) is disaggregated and ordinary citizens are enabled and given the space to influence and shape plans, policies and proposed changes that affect them.[42]

This argument, which aligns with discussions in Chapter 1 on the interpretation of Article 25 of the ICCPR, basically rests on the subjective and autonomous

37 Kweit and Kweit (n 14) 35 and 7.

38 NM Rosenbaum, 'Citizen participation and democratic theory', in Langton (ed) (n 12) 43, 44–48.

39 Ibid, 46.

40 Held (n 28) 274.

41 For example, 'Schumpeter (1943), Berelson (1954), Dahl (1956) and Lipset (1963), among others, have argued that allegedly inherent tendencies of mass publics to be authoritarian, irrational, antidemocratic, intolerant of civil liberties, and ill-informed about political issues require that mass participation in decision making be confined mainly to leadership choice in elections'. JA Booth, 'Introduction: a framework for analysis', in MA Seligson and JA Booth (eds), *Elections and Democracy in Central America Revisited* (North Carolina: University of North Carolina Press, 1995) 3–4.

42 JJ Rousseau, *The Social Contract* (F Watkins (ed & transl), University of Wisconsin Press, 1986)102–106.

nature of interests and values which, similar to Rousseau's view,[43] made Cole opine that 'no man's will can be treated as a substitute for, or representative of, the will of others'.[44] Moreover, Loughlin's point that even though politicians should be representatives, they usually do what they want as against what is the clear reflection of the general will of the people,[45] would seem to corroborate Cole's position. (The latter view is commonly the case in Nigeria, hence the need to push for deeper and more direct public participation.)

This does not, however, negate the fact that representation which is meant to interpret/articulate the public will or amplify the voices of the people – especially where those voices cannot be self-financed or lack the intellectual ability required adequately to participate – is a vital part of democracy.[46] In fact, justifying representation based on the functional need for effective political decision-making in a complex society,[47] or for a more efficient day-to-day running of the society is not unreasonable.

However, from the definition of democracy to the views of respected democrats who recognise the direct and personal public participatory element of the concept,[48] it can strongly be argued today that representation, especially through government institutions, is not enough to call a system a democracy. The public needs to participate directly in the business of government, not simply to prevent a situation where democracy degenerates into a system of elected dictatorship,[49] but to constitute a check on elected officials, and fulfil the innate desire of the average human being to speak for him or herself on certain occasions, among other reasons.[50]

However, it is important to note that two countries may in fact possess similar democratic institutions, and yet one may still be more democratic than the other.[51] This means that there can be 'more or less democracy' depending on the 'amount and quality' of public participation in governance, especially in terms of public access to (environmental) information and decision-making processes.[52] The more 'significant and comprehensive' the opportunities for public participation are, the greater the level of democracy attached to that democracy.[53] However, the main challenge democracy faces remains how to organise effective participation in such

43 Ibid, 103, 104 and 106.
44 Quoted in Rosenbaum (n 38) 44.
45 M Loughlin, *Sword and Scale: An Examination of the Relationship Between Law and Politics* (Oxford and Portland: Hart Publishing, 2000) 8.
46 E Dannenmaier, 'Democracy in development: toward a legal framework for the Americas' (1997) 11(1) *Tulane Environmental Law Journal* 1, 4–5.
47 M Mason, *Environmental Democracy* (London: Palgrave Macmillan, 1999) 22.
48 See Seligson and Booth (n 41) 5.
49 Barton (n 17) 88.
50 See Rosenbaum (n 38) 44–45.
51 E Berndtson, 'Difference, compromises and democratic theory: from pluralism to multiculturalism', a paper presented at the 31st Annual Meeting of the Finnish Political Science Association, held in Turku, Finland, on 14–15 January 1999, 3.
52 Seligson and Booth (n 41) 6.
53 Mason (n 47) 21.

a way that the voice of the public is heard, and their wish(es) met as far as possible; (to this query, the provisions of the Aarhus Convention arguably provide a very useful response).

Wengert further spells out the challenge in more dramatic terms:

> The preacher says 'Seek ye first the kingdom of God'; the responsible democrat says 'Seek ye first the public interest'. Neither is easy; with respect to both it is the *seeking* that makes the difference, even when it is recognized that we often fall short.[54]

Plato's criticism of democracy also raises serious questions about the value of public participation. He tells of a captain who has studied navigation and has the technical skills to safely direct a ship. If the ship were a democratic state, the crew members who do not possess the necessary skills will quarrel among themselves over the captaincy of the ship. With everyone thinking he ought to be the captain, they do everything they can to make him hand over the tiller to them. The ignoramus who finally takes control endangers the ship and its passengers.[55] Plato's criticism highlights the tendency for democracy to devalue technical expertise at crucial times.

The thoughts raised here are particularly important in the environmental law field, where a clash between what sciences say and what the people want is not uncommon.[56] A further criticism is that 'a participatory and accountable polity may opt for short term affluence rather than long term environmental protection', in other words, '[d]emocracies are entirely capable of environmental destruction, and may even be structurally predisposed to unfettered consumption,' the industrial democracies of the North being a good example here.[57]

However, for public participation to thrive in any society, democracy must be embraced. Yet, to avoid or mitigate the negative 'side-effects' of democracy, it would be useful for such a society to consider some level of flexibility in implementing democratic principles. Although this point is further discussed below, it suffices to note here that Eckstein elaborates on this point in his work *A Theory of Stable Democracy* (1966), where he argued that for a democracy to be stable the government authority pattern must not be 'purely' democratic, and that it must contain a 'balance of disparate elements', one of which must be a 'healthy element of authoritarianism'.[58]

54 Wengert (n 11) 39–40.

55 Plato, *The Republic* (GRF Ferrari (ed) and T Griffith (tr), Cambridge: Cambridge University Press, 2000) xxvi, 191–92.

56 See S Eden, 'Public participation in environmental policy: considering scientific, counter-scientific and non-scientific contributions' (1996) 5 *Public Understanding of Science* 183–204.

57 MR Anderson, 'Human rights approach to environmental protection: an overview', in A Boyle and MR Anderson, *Human Rights Approaches to Environmental Protection* (Oxford: Clarendon Press, 1996) 1, 10.

58 See C Pateman, *Participation and Democratic Theory* (Cambridge: Cambridge University Press, 1970) 11–13.

3.3.4 Pluralism and public participation

Pluralism, which has a strong democratic foundation, emphasises the role of interest groups as against individual rights or state sovereignty.[59] According to McLennan, 'pluralism signals a theorized preference for multiplicity over unicity, and for diversity over uniformity'.[60] Whilst placing less emphasis on the state, it focuses on the competition among numerous groups representing different interests, such as business organisations, environmental advocacy organisations, trade unions, political parties, ethnic groups, women's collectives and religious groups.[61] Pluralism asserts that through 'the mechanisms of elections and pressure politics the government is reflective of society's demands and constrained by the countervailing powers of civil society and other organisations'; this is reflective of the pluralists definition of the state as 'a discreet organisation making policy in response to the myriad of groups [sic] pressing on the government'.[62]

To the pluralist, politics and policy-making is essentially a constant process of conflict, competition, negotiation and bargaining in a bid to resolve the conflicting interests of various groups.[63] In this case, 'there are multiple centres of power, none of which is wholly sovereign'.[64] State agencies are seen as no more than interest groups themselves,[65] and the state or government as no more than a site of conflict between interest groups, and as the umpire to declare the winners.[66] In performing this function, the government must also prevent any individual group from undermining the freedom of other groups to further their own interests.[67]

Although having a participatory outlook, pluralism has been criticised on the ground that interests with more resources, in terms of wealth and close contacts with government, for instance, are more likely to have better representation and influence on political outcomes than poorer groups.[68] Whilst poorer groups can use media and campaign to influence policies,[69] happenings in developing countries such as Nigeria where buoyant extraction corporations are at loggerheads with relatively poorer environmental advocacy groups over how the government should respond to certain natural resource and environmental issues, largely validates the point of richer groups having the upper hand. However,, the solution to this power imbalance is not to 'dismantle' environmental advocacy groups, but to continue to push for their strengthening; their mere presence on the scene is usually a boost to public and environmental interests than their absence.

59 See Held (n 28) 158 ff.
60 G McLennan, *Pluralism* (Buckingham: Open University Press, 1995) 25.
61 Ibid, 160.
62 M Smith, 'Pluralism', in D Marsh and G Stoker (eds), *Theory and Methods in Political Science* (London: Macmillan, 1995) 211, 212.
63 RA Dahl, *Pluralist Democracy in the United States* (Chicago: Rand McNally, 1967) 24.
64 Ibid.
65 Smith (n 62) 211.
66 Barton (n 17) 91.
67 Held (n 28) 159.
68 Smith (n 62) 212–213.
69 Ibid.

There is also the related and largely unaddressed concern under pluralism of some interests not having the resources to compete in the political arena, and of the groups that compete not being representative of a large section of the public that may be disadvantaged in certain respects.[70] These concerns with pluralism have been aptly captured in the view that 'the flaw in the pluralist heaven is that the heavenly chorus sings with a strong upper-class accent'.[71]

Nevertheless, despite these potential shortcomings, the value of the platform of pluralistic participation in bolstering the voice of environmentalists, in contrast to days when they had next to no say over the exploration of natural resources and environmental changes, is widely recognised.[72] Indeed, the effectiveness of group voice over that of disintegrated individuals in certain cases, and the check on excesses that countervailing powers with more capacities than available to individuals may introduce into political systems, are plausible contributions pluralism could bring to the public participation discourse in an environmental context.

3.4 The value of public participation

Although the theories discussed above, and others, favour public participation to varied extents and for various reasons, it is generally agreed that democracy is the best political platform for public participation to thrive. Interestingly, Winston Churchill is reputed to have noted that '[d]emocracy is the worst possible form of government . . . except for all of the other forms'.[73] However, in practice, some elements of the various theories discussed are usually present in a democracy. In exploring the value of public participation, in terms of public access to (environmental) information, decision-making processes (and justice, to an extent), this section will discuss the arguments that justify public participation and those that are critical of it. In the end, it will be clear that a participatory democratic system would need to incorporate certain seemingly 'undemocratic' thoughts and restrictions rooted in other political traditions to reduce or avoid occasional democratic 'excesses' and its negative effects.

Basically, the argument for public participation is made on diverse grounds which have come to be popularly categorised under two broad headings; the *process rationale*, which views public participation as an end in itself – it matters for its own sake and the *substantive rationale*, which views public participation as contributing to some further outcome such as the protection of the environmental and human wellbeing.[74]

70 See Barton (n 17) 91; Wengert (n 11) 36.

71 EE Schattschneider, *The Semisovereign People* (Hinsdale IL: Dryden Press, 1960) 35.

72 Barton (n 17) 94.

73 Quoted in ES Cahn and JC Cahn, 'Maximum feasible participation: QA general overview', in ES Cahn and BA Passett (eds), *Citizen Participation: Effecting Community Change* (New York: Praeger, 1971) 9, 16.

74 See G Pring and SY Noe, 'The emerging international law of public participation affecting global mining, energy, and resources development', in Zillman, Lucas and Pring (eds) (n 17) 11, 22; and HJ Steiner, 'Political participation as a human right' (1988) 1 *Harvard Human Rights Yearbook* 77, 100.

Although this categorisation is useful in structuring discussions to an extent, one may find it somewhat confusing, if not misleading. First, whilst some writers seem to discuss the grounds for justification under the rationales as distinctive and not connected,[75] others have sought reasonably to demonstrate the unsustainable nature of that position by playing down the boundary and stressing the connectivity and intertwined nature of the grounds under both rationales. For example, Ebbesson, reasonably argues that 'legitimacy' – which some analyse only under the process rational – can indeed be viewed in a 'more complex procedural-substantive terms' and 'in terms that are entirely or mainly related to the outcomes'.[76] Barton also provides support for the inexact nature of the popular categorisation by demonstrating how 'accountability' as a value can fall under either of both rationales.[77]

This situation calls for a more flexible approach in making the categorisation. Thus, rather than wholly follow this popular path, which has been described by Richardson as 'frequently muddled',[78] the grounds for justification in this section will be addressed individually and flexibly, under loose and broadly descriptive categories to maintain a sense of order, whilst being mindful of the fact that most grounds can be reasonably argued both from an instrumental and non-instrumental/intrinsic perspective. Of course, the justifications and criticisms cannot be exhausted below. Therefore, only the major ones will be examined.

3.4.1 Justifications

The first set of arguments for public participation that will be explored are those that place more emphasis on the direct impact and benefit of participation on and for the public participants as humans, mainly from a psychological and general human rights perspective. Here, in Kaufman's words, the participatory process is seen as one which 'enriches the lives of men not only by what it does *for* them but by what it does *to* them'.[79] In this regard, participation can achieve: (1) greater individual fulfilment; (2) personal development; (3) self-awareness; and (4) self-expression.

With respect to greater individual fulfilment, participation is seen as a way of recognising the worth of a participant as a human being, and ensuring and bolstering the individual's actual, as well as his or her sense of, dignity, self-respect and personal freedom, which may not be attained by an alternative means.[80] Members of various Nigerian communities, whom the government and powerful corporations have left in the dark and excluded from environmental decision-making processes that affect their wellbeing over the years, can certainly relate

75 See e.g. Pring and Noe (n 74) 22.
76 Ebbesson (n 13) 75–76.
77 Barton (n 17) 104–106.
78 A Richardson, *Participation* (London: Routledge & Kegan Paul, 1983) 51.
79 A Kaufman, *The Radical Liberal* (New York: Atherton Press, 1968) 56.
80 Richardson (n 78) 54.

with this point. Hence the feeling in such communities that they are been treated as 'second class citizens' or 'slaves' with no voice in their own country.[81]

If the public is allowed and encouraged to participate in the making of environmental decisions that affect their lives, a strong message is sent as to their value, in terms of their potential to make useful contributions; and this should have a positive impact on their individual self-esteem.[82] The reverse may be the case if this opportunity to participate is denied the public or they are subjected to a largely passive role in the process.[83] Similarly, people's sense of dignity and respect is bolstered when they have reasonable access to information about the state of their environment, which empowers them to make personal and other decisions. In this light, there is real value in the argument that 'freedom is increased through participation . . . because it gives him a very real degree of *control* over the course of his life and the structure of his environment'.[84]

The same applies to the position that 'it is of the essence of a truly human life that certain decisions are made by the individual himself, not because they are better decisions . . . but because the "control of decisions that affect a man's life" must be his before a man can be free'.[85] Cahn and Cahn encapsulate it thus:

> Participation is, in fact, the active expression of our faith in the dignity and worth of the individual. To deny effective participation, including the opportunity to choose, to be heard, to discuss, to criticise, to protest and to challenge decisions regarding the most fundamental conditions of existence, is to deny the individual's own worth and to confirm his impotence and subservience.[86]

The next argument, which goes beyond making participants more fulfilled, stresses the value of participation in facilitating the development of the individual participant's capacities, in both a moral and intellectual context. This relates to the educative function. This is vital in an environmental context where scientific realities and lay public views are usually in friction, and a host of legal instruments have stipulated for the improvement of public education and awareness on environmental issues.[87]

This is particularly important for Nigeria, considering the relatively high level of (environmental) illiteracy especially in the rural areas where many extractive and other industries are usually located, as highlighted in Chapter 2. In the Niger

81 See I Osuoka, 'People in the Niger delta Now Recognize that Jonathan is a waste of time', *Sahara Reporters*, 8 January 2012, available at http://saharareporters.com/interview/%E2%80%9Cpeople-niger-delta-now-recognize-jonathan-waste-time%E2%80%9D-%E2%80%93-isaac-osuoka (last accessed 30 January 2015).

82 See P Burton, 'Conceptual, theoretical and practical issues in measuring the benefits of public participation' (2009) 15(3) *Evaluation* 263, 265.

83 Ibid, 266.

84 Pateman (n 58) 26.

85 Quoted in Richardson (n 78) 55.

86 Cahn and Cahn (n 73) 31.

87 See e.g. Basel Convention, art 10(4); and Desertification Convention, arts 5(d) and 19(1)(a).

Delta, for example, as documented by Amnesty International in 2009, having 'almost no information on the impacts of pollution', the ability of many to make correct personal choices diminishes: 'people drink, cook with, and wash in polluted water; they eat fish contaminated with oil and other toxins'.[88]

By granting the public wide access to information and the opportunity to become involved in 'discussion[s] . . . of varying types of issues, people are given a chance to learn about new problems and solutions . . . if they make a few mistakes, they will also learn from them'.[89] This justification goes beyond the direct benefit for members of the public as Nonet and Selznick have rightly argued that 'the enlargement of legal participation . . . contribute[s] to the competence of legal institutions',[90] in that, such procedures have the clear potential to 'generate knowledge, new options and new models' that will be useful to public authorities.[91]

Broadly, by participating in one aspect of public life and drawing on its educative effect, the skills and confidence to tackle problems in other public and private spheres, [92] especially in terms of combating 'ecological damage in political fora',[93] are developed by disadvantaged groups such as the rural population in Nigeria who are mostly illiterate in relation to the existing political system. 'Civic activities', Barber claims, 'educates individuals how to think publicly . . . Politics becomes its own university . . . and participation its own tutor.'[94] In support of Rousseau on the educative value of public participation, Pateman writes:

> The major function of participation . . . is therefore an educative one, educative in the very widest sense, including both the psychological aspect and the gaining of practice in democratic skills and procedures . . . Participation develops and fosters the very qualities necessary for it; the more individuals participate the better able they are to do so.[95]

Furthermore, although closely linked with the educative function, public participation has also been supported on the ground of self-awareness: that 'participation is necessary for individuals to discover their own real interest, to learn [more] about themselves'.[96] This justification is supported by Bachrach,

88 Amnesty International, *Nigeria: Petroleum, Pollution and Poverty in the Niger Delta* (London: Amnesty International Publication, 2009) 21.

89 Richardson (n 78) 55.

90 P Nonet and P Selznick, *Law and Society in Transition: Towards Responsive Law* (New York: Harper & Rowe, 1978) 66.

91 K Getliffe, 'Proceduralisation and the Aarhus Convention: does increased participation in the decision-making process lead to More effective EU environmental law?' (2002) 4 *Environmental Law Review* 101, 108.

92 See Burton (n 17) 266.

93 Anderson (n 57) 6.

94 BR Barber, *Strong Democracy: Participation for a New Age* (California: University of California Press, 1984) 152.

95 Pateman (n 58) 42–43, 31–33.

96 Richardson (n 78) 56.

who argues that 'participation is an essential means for the individual to discover his real needs through the intervening discovery of himself as a social human being',[97] and that those who are excluded from participatory processes would have interests buried within them, that cannot be discovered by any other means, thus hampering the state's ability to satisfy them. As against when they are being represented, participating individuals discover more about themselves as they are obliged to reflect more deeply about their 'preferences and priorities' and their 'values and beliefs'.[98]

Added to these arguments, public participation is also seen as a route for greater self-expression.[99] The major claim is that there is a natural yearning in humans generally to let others understand them, their values and what they stand for, and that participation in public matters is a vital platform for having this natural urge satisfied. This relates to the discussion in the early part of Chapter 1 where, among other aspects, it was posited that the drive to participate is part of human nature. Thus, people who feel passionately about the environment would feel a level of satisfaction if given the opportunity to make a real input into the relevant processes of governance, even if their wishes do not (fully) materialise.

This view is well captured by Barber and Roszak who stated, respectively, that '[i]n strong democratic politics, participation is a way of defining the self',[100] and 'men participate democratically for the purpose of freeing the imagination and exploring self-expression'.[101]

The four justifications for public participation outlined above are mainly seen as intrinsic values of participation. However, it will not be out of place to argue for their instrumental value, albeit from an environmental position. Of course, if the individual has the above experiences, this will, more often than not, lead to better and more environmentally protective decisions. Thus, the justifications discussed above can also be seen as 'preliminary' benefits, and as a means to other ends. These sets of benefits may as well accrue to the officials, not only the public, as they engage with and observe the reaction of the public to issues.[102]

The second set of justifications focuses less on the direct human impact of public participation, and more on its broader social benefits and value for institutions and the processes of governance. Under this category, the following main values will be discussed: (1) accountability; (2) legitimacy and acceptability; (3) conflict resolution and avoidance; and (4) social cohesion and integration.

First, beyond the intermittent opportunity to hold the government accountable during elections, it is argued that public participation increases the accountability of decision-makers in government (and, to an extent, in the private sector) as

97 P Bachrach, 'Interests, participation, and democratic theory', in JR Pennock and JW Chapman (eds), *Participation in Politics* (New York: Lieber-Atherton, 1975) 39, 40.
98 See Burton (n 17) 266.
99 Richardson (n 78) 56.
100 Barber (n 94) 153.
101 T Rozak, *The Making of a Counter Culture: Reflections on the Technocratic Society and Its Youthful Opposition* (London: Faber & Faber, 1970) 148.
102 See Richardson (n 78) 89.

should be the case in a democracy.[103] The public having wide access to environmental information and decision-making processes and the ability to subject actions of public institutions and officials to judicial process will constitute a regular check on bureaucracy and corruption, which may be harmful to the environment and public wellbeing. For example, an analysis of numerous reports on the implementation of India's 2005 Right to Information Act (RTIA) revealed, overall, how 'citizens and civil society organizations have been able to use the RTIA to fight mismanagement and corruption and improve governmental responsiveness.'[104]

In the same vein, public participation can help prevent 'agency capture'[105] – a situation where a public regulatory agency aligns itself with the industry it is charged with regulating, usually to the detriment of its ability properly to perform its duties – which mostly thrives in a closed environment. Given the historical roots the Nigerian civil service has in official secrecy and public exclusion, and its weaknesses in terms of corruption and inadequate resources, 'agency capture' is arguably commonplace. This is exemplified, as noted in Chapter 2, by the complacency and complicity of the Nigerian National Petroleum Corporation in the pollution of the Nigerian environment by huge multinational oil companies, given the government's economic interests in those companies.

It is in this light that the opening up of government and the empowerment of the public in general has been canvassed as a means of countering capture and corruption within regulatory agencies.[106] So, just as 'war is too important to leave to the generals' alone, as Clemenceau remarked,[107] in line with Pomeroy's view, information and decisions about the environment is too fundamental to human survival and thriving to leave to public officials alone.[108]

Another justification for public participation in governance is that it promotes the legitimacy and credibility of institutions and their decisions and actions, and the consequential general acceptability of the latter to the public.[109] Of course, the close connection between people and their environment suggests that if environmental policies are to be successfully implemented, the entities carrying out public services and functions must establish their legitimacy in the eyes of the public. The environment 'belongs' to everyone and is the most vital element of human existence. In that light, why should only a few people holding certain

103 Barton (n 17) 104.

104 A Roberts, 'A great and revolutionary law? The first four years of India's Right to Information Act' (2010) 70(6) *Public Administration Review* 925, 926.

105 See Barton (n 17) 104; Checkoway and Til (n 18) 33; ME Levine and JL Forrence, 'Regulatory capture, public interest, and the public agenda: towards a synthesis' (1990) 6 *Journal of Law, Economics, and Organisation* 167–97.

106 See I Ayres and J Braithwaite, *Responsive Regulation* (Oxford: Oxford University Press, 1992).

107 Quoted in H Goldblatt, 'Arguments for and against citizen participation in urban renewal', in HBC Spiegel (ed), *Citizen Participation in Urban Development* (Washington DC: National Training Laboratories Institute for Applied Behavioral Science, 1968) 31, 35–36.

108 HR Pomeroy, 'The planning process and public participation', in G Breese and DE Whiteman (eds), *An Approach to Urban Planning* (Princeton University Press, 1953) 9, 25.

109 See Barton (n 17) 105.

public-related positions exclusively administer the environment or hold information relating to it? Bodansky identified secrecy and exclusion of the public as 'destroyers' of legitimacy, especially when it comes to environmental issues.[110] Ebbesson, in support, opines that proper procedural arrangements are necessary for establishing legitimacy.[111]

Nigerians can relate with the preceding point given the long history of secrecy and public exclusion in the country, which has led to a very poor public estimation and deep mistrust of nearly all governments in power, leading to difficulty in cooperation between the government and the public. By allowing for public input, informing them 'as to what went into the decision',[112] and creating an opportunity for them to subject the institutions to judicial or administrative scrutiny, the public is enabled to build a beneficial sense of 'ownership and of commitment'[113] to the final decision, 'even among parties who have not got what they want'.[114] This argument is justified in the following urban renewal scenario:

> [H]aving had a hand in the planning, residents are already predisposed to accept the plans which they feel they have helped create, even though the plans finally involve changes in the neighbourhood they would not have agreed to without prior discussion . . .[115]

Apart from the legitimacy-boosting effect of involving the public in environmental governance, the resulting substantive entitlements for the public or public-sensitive outcomes of such a process has its separate legitimising effect on institutions.[116] This is also relevant in the Nigerian situation as part of the general public complaint in the Niger Delta, for example, is that they have seen their livelihoods and the state of their environment seriously decline with their exclusion from participation in the oil industry as engendered mainly by the promulgation of the Land Use Act as highlighted in Chapter 2. So why should they support the government and developers or believe that their proposals are in the interest of their communities?

Also put forward as a ground for taking public participation seriously is the potential it has to resolve and avoid serious conflicts among competing interests, especially by building understanding and encouraging consensus amongst the various stakeholders with diverse interests, which is necessary for communal

110 See D Bodansky, 'Legitimacy' in D Bodansky, J Brunnée and E Hey (eds), *International Environmental Law* (Oxford: Oxford University Press, 2007) 704–23, 711.
111 Ebbesson (n 13) 75–81. See also E Gellhorn, 'Standing, participation, and who pays?' (1974) 26 *Administrative Law Review* 423, 424.
112 Gellhorn (n 111).
113 A Ackland, P Hyam and H Ingram, *Guideline for Stakeholder Dialogue – A Joint Venture* (London: The Environmental Council, 1999) 8.
114 Barton (n 17) 105.
115 Quoted in Goldblatt (n 107) 33.
116 Bodansky (n 110) 711; and Ebbesson (n 13) 75–81.

development.[117] Most governments and developers usually think that, in order to ensure the smooth progress of a project, it is better not to inform or talk to the relevant public about it. However, '[a]s citizens hear about [such] plans . . . they become distressed by the absence of prior notification from relevant officials and organize to stop the project.'[118]

If correct information replaces misinformation, and various interested parties put their minds together, this will facilitate better 'understanding and tolerance', induce 'modifications of values and opinions', reduce 'bias and mistrust' and increase 'confidence and trust'.[119] Chaotic environmental conflicts could be avoided, resolved or minimised if there is smooth flow of information between relevant parties and adequate access to justice is provided through which the public could properly channel any grievances.

The relative inadequacy of such public participatory mechanisms in Nigeria is a major reason for environment-related violence and conflicts in the country, as discussed in Chapter 2, and only a commitment to adequate public participation can douse the tension that still remains in the air. In addition, a lesser point is that the mere fact that people feel respected because their opinion has been sought might make them less aggressive and more willing to engage further in the process and accept certain outcomes that they would ordinarily reject if their relevance were not recognised.

In addition, public participation, it is argued, makes the individual more sociable, and this fosters actual, as well as a sense of, social cohesion and integration.[120] This effect, it is argued, strongly 'relies on participation taking a social form – the public meeting or focus group . . . for example – rather than its more individualistic forms, such as responding in isolation to a questionnaire survey'.[121] As people exchange information and engage in deliberations together, 'disruptive divisions between rich and poor',[122] government and the governed, and between races, ethnic groups and genders, which could negate reasonable engagement in processes relevant to environmental protection, are likely to diminish, leading to an increased sense of productive social cohesion and integration.

This point is particularly vital for Nigeria, given her massive plurality – with about 250 ethno-linguistic groups with a higher awareness, generally, of their differences than their oneness as 'Nigerians', besides the assortment of pressure groups and associations – and the non-consensual manner in which the country was formed as revealed in Chapter 2. This division, for example, continues to be a major source of tension, suspicion and mistrust within and between various groups and the government when it comes to dealings that affect the environment

117 DJ Fiorino, 'Citizen participation and environmental risk: a survey of institutional mechanisms' (1990) 15(2) *Science, Technology and Human Values* 226, 234.
118 C Davies, 'Public involvement in hazardous waste siting decisions' (1986) 19(2) *Polity* 296, 297.
119 Wengert (n 11) 26–27.
120 See Burton (n 17) 266.
121 Ibid.
122 Pateman (n 58) 27.

and natural resources of a particular group or region of the country. According to Barber: '[c]ommunity grows out of participation and at the same time makes participation possible'.[123] Building on Rousseau's thoughts, Pateman writes:

> [T]he experience of participating in decision making itself, and the complex totality of results to which it is seen to lead, both for the individual and for the whole political system; this experience attaches the individual to his society and is instrumental in developing it into a true community.[124]

The third set of justifications does not directly place emphasis on the value of participation for the individual or on the social and institutional benefits, but on the 'substantive outcome'[125] of the particular participatory activity. In an environmental context, it is mainly argued that public participation helps in environmental protection by ensuring sustainable development. This view is echoed in both Agenda 21[126] and the popular Brundtland Report,[127] which holds public participation in terms of access to information, decision-making processes and justice in environmental matters to be fundamental prerequisites for achieving sustainable development, given that they enable the public to discover, scrutinise and challenge policies and practices with potentially serious negative consequences for the environment.

In fact, it has been noted in empirical research across several countries that serious environmental degradation is often made possible by the suppression of activists and the denial of opportunities for public access to environmental information and decision-making processes,[128] as the discussion of Nigeria in Chapter 2 also reveals. Hence the importance of ensuring the proper legal implementation of these participatory elements in Nigeria, where developmental and industrial activities causing serious environmental degradation and public health issues urgently need to be guided onto a more sustainable path.

Accordingly, public participation contributes to achieving sustainable development and environmental protection mainly by ensuring: (1) improved quality of decisions (made by state and non-state actors) that affect the environment; and (2) better implementation and enforcement of environment-related laws.

123 Barber (n 94) 153.

124 Ibid.

125 'Substantive outcome' is used here in a narrow sense to refer to 'substantive decisions, conclusions, or recommendations – such as whether an incinerator should be built, what environmental problems should receive priority attention [etc.]' resulting from a participatory process. TC Beierle, 'Using social goals to evaluate public participation in environmental decisions' (1999) 16(3/4) *Policy Studies Review* 75, 81.

126 See ch 23, para 23.2.

127 Report of the UN World Commission on Environment and Development, *Our Common Future* (1987), foreword, ch 2, para 77 and ch 12, para 89.

128 Human Rights Watch and Natural Resources Defense Council, *Defending the Earth: Abuses of Human Rights and the Environment* (New York: Human Rights Watch and Natural Resources Defense Council, 2012).

To start with, if individuals and institutions are positively affected by participation as discussed above, this would most likely result in 'better' or more qualitative decisions[129] from informed contributions, and the improved ability to identify violations and enforce environmental laws, for the safety of the environment and humans. As Tribe opines, the quality of an outcome ('where one ends up') is largely determined by the quality of the process ('how one gets there').[130] Also, there is the saying that 'two [good] heads are better than one'. Public participation enables the proper and adequate integration of ecological, social and other relevant considerations into development decisions made by government and developer. This will most likely produce well-informed decisions, as against one taken from a limited and narrow (and probably defective) perspective.

In that light, government agencies and private corporations may have the technical knowledge relevant for environmental management, yet important 'value judgements' cannot be measured in any technical way, but by involving the public.[131] In noting that there are questions experts can answer for the public and those only the public can answer, Wexler provides a helpful example to illustrate this: for instance, 'Should I bring a suit?' is a complex question which requires the lawyer (expert) first to answer the question – 'Have I a cause of action?', and the (lay) public to make a decision on the last question – 'Should I sue?', considering factors including personal feelings and commitments.[132] So the voice of the public on certain issues that affect them, such as the execution of environmental changes, is indispensable, considering the fact that, amongst others, 'value judgments may fill gaps in knowledge; determine appropriate levels of safety; distribute [and reveal actual] costs and benefits of pollution; decide between fundamentally divided interests'.[133]

Further, the local public are usually custodians of important information about their environment and community, which can easily elude the experts and can provide useful feedback on past decisions, 'all of which is not easily attained by other means'.[134] These are necessary for quality decisions that are more protective of the environment and human wellbeing. For instance, a World Bank review of

129 In TC Beierle, *Public Participation in Environmental Decisions: An Evaluation Framework Using Social Goals* (Washington DC: Resources for the Future, 1998) 7, the author provides a series of questions, the affirmative response to all or some of which, may constitute a strong pointer to the realisation of a 'better' or more qualitative decision; e.g. '[d]id the public . . . [participation] process clearly increase all parties' satisfaction with the outcome relative to the likely non-participatory outcome? Were new alternatives generated? Were new opportunities for trade-offs or compensation between parties identified? Were relevant new facts revealed that corrected or otherwise clearly improved the technical analysis? Were decisions, technically, financially, or otherwise achievable?'

130 L Tribe, 'Technology assessment and the fourth discontinuity: the limits of instrumental rationality' (1972) 46 *Southern California Law Review* 617, 630–33.

131 Barton (n 17) 101.

132 S Wexler, 'Expert and lay participation in decision-making', in Pennock and Chapman (eds) (n 97) 186, 186–89.

133 M Lee and C Abbot, 'The usual suspects? Public participation under the Aarhus Convention' (2003) 66 *Modern Law Review* 80, 84.

134 Richardson (n 78) 61.

164 projects in 1982 found that where local communities were not involved in project planning, 'inaccurate assessments and information about local institutions were common' and this led to 'unworkable project proposals', as against projects with community participation which were successful.[135]

Accordingly, the UK Royal Commission on Environmental Pollution – a body predominantly consisting of scientists and technologists – in asserting that 'secrecy breeds fear', has also stated that 'in a democracy it is an unhealthy sign when authority claims omniscience and dismisses grass roots concerns as irrational'.[136] No one is in a better position to know where the shoe pinches than the wearer. So, according to Anderson: '[i]f the people who make the decisions are the same as those who pay for and live by the consequences . . . then we go a long way towards protecting the environment.'[137]

This view is very instructive for the Niger Delta situation, where those mainly responsible for and who are the major beneficiaries of the destructive oil and gas activities in the region do not live. Moreover, in a participatory environment, segments of the public with relevant (technical) expertise could assist public institutions with expertise not possessed by the public institutions or when the latter is short of necessary (human) resources as ample evidence suggests.[138] Surely, public participation can help to supplement the resources available to government agencies considering the free information transfer and dissemination and the shared decision-making role they could play.[139] In filling the void created by government agencies, O'Rourke and Macey demonstrated in their empirical piece how the local group called 'bucket brigade' engaged in sampling industrial air emissions in their locality 'help to increase knowledge of emissions and potential health risks, [and] raise awareness' in their community.[140]

Also, apart from government agencies, informed public participation can regulate the behaviour of private corporations, by forcing them to make more environmentally protective decisions, which will support and reflect the public needs and values.[141] This could happen through the public playing a meaningful role in the decision-making process or by the public having access to critical environmental information about a company's activities, as O'Rourke and Macey's piece demonstrates: the fact that private corporations knew that local people were independently collating, analysing and deploying data containing their emissions, forced them to take steps to reduce their emissions level significantly.[142] Also, the potency of access to environmental information in aiding

135 A Zazueta, *Policy Hits the Ground: Participation and Equity in Environmental Policy-making* (Washington DC: World Resources Institute, 1995) 7.

136 R McCracken and G Jones, 'The Aarhus Convention' (July 2003) *Journal of Planning and Environmental Law* 802, 804.

137 Anderson (n 57) 9.

138 See Birnie and others (n 20) 100–103; and Ebbesson (n 13) 68.

139 See JW Futrell, 'Public participation in Soviet environmental policy' (1987) 5 *Pace Environmental Law Review* 487, 498.

140 O'Rourke and Macey (n 22) 403–405.

141 S Bell and D McGillivray, *Environmental Law* (7th edn Oxford: Oxford University Press, 2008) 297.

142 O'Rourke and Macey (n 22) 403–405.

individuals in making better personal and life preserving decisions has clearly been recognised.[143]

The second perspective is that informed public participation enables and creates wider space for better enforcement and implementation of laws relevant for environmental protection. Just as government agencies do not and cannot know it all, they can also not do it all: '[i]t is impossible for an agency to have its eyes and ears everywhere to detect infractions'.[144] Owing to a lack of adequate resources (human, financial and infrastructure-wise), government agencies in Nigeria, for example, are unable to respond adequately to violations of environmental laws. In such cases, any impending harm to the environment and public wellbeing caused by an extractive industry, for example, may be avoided if there are broad and adequate legal mechanisms for access to environmental information through which individuals and NGOs can discover environmental breaches and/or gather all the information relevant for them successfully to subject such (potentially) harmful activity to judicial and administrative review processes.

In addition, informed public participation in environmental decision-making processes, especially when supported by adequate legal mechanisms, can positively influence better state and developers' compliance with environmental obligations by the former benchmarking the views of the latter against the requirements of existing environmental laws in the course of participation, and pushing for compliance with such laws. There is the argument that public participation is important in ensuring that 'deference to environmental law does not depend solely on the discretion of government',[145] considering the fact that many governments may even be more inclined to favour certain economic interests at the expense of the environment and human wellbeing.

In support, it has been noted, for instance, that with respect to the Convention on the Conservation of European Wildlife and Natural Habitats, 'the attendance of NGOs at the meeting of the convention plays an essential role in relation to compliance with the obligations of the Convention. This applies . . . to areas such as *information, publicity and pressure for action*.'[146]

Although these substantive outcomes are usually discussed from an extrinsic perspective, as has been done here, their intrinsic value is not in doubt.[147] For example, it has been reasonably argued that high-quality decisions or 'accurate decisions themselves constitute an important element of fair treatment, which in turn constitutes an important element of respect for persons'.[148] It is also important to make clear that, although outcomes are important, the participatory process itself, together with its intrinsic value, also matters a great deal; i.e. public

143 See *Guerra v Italy* (1998) 26 EHRR 357; and the 2000 OAS Public Participation Strategy.

144 Barton (n 17) 100.

145 Ebbesson (n 13) 63–67.

146 V Koester, 'Pacta sunt servanda' (1996) 26 *Environmental Policy and Law* 81.

147 See TRS Allan, 'Review: procedural fairness and the duty of respect' (1998) 18(3) *Oxford Journal of Legal Studies* 497, 499–501.

148 DJ Galligan, *Due Process and Fair Procedures: A Study of Administrative Procedures* (Oxford: Clarendon Press, 1996) 78; reviewed by Allan (n 147) 497.

participation is not all about the final substantive outcome. This fact is demonstrated by an actual case where 'a women's group introduced some resolutions [in a parliament] about policies regarding women, which were immediately passed, and passed unanimously. The women concerned were furious; they had wanted to hold a discussion of the resolutions, and to be listened to.'[149]

Thus, whilst it may be the case that right outcomes, most likely by chance, may result without a participatory process or with a highly limited one, it is also true that many other benefits to the public and the society as a whole would have been lost to non-participation, which may be antithetical to the outcome achieved. In view of this fact, a wholly or largely successful public participation is not one which meets only the outcome goals, or those of the participatory process, but one which meets some balance of outcome *and* participatory process goals.[150]

A final issue here is that it is possible for there to be, in some cases, a level of disinterest on the part of the public when it comes to engaging in participatory activities. For example, it was noted in a study that only 35 out of 8315 respondents who indicated intent to participate, actually took the initiative to make an inquiry about how to join the participatory process, despite knowing the appropriate office to contact.[151] Such situations support the frustration of some experts in being burdened with a public that is really not interested in participating.[152] This situation may even bolster 'argument for a top-down administration simply on the grounds of efficiency'.[153] However, it is thought that a more beneficial approach would be for public authorities and developers to show a great deal of perseverance, and educate and motivate the public on the need to participate, given the multi-dimensional benefits of engaging the public and the value of such engagement for all parties.

3.4.2 Criticisms (and some responses)

Turning from the benefits of participation, as should be expected, there are those who, to an extent, think otherwise. Generally, critics do not advocate complete abstinence by the public from participation in environmental matters for, as Arnstein noted, 'the idea' of public participation 'is a little like eating spinach: no one is against it in principle because it is good for you'.[154] Rather, the main criticisms support some level of participation, but doubt its potential to

149 D Braybrooke, 'The meaning of participation and of demands for it: a preliminary survey of the conceptual issues', in Pennock and Chapman (eds) (n 97) 56, 84–85.
150 C Chess and K Purcell, 'Public participation and the environment: do we know what works?' (1999) 33(16) *Environmental Science and Technology* 2685–86.
151 Williams and others (n 2) 59.
152 J Petts, 'The public-expert interface in local management decisions: expert, credibility and process' (1997) 6 *Public Understanding of Science* 359.
153 RA Irvin and J Stansbury, 'Citizen participation in decision-making: is it worth the effort?' (2004) 64(1) *Public Administration Review* 55, 58.
154 SR Arnstein, 'A ladder of citizen participation' (1969) 35(4) *Journal of the American Institute of Planners* 216.

achieve certain results and highlights the drawbacks, the risks and the problems that can occur.[155]

First, on the impact of participation on humans noted above, Smith has noted that 'participation in government is neither necessary nor sufficient' for the 'full' realisation of such impact.[156] Not denying the achievability of such an impact, Smith also went on to entertain the idea of lack of opportunity to participate having a negative effect on a person's self-esteem, vision of common good and the like.[157] This is still sufficient reason to justify a call for wide public participation, as the idea of participation being a major tool in positively impacting the individual remains unscathed. Moreover, there is hardly a solid argument that participation is detrimental to innate human fulfilment or development.[158] Even the criticism that '[b]y focusing their energies and attention on themselves, participation deflects their potential concern for wider issues'[159] is less of an issue.

Many individuals are mainly focused on more substantive results of participation as against these 'human benefits' which mainly accrue indirectly in the process of participating. With the educative function of participation, such a potential problem becomes largely insignificant because as was earlier noted, engaging in the civic activity of participation has the potential to educate the individual to think more publicly in such situations. Moreover, seeking human fulfilment and that of other 'wider issues' are not necessarily opposing objectives, but may be complementary. For instance, in the women's group case noted above, the clamour for the women to be heard was supportive of the wider interest of the group, even though it would have also delivered some personal 'human benefits'.[160]

Furthermore, as against ensuring institutional accountability and legitimacy, it has been argued that participation can be used by authorities to manipulate the public into gaining awareness of government or even developers' problems in such a way and to such an extent as to inhibit the public from pressing for solutions to their own problems.[161] This way, the authorities, who are usually more skilled in participatory processes,[162] are able to legitimise their decisions with the stamp of public approval even when this is essentially against the public interest and will.[163] Here, the public is 'fooled' into believing their opinion will be taken into consideration, when in fact they are being 'used' by officials to build support for, and reduce antagonism towards, their own ends.[164] This strategy of co-option,

155 See Barton (n 17) 106–107.
156 MBE Smith, 'The value of participation', in Pennock and Chapman (eds) (n 97) 126, 127–28.
157 Ibid.
158 Richardson (n 78) 57.
159 Ibid.
160 Braybrooke (n 149).
161 J Dearlove, 'The control of change and the regulation of community action', in D Jones and M Mayo (eds), *Community Work One* (London: Routledge & Kegan Paul, 1974) 22, 37.
162 Richardson (n 78) 78 ff.
163 Dearlove (n 161). See also Wengert (n 11) 26.
164 See Checkoway and Til (n 18) 32–33; and MR Haug and MB Sussman, 'Professional autonomy and the revolt of the client' (1969) 17(2) *Social Problems* 153.

rather than cooperation, may only serve to dampen the enthusiasm of the public to 'take on' the system in the interests of change[165] and produce outcomes not reflective of public needs and values. Although these are legitimate concerns, it is still reasonable to think that, in some cases, instead of such situations taming the participant it may in fact heighten the urge to press for change.[166]

Also, whilst there is the undeniable conflict resolution and social cohesion potential of participation, the reverse may well be the case in some situations. To Offe, the 'conflict-generating potential of the institutions of the democratic polity by far outweighs their conflict-resolving capacity', as the system is usually overloaded with diverse demands.[167] On the contrary, it is argued here that the reality of Offe's view largely results from how the relevant stakeholders in the participatory process conduct themselves and how the process itself is carried out, and usually not from the idea of participation itself. Indeed, Lee and Abbot did highlight the UK Government's complaint about the need to fine-tune its system of public hearing as it usually turns out to be 'too adversarial'.[168]

Similarly, it makes sense to believe that conflict and increased polarisation may result in cases where public demands are not largely met after their hopes had been inflated by the potential benefits of participation,[169] or where the community is one with highly diverse interests,[170] or a decision-making procedure has been excessively formalised and modelled on a judicial procedure, which may create an atmosphere of confrontation.[171] Although the highly structured judicial process where parties have no option but to accept unacceptable decisions may reduce conflict,[172] the usual winner-takes-all norm of this system will increase polarisation, which is the foundation for conflict. It must also be noted that conflict can occur between professionals who represent the public and those on the other side, for although 'science may strive for the 'truth', the opinions of scientists 'are [often] coloured by their values and beliefs'.[173]

Furthermore, the idea that informed participation leads to better outcomes is not without criticism. Participation in some circumstances may not be able to produce better decisions. There may be: the difficulty or 'inefficiency in identifying public preferences and aggregating them into coherent public policy';[174] the usual power imbalance in participatory abilities earlier alluded to, which may not only negatively impact on the fairness and equitableness of the process and outcome,

165 Richardson (n 78) 59–60, 66.
166 Ibid, 60.
167 C Offe, *Contradictions of the Welfare State* (London: Hutchinson, 1984) 164.
168 Lee and Abbot (n 133) 99.
169 SP Huntington, 'The democratic distemper' (1975) 41 *Public Interest* 9–38.
170 See JD Priscoli, 'Implementing public involvement programs in federal agencies' in Langton (ed) (n 12) 97–98.
171 Barton (n 17) 108.
172 Wengert (n 11) 27.
173 MK Ewing, 'Public participation in environmental decision-making' (2003) 13, available at http://www.gdrc.org/decision/participation-edm.html (last accessed 30 January 2015).
174 Rosenbaum (n 38) 48.

but also on how much the latter reflects public values;[175] excessive compromises that may render policies too ineffectual to achieve their purpose; and the fact that 'the process [may] placate the vehemently-held opinion of the few, at the cost of an interest that is important and widely, but less vehemently, held in the larger community'.[176]

Participation is also criticised for potentially enabling small groups and individuals that do not reflect the will of the general public to reject critical decisions, especially with the wide standing granted them to obtain review.[177] As some have argued, the public is generally and usually too selfish and irrational at the cost of the wider society, as in many cases they canvass and strive to protect their own interests only.[178] By way of contrast, public participation is also criticised for providing the rich and well-organised majority a tool with which to subjugate the interests of the poor and weakly organised minority.[179] Whatever the position may be, a positive perspective here may be that both the minority and the majority have a tool with which to protect themselves from marginalisation.

In addition, as against infusing efficiency and effectiveness into institutional systems, there is the reality and potential of wide participation being time consuming[180] especially, as in many cases, the public has no clear leader with proper authority.[181] This 'additional' time the participatory process takes may inhibit reasonable development or quick action when time is of the essence; environmental cases may drag on in court and useful projects and proposals may be held up for a long time; and the complexities involved in meshing various interests to form a common decision takes time also.

The process of ensuring adequate public access to information and decision-making processes may also be quite costly as a result of the enormity of the mechanisms that may be needed to ensure their smooth running, the large number of participants, and the increased time it takes to conclude an issue.[182] For instance, Ewing provides an example of a project which was funded for three years under the EU Life Programme; after three years of intense community activity and drawing up a large volume of public participation plan, 'no further fund was available, and the project was closed down. Clearly the process was a success, but the result not.'[183]

Whilst not disproving the above criticisms, it is fair to note that early participation can help save time 'by reducing delays caused by challenges already under

175 Richardson (n 78) 78.
176 Barton (n 17) 107. See also Goldblatt (n 107) 38–39.
177 Rosenbaum (n 38) 49.
178 MF Kraft and BB Clary, 'Citizen participation and the Nimby Syndrome: public response to radioactive waste disposal' (1991) 44 *Political Research Quarterly* 299, 301.
179 See RW Collins, 'Environmental equity: a law and planning approach to environmental racism' (1992) 11 *Virginia Environmental Law Journal* 495–546; SL Cutter, 'Race, class and environmental justice' (1995) 19(1) *Progress in Human Geography* 111–22.
180 Rosenbaum (n 38) 48.
181 Goldblatt (n 107) 40.
182 Rosenbaum (n 38) 48.
183 Ewing (n 173) 11.

way'[184] as well as 'reduce cost by limiting the need to redesign projects to meet public objectives'[185] or having to spends funds to acquire knowledge that is freely obtainable from NGOs and the public. Similarly, public participation can help avoid violence, which may cost a developer loss of property and money; this is exemplified in the Niger Delta where the finances of the nation and the companies are negatively impacted by the vandalism of oil installations, kidnapping of oil company workers for ransom and the huge cost spent on providing extraordinary security for oil installations and workers, partly resulting from the disconnection between government/developers and the relevant public.

Also, public access to environmental information and decision-making processes may significantly reduce litigation, which will help to save costs and time that would have been spent on a (potential) lawsuit,[186] as well as preserve the positive image of a company in the eyes of the public, which in turn could positively impact on the company's finances. In assessing the cost to public authorities of providing (environmental) information, the position of the Information Commissioner of Canada is invaluable:

> The annual cost [to the government] of administration [of the Canadian Access to Information Law] is some $20 million by a generous estimate. That is a bargain for such an essential tool of public accountability. The law pays for itself in more professional, ethical and careful behaviour on the part of public officials who must now conduct public business in the open. Excessive fees discourage use of the law and, in the long run, that is too high a cost.[187]

Finally, it is also argued that involving the public in decision-making could hinder the creativity of agencies and corporations and prevent them from utilising their expertise and experience in problem solving,[188] considering that the public may be too emotional or ill-equipped to do the right thing. In contrast, however, the Cahns have highlighted what they termed 'the right to be wrong', which certainly has some virtue:

> [T]oday, meaningful . . . participation encompasses more than the protection of mere dissent. It entails the right of a group or a people to risk choosing wrongly where they and not others will bear the primary consequences of that choice . . . The right to be wrong . . . requires opportunity to learn from the trials and errors of others. It is not necessary that each community . . .

184 2000 OAS Public Participation Strategy.

185 Ibid.

186 J Randolph and M Bauer, 'Improving environmental decision-making Through collaborative methods' (1999) 16(3/4) *Policy Studies Review* 168, 170. Cf C Coglianese, 'Assessing consensus: the promise and performance of negotiated rulemaking' (1997) 46(6) *Duke Law Journal* 1255–1349.

187 Information Commissioner of Canada, *Annual Report 1993–94*, 9.

188 Pring and Noe (n 74) 25; Rosenbaum (n 38) 49.

repeat the process of error and suffering of others. It is not a mandate to begin from ignorance.[189]

3.4.3 A 'middle ground' theory for public participation

From the above analysis, it is clear that participation could be an unruly horse. It must be tamed to get the best out of it. The unruly horse (i.e. participation) has no responsibility in this, only the riders (i.e. the parties involved). The parties involved will tame participation by approaching it with a more cooperative motive and a give-and-take mentality that does not endanger the objective of a viable result; they must know where to draw the line on participation in order to minimise its excesses and maximise its benefits. The solution to the problems of participation is neither non-participation nor the advice of Al Smith: '[t]he only cure for the evils of democracy is more democracy.'[190] According to Huntington, this 'could well be adding fuel to the fire'.[191]

The solution is 'democratic moderation' – the introduction of some beneficial tenets of other political traditions, as discussed above, into the body of democracy, to enhance it. In clarifying this point, Huntington's comment on excessive democracy in the United States and the need for moderation, is instructive:

> [D]emocracy is only one way of constituting authority . . . A university where teaching appointments are subject to approval by students may be a more democratic university, but it is not likely to be a better university. In similar fashion, armies in which the commands of officers have been subject to veto by the collective wisdom of their subordinates have almost invariably come to disaster on the battle field . . . *The Greek philosophers argue that the best practical state – the 'mixed regime' – would combine several different principles of government in its constitution.* 'Democracy never lasts long,' John Adams observed: '. . . There never was a democracy yet that did not commit suicide'. *That suicide is more likely to be the product of overindulgence than of any other cause. A value which is normally good in itself is not necessarily optimized when it is maximized* . . . There are . . . potential desirable limits to the extension of political democracy. *Democracy could have a longer life if it has a more balanced existence.*[192]

What is, however, non-negotiable is the fact that the system adopted must provide wide access for the public to participate meaningfully, whilst maintaining some clearly defined state powers to regulate participatory processes as situations present themselves, in provable good faith, with the benefits of such a process as the driving force. However, overall, there is no doubt, from the perspectives of writers and governments, that the 'benefits' of participation 'vastly outweigh its

189 Cahn and Cahn (n 73) 43–45.
190 Quoted in Huntington (n 169) 36.
191 Ibid.
192 Emphasis added. Ibid, 36–37.

disbenefits'[193] and 'the significance of the instances of the abuse of participatory rights'.[194] This position is validated and evidenced by the fact that 'it continues to be embraced, in particular with great force, in environmental matters'.[195]

3.5 Conclusion

This chapter has addressed some theoretical issues about public participation, mainly in an environmental context, as relevant to achieving the overall aim of this book. Apart from the nature of 'the public', the place and extent of public participation in various political traditions, as well as its value mainly in terms of its benefits and criticisms, was explored in this chapter. To this end, a major conclusion similar to Gauna's was reached, which is: even though participatory democratic norms must remain the general and fundamental disposition of the polity, it is better to avoid settling with the norms of a particular tradition, and 'steer a hybrid course',[196] seeing that they 'all have strengths and weaknesses, and offer useful insights into what is happening and what should happen'.[197] This was proposed as a plausible way of overcoming the excesses of participation and maximising its benefits.

Going forward, it is argued that the implementation of the provisions of the Aarhus Convention and similar regimes (which will be discussed in the subsequent chapters) will contribute in deepening environmental democratic norms in countries such as Nigeria, and in delivering the benefits and limiting the potential excesses of environmental public participation.[198]

So much is indicated in the preamble of the Aarhus Convention: the conviction that its implementation will 'contribute to strengthening democracy'; the fact that the regime aims 'to further the accountability and transparency in decision-making' by advancing public participation; the recognition of the potential of public participation 'to strengthen public support for decisions on the environment'; and the fact that 'in the field of the environment, improved access to information and public participation in decision-making enhance the quality and the implementation of decisions, contribute to public awareness of environmental issues, give the public the opportunity to express its concerns and enable public authorities to take due account of such concerns.'

193 Pring and Noe (n 74) 26.
194 M Fitzmaurice, 'Some reflections on public participation in environmental matters as a human right in international law' (2002) 2 *Non-State Actors and International Law* 1, 12.
195 NP Spyke, 'Public participation in environmental decision-making at the new millennium: structuring new spheres of public influence' (1999) 26 *Boston College Environmental Affairs Law Review* 263, 275.
196 E Gauna, 'The environmental justice misfit: public participation and the paradigm' (1998) 17 *Stanford Environmental Law Journal* 3, 52.
197 Barton (n 17) 120.
198 See S Stec, 'EU enlargement, neighbourhood policy and environmental democracy', in M Pallemaerts (ed), *The Aarhus Convention at Ten: Interactions and Tensions Between Conventional International Law and EU Environmental Law* (Groningen: Europa Law Publishing, 2011) 35, 51.

Bibliography

Abel TD and Stephan M, 'The limits of civic environmentalism' (2000) 44(4) *American Behavioral Scientist* 614.

Ackland A, Hyam P and Ingram H, *Guideline for Stakeholder Dialogue – A Joint Venture* (London: The Environmental Council, 1999).

Allan TRS, 'Review: procedural fairness and the duty of respect' (1998) 18(3) *Oxford Journal of Legal Studies* 497.

Amnesty International, *Nigeria: Petroleum, Pollution and Poverty in the Niger Delta* (London: Amnesty International Publication, 2009) 21.

Anderson MR, 'Human rights approach to environmental protection: an overview', in Boyle A and Anderson MR, *Human Rights Approaches to Environmental Protection* (Oxford: Clarendon Press, 1996) 1.

Arnstein, SR, 'A ladder of citizen participation' (1969) 35(4) *Journal of the American Institute of Planners* 216.

Ayres I and Braithwaite J, *Responsive Regulation* (Oxford: Oxford University Press, 1992).

Bachrach P, 'Interests, participation, and democratic theory', in Pennock JR and Chapman JW (eds), *Participation in Politics* (New York: Lieber-Atherton, 1975) 39.

Barber BR, *Strong Democracy: Participation for a New Age* (California: University of California Press, 1984).

Barton B, 'Underlying concepts and theoretical issues in public participation in resource development', in Zillman DN, Lucas AR and Pring G (eds), *Human Rights in National Resource Development: Public Participation in the Sustainable Development of Mining and Energy Resource* (Oxford: Oxford University Press, 2002) 77.

Bealey F, 'Democratic elitism and the autonomy of elites' (1996) 17(3) *International Political Science Review* 319.

Beierle TC, *Public Participation in Environmental Decisions: An Evaluation Framework Using Social Goals* (Washington DC: Resources for the Future, 1998).

Beierle TC, 'Using social goals to evaluate public participation in environmental decisions' (1999) 16(3/4) *Policy Studies Review* 75.

Bell S and McGillivray D, *Environmental Law* (7th edn Oxford: Oxford University Press, 2008).

Berndtson E, 'Difference, compromises and democratic theory: from pluralism to multiculturalism', a paper presented at the 31st Annual Meeting of the Finnish Political Science Association, held in Turku, Finland, on 14–15 January 1999.

Birnie P, Boyle A and Redgwell C, *International Law and the Environment* (3rd edn, Oxford: Oxford University Press, 2009).

Bodansky D, 'Legitimacy' in Bodansky D, Brunnée J and Hey E (eds), *International Environmental Law* (Oxford: Oxford University Press, 2007) 704.

Booth JA, 'Introduction: A framework for analysis', in Seligson MA and Booth JA (eds), *Elections and Democracy in Central America Revisited* (North Carolina: University of North Carolina Press, 1995) 3.

Braybrooke D, 'The meaning of participation and of demands for it: a preliminary survey of the conceptual issues', in Pennock JR and Chapman JW (eds), *Participation in Politics* (New York: Lieber-Atherton, 1975) 56.

Burton P, 'Conceptual, theoretical and practical issues in measuring the benefits of public participation' (2009) 15(3) *Evaluation* 263.

Cahn ES and Cahn JC, 'Maximum feasible participation: a general overview', in Cahn ES and Passett BA (eds), *Citizen Participation: Effecting Community Change* (New York: Praeger, 1971) 9.

Checkoway B and Til JV, 'What do we know about citizen participation? A selective review of research', in Langton S (ed), *Citizen Participation in America* (Massachusetts: Lexington Books, 1978) 25.

Chess C and Purcell K, 'Public participation and the environment: do we know what works?' (1999) 33(16) *Environmental Science and Technology* 2685.

Coglianese C, 'Assessing consensus: the promise and performance of negotiated rulemaking' (1997) 46(6) *Duke Law Journal* 1255.

Collins RW, 'Environmental equity: a law and planning approach to environmental racism' (1992) 11 *Virginia Environmental Law Journal* 495.

Cutter SL, 'Race, class and environmental justice' (1995) 19(1) *Progress in Human Geography* 111.

Dahl RA, *Pluralist Democracy in the United States* (Chicago: Rand McNally, 1967).

Dannenmaier E, 'Democracy in development: toward a legal framework for the Americas' (1997) 11(1) *Tulane Environmental Law Journal* 1.

Davies P, 'Public participation, the Aarhus Convention, and the European Community', in Zillman DN, Lucas AR and Pring G (eds), *Human Rights in National Resource Development: Public Participation in the Sustainable Development of Mining and Energy Resource* (Oxford: Oxford University Press, 2002) 155.

Dearlove J, 'The control of change and the regulation of community action', in Jones D and Mayo M (eds), *Community Work One* (London: Routledge & Kegan Paul, 1974) 22.

Dryzek JS, *Deliberative Democracy and Beyond: Liberals, Critics, Contestations* (Oxford: Oxford University Press, 2000).

Duane TP, 'Community participation in ecosystem management' (1997) 24 *Ecology Law Quarterly* 771.

Ebbesson J, 'The notion of public participation in international environmental law' (1997) 8 *Yearbook of International Environmental Law* 51.

Eden S, 'Public participation in environmental policy: considering scientific, counter-scientific and non-scientific contributions' (1996) 5 *Public Understanding of Science* 183.

Evans M, 'Karl Marx and the concept of political participation', in Parry G (ed), *Participation in Politics* (Manchester: Manchester University Press, 1972) 127.

Ewing MK, 'Public participation in environmental decision-making' (2003) 13, available at http://www.gdrc.org/decision/participation-edm.html (last accessed 30 January 2015).

Fiorino DJ, 'Citizen participation and environmental risk: a survey of institutional mechanisms' (1990) 15(2) *Science, Technology and Human Values* 226.

Fitzmaurice M, 'Some reflections on public participation in environmental matters as a human right in internal law' (2002) 2 *Non-State Actors and International Law* 1.

Futrell JW, 'Public participation in Soviet environmental policy' (1987) 5 *Pace Environmental Law Review* 487.

Galligan DJ, *Due Process and Fair Procedures: A Study of Administrative Procedures* (Oxford: Clarendon Press, 1996).

Gauna E, 'The environmental justice misfit: public participation and the paradigm' (1998) 17 *Stanford Environmental Law Journal* 3.

Gellhorn E, 'Standing, participation, and who pays?' (1974) 26 *Administrative Law Review* 423.

Getliffe K, 'Proceduralisation and the Aarhus Convention: does increased participation in the decision-making process lead to more effective EU environmental law?' (2002) 4 *Environmental Law Review* 101.

Glicken J, 'Effective public involvement in public decisions' (1999) 20(3) *Science Communication* 298.

Goldblatt H, 'Arguments for and against citizen participation in urban renewal', in Spiegel HBC (ed), *Citizen Participation in Urban Development* (Washington DC: National Training Laboratories Institute for Applied Behavioral Science, 1968) 31.

Hardin G, *Exploring New Ethics for Survival: The Voyage of the Spaceship Beagle* (New York: Viking Press, 1972).

Haug MR and Sussman MB, 'Professional autonomy and the revolt of the client' (1969) 17(2) *Social Problems* 153.

Held D, *Models of Democracy* (3rd edn Cambridge: Polity Press, 2006).

Human Rights Watch and Natural Resources Defense Council, *Defending the Earth: Abuses of Human Rights and the Environment* (New York: Human Rights Watch and Natural Resources Defense Council, 2012).

Huntington SP, 'The democratic distemper' (1975) 41 *Public Interest* 9.

Information Commissioner of Canada, *Annual Report 1993–94.*

Irvin RA and Stansbury J, 'Citizen participation in decision-making: is it worth the effort?' (2004) 64(1) *Public Administration Review* 55.

Kaufman A, *The Radical Liberal* (New York: Atherton Press, 1968).

Koester V, 'Pacta sunt servanda' (1996) 26 *Environmental Policy and Law* 81.

Kraft MF and Clary BB, 'Citizen participation and the Nimby Syndrome: public response to radioactive waste disposal' (1991) 44 *Political Research Quarterly* 299.

Kweit MG and Kweit RW, *Implementing Citizen Participation in a Bureaucratic Society: A Contingency Approach* (New York: Praeger, 1981).

Langton S, 'What is citizen participation?' in Langton S (ed), *Citizen Participation in America* (Massachusetts: Lexington Books, 1978) 16.

Larmore C, 'The moral basis of political liberalism' (1999) 96(12) *Journal of Philosophy* 599.

Lee M and Abbot C, 'The usual suspects? Public participation under the Aarhus Convention' (2003) 66 *Modern Law Review 80.*

Levine ME and Forrence JL, 'Regulatory capture, public interest, and the public agenda: towards a synthesis' (1990) 6 *Journal of Law, Economics, and Organisation* 167.

Loughlin M, *Sword and Scale: An Examination of the Relationship Between Law and Politics* (Oxford and Portland: Hart Publishing, 2000).

McAllister ST, 'Community-based conservation: restructuring institutions to involve local communities in a meaningful way' (1999) 10(1) *Colorado Journal of International Environmental Law and Policy* 195.

McCracken R and Jones G, 'The Aarhus Convention' (July 2003) *Journal of Planning and Environmental Law* 802.

McLennan G, *Pluralism* (Buckingham: Open University Press, 1995).

Mason M, 'Information disclosure and environmental rights: the Aarhus Convention' (2010) 10(3) *Global Environmental Politics* 10.

Nonet P and Selznick P, *Law and Society in Transition: Towards Responsive Law* (New York: Harper & Rowe, 1978).

O'Rourke D and Macey GP, 'Community environmental policing: assessing new strategies of public participation in environmental regulation' (2003) 22(3) *Journal of Policy Analysis and Management* 383.

Offe C, *Contradictions of the Welfare State* (London: Hutchinson, 1984).

Omorogbe Y, 'The legal framework for public participation in decision-making on mining and energy development in Nigeria: giving voices to the voiceless', in Zillman DN, Lucas AR and Pring G (eds), *Human Rights in National Resource Development: Public*

Participation in the Sustainable Development of Mining and Energy Resource (Oxford: Oxford University Press, 2002) 549.

Ophuls W, 'Leviathan or oblivion?', in Daly HE (ed), *Towards a Steady-State Economy* (San Francisco: WH Freeman, 1973) 15.

Ortolano L, *Environmental Regulation and Impact Assessment* (New York: John Wiley & Sons, 1997).

Osuoka I, 'People in the Niger delta Now Recognize that Jonathan is a waste of time', *Sahara Reporters*, 8 January 2012, available at http://saharareporters.com/interview/%E2%80%9Cpeople-niger-delta-now-recognize-jonathan-waste-time%E2%80%9D-%E2%80%93-isaac-osuoka (last accessed 30 January 2015).

Pateman C, *Participation and Democratic Theory* (Cambridge: Cambridge University Press, 1970).

Petts J, 'The public-expert interface in local management decisions: expert, credibility and process' (1997) 6 *Public Understanding of Science* 359.

Plato, *The Republic* (Ferrari GRF (ed) and Griffith T (tr), Cambridge: Cambridge University Press, 2000).

Pomeroy HR, 'The planning process and public participation', in Breese G and Whiteman DE (eds), *An Approach to Urban Planning* (Princeton University Press, 1953) 9.

Pontius FW, 'Public involvement in regulation development', in Pontius BL, *Drinking Water Regulation and Health* (New Jersey: John Wiley & Sons, 2003) 251.

Pring G and Noe SY, 'The emerging international law of public participation affecting global mining, energy, and resources development', in Zillman DN, Lucas AR and Pring G (eds), *Human Rights in National Resource Development: Public Participation in the Sustainable Development of Mining and Energy Resource* (Oxford: Oxford University Press, 2002) 11.

Priscoli JD, 'Implementing public involvement programs in federal agencies', in Langton S (ed), *Citizen Participation in America* (Massachusetts: Lexington Books, 1978) 97.

Randolph J and Bauer M, 'Improving environmental decision-making through collaborative methods' (1999) 16(3/4) *Policy Studies Review* 168.

Report of the UN World Commission on Environment and Development: *Our Common Future* (1987).

Richardson A, *Participation* (London: Routledge & Kegan Paul, 1983).

Richardson BJ and Razzaque J, 'Public participation in environmental decision-making', in Richardson BJ and Wood S (eds), *Environmental Law for Sustainability* (Oxford: Hart Publishing, 2006) 165.

Roberts A, 'A great and revolutionary law? The first four years of India's Right to Information Act' (2010) 70(6) *Public Administration Review* 925.

Rosenbaum NM, 'Citizen participation and democratic theory', in Langton S (ed), *Citizen Participation in America* (Massachusetts: Lexington Books, 1978) 43.

Rousseau JJ, *The Social Contract* (F Watkins (ed & transl), University of Wisconsin Press, 1986).

Rozak T, *The Making of a Counter Culture: Reflections on the Technocratic Society and Its Youthful Opposition* (London: Faber & Faber, 1970).

Schattschneider EE, *The Semisovereign People* (Hinsdale IL: Dryden Press, 1960).

Slovic P, 'Perception of risk' (1987) 236(4799) *Science* 280.

Smith M, 'Pluralism', in Marsh D and Stoker G (eds), *Theory and Methods in Political Science* (London: Macmillan, 1995) 211.

Smith MBE, 'The value of participation', in Pennock JR and Chapman JW (eds), *Participation in Politics* (New York: Lieber-Atherton, 1975) 126.

Spyke NP, 'Public participation in environmental decision-making at the new millennium: structuring new spheres of public influence' (1999) 26 *Boston College Environmental Affairs Law Review* 263.

Stec S, 'EU enlargement, neighbourhood policy and environmental democracy', in Pallemaerts M (ed), *The Aarhus Convention at Ten: Interactions and Tensions Between Conventional International Law and EU Environmental Law* (Groningen: Europa Law Publishing, 2011) 35.

Steiner HJ, 'Political Participation as a human Right' (1988) 1 *Harvard Human Rights Yearbook* 77.

Tribe L, 'Technology assessment and the fourth discontinuity: the limits of instrumental rationality' (1972) 46 *Southern California Law Review* 617.

Washington HA (ed), *The Writings of Thomas Jefferson* (Vol 7, New York: Riker, Thorne & Co, 1854) 177.

Wengert N, 'Citizen participation: practice in search of a theory' (1976) 16 *Natural Resources Journal* 23.

Wexler S, 'Expert and lay participation in decision-making', in Pennock JR and Chapman JW (eds), *Participation in Politics* (New York: Lieber-Atherton, 1975) 186.

Williams BL, Suen HK, Brown S, Bruhn RA, de Blaquiere R and Rzasa SE, 'Hierarchical linear models of factors associated with public participation among residents living near the US Army's chemical weapons stockpile sites' (2001) 44(1) *Journal of Environmental Planning and Management* 41.

Zazueta A, *Policy Hits the Ground: Participation and Equity in Environmental Policy-making* (Washington DC: World Resources Institute, 1995).

4 Public access to environmental information: international best practice principles

4.1 Introduction

Considering the value of adequate and meaningful public access to environmental information as discussed earlier in this book, the issue is a core one in international environmental law. Given this premise, the aim of this chapter is critically to evaluate what may generally be considered international best practice in terms of law and practice on public access to environmental information that could effectively ensure adequate access in this regard.

The analysis in this chapter will generally clarify and further the understanding of the development of this area of procedural environmental rights, as well as provide a reasonable and useful comparative basis on which to analyse and recommend improvements to Nigerian law and practice on access to environmental information in the subsequent chapter. As alluded to in Chapter 1, the framing of the international best practice principles in this chapter will have relevant provisions of the Aarhus Convention as its central theme, and efforts will be made to demonstrate how many of the Convention's provisions overlap, emphasise or amplify existing provisions of some other international regimes to which Nigeria is directly committed.

Accordingly, the analysis below will cover four main areas: the scope of a regime on access to environmental information; the actual public access right to that information, in its passive and active contexts; the exemptions and override to the access rights; and the provisions for enforcing the access rights.

4.2 Access to environmental information: issues on scope

When putting in place legal mechanisms to enable the public to have access to environmental information, inclusiveness of some of its general conceptions and aspects is vital in deciding its value to the public and the society at large. In analysing international best practice in this regard, this section will focus on the following major themes: (1) the meaning of 'environmental information'; (2) the format of the information; (3) the beneficiary of the access right; and (4) the bodies obliged to provide access.

4.2.1 The meaning of 'environmental information'

The importance of the meaning ascribed to 'environmental information' in an environmental information access regime is self-evident; its narrowness or broadness is key to the value of the public's right of access granted by the regime.[1] A number of international instruments in this regard merely allude to or mention 'environmental information' without defining it.[2] Although the concept was defined in the (repealed) EU Directive 90/313/EC on the Freedom of Access to Information on the Environment, that definition is less comprehensive than that in the Aarhus Convention, which represents a marked improvement. For instance, as against the Aarhus Convention, the (repealed) EU's Directive 90/313/EC definition of 'information relating to the environment' does not include elements such as information on human health and safety, economic data used in reaching environmental decisions and cultural sites.

The Aarhus Convention gives the concept what may be considered its most appropriate and expansive definition yet at the international level, and one that has been widely lauded.[3] Article 2(3) of the Convention defines 'Environmental information' as 'any information . . . on':

(a) The state of elements of the environment, such as air and atmosphere, water, soil, land, landscape and natural sites, biological diversity and its components, including genetically modified organisms, and the interaction among these elements;
(b) Factors, such as substances, energy, noise and radiation, and activities or measures, including administrative measures, environmental agreements, policies, legislation, plans and programmes, affecting or likely to affect the elements of the environment within the scope of subparagraph (a) above, and cost-benefit and other economic analyses and assumptions used in environmental decision-making;
(c) The state of human health and safety, conditions of human life, cultural sites and built structures, inasmuch as they are or may be affected by the state of the elements of the environment or, through these elements, by the factors, activities or measures referred to in subparagraph (b) above.

Commendably, with words and phrases including 'such as', 'including', 'likely to affect' and 'may be affected', this definition is largely non-exhaustive in nature

1 See *European Community* ACCC/C/2007/21, ECE/MP.PP/C.1/2009/2/Add.1, 8 February 2011, para 34.
2 See e.g. Rio Declaration, Principle 10.
3 See P Davies, 'Public participation, the Aarhus Convention, and the European Community', in DN Zillman, AR Lucas and G Pring (eds), *Human Rights in National Resource Development: Public Participation in the Sustainable Development of Mining and Energy Resource* (Oxford: Oxford University Press, 2002) 155, 159–60; and P Birnie, A Boyle and C Redgwell, *International Law and the Environment* (3rd edn, Oxford: Oxford University Press, 2009) 292.

(as against its being 'vague', as some suggests).[4] This is clearly in keeping with progressive environmental politics and treaty-making practice, where the tendency is usually to be as open-ended as possible when defining key terms in an agreement, especially as 'it is [usually] not possible to determine *a priori* the user, nor their questions, nor the future problems which may be encountered'.[5]

Laudable also is the fact that, despite the definition being couched in a non-exhaustive manner, it is still largely enumerative in nature and limits the danger of undue restriction that comes with authorities having too much discretion to determine what key terms in a law mean or do not mean. Examples of information already considered by the Aarhus Compliance Committee to be 'environmental information' under this definition include a waste-related feasibility study containing technical and economic details;[6] 'financing agreements, even though not listed explicitly in the definition, may sometimes amount to "measures . . . that affect or are likely to affect the elements of the environment"';[7] and, more recently, a contract for rent of lands.[8]

4.2.2 The format of the information

Related to the above, the right given under the Aarhus Convention relates to 'information in written, visual, aural, electronic or any other material form'.[9] Elucidating on the expansiveness of this provision, the Aarhus Implementation Guide notes that any other material forms 'not mentioned, existing now or developed in the future' are captured by this provision.[10]

4.2.3 The beneficiary of the right of access

As with Principle 10 of the Rio Declaration and a number of other international agreements,[11] the beneficiary of the right to access environmental information is easily identified in the Aarhus Convention as 'the public'.[12] The Convention defines the 'the public' as 'meaning one or more natural or legal persons, and, in accordance with national legislation or practice, their associations, organisations or groups'.[13] A similar definition is given to the phrase under the Bali Guidelines.[14] Clearly, this definition of 'the public' is not limited to associations or organisations

4 ME Haklay, *Public Environmental Information Systems: Challenges and Perspectives* (PhD Thesis, University College London, 2002) 31–32.
5 RA Deininger and World Health Organisation (Regional Office for Europe), *Design of Environmental Information Systems* (Michigan: Ann Arbor Science Publishers, 1974) 4.
6 *Kazakhstan* ACCC/C/2004/1, ECE/MP.PP/C.1/2005/2/Add.1, 11 March 2005, para 18.
7 *European Community* (n 1) para 30.
8 *Moldova* ACCC/C/2008/30, ECE/MP.PP/C.1/2009/6/Add.3, 8 February 2011, para 29.
9 Article 2(3).
10 Aarhus Implementation Guide, 51.
11 See e.g. World Charter for Nature, art 16.
12 See arts 4 and 5.
13 Article 2(4).
14 See footnote to Guideline 6.

with legal personality, but can be interpreted as extending to associations or groups 'without legal personality',[15] albeit 'in accordance with national legislation or practice'[16] – a proviso that appears liberal and in line with democratic and pluralist thoughts, and the analysis of 'the public' that should be allowed to participate in environmental matters as discussed in Chapter 3.

Also, as evidenced by the Bali Guidelines,[17] 'modern practices allow *any* person to request and receive information – not only those who can prove that they have a special interest in the information'.[18] Similarly, Article 4(1)(a) of the Aarhus Convention obliges public authorities to make environmental information available to the public '[w]ithout an interest having to be stated'. This point has been endorsed by the Aarhus Compliance Committee, which found that Kazakhstan was in breach of Article 4(1)(a) for retaining a practice where people requesting information in general have to explain the reasons for which the information is requested.[19]

Furthermore, the right given to the public under the Aarhus Convention is non-discriminatory and so is exercisable by any person, irrespective of citizenship, nationality, domicile, or place of registered seat or effective centre of activities.[20] Thus, the Aarhus Compliance Committee rightly upheld this non-discriminatory provision when it noted, with respect to Turkmenistan, that the exclusion of foreign citizens and persons without citizenship from the possibility to found and participate in an NGO is a disadvantageous discrimination against them, and so constitutes non-compliance with Article 3(9) of the Aarhus Convention.[21] In addition, the Committee has noted that 'foreign or international non-governmental environmental organisations' would normally be considered part of 'the public' and so eligible to access environmental information at the national level.[22]

4.2.4 The bodies obliged to provide access

This point will receive special consideration here as it has witnessed some key changes in recent years, which has no doubt made it more susceptible to controversy. Unequivocally, based on the participatory democratic norms hitherto discussed, the obligation to provide the public access to (environmental) information is, and has historically been that of 'the government'. This is well reflected in a number of international (environmental) instruments, chiefly the Rio Declaration,

15 Aarhus Implementation Guide, 55.
16 Aarhus Convention, art 2(4).
17 Guideline 1. See World Charter for Nature, art 18.
18 S Kravchenko, 'Is access to environmental information a fundamental human right?' (2009) *Oregon Review of International Law* 227, 241. See also *Claude Reyes v Chile*, Inter-Am Ct HR (series C) No 151, 19 September 2006, para 77.
19 *Kazakhstan* (n 6) para 20. See also Aarhus Implementation Guide, 80.
20 Article 3(9).
21 *Turkmenistan* ACCC/C/2004/5, ECE/MP.PP/C.1/2005/2/Add.5, 14 March 2005, para 16.
22 *Ukraine* ACCC/C/2004/3, ECE/MP.PP/C.1/2005/2/Add.3, 14 March 2005, para 26. See also *Kazakhstan* (n 6) para 16.

which provides, without more, for public access to environmental information held by 'public authorities',[23] which phrase can easily be interpreted to mean 'the government'. Similarly, the Aarhus Convention also lays the principal obligation of providing environmental information on the 'public authority'[24] and explicitly defines this in Article 2(2)(a) to mean, amongst other things, 'Government at national, regional and other levels'.

However, as governments around the world adopt the view that 'government has no business in business', the growing private sector which now controls enormous resources is increasingly being entrusted with responsibilities with immense public and environmental implications (e.g. the provision of water and power), which were hitherto the preserve of the public sector.[25] Hence, it was fitting for the Aarhus Convention which applies only to 'public authorities', to proffer a wider and more appropriate definition for the concept, which is capable of including some private entities in recognition of their significant emerging status, thus ensuring reasonable access rights for the public with regards to environmental information.

This does indeed remove liberalism's age-old 'wedge' driven between 'public' and 'private' in order to achieve its aim of 'differential treatment of the two spheres',[26] as alluded to in Chapter 3. Article 2(2) of the Aarhus Convention expressly defines 'public authority' out of the purely government circle depicted by subparagraph (a) above, to include:

> (b) Natural or legal persons performing public administrative functions under national law, including specific duties, activities or services in relation to the environment;
> (c) Any other natural or legal persons having public responsibilities or functions, or providing public services, in relation to the environment, under the control of a body or person falling within subparagraphs (a) or (b) above.[27]

First, on Article 2(2)(b) above, it is clear that for a body to fall under that section, further than the one-dimensional opinion of Hughes (and others) that the 'public functions' of private entities 'would render them public authorities',[28] those

23 Principle 10.
24 See arts 4 and 5.
25 See JL Creighton, *The Public Participation Handbook: Making Better Decisions through Citizen Involvement* (San Francisco: Jossey-Bass, 2005) 17; and R Calland, 'Prizing open the profit-making world', in A Florini (ed), *The Right to Know: Transparency for an Open World* (New York: Colombia University Press, 2007) 214–42.
26 See Calland (n 25) 238, relying on A Robert, 'Structural pluralism and the right to information', in R Calland and A Tilley (eds), *The Right to Know, The Right to Live: Access to Information and Socio-Economic Justice* (Cape Town: ODAC, 2002) 29.
27 The definition of 'public authority' excludes bodies or institutions acting in a judicial or legislative capacity. Aarhus Convention, art 2(2).
28 D Hughes, T Jewell, J Lowther, N Parpworth and P de Prez, *Environmental Law* (4th edn, London: LexisNexis Butterworths, 2002) 157.

functions must also be *administrative functions*.[29] Also, even though the relevant entity does not have to operate in the field of the environment to fall under this subparagraph (b) as with (a), persons carrying out public administrative duties under any national law will fall under this category; such a legal basis for carrying out such a function being a prerequisite here.[30]

It is also important to note that this subparagraph (b) may arguably not include government bodies as such, which would already have been covered under subparagraph (a) of Article 2(2).[31] Perhaps, some support may be found in the fact that in cases in which the Aarhus Compliance Committee has held that a body fell under Article 2(2)(a), it has not gone on to state that they also fall under any of the other categories[32] (as it has done when a body falls under both subparagraphs (b) and (c).)[33]

It is also possible for subparagraph (b) to cover bodies which are established by statutes to be independent of government.[34] As it seems, contrary to Mason's view that it is only private entities (apart from government bodies) in the mould of Article 2(2)(c) of the Aarhus Convention that are public authorities under the regime,[35] Article 2(2)(b) arguably also covers private entities performing public administrative functions. Support for this point can be drawn from the Aarhus Implementation Guide and the UK's Department for Environment, Food and Rural Affairs (Defra) Guidance on the interpretation of the Environmental Information Regulations (EIR), which expressly entertain the idea of profit-driven 'private companies' falling under the EIR.[36] In this light, a purely private company in the UK has been held to have public administrative functions resulting from a contract with a government body, and thus falling under the EIR as a public authority.[37]

By way of contrast, for a person to fall under subparagraph (c), the person will have to be under the 'control' of those defined in subparagraph (a) or (b). With reference to a similar provision in UK's implementing EIR regime, Defra

29 A point noted in the English case: *Network Rail Ltd v Information Commissioner*, Appeal Nos EA/2006/0061 and EA/2006/0062, 17 July 2007, para 24.

30 See *Belarus* ACCC/C/2009/37, ECE/MP.PP//2011/11/Add.2, 12 May 2011, para 67.

31 Aarhus Implementation Guide, 46.

32 See *Kazakhstan* ACCC/C/2004/6, ECE/MP.PP/C.1/2006/4/Add.1, 28 July 2006, para 23; *Armenia* ACCC/C/2004/8, ECE/MP.PP/C.1/2006/2/Add.1, 10 May 2006, para 19; *Belgium* ACCC/C/2005/11, ECE/MP.PP/C.1/2006/4/Add.2, 29 July 2006, para 25; and *Denmark* ACCC/C/2006/18, ECE/MP.PP/2008/5/Add.4, 29 April 2008, para 25.

33 See note 34.

34 See *Kazakhstan* (n 6) para 17; *Hungary* ACCC/C/2004/4, ECE/MP.PP/C.1/2005/2/Add.4, 14 March 2005, para 10; and Aarhus Implementation Guide, 46.

35 M Mason, 'Information disclosure and environmental rights: the Aarhus Convention' (2010) 10(3) *Global Environmental Politics* 10, 14.

36 Chapter 2, 'Who is covered by the regulations', July 2010, para 2.16 (the 2004 EIR, No 3391, was enacted to implement in the UK the environmental information aspects of the Aarhus Convention; its equivalent in Scotland is the 2004 Environmental Information (Scotland) Regulations (EI(S)R), No 520). See also Aarhus Implementation Guide, 46–47.

37 Information Commissioner's Decision Notice – *Environmental Resources Management Ltd* (ERM), Case Ref FER0090259, 7 June 2006.

Guidance states that: 'control could mean a relationship constituted by statute, regulations, rights, licence, contracts or other means which either separately or jointly confer the possibility of directly or indirectly exercising a decisive influence on a body. Control may relate, not only to the body, but also to control of the services provided by the body'.[38] In fact, recently, the Aarhus Compliance Committee has held that where national legislation delegates some functions related to maintenance and distribution of environmental information to private entities, such entities may be treated for the purpose of access to information as being a 'public authority' under Article 2(2)(b) or (c).[39]

Furthermore, such a person (under control) is only required to perform 'public responsibilities . . . or providing public service', seemingly a broader work description than 'public administrative functions' used in subparagraph (b); but such public responsibilities or services must be related to the environment, a limited field of activity compared to subparagraph (b) which contains no such limitation.[40] At a minimum, this subparagraph may cover entities such as 'community-owned public service providers', some private companies or even public private partnerships, in areas with obvious environmental functions such as waste disposal, water, energy, transport.[41]

To an extent, this examination of Article 2(2)(b) and (c) can be taken as a rebuttal of Richardson and Razzaque's position that the 'Aarhus Convention provisions deal only with government information.'[42] Also, the analysis of those provisions refutes Wates's restrictive position which seemingly considers 'public authority' under the Convention as relating only to government bodies,[43] and does not clearly consider that some private entities fall under the definition of 'public authority' and, like government bodies, are generally and similarly subject to the Convention's obligation to grant (directly) the public access to the environmental information they hold.

Finally, to emphasise an important point, whether or not an entity or a private entity falls under Article 2(2)(b) and (c) is determined *exclusively* by the nature of the functions it performs or responsibilities it undertakes (and its controlling body – with respect the Article 2(2)(c)), and not by the nature of its corporate/organisational structure, place of registered seat, profit or non-profit-making agenda, source(s) of fund/capital, or any other criteria at all. Therefore, *any* (private) entity can *potentially* fall under Article 2(2)(b) and (c).

38 Paragraph 2.19.
39 *Belarus* (n 30) para 67.
40 Aarhus Implementation Guide, 47–48.
41 See ibid, 47; and Defra Guidance, para 2.22.
42 BJ Richardson and J Razzaque, 'Public participation in environmental decision-making', in BJ Richardson and S Wood (eds), *Environmental Law for Sustainability* (Oxford: Hart Publishing, 2006) 165, 181.
43 J Wates, 'The future of the Aarhus Convention: perspectives arising from the Third Session of the Meeting of the Parties', in M Pallemaerts (ed), *The Aarhus Convention at Ten: Interactions and Tensions Between Conventional International Law and EU Environmental Law* (Groningen: Europa Law Publishing, 2011) 384, 404.

4.2.4.1 Why directly 'bother' the private companies?

Besides the legal analysis above, a vital query might be why access to environmental information from private companies themselves is essential when environmental information can often be accessed through relevant government regulators. In response, a few possible justifications for this relatively new trend, which should persuade public authorities and other bodies from unduly restricting this paradigm shift, are highlighted below.

First, 'regulatory agency capture' (discussed in Chapter 3) by the increasingly more powerful private companies has contributed in weaken the effectiveness of government regulatory bodies generally.[44] In such circumstances, public confidence in the relevant regulatory body is largely eroded as the latter continually appears to bend to the will of the powerful private companies at the expense of performing its regulatory or public duties. It may also be unable to effectively carry out its functions of requesting, holding and deploying vital environmental information from these private companies (which information may not be supportive of the commercial interests of the companies) as it should.[45]

Lucas justifies the need for direct public participation on the basis that 'regulatory agencies generally have displayed a number of disturbing tendencies . . . [which includes the fact that] they may . . . tend, as a result of prolonged contact through regulatory process, to adopt the values and biases of the industries sought to be regulated . . . They may fail to strongly enforce their legislation . . . simply through inertia and fear of generating heat'.[46] Therefore a public right directly to access environmental information held by certain private companies is imperative to engender better transparency. Even where the regulatory agency houses the relevant information, simply giving the public an alternative of going directly to the relevant private companies may go a long way to boost public confidence in those regulatory bodies and in the information they possess.

Second, private companies may not have supplied the regulator with the necessary information in timely fashion and the regulator may not have followed this up. In some cases, it may be unreasonable to ask the public concerned to wait until such a time as this information is transmitted to the relevant regulatory agency for it to be made available to the public. In fact, it is usually the *modus operandi* for some regulatory agencies to require private companies to transmit most (environmental) information to them at long intervals. For example, the UK's Water Services

44 See e.g. M Rosenbaum, 'Tribunal to hear water information case', *British Broadcasting Corporation*, 27 October 2010. In that article, the BBC revealed internal email exchange within the Environmental Agency which suggests timidity towards powerful private water companies. Justin Neal of Fish Legal, who had earlier noted that 'the Environment Agency doesn't do a good enough job in investigating pollution incidents', stated that this is 'typical of the Environment Agency' who are 'too sensitive to [water] companies'.

45 See Ch 5 of this book, section 5.2.4.

46 A Lucas, 'Legal techniques for pollution control: the role of the public' (1971) 6 *University of British Columbia Law Review* 167, 185–86. See also JCP McLaren, 'The common law nuisance actions and the environmental battle: well-tempered swords or broken reeds?' (1972) 10(3) *Osgoode Hall Law Journal* 505, 507.

Regulation Authority (Ofwat), a regulatory agency, only requires water companies to make annual submissions (or 'June returns') about their (environmental) performance.[47] That means for the subsequent 12 months, Ofwat's records are largely left outdated, hence the need for the public to be able to head to the private companies when they require current environmental information.

Third, regulatory agencies may lack very specific environmental information the public may urgently require about the activities of a private company.[48] In fact, regulatory agencies do not necessarily hold all environmental information which the public may require, as exemplified by Ofwat's 'June returns', which is only an abridged version of the more comprehensive information held by the relevant private companies, and may not be too useful to a section of the public with interest in specifics.[49]

By the same token, much environmental information is now exclusively held by private companies around the world.[50] A case in point is the UK case of *Smartsource Drainage & Water Reports Limited v The Information Commissioner & 19 Water Companies*,[51] where some of the information requested by the appellant from the water companies was exclusively held by them and not available from government regulators.[52] Here, the activities of the water companies, which have wide public and environmental implications, can hardly be effectively checked. In this situation, the need for direct public access to this more detailed environmental information held by private companies is self-evident. Certainly, where issues of commercial confidentiality of requested information arise, this would be for the tribunals and courts to decide on based on the relevant provisions of the law.

Another very important justification for this paradigm shift, as alluded to earlier, is the increasing devolution of government responsibilities to private companies. As stated in the Aarhus Implementation Guide, this is a key reason why the Aarhus Convention 'tries to make it clear that such innovations cannot take public services or activities out of the realm of public information, participation and justice'.[53] Thus, rather than keep the law focused on only the public sector which devolves such key responsibilities to the private sector, it is reasonable to split or transfer some of its responsibilities (e.g. of directly providing the public access to environmental information) to the private sector that takes up

47 See http://www.ofwat.gov.uk/regulating/junereturn/ (last accessed 30 January 2015).

48 See e.g. *Guerra v Italy* (1998) 26 EHRR 357.

49 For example the 'sewer flooding register' and the 'water pressure register', both of which were requested by the appellant in the *Smartsource* case, are exclusively held by the water and sewage companies, except the number of properties at risk (not individual information on the properties themselves), which is held by Ofwat. Information provided by Ofwat, personal communication to author, 10 October 2011.

50 Calland (n 25) 215.

51 Case No GI/2458/2010, 23 November 2010, available at http://www.unece.org/fileadmin/DAM/env/pp/compliance/C2010-55/Communication/Judgment_UpperTribunalNov2010.pdf (last accessed 30 January 2015).

52 For example the 'water and sewerage billing records' and the 'trade effluent register'. Information provided by Ofwat, personal communication to author, 10 October 2011.

53 Aarhus Implementation Guide, 46.

the key public functions, and which now perform some regulatory functions and in certain cases even possesses rule-making and enforcement powers.[54]

Furthermore, geographical accessibility problem is another reason why it is important that the public has access to environmental information held by some private companies.[55] The relevant regulatory agency's office may be located in an area necessitating lengthy journeys and this may discourage the public from seeking information.[56] This problem will ordinarily be more pronounced for low-income groups with inadequate access to private transport, of which public transportation might be too expensive and will only serve to raise the cost of accessing information.[57] Admittedly, current legal requirements which now stipulate for environmental information to be made 'progressively' available in electronic databases which are easily accessible through public telecommunications networks might help to mitigate accessibility problems.[58] However, not all of such information is required to be so made available and there is no guarantee that other required data will be available online at the time they are needed.[59]

Other drawbacks with this electronic requirement are that it may exclude members of the public without computers, those with computers but without internet connectivity and those without the necessary skills to use the relevant electronic medium properly.[60] To an extent, these difficulties in accessing information can be further mitigated if the public is given the legal alternative of accessing information directly from the relevant private companies. In relation to geographical accessibility, this alternative will be most helpful where the relevant companies are within the concerned public's immediate locale and the information requested is not exclusively held at, for instance, a remote head office.

However, it may be quite easy and reasonable for a division of a private company to call for and collect the requested information from any of its divisions in which it is been held (especially through electronic means) and make it available within a reasonable timeframe. Possibly, this obligation on (divisions of) private companies could at least be inferred where the legal provisions enabling public access to information are drafted widely. An example of such a provision may be Article 3(2) of the Aarhus Convention which stipulates that '[e]ach Party shall endeavour to ensure that officials and authorities assist and provide guidance to the public in seeking access to information . . .'.

Finally, many private companies are beginning to realise the commercial imperative and the public relations benefits, amongst others, of being open about

54 See e.g.the UK's 1991 Water Industry Act, ch 56, ss 76, 118, 155, 157.

55 See T Burton, 'Access to environmental information: the UK experience of water registers' (1989) 1 *Journal of Environmental Law* 192, 197–98.

56 See M Poustie, 'Environmental justice in SEPA's environmental protection activities: a report for the Scottish Environment Protection Agency', 2004, 87, available at http://www.sepa.org.uk/system_pages/search.aspx?q=poustie (last accessed 15 February 2015).

57 Ibid.

58 See Aarhus Convention, art 5(3) and (9).

59 See ibid, art 5(3).

60 Poustie (n 56) 88–89.

their environmental activities. Increasingly, in the UK, for example, as with other places, they now publish environmental information about their business activities in line with the requirement of the 2006 Companies Act,[61] and the recommendations of various codes and guidelines.[62] However, such disclosure/ 'self-monitoring' or minimal legislative reporting requirements are not necessarily sufficient for proper public scrutiny of relevant private companies, seeing that the idea of being publicly transparent should ordinarily involve the public having the necessary opportunity to request and receive information that was not or would not be volunteered.

4.3 The public's right of access to environmental information

Several international environmental treaties, including the Climate Change Convention,[63] the Desertification Convention[64] and the Biosafety Protocol[65] require states, including Nigeria, to ensure public access to environmental information (as it relates to their specific focuses). As adopted in this section, this right is usually divided into two categories, i.e. 'passive' and 'active' access to environmental information.

4.3.1 'Passive' access to environmental information

4.3.1.1 The request and the right of access

In line with the import of 'passive' access to information (which is that information must be released when requested), as in Principle 10 of the Rio Declaration and the Bali Guidelines,[66] Article 4(1) of the Aarhus Convention provides for the obligation on public authorities to release environmental information to members of the public who make a request.[67] As this provision of the Aarhus Convention does not specify any particular form of 'request', oral or written requests may suffice;[68] there is also nothing to preclude an applicant from making a request electronically. If requested, the applicant is entitled to receive 'copies of the actual documentation' containing the information.[69]

In addition, the public has the right to receive environmental information 'in the form requested', except where: (1) 'it is reasonable for the public authority to

61 Chapter 46; see s 417(6)(b).
62 See OUT-LAW, 'Corporate social responsibility: the UK Corporate Governance Code', available at http://www.out-law.com/page-8221 (last accessed 30 January 2015).
63 Article 6(a)(ii).
64 Article 19(3)(b).
65 Article 23(1)(b).
66 Guideline 1.
67 See *Kazakhstan* (n 6) para 25; *Ukraine* (n 22) para 39; and *Armenia* (n 32) para 41.
68 Aarhus Implementation Guide, 79.
69 Aarhus Convention, art 4(1).

make it available in another form' – and the reason for doing so must be stated; or (2) 'the information is already publicly available in another form'.[70] A similar provision is also contained in the draft Commentary to the Bali Guidelines.[71] Importantly, the reference to 'another form' in these exceptions still means that the information contained in that other form must be the same as that in the form requested, and not a summary of it.[72]

Based on the right to receive environmental information in any form requested, the Aarhus Compliance Committee has recently held Spain in non-compliance when it provided a paper copy of a document containing 600 pages for a cost of €2.05 per page, instead of providing it in the form of a CD for a cost of €13 as requested.[73] This case clearly highlights some of the benefits of giving the public space to determine the form in which the information released, which may include ensuring cost effectiveness and convenience for both the public and possibly the public authorities. Furthermore, if the second exception to this right as stated above is taken at face value, it may pose some challenges in that the 'already publicly available information' may not reasonably be effectively accessible in view of the need to accommodate members of the public with special needs, or where the distance and/or the cost of accessing such information becomes manifestly unreasonable for the public to bear.

In such cases, against the backdrop of the obligation on public authorities to 'assist and guide' the public seeking access to information,[74] and the stipulation for environmental information to be made easily or effectively accessible in practice,[75] it is safe to conclude that public authorities would have to apply that exception in a limited way in view of the practical issues that may arise in order to comply with their overall obligation under the regime. Moreover, the application of the exception is made subject to its being 'reasonable'.

The implementing provision and tribunal decisions in the UK fully support this position: whilst the proviso in regulation 6(1)(b) of the EIR reads 'unless . . . the information is already publicly available and easily accessible to the applicant in another form or format', the tribunal rightly held in the case of *Office of Communications v Information Commissioner and T-Mobile (UK) Ltd*[76] that, amongst others, since harvesting the requested information from the authority's website would be onerous and too time-consuming for any applicant, regulation 6(1)(b) could not be relied on.[77]

Also, as stated above, under the Convention, public authorities have an obligation to assist and guide those seeking access to environmental information.

70 Ibid, art 4(1)(b)(i) and (ii).
71 Commentary to Guideline 1.
72 Aarhus Implementation Guide, 80.
73 *Spain* ACCC/C/2008/24, ECE/MP.PP/C.1/2009/8/Add.1, 30 September 2010, para 70.
74 Aarhus Convention, art 3(2).
75 Ibid, art 5(2).
76 Appeal No EA/2006/0078, 4 September 2007.
77 Ibid, paras 68–69.

One of the circumstances under which this obligation may be activated may be where a request does not describe the information sought with sufficient particularity, in which case the public authority must ask the applicant as soon as possible, or within the legal timeframe for responding to requests, to provide further particulars and generally guide the applicant on this.[78] On the other hand, the Aarhus Compliance Committee has suggested a 'common-sense' approach that information applicants should adopt to ensure expedited action on their applications, and Nigerian applicants can certainly learn from this:

> [W]hile the Convention does not require a person making an information request to explicitly refer to (a) the Convention itself, (b) the implementing national legislation or (c) even the fact that the request is for environmental information, any or all such indications in the request would, in practice, facilitate the work of the responsible public authority and help in avoiding delays.[79]

4.3.1.2 The response

4.3.1.2.1 WHERE THE PUBLIC AUTHORITY HOLDS THE ENVIRONMENTAL INFORMATION REQUESTED

In this case, under the Aarhus Convention, '[t]he environmental information . . . shall be made available as soon as possible and at least within one month after the request has been submitted . . .'.[80] The same timeframe would apply where the public authority has a reason to refuse the request.[81] The Bali Guidelines contains a similar provision.[82] The importance of stipulating such time limits, instead of merely relying on the discretion of public authorities, is underscored by the fact that the value of such information may be time-sensitive to the applicant.[83] However, as may be encountered in practice, even though not expressly provided for in the Aarhus Convention, if it happens that further particulars of the request are sought by the public authority or the latter requests advance payment of a fee, it is only reasonable that these will stop the clock until they are received.[84]

Furthermore, as an exception, where the public authority is of the view that owing to the 'volume and the complexity' of the information requested it is impracticable to deal with the request in one month, it is at liberty to extend the

78 Both the EIR, reg 9(2) and the EI(S)R, reg 9(2) of the UK, provide for this obligation.
79 See *European Community* (n 1) paras 34–35.
80 Article 4(2).
81 Article 4(7).
82 Guideline 1.
83 F Schram, 'From a general right to access to environmental information in the Aarhus Convention to a general right of access to all information in official documents: the Council of Europe's Tromsø Convention', in Pallemaerts (ed), (n 43) 67, 77.
84 See e.g. EIR, regs 9(4) and 8(5) and (6); and the EI(S)R, regs 8(6) and (7), and 9(4).

time of response by up to two months after the request;[85] in which case, it must inform the requester of the extension and its reason(s).[86]

It is useful to note at this juncture that 'volume and complexity' has recently been held not to be lawful grounds for refusal of a request.[87] However, it might be reasonable to argue that this position may not hold where the 'volume and complexity' of the information requested is to the extent that it can be described as 'manifestly unreasonable' as referred to in Article 4(3)(b) of the Aarhus Convention. Upon the lapse of the two-month extended period, the public authority must either grant access to the requested information or deny access to it, based on the exemptions in Article 4(3) and (4) of the Convention.[88]

4.3.1.2.2 WHERE THE PUBLIC AUTHORITY DOES NOT HOLD THE ENVIRONMENTAL INFORMATION REQUESTED

In this case, under Article 4(3)(a) of the Aarhus Convention, the request may be refused by the public authority as it is only obliged to give access to information it 'hold[s]'; '[t]he refusal shall be made as soon as possible and at the latest within one month, unless the complexity of the information justifies an extension of this period up to two months after the request'.[89] It has, however, been argued that the word 'hold' indicates that the 'public authority is not obliged to assemble and record what it knows nor to ascertain matters so as to produce information that answers a request'.[90]

Whilst one agrees with the second part of this statement, to an extent, the Aarhus Convention indicates the opposite with respect to the first part,[91] especially as it obliges public authorities to possess and update environmental information relevant to their functions.[92] In other words, officials may have to disclose relevant environmental information which they know about (or hold in their heads) in the appropriate form if requested in accordance with the law. Although authorities are not obliged to 'ascertain matters' in order to respond to requests, they are still not relieved of their duty to give reasonable assistance to the requester to enable the latter to procure the information sought.[93]

Also, contrary to Schram's argument that the access to information aspect of the Aarhus Convention is not applicable to information held *for*, as against information held *by*, a public authority,[94] what it means to 'hold' information in Article 4(3)(a) may not be limited to having physical possession of it. It also

85 Aarhus Convention, art 4(2) and (7).
86 Ibid.
87 *Moldova* (n 8) para 31.
88 *Spain* (n 73) para 74.
89 Article 4(7).
90 P Coppel, *Information Rights: Law and Practice* (3rd edn, Oxford: Hart Publishing, 2010) 184.
91 Aarhus Implementation Guide, 83.
92 Aarhus Convention, art 5(1)(a).
93 Ibid, art 3(2).
94 Schram (n 83) 81.

includes 'effective' possession of such information, for example, in cases where information which a public authority has the right to physically possess is left in the premises of a regulated entity,[95] or is held by a third party on its behalf.[96] After all, public authorities are obliged to possess and update environmental information relevant to their functions,[97] and cannot hide behind a breach of this provision to justify a refusal of access based on Article 4(3)(a).

However, where another public authority may hold the information requested, the public authority that does not hold the information that has been requested of it has a duty under Article 4(5) of the Aarhus Convention to 'as promptly as possible, inform the applicant' of the public authority it believes has the requested information or 'transfer the request to that authority and inform the applicant accordingly'. Although in practice a public authority may not know what type of information other public authorities have,[98] the provision on transfer does not require certainty before a transfer is made, and the obligation to provide sufficient information to the public about the type and scope of environmental information held by various public authorities would help make this process less stressful and improve access generally.[99]

4.3.1.2.3 WHERE THE REQUEST FOR ENVIRONMENTAL INFORMATION IS REFUSED

Where there is a refusal of a request or a part thereof, Article 4(7) of the Aarhus Convention provides that it must be in writing if the request was in writing or the applicant so requests; the draft Commentary to the Bali Guidelines contains a similar provision.[100] That provision clearly prohibits the use of the concept of 'positive silence' when a request is being refused, as recently held by the Aarhus Compliance Committee in a matter concerning Spain.[101] Also, the refusal notice, whether written or oral,[102] must state the reasons for the refusal, which may give the requester an opportunity to rephrase and resubmit the request. It must also provide information about the review procedure (as contained in Article 9 of the Convention), which will help applicants not to waste time and resources following the wrong procedure.[103]

Recently, in a matter concerning Moldova,[104] the failure of the public authority to state lawful grounds for refusal of access to information, and to give information on access to review procedure was held to be non-compliant with Articles 3(2) and 4(7) of the Convention.

95 Aarhus Implementation Guide, 83.
96 For example, this is consistent with EIR, reg 3(2); EI(S)R, reg 2(2).
97 Aarhus Convention, art 5(1)(a).
98 Aarhus Implementation Guide, 92.
99 Aarhus Convention, art 5(2)(a).
100 Commentary to Guideline 3.
101 *Spain* ACCC/C/2009/36, ECE/MP.PP/C.1/2010/4/Add.2, 8 February 2011, para 58.
102 Aarhus Implementation Guide, 92.
103 See *European Community* (n 1) para 31.
104 *Moldova* (n 8) para 39.

4.3.1.2.4 WHERE THE INFORMATION/DOCUMENT REQUESTED CONTAINS EXEMPTED MATERIALS

In a situation where a requested document is not made up solely of exempted information, Article 4(6) of the Aarhus Convention obliges the public authority not to refuse the request but, in the spirit of ensuring wide access, to separate out the exempted information so long as the overall confidentiality of the document will not be prejudiced, and make the remainder of the environmental information available to the requester. The same provision is contained in the draft Commentary to the Bali Guidelines.[105]

4.3.1.3 The charge

Although there is no obligation on public authorities to charge a fee, as with the Bali Guidelines that calls for 'affordable' public access,[106] Article 4(8) of the Aarhus Convention allows public authorities to charge an applicant 'for supplying information, but such charge shall not exceed a reasonable amount'; this would make the system of access financially sustainable. Although the aforementioned provision has been considered somewhat 'vague',[107] in contrast, its unequivocal message to public authorities is that they are not at liberty to transfer the entire cost of 'supplying information' to the requester, especially when it amounts to an unreasonable sum.

This interpretation is similar to the European Court of Justice's (ECJ) view as, according to Directive 90/313/EEC, the phrase 'reasonable cost' certainly 'does not authorise Member States to pass on to those seeking information the entire amount of the costs, in particular indirect ones, actually incurred for the State budget in conducting an information search'.[108] This decision was delivered during the drafting of the Aarhus Convention, and would have given 'some indication of the meaning of the term "reasonable" in the minds of the drafters who inserted it into the Convention in 1998'.[109]

In addition, similar to the ECJ's views that 'a reasonable cost' must not be one that dissuades people from seeking information or restricts their right of access,[110] the Aarhus Implementation Guide has reiterated that 'the Convention embraces the concept that if information is to be truly accessible it must be affordable',[111] at least. In fact, only recently, the Aarhus Compliance Committee in reaching a decision of non-compliance by Spain with Article 4(8), 'took note of the decisions by the Court of the European Community and national courts . . . as they shed light on how the term "reasonable" . . . may be understood and applied'.[112]

105 Commentary to Guidelines 3.
106 Guideline 1. The Commentary on Guideline 1 makes reference to 'reasonable cost'.
107 Kravchenko (n 18) 257.
108 *Commission v Germany* (Case C–217/97) [1999] ECR I–5087, para 48.
109 Kravchenko (n 18) 258.
110 Ibid, para 47.
111 Aarhus Implementation Guide, 94.
112 *Spain* (n 73) paras 77 and 79.

In that matter, the Compliance Committee held that: '[g]iving that the commercial fee for copying in Murcia is €0.03 per page, which seems to be generally equivalent to the standard commercial fee for copying in the UNECE countries . . . the charge of €2.05 per page for copying cannot be considered reasonable and constitutes non-compliance with [Article 4(8)]'.[113] In view of the above arguments, Schram's position that the stipulation of a 'reasonable' charge for supplying information under Article 4(8) does not prevent charges from legitimately exceeding the actual cost of production and delivery of the documents,[114] is arguably incorrect.

Furthermore, if an information request is refused, the applicant cannot be charged any fee, as it is clear from Article 4(8) of the Aarhus Convention that charges are only to be made for 'supplying information'.[115] Relating to this provision, Coppel has also stated that it 'appears' that public authorities are prevented from charging the public for examining *in situ* the requested information as the term 'supplying' seems to have been used 'in the sense of making a copy of some sort'.[116] There is hardly any reason to doubt that this is the right interpretation of that provision,[117] seeing that the ECJ's decision above, which has been hailed by the Aarhus Compliance Committee, expressly prohibits charging a fee to cover the cost of 'conducting an information search', which really is all that may be needed to ensure an examination *in situ* of requested information.

Article 5(2)(c) of the Convention clarifies this issue as it mandates that 'providing access to the environmental information contained in lists, registers or files' is to be done 'free of charge'. The foregoing is a firm rebuttal of Schram's position that 'a fee can be charged also for *inspection*' (emphasis added) of a document under the Aarhus Convention.[118]

Finally, any public authority that intends to charge for supplying environmental information, has an obligation to make available to requesters a 'schedule of charges' that may be levied, which must indicate 'the circumstances in which they may be levied or waived and when the supply of information is conditional on the advance payment of such a charge'.[119]

4.3.2 'Active' access to environmental information

In contrast to 'passive' access, 'active' access to environmental information touches on the positive duty on public authorities to publicly disclose environmental

113 Ibid, para 79.
114 Schram (n 83) 87.
115 This was also the position of the court in *Commission v Germany* (Case C–217/97) [1999] ECR I–5087, paras 55 and 59, where a German law permitted charges for refusing information.
116 Coppel (n 90) 188.
117 See M Poustie, 'Opening up government: paradise postponed again?', in A Miller, *Human Rights: A Modern Agenda* (Edinburgh: T&T Clark, 2000) 67, 78 and 81.
118 Schram (n 83) 87.
119 Aarhus Convention, art 4(8).

information without waiting for any request from the public, as provided for in the likes of Principle 10 of the Rio Declaration, Agenda 21,[120] the Bali Guidelines,[121] the World Charter for Nature,[122] the Basel Convention[123] and the Desertification Convention.[124] In line with these regimes, Article 5 of the Aarhus Convention – titled 'Collection and Dissemination of Environmental Information' – stipulates for free 'active' access or proactive disclosure of environmental information in generally.

Under Article 5(1)(a) of the Convention, there is also a duty on public authorities to 'possess and update environmental information which is relevant to their functions'. This includes information on which they base their decisions not minding issues of ownership (subject to relevant exemptions),[125] in order for them to be able to fulfil their active responsibility of ensuring 'transparency' and 'effective accessibility' with respect to making environmental information available to the public.[126]

4.3.2.1 Effective access to environmental information and ICT[127]

Merely providing for public access to environmental information in the law may not sufficiently guarantee actual access;[128] hence the need for 'effective' access as stressed in Agenda 21,[129] and highlighted in the Bali Guidelines,[130] or 'appropriate' access as required under Principle 10 of the Rio Declaration. In similar vein, Article 5(2) of the Aarhus Convention places a duty on public authorities to ensure environmental information made available is 'effectively accessible'. This duty goes beyond making a body of information physically available for access, and covers issues of easy access to the information itself in view of how it is prepared and presented.

Effectively accessible information is information that is accessible 'in a user-friendly form that reflects the needs and concerns of the public', and is not unwieldy and difficult to sort through, considering that research has shown that elements such as inadequate contents pages and indexing could make access ineffective.[131] It will also need to be fairly easy to access considering location, office hours, the physically disabled and illiterate, and the general

120 See e.g. ch 14, para 14.37.
121 Guidelines 2 and 4.
122 Articles 15 and 18.
123 Article 4(2)(h).
124 Article 16(f).
125 *Ukraine* (n 22) para 31.
126 Aarhus Convention, art 5(2).
127 The discussion under this sub-heading is also generally relevant to that under 'passive' access to information.
128 See Aarhus Implementation Guide, 100.
129 Chapter 40, para 40.18.
130 Guideline 1.
131 J Rowan-Robinson, A Ross, W Watton and J Rothnie, 'Public access to environmental information: a means to what end?' (1996) 8(1) *Journal of Environmental Law* 19, 34.

antipathy for or difficulty in understanding 'raw data' by lay members of the public, etc.[132]

The process of access will also need to be cost-free from the user's end, or 'pocket-friendly' and not prohibitively expensive among other requirements, which may depict a move to ensuring 'ease of access'. So, in view of the instrumental value and connotations of 'effective accessibility' as it related to environmental information under the Aarhus Convention, it may be fair to posit that the criticism by Lee and Abbott that the Convention has provided 'us with no way through the dilemma of presentation',[133] is reasonably disputable.

In fulfilling this aim of ensuring effective access, the enormous contribution that information communication technology (ICT) can make in driving this goal is well recognised: amongst others, cheap CDs can carry voluminous materials that may be relatively very expensive to print;[134] computerised information is generally easier to transfer to applicants electronically – it is also easier to sort through and it simplifies the tracking down of specific pieces of information; uploading environmental information on the internet largely ameliorates the difficulty in accessing it that comes with location (or distance), (inconvenient) office hours, and generally provides a substantial section of the public with a level of effective access that can hardly be provided by any other means.[135] These same benefits also come with creating opportunities to access some information by telephone[136] and, through electronic media, environmental information can more easily reach a wide range of people in a short time.

In that light, modern environmental laws embrace ICT as a medium for advancing public access to environmental information: the World Charter for Nature requires the broad dissemination of information 'by all possible means';[137] and Agenda 21 stresses the need to improve and 'strengthen electronic networking capabilities' to enable effective access.[138] Similarly, apart from simply '[n]oting . . . the importance of making use of the media and of electronic or other, future forms of communication'[139] and embracing environmental information in electronic forms,[140] the Aarhus Convention requires states to ensure environmental information is progressively made available in 'electronic databases' or 'computerized' forms, which are easily accessible to the public through 'public telecommunications networks'.[141]

132 See Aarhus Implementation Guide, 101; and Poustie (n 56) 87; and M Haklay, 'Public access to environmental information: past, present and future' (2003) 27 *Computers, Environment and Urban Systems* 163, 174.
133 M Lee and C Abbot, 'The usual suspects? Public participation under the Aarhus Convention' (2003) 66 *Modern Law Review* 80, 93.
134 See *Spain* (n 73) para 70.
135 Cf Poustie (n 56) 89; and Haklay (n 132).
136 Rowan-Robinson et al. (n 131) 26.
137 Articles 15 and 18.
138 See paras 40.18 and 40.25.
139 Aarhus Convention, preamble.
140 Ibid, arts 2(3), 4(1)(b).
141 Ibid, art 5(3) and (9).

4.3.2.2 Specific environmental information (and obligations) under the active duty to collect and disseminate information

The active duty on public authorities to make environmental information effectively accessible to the public cuts across different types of environmental information, including relevant texts of legislation and agreements, policies, plans and programmes related to the environment etc. However, there are certain vital and specifically defined types of information (and obligation) under this active duty to disseminate that have gained some prominence in international environmental law and may be interlinked in some cases. They are also well captured under the Aarhus Convention, four of which are discussed below.

4.3.2.2.1 EMERGENCY INFORMATION

Article 5(1)(c) of the Aarhus Convention provides that:

> In the event of any imminent threat to human health or the environment, whether caused by human activities or due to natural causes, all information which could enable the public to take measures to prevent or mitigate harm arising from the threat and is held by a public authority is disseminated immediately and without delay to members of the public who may be affected.

Whilst the above provision, which is largely contained in Agenda 21[142] and the Bali Guidelines,[143] is self-explanatory, it is important to highlight a few points. First, this obligation is triggered by an 'imminent threat' to human health or the environment, which connotes that the harm does not have to occur before the necessary information is disseminated. The fact that this provision is also focused on threats to the environment, apart from humans, is clear, and a sub-set of such a provision may be the stipulation in the World Heritage Convention that states 'shall undertake to keep the public broadly informed of the dangers threatening [cultural and natural heritage]'.[144]

Second, the provision also gives equal weight to whether the object of the threat is human health or the environment, and it also does not draw a distinction between whether the threat is caused by human activities or by natural causes;[145] a sub-set of the quoted Aarhus Convention's provision may be that in the Desertification Convention, which requires 'early warning' of local populations and the execution of other advance planning in periods of adverse climatic variations, in a manner 'suitable for practical application' by the local population.[146]

142 See ch 16, para 16.32; and ch 19, paras 19.49(h) and 19.52(c) and (i).
143 Guideline 6.
144 Article 27(2).
145 See Aarhus Implementation Guide, 98.
146 Article 16.

4.3.2.2.2 INFORMATION TO HELP OBTAIN INFORMATION

The obligation to provide this type of information is connected to the duty to ensuring effective access. Just as the Bali Guidelines, although reservedly, provide that 'advice about how to obtain information' be made public,[147] the Aarhus Convention obliges public authorities to provide sufficient information to the public about the type and scope of environmental information held, where it is held, the conditions under which such information will be made available, and the process for obtaining it.[148] The draft Commentary to the Bali Guidelines largely adopts this expanded perspective of the Aarhus Convention.[149]

Public authorities under the Convention are also required to publicise the points of contact for the public to know where and to whom they should make their applications;[150] again, a position expressly adopted in the draft Commentary to the Bali Guidelines.[151] This information may reduce the time, effort and financial resources that information applicants would have spent trying to access (non-existent) environmental information at the wrong point of contact, which ultimately may discourage the public from seeking vital environmental information.

4.3.2.2.3 NATIONAL ENVIRONMENTAL REPORT

Under Article 5(4) of the Aarhus Convention, states are required to 'publish and disseminate a national report on the state of the environment, including . . . pressures on the environment'. Although this provision requires the report to be published 'at regular intervals not exceeding three or four years', for the beneficial reasons of making comparisons and monitoring the state of the environment over a reasonable timeframe, many countries find it useful to produce their national environmental report annually,[152] which practice is in line with the recommendations for an 'annual environmental review' in Agenda 21,[153] and an 'up-to-date' report on the state of the environment disseminated at 'reasonable intervals' in the Bali Guidelines.[154]

In addition, this document is an important educative tool for the public, and will be vital in enabling them to make better personal decisions and engage better in other decision-making processes as it provides a holistic view, as against only a sectoral one, on the state of the environment.

147 Guideline 2.
148 Article 5(2)(a).
149 Commentary to Guideline 2.
150 Article 5(2)(b)(i) and (iii). See Aarhus Implementation Guide, 104.
151 Commentary to Guideline 2.
152 Aarhus Implementation Guide, 108.
153 Chapter 8, para 8.4(d).
154 Guideline 5.

4.3.2.2.4 PUBLIC ENVIRONMENTAL EDUCATION

Public environmental education and awareness-raising is an important theme in environmental participatory democracy and governance, as discussed in Chapter 3. For example, the Desertification Convention,[155] the World Heritage Convention,[156] the Biodiversity Convention,[157] the World Charter for Nature[158] and Principle 10 of the Rio Declaration all oblige or require states to support and promote environmental public education and awareness. Similarly, Article 3(3) of the Aarhus Convention expressly obliges states to 'promote environmental education and environmental awareness among the public, especially on how to obtain access to information, to participate in decision-making and to obtain access to justice in environmental matters'.[159]

This is a duty that should be fulfilled by actively disseminating environmental information to the public and targeted groups, as well as engaging with them on the information that is being disseminated, where necessary. This duty to impart environmental knowledge and build the public's capacity to effectively engage in accessing information, decision-making processes and justice is the bedrock for achieving success in procedural environmental matters and securing the likely consequential positive effect on human health and the environment,[160] as environmental awareness brings about 'the modification of behaviour in relation to the environment'.[161]

This obligation also raises the need to ensure that public officials are sufficiently educated to carry out this educational responsibility. This is apart from the need for capacity-building and training of public officials to enable them carry out other functions, including ensuring appropriate public access to environmental information, which both the Bali Guidelines[162] and the Agenda 21[163] seriously call for. Similarly, the Aarhus Implementation Guide, in relation to the Aarhus Convention's Article 5(2)(b)(ii) requirement of 'officials to support the public in seeking access to information', posits that states should 'provide training for government officials in access-to-information laws and regulations, including . . . how to ensure that the public has timely, transparent and effective access to information'.[164]

155 Article 19(3).
156 Article 27(1).
157 Article 13.
158 Article 15.
159 See also Aarhus Convention, preamble.
160 See the Thessaloniki Declaration, UNESCO-EPD-97/CONF.401/CLD.2, 12 December 1997; and UNESCO, 'Education for a sustainable future': A transdisciplinary vision for concerted effort action', UNESCO-EPD-97/CONF.401/CLD.1, November 1997.
161 Aarhus Implementation Guide, 64.
162 Guideline 7.
163 See ch 36.
164 Aarhus Implementation Guide, 104.

4.4 Exemptions to public access and the overrides

It is generally accepted that the right of the public to access environmental information is not absolute; unrestrained access to environmental information is 'incompatible with realistic, efficient and practical governance'.[165] To curtail excesses that may arise from unchecked access and protect competing legitimate interests, the public's right to 'passive' or 'active' access to environmental information is usually limited by some exemptions similar to those under the Aarhus Convention.[166]

This is part of the balancing act discussed in Chapter 3 that needs to take place if potential excesses of democracy are to be curtailed, and its benefits maximised. Nevertheless, the widely acceptable norm is that exemptions be narrowly defined so that the public can still enjoy reasonable access to environmental information.[167] In this respect, the exemptions in the Aarhus Convention have been stated to be 'undoubtedly more precise' and leave far less room for the arbitrary exercise of public authority discretion, compared with those that existed in Europe before the Convention.[168]

Under the Aarhus Convention, and largely the draft Commentary to the Bali Guidelines,[169] information requests may be refused if: (1) the public authority does not hold the requested information; (2) it is manifestly unreasonable or formulated in too general a manner; or (3) it concerns materials in the course of completion or internal communications of public authorities where such an exemption is provided for in national law or customary practice, taking into account the public interest served by disclosure.[170] Whilst some issues surrounding the first exemption have been discussed above, the second and third exemptions deserve further comment.

With regards to the second exemption, although the Aarhus Convention does not provide a definition of what may be considered 'manifestly unreasonable' or 'too general', from the common sense approach of the Defra Guidance, those terms may include 'requests for information that place a substantial and unreasonable burden on the resources of a public authority' and such that 'the work involved would require an unreasonable diversion of resources from the provision of the public services for which the public authority is mandated . . . [or is probably] vexatious'.[171] Such guidance lessens the propensity for public authorities to apply the exemption arbitrarily and guides the public in making a proper request.[172] However, there is strong argument that a public authority will

165 L Krämer, 'Transnational access to environmental information' (2012) 1(1) *Transnational Environmental Law* 95, 96.
166 Articles 4(3) and (4), and 5(10).
167 Kravchenko (n 18) 245.
168 Davies (n 3) 162.
169 See Commentary to Guideline 3.
170 Article 4(3). See note 190 below.
171 See Ch 7, para 7.4.2.
172 See Aarhus Implementation Guide, 84.

not be able to apply that exemption successfully unless it first complies with its obligation to 'advice and assist' the applicant in clarifying and narrowing down the request, if possible.[173]

Furthermore, with respect to the third exemption, 'materials in the course of completion' reflects a shift from 'unfinished documents' used in the (repealed) EU Directive 90/313/EC, and suggests that individual documents are 'actively being worked on by the public authority' or that more work will be done on them within a reasonable timeframe.[174] Thus, even if the documents are unfinished or are drafts, so long as they are not 'in the course of completion' they may be released even if they pertain to a decision that is yet to be resolved.[175]

This position was relied upon by the Scottish Information Commissioner in *Messrs McIntosh v Aberdeen City Council*[176] to hold that documents were not 'in the course of completion' as they were not having more work done on them, although they were working notes that may possibly be characterised by any 'incompleteness' or 'inchoateness' and were to be used to inform an incomplete EIA. By way of contrast, the second part of this exemption on 'internal communications' could include correspondence between staff of a public authority in the course of their duties, internal minutes, briefs and submissions.[177]

Moving on, in addition to these exemptions, under Article 4 of the Aarhus Convention a request may be refused if disclosure would 'adversely affect': international relations, national defence or public security;[178] the confidentiality of the proceedings of public authorities which are protected by law;[179] intellectual property rights;[180] the fair administration of justice;[181] the confidentiality of commercial and industrial information where such is protected by law in order to protect a legitimate economic interest – this will exclude information on emissions[182] which is relevant for the protection of the environment;[183] confidential personal data relating to a *natural* person where such confidentiality is provided in law;[184] the interests of a third party voluntary informant, where the third party has not consented to the release;[185] or '[t]he environment to which the

173 For example this is the position in the UK. See EIR, reg 9, EI(S)R, reg 9 and *Mersey Tunnel Users Association v IC and Halton BC*, Appeal No EA/2009/0001, 24 June 2009, para 95; and Defra Guidance, ch 7, paras 7.4.2.4 and 7.4.3.

174 See Aarhus Implementation Guide, 85.

175 Ibid.

176 Case No 200502963, 11 December 2006.

177 See Defra Guidance, ch 7, para 7.4.5; and Aarhus Implementation Guide, 85.

178 Article 4(4)(b).

179 Article 4(4)(a).

180 Article 4(4)(e).

181 Article 4(4)(c).

182 Not defined in the Convention, the EU Directive 96/61/EC on Integrated Pollution Prevention and Control [1996] OJ L257, gives insight into the meaning of 'emissions', thus: 'direct or indirect release of substances, vibrations, heat or noise from individual or diffuse sources in the installation into the air, water or land'. This generally resonates with the Aarhus Convention's art 2(3)(b).

183 Article 4(4)(d).

184 Article 4(4)(f). See Aarhus Implementation Guide, 89.

185 Article 4(4)(g).

information relates, such as the breeding sites of rare species'.[186] Exemptions similar to these are contained in the draft Commentary to the Bali Guidelines.[187]

Despite the above, there is the view that '[t]he best access to information legal regimes have a public interest limitation, or override, on *all* exemptions to disclosure' (emphasis added).[188] To reinforce this point, the Bali Guidelines provide that the grounds for refusal be interpreted 'narrowly' in view of the public interest served by disclosure.[189] Similarly, Article 4(4)(h) of the Aarhus Convention stipulates that all Article 4(4) exemptions 'shall be interpreted in a restrictive way', (1) 'taking into account the public interest served by disclosure'[190] (i.e. if the interest in maintaining the exemption does not outweigh the public interest in disclosing the information, the information must be disclosed);[191] and (2) 'taking into account whether the information requested relates to emissions into the environment'.[192]

Thus, the fact that the requested information falls under an exemption does not in itself justify the immediate application of the exemption. The relevant public authority must do the necessary balancing exercises with the 'public interest' and 'emissions' safeguards to be able to determine properly whether or not it is right to apply an exemption. Even though it has been argued that some of the exemptions are too generally defined and that the overrides provided will not eliminate the risk of self-serving interpretation that comes with discretion,[193] certainly the overrides greatly reduce such chances of abuse of discretion. Also, the overrides not only reduce the scope of the exemptions; they constitute an important instrument with which the courts/tribunals can overturn decisions that should have been decided in favour of the applicant had the balancing test been properly applied.

4.5 Enforcing the right to access environmental information

Effective and adequate enforcement mechanisms are required to strengthen and give teeth to legal provisions for public access to environmental information,

186 Article 4(4)(h).
187 Commentary to Guideline 3.
188 Kravchenko (n 18) 252.
189 Guideline 3.
190 'Public interest' is usually construed broadly and described in relation to public health and safety, and the quality of the environment. See Aarhus Implementation Guide, 117.
191 Sofia Guidelines on access to environmental information and public participation in environmental decision-making, ECE/CPE/24, 25 October 1995, Principle 6, referred to in the Aarhus Convention's preamble. See also *European Community* (n 1) para 30, where the Aarhus Compliance Committee held the above 'public interest' proviso to mean that 'in situations where there is a significant public interest in disclosure of certain environmental information and a relatively small amount of harm to the interests involved, the Convention would require disclosure'.
192 EC Regulation No 1367/2006 on the Application of the Aarhus Convention to the European Community Institutions and Bodies [2006] OJ L264/13, art 6(1), establishes that 'an overriding public interest in disclosure shall be deemed to exist where the information requested relates to emissions into the environment'.
193 J Ebbesson, 'The notion of public participation in international environmental law' (1997) 8 *Yearbook of International Environmental Law* 51, 92.

and help to ensure their consistent and effective implementation.[194] Therefore, as entrenched in Principle 10 of the Rio Declaration, there is the widely recognised need to provide for '[e]ffective access to judicial and administrative proceedings, including redress and remedy' as it relates to provisions for access to environmental information. In this light, as with the Bali Guidelines,[195] the Aarhus Convention in Article 9(1) requires that national legislation ensures that:

> . . . *any person* who considers that his or her request for information under Article 4 has been ignored, wrongfully refused, whether in part or in full, inadequately answered, or otherwise not dealt with in accordance with . . . [Article 4], has access to a review procedure before a court of law or another independent and impartial body established by law. (emphasis added)

In other words, in view of the reference to 'any person', 'no standing requirements [but the fact that the person has made a request under Article 4] are allowed under this category of access to justice.'[196]

More generally, Article 9(3) of the Aarhus Convention requires that members of the public meeting relevant criteria stipulated in national law have access to administrative or judicial procedures to challenge acts and omissions of public authorities that contravene any 'national law relating to the environment'. By this provision, alleged violations of other binding provisions of the Aarhus Convention (apart from Article 4, discussed above) relating to access to information can be legally challenged; examples of such provisions will be Articles 3 and 5 (especially those that impose a clear obligation, e.g. Article 5(1)(c)), which are also generally relevant for the implementation of some Article 4 obligations. The Bali Guidelines contain a similar provision to Article 9(3), which allows members of the public concerned to challenge alleged violations of 'procedural legal norms of the State related to the environment'.[197]

These enforcement procedures, both as commonly accepted norms and as reflected in the Aarhus Convention and the Bali Guidelines, are required to provide adequate and effective remedies, be fair and equitable, and be timely and not prohibitively expensive.[198] Reasonable progress can be made in fulfilling these requirements if the Aarhus Convention's requirement in Article 9(1) for states, if they already provide for review by a court of law, also to ensure that aggrieved applicants have access 'to an expeditious procedure established by law that is free of charge or inexpensive for reconsideration *by a public authority or review by an independent and impartial body other than a court of law*' (emphasis added), is implemented. According to the Aarhus Convention and the Bali Guidelines, states should

194 Aarhus Implementation Guide, 187.

195 Guideline 15.

196 F de Lange, 'Beyond *Greenpeace*, courtesy of the Aarhus Convention', in H Somsen (ed), *The Yearbook of European Environmental Law* (Vol 3, Oxford: Oxford University Press, 2003) 227, 239.

197 Guideline 17.

198 See Aarhus Convention, art 9(4); A Andrusevych, T Alge and C Konrad (eds), *Case Law of the Aarhus Convention Compliance Committee (2004–2011)* (Lviv: Resource & Analysis Center 'Society and environment', 2011) 81–88; and Bali Guidelines 19–22.

'consider the establishment of appropriate assistance mechanisms to remove or reduce financial and other barriers to access to justice'.[199]

4.6 Conclusion

The above analysis elucidates what may be considered as international best practice for laws and practices with respect to access to environmental information, which is capable of maximising the benefits of open environmental governance and striking a largely appropriate balance between legitimate competing interests. As argued in Chapter 2, the implementation of similar norms in Nigeria will contribute in ensuring a more open and transparent form of environmental governance, which will also engender meaningful public participation in environmental decision-making processes. In addition, if Nigeria is to comply with its international environmental law commitments on access to environmental information, this book argues that those are the norms it should generally follow in designing its laws and guiding its practices. The extent to which this is the case in Nigeria, and recommendations for improvement if need be, are dealt with in the next chapter.

Bibliography

Andrusevych A, Alge T and Konrad C (eds), *Case Law of the Aarhus Convention Compliance Committee (2004–2011)* (Lviv: Resource & Analysis Center 'Society and Environment', 2011).

Birnie P, Boyle A and Redgwell C, *International Law and the Environment* (3rd edn, Oxford: Oxford University Press, 2009).

Burton T, 'Access to environmental information: the UK experience of water registers' (1989) 1 *Journal of Environmental Law* 192.

Calland R, 'Prizing open the profit-making world', in Florini A (ed), *The Right to Know: Transparency for an Open World* (New York: Colombia University Press, 2007) 214.

Coppel P, *Information Rights: Law and Practice* (3rd edn, Oxford: Hart Publishing, 2010).

Creighton JL, *The Public Participation Handbook: Making Better Decisions through Citizen Involvement* (San Francisco: Jossey-Bass, 2005).

Davies P, 'Public participation, the Aarhus Convention, and the European Community', in Zillman DN, Lucas AR and Pring G (eds), *Human Rights in National Resource Development: Public Participation in the Sustainable Development of Mining and Energy Resource* (Oxford: Oxford University Press, 2002) 155.

Deininger RA and World Health Organisation (Regional Office for Europe), *Design of Environmental Information Systems* (Michigan: Ann Arbor Science Publishers, 1974).

Draft Commentary to the UNEP Guidelines for the development of national legislation on information, public participation and access to justice in environmental matters, available at http://www.unep.org/civil-society/Portals/24105/documents/Guidelines/Commentary-to-the-guidelines-for-the-development-of-national-legislation.pdf (last accessed 30 January 2015).

Ebbesson J, 'The notion of public participation in international environmental law' (1997) 8 *Yearbook of International Environmental Law* 51.

199 Aarhus Convention, art 9(5); and Bali Guidelines 20.

Ebbesson J, Gaugitsch H, Jendroska J, Marshal F and Stec S, *The Aarhus Convention: An Implementation Guide* (2nd edn, New York and Geneva: UN, 2014).

Haklay ME, *Public Environmental Information Systems: Challenges and Perspectives* (PhD Thesis, University College London, 2002).

Haklay M, 'Public access to environmental information: past, present and future' (2003) 27 *Computers, Environment and Urban Systems* 163.

Hughes D, Jewell T, Lowther J, Parpworth N and de Prez P, *Environmental Law* (4th edn, London: LexisNexis Butterworths, 2002).

Krämer L, 'Transnational access to environmental information' (2012) 1(1) *Transnational Environmental Law* 95.

Kravchenko S, 'Is access to environmental information a fundamental human right?' (2009) *Oregon Review of International Law* 227.

Lange F de, 'Beyond *Greenpeace*, courtesy of the Aarhus Convention', in Somsen H (ed), *The Yearbook of European Environmental Law* (Vol 3, Oxford: Oxford University Press, 2003) 227.

Lee M and Abbot C, 'The usual suspects? Public participation under the Aarhus Convention' (2003) 66 *Modern Law Review* 80.

Lucas A, 'Legal techniques for pollution control: the role of the public' (1971) 6 *University of British Colombia Law Review* 167.

McLaren JCP, 'The common law nuisance actions and the environmental battle: well-tempered swords or broken reeds?' (1972) 10(3) *Osgoode Hall Law Journal* 505.

Mason M, *Environmental Democracy* (London: Palgrave Macmillan, 1999).

OUT-LAW, 'Corporate social responsibility: the UK Corporate Governance Code', available at http://www.out-law.com/page-8221 (last accessed 30 January 2015).

Poustie M, 'Opening up government: paradise postponed again?', in Miller A, *Human Rights: A Modern Agenda* (Edinburgh: T&T Clark, 2000) 67.

Poustie M, 'Environmental justice in SEPA's environmental protection activities: a report for the Scottish Environment Protection Agency', 2004, 87, available at http://www.sepa.org.uk/system_pages/search.aspx?q=poustie (last accessed 15 February 2015).

Richardson BJ and Razzaque J, 'Public participation in environmental decision-making', in Richardson BJ and Wood S (eds), *Environmental Law for Sustainability* (Oxford: Hart Publishing, 2006) 165.

Robert A, 'Structural pluralism and the right to information', in Calland R and Tilley A (eds), *The Right to Know, The Right to Live: Access to Information and Socio-Economic Justice* (Cape Town: ODAC, 2002) 29.

Rosenbaum M, 'Tribunal to hear water information case', *British Broadcasting Corporation*, 27 Oct 2010.

Rowan-Robinson J, Ross A, Walton W and Rothnie J, 'Public access to environmental information: a means to what end?' (1996) 8 (1) *Journal of Environmental Law* 19, 34.

Schram F, 'From a general right to access to environmental information in the Aarhus Convention to a e gneral right of access to all information in official documents: the Council of Europe's Tromsø Convention', in Pallemaerts M (ed), *The Aarhus Convention at Ten: Interactions and Tensions Between Conventional International Law and EU Environmental Law* (Groningen: Europa Law Publishing, 2011) 67.

UNESCO, 'Education for a sustainable future: a trans-disciplinary vision for concerted effort action', UNESCO-EPD-97/CONF.401/CLD.1, November 1997.

Wates J, 'The future of the Aarhus Convention: perspectives arising from the Third Session of the Meeting of the Parties', in Pallemaerts M (ed), *The Aarhus Convention at Ten: Interactions and Tensions Between Conventional International Law and EU Environmental Law* (Groningen: Europa Law Publishing, 2011) 384.

5 Public access to environmental information: Nigerian law and practice in comparative perspective

5.1 Introduction

In view of the international best practice principles on public access to environmental information critically set out in the preceding chapter, this chapter seeks comparatively to analyse the Nigerian law and practice in that regard and, where necessary, make recommendations for improvement in that light, considering some relevant non-legal realities of the country. From the Nigerian perspective, apart from a few other local instruments that will be referred to, the 2011 FOI Act will be at the heart of the (comparative) discussion in this chapter, being the flagship and detailed law for public access to (environmental) information in Nigeria.

The 2013 FOI Act Implementation Guidelines[1] published under the authority of the Attorney-General of the Federation and Minister of Justice (Attorney-General) (who is charged with ensuring that all public institutions comply with the FOI Act)[2] to enable public institutions better to understand and fulfil their obligations under the Act, will also be referred to. Although the FOI Act is a general information legislation, Shelton and Kiss have rightly stated that 'where national law includes a Freedom of Information Act, issues of access to environmental information . . . arise'.[3] The discussion in this chapter will follow a similar progression as that in the preceding chapter.

5.2 Access to environmental information: issues on scope

In determining the scope, and hence partly the value to the public of the Nigerian regime that enables public access to environmental information vis-à-vis best practice, the focus in this section will be on: (1) the meaning of 'environmental information'; (2) the format of the information; (3) the beneficiary of the right of access; and (4) the bodies obliged to provide access.

1 Available at http://foia.justice.gov.ng/pages/resources/REVISED_GUIDELINES_ON_THE_IMPLEMENTATION_OF_THE_FOIA_2013.pdf (last accessed 1 February 2015).

2 FOI Act, s 29.

3 D Shelton and A Kiss, *Judicial Handbook on Environmental Law* (Nairobi: UNEP, 2005) 27.

5.2.1 The meaning of 'environmental information'

In Nigerian law, there is no express definition of 'environmental information', even though the term has been used repeatedly in vital environment-specific policy documents.[4] Under the FOI Act, as in several countries in the UNECE region and around the world,[5] 'environmental information' is not differentiated from other types of information held by public institutions in Nigeria, given that the Act is a general information law. Rather, it provides for access to 'information', which 'includes all records, documents and information stored in whatever form',[6] subject to some exemptions. This comparatively broader approach, which includes 'environmental information', is in alignment with best practice and the Aarhus Convention, which only seeks to provide minimum standards.[7]

Nevertheless, the broad and enumerative nature of the Aarhus Convention's definition of 'environmental information' could serve as a useful guide to public institutions in Nigeria, which have specific responsibilities to collect and ensure public access to environmental information. An example of such an institution is the Nigerian apex environmental body – National Environmental Standards and Regulations Enforcement Agency (NESREA) – which is expected to 'collect and make available . . . in co-operation with public or private organisations, basic scientific data and other information pertaining to environmental standards'.[8] In order for NESREA's effort in this regard reasonably to align with international best practice and adequately to serve the interests of the Nigerian public, it might have to interpret 'information pertaining to environmental standards' in the light of the definition of 'environmental information' espoused in the Aarhus Convention, at least.

5.2.2 The format of the information

Commendably, the Nigerian law is in line with best practice as the public right to information under the FOI Act covers 'information stored in whatever form, including written, electronic, visual images, sound, audio recording, etc.'.[9]

5.2.3 The beneficiary of the right of access

In line with the liberal current reflected by best practice, the beneficiary of the right of access to environmental information in Nigeria is 'any person', as provided

4 See the 1998 Nigerian National Policy on the Environment, para 6.6(f); and Draft Objectives and Strategies for Nigeria's Agenda 21, done under the auspices of the UNDP, (Nigeria's Agenda 21), para 2.5(3)(f), available at http://www.nesrea.org/images/NIGERIA'S%20AGENDA%2021.pdf (last accessed 1 February 2015).

5 For example Finland, Sweden, the Netherlands, United States etc. See Aarhus Implementation Guide, 50.

6 FOI Act, ss 1(1) and 31.

7 Article 3(5).

8 NESREA Act, s 8(p).

9 Section 31.

in section 1 of the FOI Act. The two initial versions of the FOI Bill[10] that were passed by the Nigerian National Assembly (Parliament) in 2004 and 2007 (but did not received the president's assent to make it an Act) gave the right of access only to 'every citizen' of Nigeria, as against the term 'any person', which was contained in the original FOI Bill[11] sent to the National Assembly in 1999. This shows a conscious attempt to limit the scope of the access right, in line with President Obasanjo's erroneous view (discussed in Chapter 2) that allowing non-citizens to access information is not done anywhere in the world and should be prevented. Thus, it is gratifying that the term 'any person' was finally used.

Going beyond the individual, 'person' is defined in section 31 of the Act as 'including a corporation sole and body of persons whether corporate or incorporate; acting individually or as a group'. In line with best practice, in the absence of an express non-discriminatory provision, the right given to 'any person' to access environmental information under the FOI Act is clearly non-discriminatory, embracing all irrespective of race, gender, nationality or domicile, or other distinguishing factors. This is especially so considering that the non-discriminatory principle has been largely accepted as a principle of international environmental law and argued as having attained the status of 'general international law',[12] and so would arguably be applicable to Nigeria from that perspective as well.[13] In addition, the FOI Act goes on expressly to empower illiterate and disabled applicants to make their applications through a third party.[14]

In accordance with best practice, section 1(2) of the FOI Act also provides that an applicant does not need to demonstrate any specific interest in the information being applied for. Any provision requiring the public to have and show 'sufficient interest' in the requested information would simply mean granting Nigerian public institutions an unhealthy level of discretion that could easily be exercised to restrict public access to environmental information, especially in view of the country's lingering culture of official secrecy.

This culture of secrecy reared its head in the recent FOI Act case of *Paradigm Initiative Nigeria v Dr Reuben Abati*,[15] where the judge, Justice Gabriel Kolawole, expressed shock at the openness of section 1(2) of the Act, calling on the legislators to amend it, such that it requires information applicants to show sufficient interest before their application is attended to. According to the judge, this was to prevent a situation where scarce public resources are squandered on information requests by irate litigants and busybodies.

The position of Justice Gabriel Kolawole's above is problematic on many levels and should not be accepted: first, it does not take cognisance of the fact that

10 On file with author.

11 On file with author.

12 J Ebbesson, 'The notion of public participation in international environmental law' (1997) 8 *Yearbook of International Environmental Law* 51, 81–83.

13 See C Nawpi, 'International treaties in Nigerian and Canadian courts' (2011) 19(1) *African Journal of International and Comparative Law* 38, 54–57.

14 Section 3(3).

15 Unreported, Suit No FHC/ABJ/CS/02/2013, 3 July 2013.

people have the right simply to 'know' about the activities of public authorities that act on their behalf; referring to resources spent on ensuring wide access as a waste does not show a good appreciation of the value of access to information in a democratic setting, even when public institutions in the country are not complaining about an unreasonable increase in running cost owing to the implementation of the Act.[16] Moreover, it is hardly conceivable or reasonable to suggest that a person who has no interest in information will spend his/her money, time and energy trying to procure it for the purpose of 'burdening' public institutions.

5.2.4 The bodies obliged to provide access

The preceding chapter elaborates on a number of points as to why it is reasonable to place not only government bodies, but also some private entities, under the obligation to ensure access to the environmental information which they hold. Those reasons equally apply to Nigeria, and necessitate the imposition of environmental information access obligations on similar private entities. For example, the 'regulatory agency capture' phenomenon cited in the preceding chapter as one of the reasons for extending access obligations, has been a major issue in Nigeria where, according to Osaghae, the apparatuses of government generally 'lack autonomy in the sense that they are not well developed, and not insulated from private capture. This means that the legal-rational and bureaucratic ethos of impersonality, impartiality and rationality has not been entrenched, making it possible to be captured by hegemonic classes and groups.'[17] In support, Amnesty International has, with respect to Nigeria, noted how 'powerful business actors whose word appears to be law in some cases' have seemingly grown above effective regulation by their regulator.[18]

Another reason given in the previous chapter for the paradigm shift is the increasing devolution of government responsibilities to private entities. This is also a major drive in Nigeria where, amongst other measures, there is the 1999 Public Enterprises (Privatisation and Commercialisation) Act[19] that provides for the privatisation and commercialisation of some traditional government functions in the country. All other reasons why it is vital to open up some private entities provided in the preceding chapter – as they relate to geographic accessibility and holder/flow of information between the regulator and the regulated – apply to Nigeria. This is in addition to the fact that enabling the public to access environmental information from multiple non-government sources will

16 E Ojo, 'FOI Act: where his lordship got it wrong', *Vanguard*, 6 August 2013, available at http://www.vanguardngr.com/2013/08/foi-act-where-his-lordship-got-it-wrong/ (last accessed 1 February 2015).

17 EE Osaghae, *Crippled Giant: Nigeria since Independence* (London: Hurst & Co Publishers Ltd, 1998) 23.

18 Amnesty International, *Nigeria: Petroleum, Pollution and Poverty in the Niger Delta* (London: Amnesty International Publications, 2009) 48.

19 Cap P38, Laws of the Federation of Nigeria, 2004.

reduce the pressure on the human and financial resources of government bodies, especially in a developing country such as Nigeria.

Also, in line with a growing trend as noted in the preceding chapter, some private entities in Nigeria, whose activities have immense public and environmental implications, have voluntary codes and guidelines which are aimed at ensuring reasonable direct public access to the environmental information about their activities. However, generally, private entities in Nigeria hardly take seriously their adopted voluntary initiatives. For example, the Nigerian subsidiary of the multinational oil and gas firm, Shell, is supposed to be operating under such a voluntary initiative that aims to ensure direct public access to information.[20]

Yet, it has been noted as common knowledge that neither Shell Nigeria nor other similar multinational companies in Nigeria hardly ever allow public access to the environmental information they hold; usually, they provide the public with inaccurate environmental information (so as to escape liability or appear responsible), and do not do enough gathering of information about the environmental impact of their activities.[21] This clearly substantiates the argument in the preceding chapter that such voluntary measures are insufficient to ensure adequate access to information held by private entities, and hence the need for a binding law on the matter.

This is why it is commendable that the Nigerian law has moved forward in this regard. The body obliged to provide public access to environmental information under the FOI Act is the 'public institution'. Strangely, however, the Act defines 'public institution' twice, using slightly different wordings, thus:

> Public institutions are all authorities whether executive, legislative or judicial agencies, ministries, and extra-ministerial departments of the government, together with all corporations established by law and all companies in which government has a controlling interest, and private companies utilizing public funds, providing public services or performing public functions.[22]
>
> '[P]ublic institution' means any legislative, executive, judicial, administrative or advisory body of the government, including boards, bureau[x], committees or commissions of the State, and any subsidiary body of those bodies including but not limited to committees and sub-committees which are supported in whole or in part by public fund[s] or which expends public fund[s] and private bodies providing public services, performing public functions or utilizing public funds.[23]

20 Shell Group, 'Shell general business principles', 1976 (last revised in 2005), Principle 7 (on 'Communication and engagement'), available at http://www.shell.com/content/dam/shell/static/public/downloads/corporate-pkg/sgbp-english.pdf (last accessed 15 February 2015).

21 See Amnesty International (n 18) 48, 50, 59, 68 and 69.

22 Section 2(7).

23 Section 31.

Arguably, there is no real difference between both provisions in terms of substance, even though the inclusion of two definitions is presumably a mistake that should be corrected. However, in accordance with the established rule of statutory interpretation espoused by the Nigerian Court of Appeal in *Crownstar and Company Ltd v The Vessel MV Vali P*,[24] and further developed and followed in *Ziza v Mamman*,[25] to the effect that where there is a potential conflict between two provisions of the same statute the latter provision supersedes the former, it is submitted that the latter section 31 definition is the operative definition of 'public institution' in the FOI Act. Nevertheless, that is not to say it is impossible for this unnecessary double definition to give rise to unwarranted delays and conflicts between information applicants and the relevant public institutions, as the wording difference of the provisions may give a false sense of difference in scope.

Some public institutions may seek to exploit this situation unjustly to prevent or discourage the public from gaining access to environmental information by claiming not to be public institutions under the FOI Act and so not subject to it. If this happens, access to information might be prohibitively expensive as some applicants may be forced to seek judicial review, whilst others without the financial means or the time to pursue a judicial review may ultimately have to forfeit their requests.

Already, possibly the first of such unnecessary delay and conflict cases has been recorded. In response to a request for certain information, the Nigerian National Petroleum Corporation (NNPC) in a letter stated that it is a 'statutory corporation' (or a 'corporation established by law') and is not bound by the FOI Act by virtue of the definition of 'public institution' in section 31 of the Act, which does not extend to 'statutory corporation'.[26] The NNPC, which is the foremost entity in Nigeria's oil and gas industry that has impacted enormously on the country's environment, perhaps erroneously believed or disingenuously tried to foster the argument that since the section 31 definition excludes a direct reference to statutory bodies, which is included in the section 2(7) definition, it means it is automatically excluded from the scope of section 31 upon which it relied.

That position is flawed and it is submitted that the NNPC is a 'public institution' under the section 31 definition.[27] It is an 'administrative' or, at the very least, a 'subsidiary' body of the government which, according to the long title of its enabling statute, is 'empowered to engage in all commercial activities relating to the Petroleum industry and to enforce all regulatory measures relating to the general control of the Petroleum sector',[28] considering that section 44(3) of the

24 (2000) 1 NWLR (pt 639) 37, 62.

25 (2002) 5 NWLR (pt 760) 243, 265.

26 NM Abdallah, 'We are not bound by FOI Act – NNPC', *Daily Trust*, 31 July 2012.

27 The NNPC has subsequently accepted that it is bound by the FOI Act. See C Okafor, 'NNPC says it is bound by provisions of FOI Act', *ThisDay*, 11 August 2012, available at http://www.thisdaylive.com/articles/nnpc-says-its-bound-by-provisions-of-foi-act/122090/ (last accessed 1 February 2015).

28 NNPC Act, Cap N123, Laws of the Federation of Nigeria, 2004.

Nigerian Constitution provides that 'the entire property in and control of all minerals, mineral oils and natural gas in under or upon any land in Nigeria or in, under or upon the territorial waters and the exclusive economic Zone (EEZ) of Nigeria shall vest in the Government of the Federation and shall be managed in such manner as may be prescribed by the National Assembly.'

Apart from the fact that the NNPC is established by statute, some of its other governmental ties include the fact that it is fully under the control of government appointees, performs regulatory functions in the petroleum industry and is wholly supported by public funds.[29] Therefore, to forestall confusion and align with the general principle espoused in Article 3(1) of the Aarhus Convention, which obliges states to ensure that legislative measures taken to guarantee public participatory rights are 'clear, transparent and consistent', the FOI Act should be amended to provide for a single definition of 'public institution'.

That aside, the latter definition in section 31 (and even that of section 2(7)) would generally cover the entities, and more, that are covered by the Aarhus Convention's definition of 'public authority'. Like the Aarhus Convention, in the Nigerian context, it covers all government bodies, including bodies established by statute. For the first time in Nigeria, 'public institution' is also regarded as stretching beyond government-related bodies, to include some private entities – those 'providing public service', 'performing public functions' or 'utilizing public funds' – and, unlike the Aarhus Convention, there are no restrictions that these public services or functions must be 'administrative', done based on 'national law' or done 'in relation to the environment'; or even that the private entity be under the control of any other (government) body. Importantly also, and going beyond the Aarhus Convention, the mere fact that a 'private body . . . [is] utilizing public funds' makes it a public institution under the FOI Act.

For example, in view of the above discussion, major private entities involved in oil and gas exploration and exploitation in Nigeria, whose activities have had serious environmental implications over the years, can arguably now be considered as 'public institutions' under the FOI Act. These entities include Shell Petroleum Development Company of Nigeria Limited, Chevron Nigeria Limited, Mobil Producing Nigeria Unlimited, Nigerian Agip Oil Company Limited, NNPC Texaco-Chevron Joint Venture and Total E & P Nigeria Limited – all operators of joint venture agreements involving the NNPC as the government representative (holding the majority stake).[30]

Given that these private companies explore and exploit state-owned natural resources (and the mainstay of the nation's economy) in partnership with the NNPC, a government administrative/subsidiary body, under a special arrangement that enables the latter to fulfil its statutory duties of exploring and exploiting

29 See ibid generally.

30 International Business Publications, *Nigeria: Mineral, Mining Sector Business investment Guide – Volume 1 – Oil and Gas Industry Strategic Information and Regulations* (Washington DC: International Business Publications, 2013) 76–77.

oil and gas resources for the overall interest of Nigeria,[31] they can arguably be considered as 'private bodies providing public services' under section 31 of the FOI Act, and thus obliged to ensure public access to the (environmental) information they hold.

What is more, unlike the Aarhus Convention that excludes 'bodies or institutions acting in a judicial or legislative capacity'[32] from its definition of 'public authority', the FOI Act does not contain such exclusion in its definition of 'public institution'. However, there are exemptions under the FOI Act that bodies can easily take advantage to withhold information from the public when they are acting in a judicial capacity in order to ensure their independence whilst acting in such a capacity and to protect the rights of parties during such proceedings.[33]

5.3. The public's right of access to environmental information

5.3.1 'Passive' access to environmental information

5.3.1.1 The request and the right of access

In Nigeria, in line with best practice, section 1(1) of the FOI Act provides that 'the right of any person to access or request information . . . which is in the custody or possession of any public official, agency or institution howsoever described, is established'. As against best practice that is silent on the point, the FOI Act erases all doubt by expressly giving the applicant an option of making an 'oral application for information', which the relevant official of the public institution 'shall reduce . . . into writing . . . and shall provide a copy of the written application to the applicant'.[34]

Apart from creating that level of flexibility for applicants, the Act seemingly goes further than best practice and, indeed, aligns with recommendations in the draft Commentary to Bali Guidelines referred to in Chapter 2, by expressly widening access opportunity for illiterate and disabled applicants by giving them the right to 'make an application through a third party',[35] or personally, if they are able to.

Also, sections 1(1) and 3 of the FOI Act, which deal with the application for access to information seem capable of accommodating electronic applications in line with best practice. This should certainly be encouraged as it can help to remove barriers of access such as distance to the offices of public institutions and the financial cost of making the trips, and make access generally easier and cheaper for the substantial and growing section of the Nigerian public with

31 See generally NNPC Act, s 5.
32 See proviso to art 2(2); and Aarhus Implementation Guide, 49.
33 For example see FOI Act, s 12.
34 Section 3(4).
35 Section 3(3).

internet and mobile telecommunications connectivity and skills, as indicated in Chapter 2. In furtherance of this, the FOI Act Implementation Guidelines provide that:

> [w]ritten applications may be transmitted electronically (email), by courier, post or delivery in person. To facilitate requests made via email, public institutions are advised to dedicate an email address which should be adequately publicised and should be configured to automatically generate an acknowledgment/receipt of the request.[36]

The Attorney-General also directed elsewhere that 'public institutions must establish a telephone line or internet service that persons requesting information under the Act may use to inquire about the status of their request.'[37]

These measures could be enhanced by adopting similar measures taken by a state in India (in partnership with an NGO) to overcome many barriers of access. These measures include: 'allowing individuals to make . . . [information] request through a single *toll-free* number. Service is provided in *four languages.* The application fee is charged to the caller's phone bill, and a reply is sent directly from the [public information officer]' (emphasis added).[38] However, so far, only very few public institutions in Nigerian have even established the FOI Unit proposed in the FOI Act Implementation Guidelines[39] (as a way of fulfilling their obligation under section 2(3)(f) of the Act) that should be dedicate to organising and dealing effectively with all such access-related issues in the organisation.[40] It is hoped that those recommendations are taken seriously by public institutions and adequate resources are allocated progressively to make them a widespread reality.

Furthermore, section 1(1) of the FOI Act, which empowers an applicant to request information 'which is in the custody or possession' of a public institution indicates that they are entitled to 'copies of the actual documentation' rather than an excerpt prepared by a public authority, as provided in the Aarhus Convention;[41] a major benefit here being the opportunity to appreciate the information better by viewing it in its original language and context.[42] Furthermore, unlike the Aarhus Convention, the FOI Act does not directly provide for the applicant's right to

36 Paragraph 1.9.
37 Attorney-General of the Federation, 'Implementation of the Freedom of Information Act 2011 and the Reporting Requirements under Section 29 Thereof', a Memorandum (HAGF/MDAS/FOIA/2012/I) issued on 28 January 2012 to all public institutions (Attorney-General's FOI Act Memorandum).
38 A Roberts, 'A great and revolutionary law? The first four years of India's Right to Information Act' (2010) 70(6) *Public Administration Review* 925, 931.
39 Paragraph 1.16.1.
40 Right to Know, 'A report on the level of awareness, compliance and implementation of the Freedom of Information Act, 2011, 18 months after its enactment' (2012), available at http://r2knigeria.org/index.php/downloads/foi-assessments-a-reports (last accessed 1 February 2015).
41 Aarhus Convention, art 4(1).
42 Aarhus Implementation Guide, 80.

request that the environmental information be provided in a particular form other than that in which it is held. The only suggestion of a similar right in the Act is the provision for fees to be charged for 'document duplication and *transcription* where necessary' (emphasis added).[43] A more explicit provision in this regard would be preferable as attempting to argue for a right from this indirect perspective could be problematic.

Nonetheless, the term 'duplication' in the aforementioned provision allows members of the public to request environmental information in a variety of (possibly cheaper) forms than that in which it is held – e.g. on CDs and USB drives, or freely sent to the applicant's email address – going by the schedule to the FOI Act Implementation Guidelines.[44] The same applies to 'transcription' used in that provision, which in addition, arguably enables the public to request that environmental information be translated and made available in a language they understand (an issue arguably not covered in the Aarhus Convention as Article 4(1)(b) seemingly only contemplates 'material form[s]'[45] and not immaterial forms such as 'language'), or that recorded speech sounds be made available in written format, amongst other possible scenarios.

These provisions, which allow some flexibility in accessing environmental information, are highly useful in ensuring effective access for illiterate, disabled and poor people. They are also important to those only able to read and write in a Nigerian indigenous language and not in English, and the government acknowledges that the provision of environmental information in native languages is necessary for Nigeria to 'attain full compliance with international regulations, standards and guidelines' in the environmental law field.[46]

Finally, unlike the Aarhus Convention which obliges public authorities to assist and guide those seeking access to environmental information, the FOI Act contains no such provision. As it relates to applications for environmental information under the Act, this could mean that public institutions might be able legitimately to refuse improperly made information applications in cases where they could easily have assisted and guided the applicants in making a proper one.

Again, this is an important issue in Nigeria especially as the level of illiteracy is relatively high and a reasonable number of applicants may well need some form of assistance and guidance in order properly to apply for environmental information, the absence of which could negatively affect public access. In fact, a recent empirical study in India (which shares a similar history of secrecy and level of literacy with Nigeria) identified 'no assistance in drafting and filing . . . requests' as a major barrier to public access to information in the country.[47]

It would seem, however, that the Nigerian authorities have become aware of this gap and have taken steps to 'patch it up' using Paragraph 1.10 of the FOI Act

43 FOI Act, s 8.
44 See section 5.3.1.3 below.
45 Aarhus Convention, art 2(3).
46 Nigeria's Agenda 21, para 2.12.
47 Roberts (n 38) 927–28.

Implementation Guidelines, which urges public institutions urgently to consult with applicants to clarify or make more specific, an unclear or too general application, as well as help inform applicants of information that is readily available. Although welcomed, this provision is merely advisory and is subject to the whims of public institutions. It is therefore advisable for Paragraph 1.10 to be entrenched within the FOI Act itself in order to prevent it from being ignored without legal consequences by public institutions that have existed under the culture of secrecy for so many years, and arguably need tougher provisions to enable them to make the necessary cultural change.

5.3.1.2 The response

5.3.1.2.1 WHERE THE PUBLIC INSTITUTION HOLDS THE ENVIRONMENTAL INFORMATION REQUESTED

In the Nigerian situation the case is somewhat different from the best practice position: '[w]here information is applied for under this [FOI] Act, the public institution to which the application is made shall . . . within 7 days after the application is received' make the information available to the applicant or refuse the application.[48] However, upon notifying the applicant, the public institution may extend this time limit by another seven days in cases where 'the application is for a large number of records' or 'consultations are necessary to comply with the application' and these cannot reasonably be completed within the original time limit.[49] In this regard, the FOI Act is in line with best practice and is even more demanding of public authorities than the Aarhus Convention, which allows public authorities to grant or refuse a request one month after the request is made and another month if an extension is needed.

However, especially in view of the generally low employment of technology in information management in most of Nigeria's public institutions, current implementation reports show that 'public institutions respond to request . . . many times beyond the statutory 7-day limit'.[50] In fact, some applicants who saw the unfeasibility of the seven-day period in a particular case voluntarily gave the public institution concerned 28 days to respond to their application.[51]

In this light, the Head of Civil Service of the Federation, Bukar Aji, has reasonably recommended the review of the FOI Act to extend the seven-day period to 14 days (as contained in the 2007 version of the FOI Bill).[52] Admitting

48 FOI Act, s 4(a) and (b).

49 Ibid, s 6.

50 Right to Know (n 40).

51 See B Aturu, 'CBN governor replies to freedom of information request', *Sahara Reporter*, 3 February 2013, available at http://saharareporters.com/article/cbn-governor-replies-freedom-information-request-bamidele-aturu (last accessed 1 February 2015).

52 'Head of service want review of FOI timeline', *Punch*, 31 July 2013, available at http://www.punchng.com/news/head-of-service-wants-review-of-foi-timeline/ (last accessed 1 February 2015).

that the nation's civil service mostly use the 'analogue system of record keeping [and so] retrieval of information within the specific time limit has been practically difficult', he rightly stressed the need for proper and systematic record-keeping that aids easy accessibility and the eventual digitalisation of public records, which in turn will aid quick retrieval and proactive disclosure.[53] The Right to Know NGO made a similar point when it noted that records in many public institutions 'are still paper based and tied up in bundles of stacks of files' (with only a few having computerised their documents), thus making retrieval difficult.[54]

Even with an extended time limit, for the public institutions in Nigeria to effectively respond to requests, they will still need seriously to address red tape, rigidity, centralisation and excessive bureaucratic layers that largely characterise the present system,[55] and set themselves on a more decentralised, flexible and efficient path. Adequate funding must also be made available for the modernisation of the record-keeping system in public institutions, considering, for example, the report that the 2012 national budget made no provision for the implementation of the Act by government agencies,[56] some of which have complained about financial constraints in implementing the Act.[57]

However, for now, the current seven- to14-day time limit is commendable for its ambition of providing applicants with timely access to environmental information. It also has the side-effect of putting pressure on public institutions to improve and computerise their information management systems to ensure quick and easy retrievals.

However, certain environmental information should ordinarily be accessible well before the seven-day time limit. This may be the case when applicants need access urgently, or have opted to view the requested information only within the premises of the public institution, instead of receiving copies or transcriptions. In these situations, the best practice approach of making the information available 'as soon as possible' (before trying to take advantage of the maximum time limit) becomes relevant. Such a condition helps to forestall undue delay.

This form of base standard approach was not followed by the FOI Act, which contains only a maximum time limit. It is submitted that this is a weakness in the FOI Act that needs to be addressed as it could otherwise encourage undue delay in providing requested environmental information, which will arguably be contrary to the notion of 'appropriate access' under Principle 10 of the Rio Declaration. For the time being, public institutions should be encouraged strictly to follow the wording of the FOI Act Implementation Guidelines that refers to responding to applications '*promptly* and in any event within 7 days' (emphasis

53 Ibid.
54 Right to Know (n 40).
55 O Okontoni, 'Problems and prospects of Nigerian bureaucracy' (2001) 7(3) *Journal of Social Science* 223–29.
56 Right to Know (n 40).
57 M Kadiri, 'Implementing Nigeria's Freedom of Information Act, 2011: the journey so far', a paper presented at the National Conference on the Freedom of Information Act (2011), held in Abuja, Nigeria, on 30–31 July 2013.

added),[58] as well as the memorandum issued by the Attorney-General, which states that '[public institutions should] work proactively and respond to requests *promptly* . . . [they] should make it a priority to respond in a *timely manner*. Timely disclosure of information is an essential component of transparency' (emphasis added).[59]

Furthermore, section 6 of the FOI Act, which should ordinarily provide for '[e]xtension of time limit for granting or refusing application' as its marginal note states, is poorly drafted, and this can potentially result in unwarranted conflicts and court actions that may discourage the public from engaging their FOI rights. Section 6 of the Act provides that: '[t]he public institution may extend the time limit set out in section 5 or section 6 in respect of an application for a time not exceeding 7 days', for the two reasons stated earlier. This excludes section 4 of the FOI Act, which is the main provision dealing with time limit for granting or refusing applications.

However, section 4 largely helps to 'clear the mist' here as it expressly states that it (section 4) is 'subject to section 6'. But, in addition, that aspect of section 6 goes on to include 'section 6', which arguably does not set out any extendable time limit; this may be (mischievously) read as empowering public institutions to extend the relevant time for multiples, as against a single extension, of seven days. These issues should ordinarily attract correctional amendments to section 6 in line with the general principle espoused in the Aarhus Convention that legislative measure on environmental participatory right should be 'clear, transparent and consistent'.[60]

5.3.1.2.2 WHERE THE PUBLIC AUTHORITY/INSTITUTION DOES NOT HOLD THE ENVIRONMENTAL INFORMATION REQUESTED

In Nigeria, the public institutions are allowed to refuse an application for information which they do not hold as section 1(1) of the FOI Act limits the access rights of applicants to information 'in the custody or possession' of public institutions; generally, the refusal must be effected within seven days after the application is received.[61] The discussion in Chapter 4 that the meaning of 'hold' under the counterpart Aarhus Convention provision may not be limited to physical possession alone but includes 'effective' possession, is arguably applicable to what 'custody or possession' of information under the Act means, especially as the Act also mandates public authorities to maintain and update all information relating to their functions.[62]

However, as against the Aarhus Convention where it has been argued that public authorities are still obliged reasonably to assist and guide applicants for environmental information which they do not hold in their quest to access that

58 Paragraph 1.6.
59 Attorney-General's FOI Act Memorandum.
60 Article 3(1).
61 Section 4.
62 Section 9(1).

information, there is no similar obligation under the FOI Act. The FOI Act could be better placed to fulfil its objective of '[making] . . . information more freely available'[63] if such a general obligation to assist and guide applicants is contained in it.

The FOI Act further fails to achieve best practice by not making any provision to ensure the transfer of applications from a public institution that does not hold requested information to one which it believes holds the requested information, or at least informing the applicant of such an institution. Arguably, such a provision is useful in entrenching the principle that 'public authorities have a collective responsibility for dealing with information requests from the public, irrespective of the particular agency or department to which a request is submitted'.[64]

This lacuna in the FOI Act, which its Implementation Guidelines have attempted to plug,[65] needs to be filled with a *binding* referral provision as it potentially places an avoidable burden on applicants to find the actual public institution that holds the required information. Such burden may discourage applicants from accessing vital environmental information, when in fact the public institution that was the first port of call could more easily have made this process more efficient and less stressful for the applicant by directing the latter or referring him or her to the relevant institution.

Such a lacuna, which is consistent with the failure to impose a general obligation to assist applicants, might suppress the provision of relevant environmental information in Nigeria, where there is still a lingering culture of secrecy in most public institutions. However, empirical enquiries have identified the problem of 'inadequate . . . inter-sectoral communication and co-ordination' amongst public institutions concerning environmental issues.[66] In order to make the proposed referral provision work effectively in Nigeria, this problem must be addressed by reducing bureaucratic bottlenecks and taking practical and policy-integrating measures to bridge the gap between relevant public institutions.

Despite the above limitation, the FOI Act makes an arguably awkward 'referral' provision, which allows for the transfer of an application and, where necessary, the requested information, by a public institution which *holds* the requested information to another public institution which is viewed as '[having] greater interest in the [requested] information'.[67]

This provision is arguably influenced by the historical culture of secrecy in public institutions in Nigeria, and should be expunged from the FOI Act (and

63 See the long title of the FOI Act.

64 Aarhus Implementation Guide, 91.

65 See the FOI Act Implementation Guidelines, Template 1.

66 Nigeria, 'Institutional aspects of sustainable development in Nigeria', presented by the Government of Nigeria to the 5th session of the United Nations Commission on Sustainable Development, held in New York, on 7–25 April 1997, available at http://www.un.org/esa/agenda21/natlinfo/countr/nigeria/inst.htm#info (last accessed 1 February 2015). See also Amnesty International (n 18) 29.

67 Section 5(1). According to s 5(3) of the FOI Act, 'a public institution has "a greater interest" in information if – (a) the information was originally produced in or for the institution; or (b) . . . the institution was the first public institution to receive the information.'

replaced with the referral provision suggested above) as it is contrary to best practice and potentially weakens effective/efficient access to environmental information. The provision, it would seem, is geared towards frustrating and wasting the time of applicants. Why else should such transfers be made to a public institution that has the same responsibility to ensure access to information under the FOI Act as the one doing the transfer?

5.3.1.2.3 WHERE THE REQUEST FOR ENVIRONMENTAL INFORMATION IS REFUSED

Commendably, and largely in line with best practice, section 7(1) of the FOI Act also provides that where a public institution refuses access to requested information, or a part of it, 'the institution shall state in the notice given to the applicant the grounds for refusal, the specific provision of this Act that it relates to and that the applicant has a right to challenge the decision refusing access and have it reviewed by a court'.[68]

As mentioned in the counterpart section of Chapter 4, whilst the first part of this provision may give an applicant the opportunity to rephrase and resubmit the request, the latter part will help ensure that an applicant does not waste resources following the wrong procedure in addition to its specific importance in the Nigeria context where empirical studies have shown that 'ignorance of legal rights' is a major barrier to access to courts in the country.[69]

However, one can also find in section 4(b) of the Act a similar provision as section 7 for written notice to be given to the applicant upon refusal of a request; it is submitted that this provision is largely superfluous and can result in confusion that can limit the public's right to access environmental information as it only provides that the relevant notice should contain 'reasons for the denial, and the section of this Act under which the denial is made'. Apart from failing to meet best practice especially as it does not provide for applicants to be informed of the judicial review process, the scope of the section 4(b) notice is clearly at variance with that of section 7. Therefore, it should be expunged from the FOI Act for the sake of clarity and consistency, which Article 3(1) of the Aarhus Convention mandates. Nevertheless, a later section 7 of the FOI Act is the operative provision dealing with notice of refusal in accordance with the rule of statutory interpretation espoused by the Nigerian Court of Appeal in the decisions referred to earlier.[70]

5.3.1.2.4 WHERE THE INFORMATION/DOCUMENT REQUESTED CONTAINS EXEMPTED MATERIALS

Aligning with best practice, the FOI Act provides that 'where an application is made to a public institution for information which is exempted from disclosure by

68 See further s 7(2) and (3).
69 JG Frynas, 'Problems of access to courts in Nigeria: results of a survey of legal practitioners' (2001) 10(3) *Social and Legal Studies* 397, 408.
70 *Crownstar and Company Ltd* (n 24) and *Ziza* (n 25).

virtue of this Act, the institution shall disclose any part of the information that does not contain such information'.[71] In practice, such exempted information will be marked out or deleted.[72]

5.3.1.3 The charge

Expectedly, the FOI Act provides for fees to be charged for supplying requested information. Section 8 of the Act provides that '[f]ees shall be limited to standard charges for document duplication and transcription where necessary'. It is commendable that this provision expressly states the two activities that will be charged; this will help to avoid the difficulty of determining what is or is not to be charged. Obviously, activities such as public institutions conducting an information search or the applicant examining the requested information in situ, are not chargeable, especially as charges for 'document search' which was contained in the 1999, 2004 and 2007 versions of the FOI Bill was excluded from the FOI Act in line with best practice.

However, even though it is appropriate for the public to bear some financial burden for acquiring environmental information, it may be argued that the above provision, to an extent, falls below best practice as it does not contemplate the affordability or reasonableness of the cost of securing (environmental) information. By permitting the 'standard charges' for duplication and transcription, public institutions are free to transfer the entire cost of these to applicants, irrespective of how prohibitive the cost might be. It is noteworthy that, whilst the 1999, 2004 and 2007 versions of the FOI Bill used the phrase 'reasonable standard charges', 'reasonable' was carefully excluded from the FOI Act, as it appears, to make way for the public to be fully charged in all instances.

As a result, considering the relatively high level of poverty in the Nigeria, many potential applicants are likely to be dissuaded from seeking environmental information,[73] and this will be counter-productive to the aim of the FOI Act, which is to make 'public records and information more freely available'.[74] This is contrary to best practice, which anticipates the public authority picking up a part of the bill incurred by administering the public information access law, especially when in view of the nature of the request the access charge appears prohibitive. For example, the cost of translating requested environmental information to an indigenous Nigerian language may be quite high, especially when the document is relatively voluminous.

Those in the rural areas where English is less commonly spoken will be hit the hardest, considering that poverty is also more prevalent in those areas. Thus, on

71 Section 18.

72 Aarhus Implementation Guide, 92.

73 See Australian Law Reform Commission, *Open Government: A Review of the Federal Freedom of Information Act 1982* (Report 77, January 1996), paras 2.11 and 14.2., available at http://www.alrc.gov.au/sites/default/files/pdfs/publications/ALRC77.pdf (last accessed 1 February 2015).

74 Long title.

the basis that there is already some awareness amongst Nigerian public institutions that the provision of environmental information in local languages is necessary for Nigeria to comply with international best practice,[75] ways of cushioning the cost burden on the public, especially poorer communities, must be explored.

This 'additional' cost on public institutions of providing environmental information is arguably offset by the major contributions of a functional access law to the polity, e.g. in terms of ensuring public accountability and fighting corruption, as well as ensuring that public officials are more professional, ethical and careful in conducting their affairs,[76] the opposite of which usually leads to a huge loss of public funds. Therefore, legal precaution must be taken against the public being dissuaded from using the FOI Act because of high costs on their part. Moreover, over time, as public institutions in Nigeria become more efficient at dealing with public requests and at properly organising and maintaining all information in their custody 'in a manner that facilitates public access to such information' (following section 2(2) of the FOI Act), it is expected that the cost they bear would reduce.[77]

In addition, it is reasonable to expect that the continued advancement of information technology would help make it easier and cheaper for public institutions to provide information to the public.[78] In particular, for example, effort should be put into the development and use of local language translation computer software that will greatly cheapen and accelerate the translation of (large volumes of) requested environmental information from English to a local language; the starting point may well be the three local languages understood by more than half of Nigeria's population – Hausa, Igbo and Yoruba. Also, governmental effort in further increasing the level of public literacy in the English language than is presently the case will eventually help to reduce the need and cost that comes with translation.

Furthermore, contrary to best practice as reflected in the Aarhus Convention, the FOI Act contains no provision for a 'schedule of charges', or the like, to be made available to potential applicants. In view of the benefits relating to clarity and certainty that a 'schedule of charges' can deliver to the system of access to environmental information, including such an obligation in the FOI Act would be a welcome development. A 'schedule of charges' can go a long way to help protect against abuse and inconsistency of charges.[79]

It is impossible to overstate the relevance of such a device in Nigeria where financial corruption is rife in public institutions. Also, a 'schedule of charges' has the potential to encourage the public to access information if they know in advance what it will cost.[80] Nevertheless, despite this lacuna in the Act, the

75 Nigeria's Agenda 21, para 2.12.
76 Information Commissioner of Canada, *Annual Report 1993–94*, 9.
77 See RA Mmadu, 'A critical assessment of Nigeria's Freedom of Information Act 2011' (2011) 1(1) *Sacha Journal of Human Rights* 118, 141.
78 Australian Law Reform Commission (n 73) para 14.19.
79 Aarhus Implementation Guide, 94.
80 Ibid.

schedule to the FOI Act Implementation Guidelines contains a breakdown of the range of costs of the various methods of duplicating records, namely: copying to CD or USB drives (if provided by the public institution), photocopying, scanning and printing. However, the schedule does not provide information about the cost of various types of transcription. It is advisable that the schedule, supported by a binding provision in the FOI Act, be further developed to include such information.

Finally, it is rather disappointing that the FOI Act does not provide for fee waivers at all, as recommended by the Aarhus Convention. As the Aarhus Implementation Guide states, some countries may decide not to levy charges for 'copies of a limited number of pages . . . for non-commercial use or for limited postage'.[81]

Fee waivers would be invaluable in the case of environmental NGOs – many of which have very limited funds to carry out their public interest activities – and members of the public who reside in some of the poorest regions of Nigeria. Generally, such waivers would serve to motivate the public to take advantage of the access rights granted by the FOI Act. The FOI Act Implementation Guidelines provide limited respite in this regard by advising public institutions that: '[w]here the cost of copying or transcription is negligible or where the cost of collecting or recovering the fees would be equal to or greater than the amount being collected, you may provide the information at no cost to the applicant'.[82]

5.3.2 'ACTIVE' ACCESS TO ENVIRONMENTAL INFORMATION

As stated in the preceding chapter, in contrast to 'passive' access, 'active' access to environmental information touches on the positive duty on public institutions publicly to disclose environmental information without waiting for any request from the public. That is, they are generally expected, as required by best practice, proactively to disclose environmental information. The FOI Act makes a similar provision for free proactive disclosure and dissemination of a wide range of information (including environmental information) held by public institutions to the public through various means, including print and electronic media.[83]

The Nigerian National Policy on the Environment is geared towards, amongst other things, achieving 'the publication of up-to-date environmental data and the dissemination of relevant environmental information'.[84] As noted above, the progressive active provision of environmental information in local languages is also necessary to ensure access for those who do not (adequately) understand the English language, and for Nigeria reasonably to comply with best practice on active access. Whilst this will have some cost implications for public institutions, as noted above, the development of language translation computer software can help lessen the cost. This is, however, a wake-up call for the government seriously

81 Ibid.
82 Paragraph 1.11.
83 Section 2(3) and (4).
84 Paragraph 4.0(b).

to focus resources on improving public literacy in the English language, which will over time reduce the need for translation.

As with best practice also, and fundamental to both passive and active access to environmental information, the FOI Act obliges public institutions to possess and update information relevant to their functions.[85] Commendably, the Act goes even further to make it a criminal offence punishable with a minimum of one year's imprisonment for any official of a public institution to destroy wilfully or attempt to doctor or alter records in his/her custody.[86] These provisions are hugely important in ensuring that the Nigerian public has appropriate access to environmental information, considering that it is impossible to give away something that is not owned.

In that regard, the Right to Know NGO has 'learnt of a dangerous practice in the public service of destroying certain documents after a period of seven years'.[87] This is in addition to the alarm raised by Amnesty International based on empirical studies, about the inadequate collection of relevant environmental information by government agencies and oil companies in the Niger Delta,[88] and it aligns with the complaint of 'weak databases and inadequate/inaccurate data' adversely affecting environmental governance in Nigeria.[89]

It is in this light that the implementation of the above provisions is relevant in improving and preserving the stock of environmental information held for public access by public institutions. Moreover, the provisions are, happily, also enforceable by the public (as will be discussed below), which is vital considering that the government barely enforces (environmental) laws against its erring agencies or powerful private enterprises.

5.3.2.1 Effective access to information and ICT[90]

The counterpart section of the preceding chapter refers to how best practice places a responsibility on public institutions to ensure that environmental information is 'effectively accessible'. What this means, and how best practice has embraced ICT for the major role it can and does play in ensuring and delivering the many benefits of effective access, was also discussed.

With respect to electronic access to environmental information in Nigeria, the FOI Act obliges public institutions to 'ensure' that certain enumerated and detailed information about themselves, a list of the information they hold, as well as some specified documents, are 'widely disseminated and made readily available to members of the public through various means, including print, *electronic and*

85 See ss 2(1) and 9(1).
86 Section 10.
87 Right to Know (n 40).
88 Amnesty International (n 18) 48 and 50.
89 Nigeria (n 66).
90 Although treated under 'active' access, the discussion under this sub-heading is generally relevant to 'passive' access to information.

online sources, and at the offices of such public institutions' (emphasis added).[91] And 'although electronic databases can be expensive initially for a public authority, they can later pay for themselves in time and resources saved, not only in answering information requests, but also in providing information for the public authority's own implementation and enforcement initiatives.'[92]

Even though this signifies some progress in the law in Nigeria, on a careful examination of this provision, or any other provision in the FOI Act, one can find that when it comes to 'active' access to information, the emphasis is largely skewed towards making information available to the public and, seemingly contrary to best practice, there is barely any clear mention or allusion to the fact that such information must be effectively accessible in terms of it being presented 'in a user-friendly form that reflects the needs and concerns of the public'[93] as elaborated on in the preceding chapter.

However, it might be possible to infer a level of 'effective accessibility' being called for under sections 9(2) or 2(2) of the FOI Act, which obliges public authorities to 'ensure the *proper organisation* and maintenance of all information in its custody in a manner that facilitates public access to such information' (emphasis added).

Whilst this provision may be sufficient to deal with the very limited issue of properly classifying information (perhaps by making use of a better reference system, which will contribute to effective accessibility), it is arguably too narrow to effectively respond to wider issues of effective accessibility, , including the general public antipathy for, and difficulty in understanding 'raw data', the adequacy of content page, indexing and other guiding tools, the special needs of disabled and illiterate people and, importantly, the cost effectiveness of accessing the information, as well as Nigeria's language diversity. To an extent, in this aspect of effective access, the FOI Act may be argued as falling short of best practice, and should be strengthened to contribute in driving and sustaining better access to environmental information.

What is more, the use of ICT and internet connectivity is growing rapidly in Nigeria among the populace, as noted in Chapter 2. Hence, if public institutions in Nigeria were to begin taking serious and progressive steps towards implementing their obligation proactively to disseminate (environmental) information through 'electronic and online sources', that will go a long way to make access effective and efficient for many of Nigerians with the capacity to take advantage of the opportunity, and reduce the volume of direct requests. This will reduce the resources – in terms of time, personnel and money – that public institutions may need to expend in dealing with direct requests.

However, current reports suggest that public institutions in general are yet to 'fully appreciate the utmost importance of proactive disclosure' as a key

91 See s 2(3) and (4).

92 Aarhus Implementation Guide, 106.

93 J Rowan-Robinson, A Ross, W Walton and J Rothnie, 'Public access to environmental information: a means to what end?' (1996) 8(1) *Journal of Environmental Law* 19, 34.

component of their FOI Act obligation.[94] So they have generally done nothing significant to improve their practice in this regard, especially as it relates to the ICT aspect; e.g. many of them have no functional website with which to share information, and many of those with websites have left them outdated.[95]

Proactive disclosure will usually mean additional cost to public authorities. Therefore, the government and other public institutions must make plans to provide the necessary funding. Obviously, apart from the need for capacity building, public institutions may also have to partner with interested non-governmental bodies with the requisite expertise and resources in order to build and maintain a robust system of (environmental) information dissemination.

5.3.2.2 Specific environmental information (and obligations) under the active duty to collect and disseminate information

As best practice indicates, the active duty on public authorities to make environmental information available to the public cuts across different types of environmental information and obligation. Four of such types which were specifically explored in the previous chapter will now be discussed in comparative perspective with the Nigerian position.

5.3.2.2.1 EMERGENCY INFORMATION

Unlike best practice, neither the FOI Act nor any other Nigerian law specifically addresses dissemination of information in cases of emergency. Even so, to an extent, it might be possible to infer such an obligation from section 2(4) of the FOI Act, which generally obliges public institutions to 'ensure that information referred to in this section [of which section 2(2) makes reference to 'all information' in the custody of public institutions] is widely disseminated . . . to members of the public'. Nonetheless, this provision does not reflect the same level of urgency depicted by best practice.

Whilst the focus of section 2(4) is only on the general public and the obligation it imposes would seem to have been fulfilled once the required information is places in the public domain (e.g. on a website), this arguably falls short of best practice, which expressly requires that 'the public who may be affected'[96] be specifically targeted with the specific information to deal with the emergency situation at hand *every time* there is an 'imminent threat' to humans and the environment. This is as against leaving them to rummage through the diverse information that has been placed in the public domain, seeing that, at such a time, they may not be aware of the information specifically relevant for that situation.

94 Kadiri (n 57).
95 See Right to Know (n 40).
96 For example see Aarhus Convention, art 5.

This is a major gap in the Nigerian regime that will need to be seriously and clearly addressed and made enforceable by the public (in line with best practice), especially for the sake of those in the Niger Delta whose lives and environment are more frequently faced with imminent threats (and eventually negatively impacted) from oil exploration activities. According to information gathered by Amnesty International, even at such times of imminent threat to lives and the environment in the Niger Delta, both the Nigerian Government and the oil companies in which they hold majority stakes usually keep mute and do not release information to the communities that are likely to be affected in order for them to be able to respond appropriately to the imminent danger, especially as no law obliges such disclosure.[97]

On a weaker level, however, the Nigerian National Policy on the environment makes some specific provisions for the gathering and dissemination of emergency information related to natural or man-made environmental disasters. The policy calls for the 'building of a viable network for early warning information dissemination'[98] and for NESREA to pursue strategies that include 'compiling and disseminating information on health and environmental risks from various sources'.[99]

Obviously, these provisions fall short of imposing a duty on (individual) public institutions in times of emergency, even though its implementation might partly improve public access to relevant emergency information. NESREA has the key responsibility to ensure the fulfilment of those provisions of the policy – especially giving section 7(a) of the NESREA Act which obliges it to 'enforce compliance with . . . policies . . . on environmental matters' – but that has not been achieved.

5.3.2.2.2 INFORMATION TO HELP OBTAIN INFORMATION

To a great extent, the Nigerian FOI Act addresses the issue of providing information about the information held by public institutions in order to aid public access to them, in line with best practice. Section 2(3) of the Act obliges public institutions to publish widely, in accordance with sub-section 4, first, a description of the organisation and its responsibilities including that of its divisions, branches and department,[100] and then a list of all classes of information under the control of the institution 'in sufficient details to facilitate the exercise of the right to information',[101] as well as other enumerated classes of information.[102]

Commendably, section 2(3)(f) goes further to provide that 'the title and address of the appropriate officer of the institution to whom an application for information' should be sent, as part of the information to be widely disseminated to the public, even though failure to publish this information 'shall not prejudicially affect the

97 Amnesty International (n 18) 21, 24 ff.
98 Paragraph 5.1(B)(e). See also Nigeria's Agenda 21, para 2.13(1).
99 Paragraph 4.16(l).
100 Section 2(3)(a).
101 Section 2(3)(b)(i).
102 See s 2(3)(b)(ii), (c), (e).

public's right of access to information in the custody of such a public institution'. As at mid-2012, reports suggest that only a very few public institutions have complied with section 2(3)(f), demonstrating a need to enlighten public institutions that implementation of these provisions is vital considering their potential to encourage and make access to environmental information easier and quicker for the public.

5.3.2.2.3 NATIONAL ENVIRONMENTAL REPORT

In Nigeria, even though no such report is usually published contrary to best practice, whatever responsibility there is to publish a national environmental report would naturally fall on the country's apex environmental agency – NESREA. There is no provision in the Nigerian FOI Act from which an obligation on NESREA to produce and disseminate a national environmental report can be clearly inferred, and the only annual report NESREA is expressly mandated to prepare and submit to the Federal Executive Council is limited to 'the activities of the agency' and its 'audited accounts' and does not include information on the state of the environment.[103]

However, here it is argued that it appears NESREA is obliged to publish a national environmental report in accordance with Paragraph 12.1(c) of Nigeria's National Policy on the Environment, 1998, and Paragraph 3.1 (2) of Nigeria's Agenda 21, both of which call for the publication of a periodic national report on the state of the environment, as Section 7(a) of the NESREA Act obliges it to 'enforce compliance with . . . policies . . . on environmental matters'. It is essential that NESREA fulfils this obligation, considering, as noted in the preceding chapter, the importance of a national environmental report as an educative tool in the hands of the public, and one that will be vital in enabling the public to make better personal decisions and engage better in other decision-making processes, especially as it provides a holistic view of the state of the environment.

5.3.2.2.4 PUBLIC ENVIRONMENTAL EDUCATION

The positive impact of widespread public environmental education on environmental participatory democracy and governance, and on the environment itself, has already been discussed in Chapter 3. In Nigeria, the issue is stressed in section 7(i) of the NESREA Act, which obliges NESREA to 'create public awareness and provide environmental education on sustainable environmental management'. Apart from other substantive environmental issues, this will include NESREA and other bodies with responsibility for the environment having to educate the public on their right to access information, decision-making and justice in environmental matters, in order to increase and make actual public access effective, and for its benefits to be realised in society.

103 NESREA Act, s 18.

With reference to the FOI Act, for example, even though there is growing public awareness of the Act and an increasing number engaging their rights under it, 'there is still considerable widespread ignorance about the FOIA among many in Nigeria',[104] especially in the rural areas (with substantial environmental challenges),[105] that needs to addressed by widespread sensitisation campaigns.

In fact, as the Nigerian National Policy on the Environment provides, action must be taken to not only 'review curricula at all levels of the educational system to promote the formal study of environmental concepts and sciences'[106] and foster 'non-formal [environmental] education',[107] but importantly to 'boost environmental awareness and education through the involvement of indigenous social structures, voluntary associations and occupational organizations'[108] and engage 'traditional . . . media'[109] or 'mass and folk media at all levels in the task of public enlightenment'.[110] Furthermore, as argued above, NESREA has the responsibility to ensure that this policy is actioned, even though Nigerian-based empirical research indicates, possibly to a limited extent, that '[c]ompanies have begun educating and sensitising their staff and the communities where they work on environmental issues.'[111]

Relevant public officials will need to be trained to effectively execute their general educative responsibilities. In particular, they will need to be trained, first, as to the import of the FOI Act so they can better educate the public on their rights under it, then, as to the changes that should take place in their operations so that they can better fulfil their obligations under the FOI Act and ensure adequate access for the public. Indicating the importance of this, section 13 of the FOI Act provides that 'every government or public institution must ensure the provision of appropriate training for its officials on the public's right to access to [sic] information . . . held by government or public institutions.'

Although recent reports show that a lot of training workshops are being organised for public officers under the Act,[112] there is the obvious need for that momentum to be sustained and for more to be done considering that current reports also indicate 'low level of understanding of the Act amongst civil servants',[113] which will negatively affect public access to environmental information

104 Right to Know (n 40).

105 E Enonche-Nwankpa, *Communiqué Issued at the End of a Two-day National Conference on the FOI Act 2011 Organised by Right to Know Initiative (r2k), Nigeria*, held in Abuja, Nigeria, on 30–31 July 2013.

106 Paragraph 6.6(c). See also Nigeria's National Agenda 21, paras 5(8) and 9.

107 See para 4.17.

108 Paragraph 6.6(d).

109 Paragraph 4.17(p).

110 Paragraph 6.6(b).

111 R Adomokai and WR Sheate, 'Community participation and environmental decision-making in the Niger delta' (2004) 24 *Environmental Impact Assessment Review* 495, 510.

112 Kadiri (n 57). See also MB Adoke, 'Highlights of the achievements of the Ministry of Justice 2011–2012', presented at the Ministerial Platform at the National Press Centre, Abuja, Nigeria, on 21 May 2012, 7, available at http://fmi.gov.ng/wp-content/uploads/2012/05/ACHIEVEMENTS-OF-THE-MINISTRY-OF-JUSTICE-2011-2012.pdf (last accessed 1 February 2015).

113 See Kadiri (n 57).

and could even increase the amount of court action against the institutions owing to erroneous judgments made by their officials.

Whilst many public institutions are still undergoing FOI training, current reports have noted a lack of capacity building and training in the Nigerian judiciary.[114] In the *Paradigm* case discussed above, Justice Gabriel Kolawole's unacceptable position on section 1(2) of the FOI Act, coupled with his erroneous assertion that such a law, which releases applicants from the need to show a specific interest in the information being applied for does not exist in any other country in the world, highlights the need for even judicial officers and administrative staff of the judiciary to be properly educated on issues relating to the FOI Act and its underlying tenets. This is the responsibility of the Nigeria National Judicial Institute.[115]

On the whole, and in the context of public access to environmental information in Nigeria, this obligation to educate public officers is vital in reorienting them to appreciate the fact that information is held for the benefit of the public and is a developmental tool that must be freely and widely available, as they are used to 'a culture that brands the most innocuous public information as "secret"'.[116]

5.4 Exemptions to public access and the overrides

As expected, the Nigerian FOI Act provides for some exemptions to the right of access to information in order to curtail the excesses of unchecked access that may come with 'undiluted democracy', as discussed in the previous chapters. However, the important question is whether or not the exemption provisions are in line with best practice, that is: narrow enough to allow and sustain adequate access to environmental information, precise enough to curtail the arbitrary exercise of public authority discretion in a manner that would impede appropriate access, and adequately curtailed by a 'public interest override'.

5.4.1 An analysis of the exemptions and overrides

The FOI Act allows public institutions to deny an application for information in the following instances: where its disclosure 'may be injurious to the conduct of international affairs and the defence of . . . Nigeria';[117] where it contains records that, if disclosed, could potentially interfere with a law-backed administrative or law enforcement proceedings conducted by any public institution, or could deprive a person of a fair trial or obstruct an ongoing criminal investigation;[118]

114 Ibid.

115 See http://nji.gov.ng/.

116 See L Idowu, 'Nigeria's new FOI law brings celebration, challenges', *Committee to Protect Journalists*, 7 July 2011, available at http://cpj.org/blog/2011/07/nigerias-new-foi-law-brings-celebration-challenges.php (last accessed 1 February 2015).

117 Section 11(1).

118 Section 12(1)(a)(i), (ii), (iii) and (vi). See also s 12(4).

where the information contains personal details of an individual who has not consented to its disclosure;[119] where the information contains confidential or proprietary trade secrets and commercial or financial information obtained from a person or business, or its disclosure may cause harm to a third party;[120] where the information, if disclosed, would frustrate procurement or give an advantage to any person;[121] where the information is subject to professional confidential privileges conferred by an Act;[122] and where the information contains research material prepared by faculty members.[123] These are all consistent with best practice as reflected in Article 4(4) of the Aarhus Convention.

The FOI Act, however, diverges from best practice by including an exemption that directly and negatively impacts on public access to environmental information and its benefits to society. Section 15(2) of the Act provides that '[a] public institution shall . . . deny disclosure of a part of a record if that part contains the result or product of environmental testing carried out by or on behalf of a public institution' whether or not any interest is adversely affected;[124] unlike a similar provision in the Canadian information law which generally obliges government institutions *not* to refuse disclosure of 'results of product or environmental testing'.[125] In addition, the FOI Act does not provide any (restrictive) details as to the scope of the broad and ambiguous 'environmental testing' phrase. The term may mean only the testing of a product to determine its suitability in certain environmental conditions or its potential impact on the environment; or it could simply mean the testing of the quality of the environment, amongst others.

This gap in the FOI Act leaves the interpretation to the discretion of public institutions, which they may choose to exercise in a manner that considerably limits public access to environment information. Therefore, it is submitted that section 15(2) should be revised or struck from the Act as it runs contrary to both international best practice, as well as the Nigerian National Policy on the Environment, which arguably advocates wide access to environmental information.[126] The section could be replaced with an exemption similar to the one set out in Article 4(4)(h) of the Aarhus Convention that seeks to protect certain aspects of the environment where disclosure of information relating to it would adversely affect it.

Furthermore, it can be argued that a number of other exemptions under the FOI Act have been drafted too broadly and their operation has been left entirely to the discretion of public institutions. In line with best practice, some exemptions provide for the 'public interest test' (or override) to the effect that 'an application

119 Section 14(1) and (2).
120 Section 15(1)(a).
121 Section 15(1)(c).
122 Section 16.
123 Section 17.
124 See s 15(3) of the Act.
125 See s 20(2) of the Access to Information Act, RSC, 1985, c A-1, available at http://laws-lois.justice.gc.ca/PDF/A-1.pdf (last accessed 1 February 2015).
126 Paragraph 6.6(f).

for information shall not be denied where the public interest in disclosing the information outweighs whatever injury that disclosure would cause'.[127] However, the section 15(2) 'environmental testing' exemption discussed above is not made subject to the 'public interest override', contrary to best practice.

Similarly, the exemption on 'research materials' in section 17 fails to provide for the 'public interest override'. In addition, even though the 'personal information' exemption in section 14 contains a 'public interest override' in sub-section 3, the effect of this override is largely nullified as it is made subject to section 14(2), which provides for public disclosure of personal information where 'the individual to whom it relates consents to the disclosure' or where 'the information is [already] publicly available'. Indeed, the 'public interest override' is needed when the individual to whom the information relates is yet to consent to its disclosure and the information is not publicly available.

Blatantly, the FOI Act Implementation Guidelines refers to the exemptions in sections 15(2) and 17 as 'unqualified exemptions' which 'contain an inbuilt prejudice test' (rather than a 'public interest' test).[128] This test means that 'the harm to the public interest that would result from the disclosure of information falling within an unqualified exemption has already been established.'[129] This position is unacceptable as it falls below international best practice, especially as no authority can rightly foresee, in absolute terms, the fact that there would never be a stronger public interest which would warrant disclosure of exempted information.

Furthermore, given that the FOI Act is not focused on environmental matters alone, it makes no express provision for an 'emissions' override, as the Aarhus Convention does. However, it is reasonable to argue that in cases where there are emissions, information about the emissions should be disclosed or disclosable, at least under the public interest override, in view of the fact that such emissions have the potential seriously to affect public health and wellbeing, as well as the environment.

There is the further issue that even though section 1(1) of the FOI Act guarantees the public's right of access to (environmental) information '[n]otwithstanding anything contained in any Act, law or regulation', this may not apply to the Public Complaints Commissions (PCC) Act and the National Security Agencies (NSA) Act, both of which contain general provisions empowering the bodies they create to withhold information from the public. These Acts are entrenched in the Nigerian Constitution (to which all laws are subject) by virtue of section 315, and this provision has not been amended in line with section 9(2) of the Constitution to exclude those Acts.

To achieve international best practice, it is imperative that the PCC Act and the NSA Act be made subject to the FOI Act, even though most of the environmental

127 For example see s 11(2).
128 Paragraph 1.13.1. Section 16 also contains one of the unqualified exemptions.
129 FOI Act, s 11(2).

information that they may hold may legitimately fall under the exemptions pertaining to national security and enforcement procedures under the FOI Act. However, if they were made subject to the FOI Act, the bodies created under them would have to apply the 'public interest test' when deciding whether or not to make relevant environmental information available to the public, unlike the current situation where those bodies are not clearly obliged to do so.

Surprisingly, section 26(a) of the FOI Act completely exempts 'published material or material available for purchase by the public' from the application of the Act. Whilst this exemption might refer to materials covered by intellectual property rights, which could potentially justify their exclusion under best practice (although it could still fall short for not being made subject to the 'public interest test'), the use of an open phrase such as 'published material' to describe the exempted material can easily foster broad interpretations. It could mean that *any* information that has been put into the public domain through *any* medium is not subject to the FOI Act.

This is the interpretation given to that provision in the FOI Act Implementation Guidelines.[130] The Guidelines justify this position by stating that: 'if there is another route by which someone can obtain information, there is no need for the Act to provide the person with further means of access to records.'[131] This is an unacceptable justification for the exclusion for a number of reasons, which is arguably contrary to best practice.

First, the public might face prohibitive costs for accessing or obtaining a copy of such environmental information, costs that could have been mitigated if the applicant had been able to request a cheaper (or possibly free) version of the same information. Second, there might be geographical (and resulting cost) barriers to the access of environmental information that is made publicly accessible only from a single point, say, a relatively remote public library. Third, publicly available environmental information may not be effectively accessible to members of the public with special needs who no longer have the right to request transcribed or useful versions of this information from the relevant public institution. The section 26(a) exemption is also capable of undermining section 2(4) of the FOI Act, which obliges public institutions to make information 'readily available to members of the public through various means, including print, electronic and online sources, and at the office of such public institution', as materials could have been 'published' through a single medium and, it can be argued, based on section 26(a), not to be subject to section 2(4), which is largely in line with best practice.

In summary, it is argued that generally the exemptions in the FOI Act are too broad, with the override failing to cover all exemptions in line with best practice. This is arguably a reflection of the Nigerian Government's culture of official secrecy, and its practice of exclusionism in law-making and governance discussed

130 See paras 1.2 and 12.1.1.
131 Paragraph 12.1.1.

in Chapter 2, even though the present provisions are a marked improvement from the days when the Official Secrets Act held sway.

5.4.2 Exemptions not provided for

The FOI Act does not contain an exemption similar to that in Article 4(3)(b) of the Aarhus Convention pertaining to where '[t]he request is manifestly unreasonable or formulated in too general a manner'. To avoid conflict and promote the efficient implementation of the law, it may be vital for a similar provision to be included in the FOI Act because in reality some requests would be 'manifestly unreasonable' and so incapable of being granted, or be 'formulated in too general a manner' such that a refusal might be the only rational decision.

Considering that the Article 4(3)(b) exemption is not specifically made a ground for refusal in the FOI Act and that section 7(1) of the Act mandates public institutions to state 'the specific provision' of the Act that relates to its ground(s) for refusal in the written notice to the applicant, it becomes obvious that a public institution would have been placed in a dilemma or a legally impossible position when such a situation occurs. However, if this Article 4(3)(b) exemption is subsequently enshrined in the FOI Act, it must be made subject to an obligation on public institutions to make a reasonable effort to assist and guide the applicant in making a grantable request, as indicated under the Aarhus Convention, to ensure that it is not used unjustifiably or unreasonably to restrict access to environmental information.

Likewise, it may be important for an exemption similar to that in Article 4(3)(c) of the Aarhus Convention, which 'concerns material in the course of completion or concerns internal communications of public authorities', to be made part of the FOI Act. This is because materials in the course of completion may not be suitable for public consumption, and its disclosure may even serve as a major source of distraction for the officials of the public institution actively working on the issue(s) to which that incomplete material relates.

Also, with respect to 'internal communications' of public institutions, amongst others, its protection is important because in reality officials in such institutions routinely share information that helps the institution fulfil its responsibility to the public, which information these officials may not be willing to disclose if it might easily become public knowledge. In other words, the exemption in Article 4(3)(c) may be necessary to allow public institutions to function properly for the public good, and to avoid a situation where public access rights breed consequences that are not in the interest of the public in the long run.

5.5 Enforcing the right to access (environmental) information

According to Neuman, '[i]f there is a widespread belief that the access to information law will not be [adequately] enforced, this right to information becomes meaningless'.[132] Generally in line with best practice, section 1(3) of the FOI Act provides a general right to 'any person entitled to the right to information under the Act' to 'institute proceedings in Court to compel any public institution to comply with the provisions of this Act',[133] including as it relates to active and passive access rights. Specifically on passive access and largely in line with best practice on this note, the FOI Act provides that:

> *[a]ny applicant* who has been denied access to information, or a part thereof, may apply to the Court for a review of the matter within 30 days after the public institution denies or is deemed to have denied the application, or within such further time as the Court may either before or after the expiration of the 30 days fix or allow.[134]

Unlike the Aarhus Convention, the FOI Act does not provide for review by an administrative authority or an independent and impartial body other than a court of law. The provision for such (a usually first tier) alternative access route to justice would have been a major way of reducing the cost of review procedures for the public, many of whom may not be able to access the courts owing to the high costs involved and considering the relatively high level of poverty in the country, as empirical research shows.[135]

Currently, Nigeria's legal aid scheme does not apply to the enforcement of the public rights under the FOI Act. However, if a current proposition by some civil society groups in Nigeria for NGOs (such as the Right to Know) to 'maintain and publicise a database of lawyers offering *pro bono* services on the FOIA'[136] does materialise, that will certainly contribute to widening access to justice for the public. The civil society groups may consider partnering with the Nigerian Legal Aid Council to realise this ideal, as well as with the National Youth Service Corps to make provision for lawyers on national service to contribute to the scheme.

However, an alternative administrative review procedure would at least save many aggrieved applicants the high cost of filing court processes and paying a lawyer, as a way of reducing the cost barrier of access to justice, whilst seeking additional measures to reduce such barriers. Chidi Odinkalu, who chairs the Governing Council of the National Human Rights Commission (and a key player in the fight for the FOI Act), has reasonably suggested the Commission (which is largely independent of government) as such a forum for enforcing the rights in the FOI Act;[137] this is a good idea (especially when one considers the human rights

132 L Neuman, *Enforcement Models: Content and Context* (Washington DC: World Bank, 2009) 1, available at http://siteresources.worldbank.org/EXTGOVACC/Resources/LNEumanATI.pdf (last accessed 1 February 2015).
133 See also s 2(6).
134 Section 20 (emphasis added).
135 Frynas (n 69) 406.
136 Enonche-Nwankpa (n 105).
137 CA Odinkalu, 'Myths about the FOI Act', *Right to Know*, 25 August 2011, available at http://www.r2knigeria.org/index.php/undestanding-the-foia-2011 (last accessed 1 February 2015).

nature of the right of the public to access (environmental) information as explored earlier), and the Commission's capacity can certainly be bolstered to enable it to play this vital role. Administrative review procedures are generally less complex than even summary court procedures, and so will be easier for the public, in a country such as Nigeria with a relatively high level of illiteracy, to access.

The general principle of law, as well as best practice, which stipulates that such review procedures provide 'adequate and effective remedies', seems generally to have been met by the FOI Act, which empowers the court to order the disclosure of the information in question (subject to such conditions as the court deems appropriate) if it makes a finding of wrongful denial.[138] This is in addition to wrongful denial being criminalised and the defaulting public institution or officer (potentially) held liable to a fine of ₦500,000 (£2000).[139]

The general principle and best practice of being 'fair and equitable' in review procedures is also partly reflected in section 24 of the FOI Act, which places the burden of proof on the public authority concerned to establish that it is authorised to deny an application. Acknowledging that being fair and equitable is mostly an issue of practice, there is as yet no known complaint from those who have litigated based on the FOI Act that the procedure is otherwise from the various reports written on the process.

Furthermore, in line with best practice as it relates to the review process being 'timely', the deputy executive director of Media Rights Agenda (MRA) (a major player in the fight for the FOI Act), Ms Jennifer Onyejekwe, has noted that: '[w]e are even more delighted that despite the notorious slow pace of adjudication of cases in Nigerian courts, all of these cases [which MRA has litigated based on the FOI Act] have been decided relatively speedily.'[140] In the main, this good news is made possible by section 21 of the FOI Act, which provides that an application for review of a matter made to the court 'shall be heard and determined summarily'.

In the recent case of *Legal Defence and Assistance Project (Gte) Ltd v Clerk of the National Assembly of Nigeria*,[141] where the court held the respondent had wrongfully denied disclosure, the judge, Hon. Justice Balkisu Aliyu, held that 'summarily' under section 21 of the Act means that such application be heard and determined 'promptly and in a simple manner' void of the usual procedural technicalities (under which some respondents/defendants hide to prolong cases unduly and frustrate applicants/plaintiffs).[142] In addition, the relatively less complex administrative review procedure can ensure a similar, if not a faster, review process.

138 Section 25.
139 FOI Act, s 7(5).
140 'MRA lauds judiciary for upholding right to information', *ThisDay*, 30 May 2013, available at http://www.thisdaylive.com/articles/mra-lauds-judiciary-for-upholding-right-to-information/148909/ (last accessed 1 February 2015).
141 Unreported, Suit No FHC/ABJ/CS/805/2011, 25 June 2012.
142 Ibid, 11–12.

From the few reports available, one can say the Nigerian courts have largely done well in ensuring access to information. In support, Ms Jennifer Onyejekwe stated that MRA was 'heartened to note that in almost all the cases that have gone to court, the courts have unequivocally upheld the right of members of the public to access information under the Act and have accordingly ordered the concerned public institutions to disclose the information requested'.[143] However, the rate at which applicants whose requests have been refused have had to head to court before the public institution concerned released the requested information is worryingly high. According to Chino Obiagwu of Legal Defence and Assistance Project, they have 'made request to more than 30 organisations, it is only in one case that the information was provided unhindered and in most cases we had to go to court and ask the court to order that the information be provided'.[144]

The Right to Know NGO has a similar experience.[145] Ms Jennifer Onyejekwe has also noted that: 'it is regrettable that most public institutions are leaning in favour of the option of being dragged to court, where they proffer ridiculous defences that are invariably slammed by the courts.'[146] In fact, in one of such recent cases – *Public and Private Development Centre Ltd v Power Holding Company of Nigeria Plc and the Attorney General of the Federation*[147] – the court held that the respondent's (a public institution) 'processes and arguments lack substance, [are] frivolous, time wasting and an abuse of Court process', having no justification whatsoever to deny the applicant's information request.[148]

This attitude of public institutions in general only goes to show the 'lack of desire by public officers to shift [willingly] from a culture of secrecy to that of transparency', given their century-long operation under various laws of secrecy, as even the Head of Civil Service of the Federation, Bukar Aji, admitted.[149] This attitude has the potential to affect the implementation of the Act negatively, considering its potential to discourage members of the public who may not be able to access the courts from seeking relevant information and the costly nature of access for those who choose to engage the review procedure. It is also a waste of time, especially if the decisions are appealed, and may even render the information useless where its use is time sensitive, e.g. in cases of participation in environmental decision-making processes. Such attitude is also costly for the public institution that will frequently be sued, and this amounts to a regrettable waste of public resources that ought to have been spent improving the information access procedures in the various public institutions.

All this highlights the need (continually) to ensure, on the whole, an effective and easy-to-access review mechanism, considering its importance in trumping the

143 *ThisDay* (n 140).
144 A Bamgboye, 'Nigeria: officials yet to come to terms with FOIA', *Daily Trust*, 12 September 2013.
145 Right to Know (n 40).
146 Ibid.
147 Unreported, Suit No FHC/ABJ/CS/582/2012, 1 March 2013.
148 Ibid, 10.
149 *Punch* (n 52).

lingering culture of secrecy amongst public institutions in Nigeria: 'Weak or ineffectual enforcement mechanisms can lead to arbitrary denials or encourage agency silence.'[150] So far, from the available cases in which the court held that there had been wrongful denial of access, the court has only ordered a release of the information in line with the pleadings filed; it is submitted that the additional imposition of the section 7(5) fine will contribute in making public institutions/ officers lean towards better compliance with their obligation to ensure access (and not unduly pursue an appeal to the court if there were to be a first tier administrative review procedure) and this will ultimately reduce the number of FOI cases brought to court. However, since criminal cases are currently only instituted by the government or with its permission, it is doubtful whether an Attorney-General will (effectively) prosecute a public institution/officer under section 7(5).

5.6 Conclusion

The above comparative analysis and discussion shows that Nigerian law on access to environmental information has made considerable strides towards achieving the standards reflected in international best practice. The small case law and practice of ensuring access to information which has developed so far in the field also shows a level of advancement from what used to be the case in Nigeria, judging from the discussions in Chapter 2.

Nevertheless, the analysis shows some critical gaps in the Nigerian law and practice of ensuring access to environmental information and, generally, recommends that more still needs to be done in that regard for Nigeria to meet the standards of its international commitments as reflected by best practice, which will ensure better access for the Nigerian public. The discussion also indicates that whatever steps will be taken to improve the information to access law and practice in Nigeria in an environmental context must be taken in consideration of the relevant prevailing non-legal factors in the country, including corruption, language diversity, poverty, ICT penetration, etc.

The improvement of any law and practice, including Nigeria's, with respect to public access to environmental law is crucial for the many reasons previously highlighted, not the least of which is its vital contribution to enabling the public to participate effectively in environmental decision-making processes. It is to this – public participation in environmental decision-making – that we now turn.

Bibliography

Abdallah NM, 'We are not bound by FOI Act – NNPC', *Daily Trust*, 31 July 2012.

Adoke MB, 'Highlights of the achievements of the Ministry of Justice 2011–2012', presented at the Ministerial Platform at the National Press Centre, Abuja, Nigeria, on 21 May 2012, available at http://fmi.gov.ng/wp-content/uploads/2012/05/

150 Neuman (n 132).

ACHIEVEMENTS-OF-THE-MINISTRY-OF-JUSTICE-2011-2012.pdf (last accessed 1 February 2015).

Adomokai R and Sheate WR, 'Community participation and environmental decision-making in the Niger delta' (2004) 24 *Environmental Impact Assessment Review* 495.

Amnesty International, *Nigeria: Petroleum, Pollution and Poverty in the Niger Delta* (London: Amnesty International Publication, 2009).

Attorney-General of the Federation, 'Implementation of the Freedom of Information Act 2011 and the Reporting Requirements under Section 29 Thereof', a Memorandum (HAGF/MDAS/FOIA/2012/I) issued on 28 January 2012.

Aturu B, 'CBN governor replies to Freedom of information request', *Sahara Reporter*, 3 February 2013, available at http://saharareporters.com/article/cbn-governor-replies-freedom-information-request-bamidele-aturu (last accessed 1 February 2015).

Australian Law Reform Commission, *Open Government: A Review of the Federal Freedom of Information Act 1982* (Report 77, January 1996), available at http://www.alrc.gov.au/sites/default/files/pdfs/publications/ALRC77.pdf (last accessed 1 February 2015).

Bamgboye A, 'Nigeria: officials yet to come to terms with FOIA', *Daily Trust*, 12 September 2013.

Ebbesson J, 'The Notion of public participation in international environmental law' (1997) 8 *Yearbook of International Environmental Law* 51.

Ebbesson J, Gaugitsch G, Jendroska J, Marshal F and Stec S, *The Aarhus Convention: An Implementation Guide* (2nd edn, New York and Geneva: UN, 2014).

Enonche-Nwankpa E, *Communiqué Issued at the End of a Two-day National Conference on the FOI Act 2011 Organised by Right to Know Initiative (r2k), Nigeria*, held in Abuja, Nigeria, on 30–31 July 2013.

Frynas JG, 'Problems of access to courts in Nigeria: results of a survey of legal practitioners' (2001) 10(3) *Social and Legal Studies* 397.

Idowu L, 'Nigeria's new FOI law brings celebration, challenges', *Committee to Protect Journalists*, 7 July 2011, available at http://cpj.org/blog/2011/07/nigerias-new-foi-law-brings-celebration-challenges.php (last accessed 1 February 2015).

Information Commissioner of Canada, *Annual Report 1993–94*, 9.

International Business Publications, *Nigeria: Mineral, Mining Sector Business investment Guide – Volume 1 – Oil and Gas Industry Strategic Information and Regulations* (Washington DC: International Business Publications, 2013).

Kadiri M, 'Implementing Nigeria's Freedom of Information Act, 2011: the journey so far', presented at the National Conference on the Freedom of Information Act (2011), held in Abuja, Nigeria, on 30–31 July 2013.

Mmadu RA, 'A critical assessment of Nigeria's Freedom of Information Act 2011' (2011) 1(1) *Sacha Journal of Human Rights* 118.

Nawpi C, 'International treaties in Nigerian and Canadian courts' (2011) 19(1) *African Journal of International and Comparative Law* 38.

Neuman L, *Enforcement Models: Content and Context* (Washington DC: World Bank, 2009), available at http://siteresources.worldbank.org/EXTGOVACC/Resources/LNEumanATI.pdf (last accessed 1 February 2015).

Nigeria, 'Institutional aspects of sustainable development in Nigeria', presented by the Government of Nigeria to the 5th session of the United Nations Commission on Sustainable Development, held in New York, on 7–25 April 1997, available at http://www.un.org/esa/agenda21/natlinfo/countr/nigeria/inst.htm#info (last accessed 1 February 2015).

Odinkalu CA, 'Myths about the FOI Act', *Right to Know*, 25 August 2011, available at http://www.r2knigeria.org/index.php/undestanding-the-foia-2011 (last accessed 1 February 2015).

Ojo E, 'FOI Act: where his lordship got it wrong', *Vanguard*, 6 August 2013, available at http://www.vanguardngr.com/2013/08/foi-act-where-his-lordship-got-it-wrong/ (last accessed 1 February 2015).

Okafor C, 'NNPC Says it's bound by provisions of FOI Act', *ThisDay*, 11 August 2012, available at http://www.thisdaylive.com/articles/nnpc-says-its-bound-by-provisions-of-foi-act/122090/ (last accessed 1 February 2015).

Okontoni O, 'Problems and prospects of Nigerian bureaucracy' (2001) 7(3) *Journal of Social Science* 223.

Osaghae EE, *Crippled Giant: Nigeria since Independence* (London: Hurst & Co Publishers Ltd, 1998).

Punch, 'Head of service want review of FOI timeline', *Punch*, 31 July 2013, available at http://www.punchng.com/news/head-of-service-wants-review-of-foi-timeline/ (last accessed 1 February 2015).

Right to Know, 'A report on the level of awareness, compliance and implementation of the Freedom of Information Act, 2011, 18 months after its enactment' (2012), available at http://r2knigeria.org/index.php/downloads/foi-assessments-a-reports (last accessed 1 February 2015).

Roberts A, 'A great and revolutionary law? The first four years of India's Right to Information Act' (2010) 70(6) *Public Administration Review* 925.

Rowan-Robinson J, Ross A, Watton W and Rothnie J, 'Public access to environmental information: a means to what end?' (1996) 8(1) *Journal of Environmental Law* 19.

Shell Group, 'Shell general business principles', 1976 (last revised in 2005), Principle 7 (on 'Communication and Engagement'), available at http://www.shell.com/content/dam/shell/static/public/downloads/corporate-pkg/sgbp-english.pdf (last accessed 15 February 2015).

Shelton D and Kiss A, *Judicial Handbook on Environmental Law* (Nairobi: UNEP, 2005).

ThisDay, 'MRA lauds judiciary for upholding right to information', *ThisDay*, 30 May 2013, available at http://www.thisdaylive.com/articles/mra-lauds-judiciary-for-upholding-right-to-information/148909/ (last accessed 1 February 2015).

6 Public participation in environmental decision-making: international best practice principles

6.1. Introduction

In view of the established invaluableness of adequate and meaningful public participation in environmental decision-making processes, the concept is a fundamental one in international environmental law. Given this premise, the aim of this chapter is critically to evaluate what may generally be considered international best practice in terms of law and practice on public access to, or participation in, environmental decision-making processes that could effectively ensure adequate access in this regard. This discussion will generally clarify and provide further understanding of the development of this area of procedural environmental rights, as well as providing a reasonable and useful comparative basis on which to analyse and recommend improvements to Nigerian law and practice on access to environmental decision-making processes in the subsequent chapter.

The framing of the international best practice principles in this chapter will have the relevant provisions of the Aarhus Convention as its central theme, which Convention, according to Applestrand, can ensure that public participation has 'a decisive influence on the outcome of the decision-making process' and is 'neither an illusory spectacle, delivering nothing more than a veneer of democratic participation, nor merely a pro forma matter'.[1] There is also the publication by the International Association for Impact Assessment (IAIA)[2] entitled 'Public Participation – International Best Practice Principles',[3] which principles are generally in alignment with the relevant provisions of the Aarhus Convention and will be referred to below.

1 M Appelstrand, 'Participation and societal values: the challenge for lawmakers and policy practitioners' (2002) 4 *Forest Policy and Economics* 281, 288.

2 IAIA is 'the leading global network on best practice in the use of impact assessment for informed decision making regarding policies, programs, plans and projects' with members from diverse professions representing more than 120 countries. See http://www.iaia.org/about/ (last accessed 2 February 2015).

3 P André with B Enserink, D Connor and P Croal, *Public Participation: International Best Practice Principles* (Special Publication Series No 4, North Dakota: IAIA, 2006) 1–3.

In support of the functionality of IAIA's international best practice principles, they were 'built on the experience in PP [public participation] of many IAIA members . . . Accordingly, the principles . . . are broad, generic, and non-prescriptive',[4] allowing for adaptation in various contexts. Also, in elucidating best practice, effort will be made to demonstrate how the relevant Aarhus Convention's provisions generally overlap, emphasise or amplify existing provisions of some other international regimes to which Nigeria is directly committed.

In view of the above, the analysis below will cover three main areas: public participation and the concept of 'good faith'; public participation in activity-specific decisions; and public participation in non-activity-specific decisions.

6.2 Public participation in good faith

It is important to note a key principle that should guide authorities involved in ensuring public participation in environmental decision-making and under which they could be held accountable: the general principle of 'good faith'. Good faith is generally 'an open norm, a norm the content of which cannot be established in an abstract way but which depends on the circumstances of the case in which it must be applied, and which must be established through concretisation'.[5] At the very least, one can generally describe it as dealing with the duty on parties having legal relations to act in a fair and equitable manner towards each other, eschewing undue influence, fraud or any malicious intent.[6] In the context of public participation, it would also mean that such an exercise is genuine and considerate of the special capacities of the parties, and that the outcome is not pre-determined.

Upholding good faith as a general principle of law, the International Court of Justice (ICJ) and arbitral tribunals have severally used it to hold states accountable for their actions in cases dealing with international environmental issues.[7] Also, this principle that public participation in environmental decision-making should be carried out in good faith takes central place in a number of treaties[8] and soft laws[9] which are relevant to Nigeria, the implementation of which will significantly increase the possibility of successful public participation in decision-making. Similarly, even though the Aarhus Convention does not mention good faith, it

4 Ibid, 1.

5 MW Hesselink, 'The concept of good faith', in AS Hartkamp; MW Hesselink, E Hondius, C Mak and E du Perron, *Towards a European Civil Code* (4th edn, The Hague: Kluwer Law International, 2010) 619, 622.

6 See *Black's Law Dictionary* (8th edn, 2004), 'Good faith'.

7 For example see *Nuclear Test Cases*, judgment, ICJ Reports 1974, 475, para 49, available at http://www.icj-cij.org/docket/files/59/6159.pdf (last accessed 2 February 2015); and *Pacific Fur Seal Arbitration* (1893) 1 Moore's International Arbitration 755. See also P Sands and J Peel, *Principles of International Environmental Law* (3rd edn, Cambridge: Cambridge University Press, 2012) 118.

8 For example International Labour Organisation Convention Concerning Indigenous and Tribal Peoples in Independent Countries (No 169), 27 June 1989, (1989) 28 ILM 1382, art 6(2).

9 See Rio Declaration, Principles 10, 19 and 27. See also Agenda 21, ch 27, para 27.2; and André and others (n 3) 3 and 2.

obliges states to ensure that authorities 'assist and provide guidance to the public . . . in facilitating participation in decision-making'.[10]

This duty arguably has a similar effect to the good faith principle as, for instance, it would be unacceptable for authorities entrusted with such a responsibility to take undue advantage of the public during participation by exploiting whatever imbalance of power or influence existing between the parties in order to co-opt them, rather than cooperate with them. In support, the Aarhus Compliance Committee, which interprets the Convention in a purposive manner,[11] would arguably agree with that position and not allow authorities to use the participation process to manipulate the public in ways not in line with the objective and purpose of the regime.

The principle of good faith also extends to the manner in which laws are interpreted where the interests of various parties are at stake. It is a 'criterion of interpretation. To interpret a legal text be it a contract or a treaty or a statute in accordance with good faith is to interpret it according to its real spirit and not to interpret it strictly.'[12] Although a particular regime concerning public participation may not expressly mention 'good faith', there is hardly a reasonable reason to doubt that its interpretation and implementation should in fact be based on it.[13]

6.3 Public participation in activity-specific decisions

6.3.1 Issues on scope

No matter how elaborate the rights and duties created by a regime on public participation in environmental decision-making on specific activities may be, if its scope, in terms of the general aspects of the holders of rights and obligations and the activities covered, is unreasonably narrow or unclear, the worth of that regime is automatically put in question. In analysing international best practice with respect to these issues of scope, the focus in this section will be on: (1) the issue of who can participate; (2) the body required to ensure participation; and (3) the activities open for participation.

6.3.1.1 Who can participate?

'The public concerned' can clearly be identified as holding the rights to participate in environmental decision-making on specific activities under Article 6 of the Aarhus Convention, as well as under the Bali Guidelines[14] and Principle 10 of

10 Article 3(2).

11 For example see *Belgium* ACCC/C/2005/11, ECE/MP.PP/C.1/2006/4/Add.2, 28 July 2006, para 34. See also V Koester, 'The Compliance Committee of the Aarhus Convention: an overview of procedures and jurisprudence' (2007) 37(2–3) *Environmental Policy and Law* 83, 91.

12 See 'Bonne foi' in Dictionnaire de la culture juridique (2003) (meaning: 'Good faith' in Dictionary of Legal Culture).

13 See Hesselink (n 5) 620–21.

14 See Guidelines 8–10.

the Rio Declaration, amongst others. 'The public concerned' has been defined broadly as:

> . . . the public affected or likely to be affected by, or having an interest in, the environmental decision-making; for the purposes of this definition, non-governmental organizations promoting environmental protection and meeting any requirements under national law shall be deemed to have an interest.[15]

Although the above definition is obviously narrower than that of 'the public',[16] it is quite broad and in line with the discussion on the concerned public in Chapter 3: it goes further than the usual restrictive 'sufficient interest' phrase found in many legal texts and case law, to apply to members of the public with merely 'an interest' or 'likely to be affected'; it does not require that a person shows *legal* interest, *factual* interest may be sufficient; and although the inclusion of NGOs may be based on requirements set in national law, there are limits to such requirements as they must be consistent with the objectives and principles of the Aarhus Convention, which includes non-discrimination[17] and avoidance of 'technical or financial barriers to registration' – only objective requirements that are not unnecessarily exclusionary, overly burdensome or politically motivated, will be lawful.[18]

This liberality with which NGOs must be welcomed into the participatory process, a positive influence of the pluralist thoughts discussed in Chapter 3, is further espoused under Article 3(4) of the Aarhus Convention, which places an obligation on states to 'provide for appropriate recognition of and support' to bodies promoting environmental protection, 'and ensure that its national legal system is consistent with this obligation'.[19]

An important query here is whether 'the public concerned' relates only to the domestic public or includes the public abroad. In view of the manner in which the definition of 'the public concerned' is couched, there is no difficulty in concluding that relevant foreign public may fall within it and so be entitled to participate in relevant environmental decision-making processes.[20] This position is established by Article 3(9) of the Aarhus Convention, which prohibits discrimination in the application of the Convention's provisions on the grounds of nationality, domicile,

15 Aarhus Convention, art 2(5). See also footnote to Bali Guideline 8.
16 See ibid, art 2(4).
17 See ibid, art 3(9); and *Ukraine* ACCC/C/2004/3, ECE/MP.PP/C.1/2005/2/Add.3, 14 March 2005, paras 26–28.
18 Aarhus Implementation Guide, 58.
19 Agenda 21, ch 27, para 27.1.
20 J Jendroska, 'Public participation in environmental decision-making: interactions between the convention and EU law and other key legal issues in its implementation in the light of the opinion of the Aarhus Convention Compliance Committee', in M Pallemaerts (ed), *The Aarhus Convention at Ten: Interactions and Tensions Between Conventional International Law and EU Environmental Law* (Groningen: Europa Law Publishing, 2011) 92, 129.

citizenship or seat. Based on that provision, the Aarhus Implementation Guide has stated that: 'where the area potentially affected by a proposed activity crosses an international border, members of the public in the neighbouring country might be members of the "public concerned" for the purpose of Article 6'.[21]

In agreement with that view, the Aarhus Compliance Committee has held, in a case related to Ukraine, that foreign or international environmental NGOs that had 'expressed an interest in or concern about the procedure' fall under Article 2(5) as 'the public concerned', and that provision for notification and participation in accordance with Article 6 ought to have been made for individuals and NGOs in neighbouring Romania who expressed, to the Romanian authorities, an interest in or concern about the project in issue to the knowledge of the Ukrainian Government.[22] The Committee further stated that 'such notification and participation could have been undertaken by Ukraine via the Romanian authorities', whilst admitting the need to develop clear guidance on exactly how members of the public in one country can be involved in the decision-making process of another.[23]

Moving on, it has been posited that 'the public'[24] in general is entitled to some limited participation under Article 6 of the Aarhus Convention.[25] This position arises from Article 6(7) and (9) which, respectively, expressly empowers 'the public' to submit comments for consideration, and be informed of the final decision. The Bali Guidelines adopts a similar approach.[26] Nonetheless, in practice, one may find that the right under Article 6(7) is mainly, if not only, exercisable by 'the public concerned', which to an extent may arguably make compliance with Article 6(9) seem somewhat absurd in this context. This might be the case because it is only 'the public concerned' that may have access to the extensive information that is necessary to make proper participation possible (e.g. the right to be informed of the existence of an application for a proposed activity, time and venue of public hearing, information on which public authority or body comments should be submitted to, the potential impact of the proposed activity on the environment etc.).[27]

So if 'the public' in general does not have the above information targeted at them, except if they come across it by chance, only 'the public concerned' would

21 Aarhus Implementation Guide, 57.
22 *Ukraine* (n 17).
23 Ibid, para 28.
24 See Aarhus Convention, art 2(4).
25 See Aarhus Implementation Guide, 153–58; *Lithuania* ACCC/C/2006/16, ECE/MP.PP/2008/5/Add.6, 4 April 2008, para 80.
26 See Guideline 11.
27 See Aarhus Convention, arts 2 and 6. Although art 6(3), when referring to art 6(2), refers to 'informing the public' and not 'informing the public concerned' as required in art 6(2), art 6(3) may arguably be read as referring to 'informing the public concerned' since it is expressly meant to be interpreted 'in accordance with [art 6(2)]'. See P Davies, 'Public participation, the Aarhus Convention, and the European Community', in DN Zillman, AR Lucas and G Pring (eds), *Human Rights in National Resource Development: Public Participation in the Sustainable Development of Mining and Energy Resource* (Oxford: Oxford University Press, 2002) 155, 172.

be able to participate and submit comments. Even if the general public came across the above information by chance, it is unlikely that members of the public would participate and submit comments in processes that are not likely to affect them and in which they have no interest. Nevertheless, there may be situations where the nature of the activity in question assumes a national dimension, in which case, 'the public concerned' may effectively be 'the public' in general. In summary, what is certain as a minimum with respect to international best practice is that 'the public concerned' must have the right to participate.

6.3.1.2 The body required to ensure participation

Although Principle 10 of the Rio Declaration and the Bali Guidelines[28] broadly point to the state/public authority as the body generally responsible for ensuring participation, when examined in detail, Article 6 of the Aarhus Convention demonstrates that the issue could be rather more complicated.

First, in Article 6(6) the 'public authority' is expressly stated as responsible for giving 'the public concerned access . . . to all information relevant to the decision-making', and receiving comments from the public as provided in Article 6(2)(d)(v). As those provisions actually used the terminologies 'competent public authority' and 'relevant public authority', states have some discretion to specify the particular authority to make responsible for those obligations.[29] The choices available to states may be the public authority competent to make a decision on whether or not to permit the activity in question, or any other public authority they consider fit to perform the duties.[30]

However, with respect to Article 6(8), which obliges states 'to ensure that in the decision due account is taken of the outcome of the public participation', from a practical perspective, although the provision does not expressly stipulate thus, it has been reasonably posited that this obligation is one that must be implemented by the authority competent to take a decision on whether to permit the activity in question.[31]

Apart from the above, Article 6 of the Aarhus Convention does not specify who should be responsible for the other procedural steps, such as informing the public concerned about the procedure and opportunity to participate,[32] organising early public participation[33] and promptly informing the public of the decision taken.[34] Again, this leaves the states some freedom to choose the body on which to place these responsibilities. In exercising this discretion, some seemingly efficient and Aarhus Convention-compliant options or practices are available for states to learn

28 See Guidelines 8–11.
29 Jendroska (n 20) 119.
30 Ibid.
31 Ibid.
32 Aarhus Convention, art 6(2) and (3).
33 Ibid, art 6(4).
34 Ibid, art 6(9).

from. In practice, most (EU) states place the entire responsibility of ensuring public participation and carrying out all necessary procedural steps on the public authority competent to take the decision.[35] However, the Aarhus Compliance Committee has noted that the responsibility of performing some or all the administrative functions related to public participation need not always be placed on the public authority responsible for taking the decision on whether or not to permit the activity in question.[36] On this note, it expounded that in many states:

> . . . the . . . functions [of organising the participation procedure] are being delegated to various bodies or even private persons [who are often specialising in public participation or mediation, are impartial and do not represent any interests related to the proposed activity]. Such bodies or persons, performing public administrative functions in relation to public participation in environmental decision-making, should be treated, depending on the particular arrangements adopted in the national law, as falling under the definition of a 'public' authority in the meaning of Article 2, Paragraph 2(b) or 2(c).[37]

Another way in which this discretion has been exercised, mainly by eastern Europe and central Asian states, is to place the responsibility for organising the entire public participation (including notification, providing information and collecting comments) on the developer/applicant.[38] For good reasons, the Aarhus Compliance Committee does not agree with this approach: 'placing *undue* reliance on the developer to provide for public participation would not be in line with the Convention' (emphasis added), partly because 'it is implicit in certain provisions of Article 6 . . . that the relevant information should be available directly from the relevant public authority, and that comments should be submitted to the relevant public authority'.[39]

Clearly, the Compliance Committee does not exclude the possibility of saddling applicants with some responsibilities related to the participation process, so long as such functions are carried out 'under the control of the public authorities'; an example of such responsibility being the imposition on applicants of 'special fees to cover the costs related to public participation'.[40] Also, whilst 'developers . . . may hire consultants specialising in public participation, neither the developers themselves nor the consultants hired by them can ensure the degree of impartiality necessary to guarantee proper conduct of the public participation procedure';[41]

35 Jendroska (n 20) 120.
36 *Belarus* ACCC/C/2009/37, ECE/MP.PP//2011/11/Add.2, 12 May 2011, paras 78–79.
37 Ibid.
38 Jendroska (n 20) 121.
39 See Aarhus Convention Compliance Committee, *Report of the Compliance Committee to the 3rd Session of the Meeting of the Parties*, ECE/MP.PP/2008/5, 22 May 2008, para 59; and *Lithuania* (n 25) para 78.
40 *Belarus* (n 36) para 81.
41 Ibid, 80.

thus, the need to ensure that the applicant's involvement in the process is limited and public authority-controlled.

In summary, one can conclude that the obligations under Article 6 are those of the public authority responsible for making the decision; a specially appointed public authority, where provided for; and the applicant, if assigned a limited role.

6.3.1.3 Activities in which public participation is required

In the light of Article 6(1)(a) of the Aarhus Convention, the requirements for public participation in Article 6 must be complied with in 'respect to decisions on whether to permit proposed activities listed in annex I' of the Convention. Annex I of the Convention contains a fairly broad list of activities with varying sizes and qualities, and it draws heavily on the annexes of the Convention on Environmental Impact in a Transboundary Context (Espoo Convention),[42] the EC Directives on Environmental Impact Assessment (EIA Directive),[43] and the Integrated Pollution, Prevention and Control (IPPC) Directive.[44]

That list broadly covers the following 19 activities and includes an omnibus clause (excluding the further specifications under each sector): energy sector, production and processing of metals, mineral industry, chemical industry, waste management, waste-water treatment plants, specific industrial plants, railways and airports, inland waterways and ports, groundwater abstraction or recharge schemes, works for the transfer of water resources, extraction of petroleum and natural gas, dams, pipelines, installations for the intensive rearing of poultry or pigs, quarries and opencast mining, construction of overhead electrical power lines, installations for the storage of petroleum, other specific activities (e.g. textile pre-treatment plants etc.), and any activity not covered under the preceding activities where public participation is provided for under an environmental impact assessment procedure in accordance with national legislation.[45]

However, quite reasonably, Article 6(1)(a) does not apply to any of the listed activities in annex I when undertaken 'exclusively or mainly for research, development and testing of new methods or products for less than two years unless they would be *likely* to cause a significant adverse effect on environment or health' (emphasis added).[46]

Furthermore, states are obliged to apply the provisions of Article 6, 'in accordance with its national law . . . to decisions on activities not listed in annex

42 25 February 1991 (1991) 130 ILM 800.
43 Council Directive 85/337/EEC [1985] OJ L175/40, as amended by Council Directive 97/11/EC [1997] OJ L73/5, and then Council Directive 2003/35/EC [2003] OJ L156/17.
44 Council Directive 96/61/EC [1996] OJ L257/26, now contained in Council Directive 2008/1/EC [2008] OJ L24/8.
45 In *United Kingdom* ACCC/C/2008/27, ECE/MP.PP/C.1/2010/6/Add.2, 24 August 2011, para 38, and in *United Kingdom* ACCC/C/2009/38, ECE/MP.PP/C.1/2011/2/Add.10, 24 August 2011, para 80, the Aarhus Compliance Committee held the UK in breach of annex I, para. 8(a) and annex I, para 8(c), respectively.
46 Aarhus Convention, annex I, para 21.

I which *may have* a significant effect on the environment' (emphasis added);[47] a similar obligation is alluded to under Agenda 21,[48] and can be inferred from the Rio Declaration.[49] Also, even though the Aarhus Convention provides no guidance as to what may be considered 'significant' under this provision, some criteria for determining what the term might mean can be found in Appendix III of the Espoo Convention and Annex III of the EIA Directive.

Cumulatively, the two instruments above point to the fact that the size of the proposed activity, its location (considering the environmental sensitivity or importance of the relevant geographic area, and the (density of the) population in the area), and its potential impact (on humans and the environment, including the frequency and reversibility of the impact), would be relevant in defining what is 'significant'. It goes without saying that the test of significance should be applied objectively and in good faith and not in a manner so as to avoid public participation which, as is frequently the case in some countries with developed EIA practices, has resulted in the courts overturning determinations that potential impacts are not significant.[50]

The flexibility offered by Article 6(1)(b) will enable Article 6 to be applied to decision-making on additional activities as their environmental significance is realised.[51] The character of the activities in Annex I, apart from limiting cases of unruly exercise of discretion by authorities, may also serve as a guide in making the determination of significance.

In addition, '[a]ny change to or extension of activities, where such a change or extension in itself meets the criteria/thresholds set out in [annex I]' shall be subject to Article 6(1)(a), whilst '[a]ny other change or extension of activities' shall be subject to Article 6(1)(b).[52] This provision effectively captures future physical modification of permitted activities. In a decision concerning Slovakia, the Aarhus Compliance Committee held that even though the original construction permit for a nuclear power plant (which is covered under Article 6(1) and Annex I, Paragraph 1) was issued long before the Aarhus Convention entered into force for Slovakia, that would not prevent the Convention from being applicable to subsequent reconsiderations and updates or extension of the activity by the public authority.[53]

Finally, states may choose not to apply the provisions of Article 6 to 'proposed activities serving national defence purposes' where it deems that such application would have 'an adverse effect on these purposes'.[54] This decision whether or not to apply Article 6 must, however, be made on a 'case-by-case basis if provided

47 Ibid, art 6(1)(b). See Aarhus Implementation Guide, 132–33.
48 See ch 15, para 15.5 and ch 23, para 23.2.
49 See Principles 17 and 19.
50 Aarhus Implementation Guide, 132.
51 Ibid.
52 Aarhus Convention, annex I, para 22.
53 *Slovakia* ACCC/C/2009/41, ECE/MP.PP/2011/11/Add.3, 12 May 2011, para 44.
54 Aarhus Convention, art 6 (1)(c).

under national law',[55] meaning that there would need to be some sort of national legal criteria for using this exemption in order to engender transparency and minimise arbitrariness.[56]

6.3.2 The public participation process

6.3.2.1 The duty to effectively inform the public concerned

Generally, after a project approval application has been made, the first step in the public participatory procedure is for the relevant public authority to inform the public concerned about the proposed activity and the opportunities open to them to participate in the decision-making, and ensure public access to other vital information related thereto in a timely and effective manner. This duty on public authorities is well reflected in the IAIA's best practice principles,[57] the Bali Guidelines[58] and the Rio Declaration.[59] However, the Aarhus Convention in Article 6(2) makes more detailed provision thus:

> The public concerned shall be informed, either by public notice or individually as appropriate, early in an environmental decision-making procedure, and in an adequate, timely and effective manner, *inter alia*, of:
>
> (a) The proposed activity and the application on which a decision will be taken;
> (b) The nature of possible decisions or the draft decision;
> (c) The public authority responsible for making the decision;
> (d) The envisaged procedure, including, as and when this information can be provided:
>
> i) The commencement of the procedure;
> ii) The opportunities for the public to participate;
> iii) The time and venue of any envisaged public hearing;
> iv) An indication of the public authority from which relevant information can be obtained and where the relevant information has been deposited for examination by the public;
> v) An indication of the relevant public authority or any other official body to which comments or questions can be submitted and of the time schedule for transmittal of comments or questions; and
> vi) An indication of what environmental information relevant to the proposed activity is available; and

55 Ibid.
56 Aarhus Implementation Guide, 133–34.
57 André et al. (n 3) 2.
58 Guidelines 8 and 10. See also draft Commentary to Bali Guidelines 8.
59 See Principle 10, in conjunction with Principle 19.

(e) The fact that the activity is subject to a national or transboundary environmental impact assessment procedure.

From the above provision, the public concerned may be informed, as appropriate, either by public notice or individually, through such means as the print media (with local or national coverage), electronic mass media (TV, radio, internet), posting of notices, bill-posting etc. Also, a key aspect of Article 6(2) is the requirement for the public concerned to be informed in an 'adequate, timely and effective manner'. In this regard, the Aarhus Compliance Committee has held that it 'is not convinced' that failure to use the express terms 'adequate, timely and effective manner' in the implementing provisions of an EIA in itself amounts to non-compliance with the Convention, especially as the EIA in question contained certain requirements 'aiming to ensure' effective and timely public notification.[60]

The Compliance Committee, however, noted with concern that the lack of those express terms in the EIA regime may adversely affect the implementation of Article 6;[61] such lack may heighten the possibility of relevant authorities overlooking the need for notifications to comply strictly with those express standards where they are simply implied.

Apart from cases where states have been held in breach of Article 6(2) for not providing the 'public concerned' with the details under that provision,[62] the Aarhus Compliance Committee has had ample opportunity to clarify that provision further. First, the Compliance Committee has defined the requirement for the public to be informed in an 'effective manner' as meaning that 'public authorities should seek to provide a means of informing the public, which ensures that all those who potentially could be concerned have a reasonable chance to learn about proposed activities and their possibilities to participate.'[63]

In that light, whether or not a notification is effective (or even adequate) will depend on the circumstances of each case and the extent to which the notification penetrates the relevant segment of the public. Based on this view, the Compliance Committee has once held that 'considering the nature of the project and the interest it has generated', the requirement for proper notification could only have been met if the nationwide media had been engaged as well as individual notification of organisations that explicitly expressed their interest in the matter.[64] '[I]t may also be necessary to have repeat notifications so as to ensure that the public concerned have been notified'[65] effectively, especially where the means

60 *European Community* ACCC/C/2006/17, ECE/MP.PP/2008/5/Add.10, 2 May 2008, paras 48–50, and 59.

61 Ibid, 59.

62 For example *Kazakhstan* ACCC/C/2004/2, ECE/MP.PP/C.1/2005/2/Add.2, 14 March 2005, para 23.

63 *Lithuania* (n 25) para 67.

64 *Ukraine* (n 17) para 28. See also *France* ACCC/C/2007/22, ECE/MP.PP/C.1/2009/4/Add.1, 8 February 2011, para 42.

65 *Armenia* ACCC/C/2009/43, ECE/MP.PP/2011/11/Add.1, 12 May 2011, para 70.

employed are somewhat transient in nature, e.g. TV and newspaper adverts. The timing of such notifications through such transient means as TV/radio broadcasts will also be vital; e.g. if the broadcast comes up at a time when people are usually at work, it might be considered ineffective.[66]

In addition, the Aarhus Compliance Committee has held that an inaccurate notification of the nature of the decision-making process in which participation was required cannot be considered 'adequate' (or indeed effective) and to have properly described the 'nature of possible decisions' as required under Article 6(2).[67] The adequacy (and, indeed, effectiveness) of a notification may also be judged by whether or not its content was understandable enough or, where relevant, contains satisfactory translations.[68]

Also, the Compliance Committee has provided some guidance on what it means to provide the relevant information in a 'timely' fashion. In a case concerning Armenia, the Committee, in consideration of the 'voluminous [EIA] documentation' relating to the project in issue and its 'technical nature', as well as the fact that this document was to be examined for the 'first hearing' and the public concerned only had 'one week' to examine the document, rightly held that early notice in the meaning of Article 6(2) was not achieved.[69]

Furthermore, as provided in Article 6(6) of the Aarhus Convention, the competent public authorities are under an obligation to ensure public access, upon request if required, to a different set of information relating to the activity, which should include, as a minimum:

(a) A description of the site and the physical and technical characteristics of the proposed activity, including an estimate of the expected residues and emissions;
(b) A description of the significant effects of the proposed activity on the environment;
(c) A description of the measures envisaged to prevent and/or reduce the effects, including emissions;
(d) A non-technical summary of the above;
(e) An outline of the main alternatives studied by the applicant; and
(f) In accordance with national legislation, the main reports and advice issued to the public authority at the time when the public concerned shall be informed in accordance with paragraph 2 above.

This list draws heavily on domestic and international experience relating to EIA.[70] Article 6(6) is essentially 'aimed at providing the public concerned with an

66 Aarhus Implementation Guide, 135.
67 *Lithuania* (n 25) para 66.
68 *Armenia* (n 65) para 71; Aarhus Implementation Guide, 135.
69 Ibid, para 67.
70 Aarhus Implementation Guide, 148.

opportunity to examine relevant details to ensure that public participation is informed and therefore more effective'.[71] Apart from the enumerated information above which is considered fundamental to the procedure and must be made available, Article 6(6) actually gives the public concerned access to 'all information relevant to the decision-making' covered by Article 6. Again, although subject to the exemptions provided in Article 4(3) and (4) of the Aarhus Convention, this obligation (similar to that in Article 6(2)(d)(iv) quoted above) seemingly includes information outside the scope of 'environmental information' as defined in Article 2(3) of the Aarhus Convention.[72]

However, with respect to EIA studies which are fundamental to this participatory procedure, the Aarhus Compliance Committee has rightly held that a 'general exemption of EIA studies from disclosure' is not in compliance with Article 6(6) in conjunction with Article 4(4) of the Convention.[73] It further held that 'disclosure of EIA studies in their entirety should be . . . the rule, with the possibility of exempting parts of them' being the exception.[74] Importantly, the Committee 'doubts very much that this exemption [as it relates to intellectual property rights] could ever be applicable in practice' to EIA studies.[75]

The public concerned must also be given access to relevant information 'as soon as it becomes available'.[76] Taken together with Article 6(2)(d)(iv), and in good faith, the relevant authority may be obliged to bring new and relevant information to the attention of the public concerned, as soon as possible. Also, Article 6(6) requires the authorities to give the public concerned access to information 'free of charge' for 'examination'; it 'does not forbid making a charge for copying'.[77] In addition, even though not expressly stipulated, the Aarhus Compliance Committee has, in line with the principle of good faith, posited that such access to information must be 'effective', especially in terms of the location of the information and the time allowed the public concerned to examine them properly.[78]

Furthermore, Article 6(6) only applies to information that is available 'at the time of the public participation procedure', and according to the Aarhus Compliance Committee, outside such a time, the right to examine information under that provision does not apply and the public concerned would then need to rely on Article 4 for access.[79] As it seems, the significance of this position is that they may then be able to access only 'environmental information'.

71 *Ukraine* (n 17) para 32.
72 See Aarhus Implementation Guide, 147.
73 *Romania* ACCC/C/2005/15, ECE/MP.PP/2008/5/Add.7, 16 April 2008, paras 29–30.
74 Ibid.
75 Ibid.
76 Aarhus Convention, art 6(6).
77 *Spain* ACCC/C/2008/24, ECE/MP.PP/C.1/2009/8/Add.1, 8 February 2011, para 95.
78 *Spain* ACCC/C/2009/36, ECE/MP.PP/C.1/2010/4/Add.2, 8 February 2011, para 62.
79 *Spain* (n 77) para 96.

6.3.2.2 Early public participation

One of the key shortcomings of traditional public participation procedures is that it comes too late during the decision-making process with respect to specific activities.[80] It is this problem that Article 6(4) of the Aarhus Convention, which stipulates that '[p]arties shall provide for early public participation, when all options are open and effective public participation can take place', aims to solve. A similar requirement is also provided under the Bali Guidelines,[81] and is critical to compliance with Principle 10 of the Rio Declaration, as well as Article 23 of the World Charter for Nature, which obliges states to ensure that the relevant public has 'the opportunity to participate'.

Jurisprudence from the Aarhus Compliance Committee has provided some light on what might (not) be considered early participation. With respect to participation after the relevant activity has commenced or after the required permit or licence has been issued, the Compliance Committee has held that this in itself is not in conflict with the requirement of Article 6(4), so long as all options remain open and the public can still question the permit or the activity in subsequent participatory procedures and its views can be fully taken into account.[82]

However, in recognition of the fact that this may not be realistic and may only be possible in theory in view of political and commercial pressures, as well as notions of legal certainty, the Committee is of the view that certain options (e.g. as to technology, infrastructure etc.) would have been effectively foreclosed after the grant of permit/licence or commencement of the activity, and so participation thereafter would not be in line with Article 6(4).[83] There is also the possibility of the environment being irreversibly altered after a permit/licence has been granted and the activity commences, such that subsequent public participation that would have objected to the environmental implications of the project would be meaningless. In that light, the Aarhus Compliance Committee in a recent case concerning Armenia, posited that:

> Providing for public participation only after the licence has been issued reduced the public's input to only commenting on how the environmental impact of the mining activity could be mitigated, but precluded the public from having input on the decision on whether the mining activity should be pursued in the first place, as that decision had already been taken. Once a decision to permit a proposed activity has been taken without public involvement, providing for such involvement in the other subsequent decision-making stages can *under no circumstances* be considered as meeting the requirement under Article 6, Paragraph 4, to provide "early public

80 Jendroska (n 20) 133.
81 See Guideline 8, and the draft Commentary to Bali Guideline 8.
82 See *European Community* (n 60) para 54; *Slovakia* (n 53) paras 63–64; and *Kazakhstan* (n 62) para 25.
83 Ibid.

participation when all options are open". This is the case even if a full EIA is going to be carried out.[84]

In particular, there is also the issue of when, in the stages of an EIA procedure, would it be considered appropriate and in line with Article 6(4) for public participation to be introduced. This is one issue that the Aarhus Compliance Committee is yet to give a clear opinion on, as it admits that 'the Convention does not in itself clearly specify the exact phase from which the EIA should be subject to public participation. Indeed, to do so would be particularly difficult, taking into account the great variety of approaches to conducting EIA that exist in the region'[85] and the world at large. However, in a more recent decision, which provides some guidance: 'the Committee welcomes the approach of the Lithuanian law which envisages public participation at the stage of scoping.[86] This appears to provide for early public participation in EIA decision-making.'[87]

Regardless of the Compliance Committee's view above, it is arguably more proper for public participation to begin at the 'screening'[88] stage of the EIA which precedes the 'scoping' stage.[89] In support, one of the IAIA's international best practice principles states that '[t]he public should be involved early . . . and regularly in the IA [impact assessment] process . . . [as this] builds trust among participants, gives more time for PP, improves community analysis [etc.]'; this principle goes on to refer to the '*screening* and scoping of the [impact assessment]' as early stages in which public participation is required.[90]

Arguably, public participation at the 'screening' stage is much more significant than in any other stage of the EIA process, since that is where a decision is taken whether to have an actual EIA or not, which is often the key issue. At this stage, the public, from local experience especially, will be helpful in identifying the potentially significant impacts of a proposed activity on the environment and the wellbeing of the locals that may elude project proponents and public officials. A number of countries provide for mandatory public participation in the 'screening' of projects,[91] and others should be encouraged to so do.

Furthermore, there may be cases where relevant public authorities may have concluded contracts or agreements between themselves or with private entities,

84 *Armenia* (n 65) para 76, emphasis added.
85 *Hungary* ACCC/C/2004/4, ECE/MP.PP/C.1/2005/2/Add.4, 14 March 2005, para 11.
86 Scoping 'is a procedural stage within the EIA procedure at which the scope of studies and information to be assessed (in particular to be covered in the EIA report) is being decided. Sometimes this is called "designing the EIA programme".' Jendroska (n 20) 135.
87 *Lithuania* (n 25) para 73.
88 Screening 'is a procedural stage preceding the actual EIA procedure at which it is decided whether an activity is likely to have a significant impact on the environment and therefore require an EIA to be carried out'. Jendroska (n 20) 135.
89 BJ Richardson and J Razzaque, 'Public participation in environmental decision-making', in BJ Richardson and S Wood (eds), *Environmental Law for Sustainability* (Oxford: Hart Publishing, 2006) 165, 179.
90 André et al. (n 3) 2.
91 Jendroska (n 20) 135.

which may have various legal characters and the capacity to limit the range of options available during public participation. On this note, the Aarhus Compliance Committee has signified that 'public authorities that enter into agreements relevant to the Convention that would foreclose options without providing for public participation may be in conflict with Article 6 of the Convention.'[92]

Indeed, Article 6(4) is clear on the fact that 'all' options should be open during participation, and does not accommodate the exception of public authorities compromising the process with pre-dated agreements. This position is buttressed by the reasoning of the Aarhus Compliance Committee to the effect that Article 6(4) implies that: 'the permit authority must be neither formally nor informally prevented from fully turning down an application on substantive or procedural grounds. If the scope of the permitting authority is already limited due to earlier decisions, then the Party concerned should have also ensured public participation during the earlier stages of decision-making.'[93]

Finally, environmental decision-making with respect to specific activities may consist of various stages where a number of consecutive decisions (e.g. on location, technical design etc.) relating to the activity in question may be made. In this case, the requirement of 'early public participation' would not only apply to the chain of the decision-making procedure as a whole, but to each of the decisions constituting consecutive stages of this chain.[94] This position is shared by the Aarhus Compliance Committee, as revealed in a case concerning Lithuania.[95]

6.3.2.3 Reasonable timeframes between phases of public participation

Whilst 'early' participation in decision-making process as discussed above relates to getting started with the participation procedure, Article 6(3) of the Aarhus Convention deals with the pace.[96] The latter provides that 'public participation procedures shall include reasonable time frames for the different phases, allowing sufficient time for informing the public in accordance with Paragraph 2 above and for the public to prepare and participate effectively during the environmental decision-making', a near word-for-word provision as the latter is contained in the draft Commentary to the Bali Guidelines.[97] The aforementioned provision obliges states to ensure effective pacing of 'the difference phases' of participation so as to allow for effective implementation of other Article 6 requirements, 'including time for the public to digest the information provided in the [Article 6(2)] notification . . ., time to seek additional information from the public authorities identified in the notification, time to examine information available . . ., time to participate in a hearing or commenting opportunity,

92 *Spain* (n 77) para 119(a)(iii).
93 *France* (n 64) para 38.
94 See Jendroska (n 20) 133–35.
95 *Lithuania* (n 25) para 71.
96 Aarhus Implementation Guide, 144.
97 Commentary to Guideline 8.

and time to participate effectively in those proceedings'.[98] According to the Aarhus Compliance Committee:

> The requirement to provide 'reasonable time frames' implies that the public should have sufficient time to get acquainted with the documentation and to submit comments taking into account, inter alia, the nature, complexity and size of the proposed activity. A time frame which may be reasonable for a small simple project with only local impact may well not be reasonable in case of a major complex project.[99]

Accordingly, the Compliance Committee has held that '[t]he time frame of only 10 working days, set out in the Lithuanian EIA Law, for getting acquainted with the documentation . . . and for preparing to participate in the decision-making process concerning a major landfill, does not meet the requirement of reasonable time frames in Article 6, Paragraph 3.'[100] The Compliance Committee reached the same conclusion in a case where a Spanish authority had only allowed 'access to thousands of pages of documentation from only two computers without permitting copies to be made on CDROM or DVD, and . . . setting a time frame of one month for the public to examine all this documentation on the spot'.[101]

In a different case, however, the Compliance Committee was convinced that the provision of 'a period of approximately six weeks for the public to inspect the documents and prepare itself for the public inquiry' and 'exercise its rights under Article 6(6)', and '45 days for public participation and for the public to submit comments, information, analyses or opinions relevant to the proposed activity', 'in this case', was in accordance with Article 6(3).[102]

Apart from those criteria indicated above, the timing of the public participation is also vital in ensuring a 'reasonable timeframe' for the different phases of participation. In a recent case concerning Spain, the question in issue was not only the time span itself 'but most importantly the timing of the commenting period, which was during the summer holiday season or during the Christmas holiday season'.[103] On that basis, the Aarhus Compliance Committee found that 'a period of 20 days for the public to prepare and participate effectively cannot be considered reasonable, in particular if such period includes days of general celebration in the country' even though 'officially many offices work during that time'.[104]

Importantly, the Aarhus Compliance Committee has indicated a 'flexible approach' to setting timeframes as a way of ensuring that the obligation under

98 Aarhus Implementation Guide, 142.
99 *Lithuania* (n 25) para 69.
100 Ibid, para 70.
101 *Spain* (n 78) para 62.
102 *France* (n 64) para 44.
103 *Spain* (n 77) paras 90–91.
104 Ibid, paras 91–92.

Article 6(3) is well implemented. In particular, the Compliance Committee appreciates the flexibility that is presented by setting a reasonable minimum timeframe for a participatory procedure as this will allow for the extension of this minimum period as may be necessary taking into account the nature, complexity and size of the proposed activity, as well as other realities on ground.[105] However, according to the Compliance Committee, where only a maximum timeframe is set, 'regardless of how long the maximum time frame is, [it] runs the risk that in individual cases time frames might be set which are not reasonable. Thus, the approach of setting only maximum time frames for public participation cannot be considered as meeting the requirement of setting reasonable time frames under [Article 6(3)].'[106]

In light of the above, a reasonable timeframe may not only be favourable to the public, but may also benefit the public authorities as it will provide 'sufficient time to manage the process of public participation and to [properly] process the information provided by the public'.[107]

6.3.2.4 The right of the public to contribute

Under Article 6(7) of the Aarhus Convention, and as generally reflected in the Bali Guidelines,[108] Agenda 21,[109] the Biodiversity Convention[110] and others, a fundamental aspect of the public participatory procedure is that 'the public' must be allowed to submit to the relevant public authority 'in writing or, as appropriate, at a public hearing or inquiry with the applicant, any comments, information, analyses or opinions that it considers relevant to the proposed activity'.[111] This level of public participation may also be argued as being a general principle of law, with international applicability, with respect to EIA processes as noted in Chapter 1.

The scope of the above provision is signified by the Aarhus Compliance Committee's decision that the Lithuanian law, which limited the right to submit comments to 'the public concerned' (instead of 'the public') and required these comments to be 'motivated proposals', that is, containing reasoned argumentation, failed to guarantee the full scope of the right under Article 6(7).[112]

The Compliance Committee has also recently held that Belarusian legislation that did not envisage the possibility of public comments being submitted directly to the authority that was to take them into account and make the final decision, but only to the applicants and the consultants handling the public hearing, is a

105 *Belarus* (n 36) para 89. In this case, the Belarusian law, which was acceptable, provided that public hearings shall be organised no *earlier* (as against *later*) than 30 days from the date of public notice.
106 Ibid, para 90.
107 Aarhus Implementation Guide, 142.
108 Guidelines 9 and 11.
109 For example see ch 16, para 37.
110 Article 14(1)(a).
111 See art 6(2)(d)(v).
112 *Lithuania* (n 25) para 80.

limitation to the public's right and was not in compliance with Article 6(7) in conjunction with Article 6(2)(d)(v).[113]

Furthermore, in implementing the above provision, the relevant public authority responsible for receiving the comments should have been identified in the notification to the public concerned under Article 6(2)(d)(v), along with the timeframe for submitting the information. Members of the public must also be given reasonable time to put together and make their contributions.[114] In a Ukrainian case, only seven days were given between the publication of the environmental impact statement and the final decision, and the Aarhus Compliance Committee held that this short period 'failed to allow the public to study the information . . . and prepare and submit its comments'.[115]

However, in a French case, the Compliance Committee noted that the provision of 45 days for actual public inquiry/participation and for the public to submit comments, information, analyses or opinions relevant to the proposed activity in issue, was adequate to fulfil the requirement under Article 6(7) in connection with Article 6(3).[116] Nonetheless, depending on the nature of a proposed activity and the surrounding circumstances, 45 days may not be seen as a reasonable timeframe to participate and make the necessary submissions.

In addition, Article 6(7) gives the public two possible means of making their contributions – in writing, or in public hearings or inquiries with the applicant. The latter means, which allows physical encounter with the applicant, provides a beneficial avenue for the applicant to present the project, and for the public to ask questions, make comments and receive a direct response that could shape any further written public submissions that will be taken into account when the decision is to be made,[117] or even cause the applicants independently to reconsider and make useful variations to their projects before the final decision stage. Similarly, the draft Commentary to the Bali Guidelines also proposed that 'the right to be heard' and the 'holding [of] oral hearings' be made part of domestic legislation in order to ensure adequate public participation.[118]

6.3.2.5 The duty to consider and communicate

After the relevant public has made their contributions to the decision-making, in its decision, the relevant public authority is obliged to take due account of the outcome of the public participation, as provided in Article 6(8) of the Aarhus Convention, the Bali Guidelines[119] and the IAIA's international best practice principles.[120] Clearly, this obligation does not give the public a right to

113 *Belarus* (n 36) para 94.
114 See Aarhus Convention, art 6(3).
115 *Ukraine* (n 17) para 29.
116 *France* (n 64) para 44.
117 Aarhus Implementation Guide, 154.
118 Commentary on Guideline 8.
119 Guideline 11.
120 André et al. (n 3) 2.

veto the decision, neither does it require the relevant authority to accept and align the final decision to suit the outcome of the public participation or the comments received.[121]

That may not be a practicable even under a well established democracy in view of other relevant interests and the need to curtail democratic excesses as discussed in Chapter 3, the core of which Popovic ably summaries thus: '[a] tyrannical majority can be as harmful to the environment as it can be to the rights of minorities in other contexts.'[122] This is where the view of the rational elitist theorists finds some positive relevance as noted in Chapter 3. Accordingly, Popovic continues, 'public participation should fit into an environmental scheme that also includes substantive baselines'[123] arguably provided by a measure such as Article 6(8) of the Aarhus Convention.

Article 6(8), however, requires the relevant authority, which should be the authority competent to make the final decision,[124] seriously to consider the substance of the outcome of the process, including the comments received, and include them in the motivation of the final decision, in such a way that the authority is able to show why particular outcomes or comments were rejected on substantive grounds.[125]

A similar interpretation is adopted in the draft Commentary to Bali Guideline 11. In a case concerning Ukrainian, the decision on the project was taken seven days after the publication of the environmental impact statement, and the Aarhus Compliance Committee held that this 'did not allow the public officials responsible for making the decision sufficient time to take any comments into account in a meaningful way, as required under [Article 6(8)]'.[126] In other words, a reasonable time must be spent on this process of taking due account of outcomes, failing which a presumption of non-compliance with Article 6(8) may be raised. A failure to implement this obligation may invalidate the final decision; 'members of the public whose comments were not duly taken into account will be able to challenge the final decision in an administrative or judicial proceeding on this basis', under Article 9(2) of the Aarhus Convention.[127]

In addition, under the Aarhus Convention, states are required to 'ensure that, when the decision has been taken by the public authority, the public is promptly informed of the decision in accordance with the appropriate procedures', and that 'the text of the decision along with the reasons and considerations on which the decision is based' be made 'accessible to the public'.[128] A similar provision is contained in the Bali Guidelines and in its draft

121 *Spain* (n 77) paras 98–99.
122 NAF Popovic, 'The right to participate in decisions that affect the environment' (1993) 10(2) *Pace Environmental Law Review* 683, 702.
123 Ibid.
124 *Belarus* (n 36) para 96.
125 Aarhus Implementation Guide, 155–56. See also Aarhus Convention, art 6(9).
126 *Ukraine* (n 17) para 29.
127 Ibid, para 110.
128 Aarhus Convention, art 6(9). For non-compliance see *Belarus* (n 36) para 98.

Commentary.[129] As highlighted by the Aarhus Compliance Committee, this obligation does not require the relevant authority to publicise the decision itself, but to inform the public about the decision and ensure its right to have access to it, including the reasons and considerations on which it is based.[130]

The aforementioned obligation must also be fulfilled 'promptly'; what may be considered 'prompt' notification must be judged in the context of other legal requirements – e.g. the time limit for appealing the decision – and the specific circumstance of the case – e.g. the kind of decision, the type and size of the activity in question, and even the opportunity a certain time lag may present the applicant substantially to alter the subject matter before there is an opportunity to appeal the decision.[131]

Also, it has been stated that it is customary for notifications of decisions to include information about opportunities to appeal;[132] apart from the fact that a similar requirement is provided for with respect to information refusal notices under Article 4(7) of the Aarhus Convention discussed in Chapter 4, it is arguably in accordance with the principle of good faith and the authority's obligation to assist and guide the public under Article 3(2) of the Convention.

Finally, providing the written 'reasons and considerations on which the decision is based', as alluded to above and recently supported by the Aarhus Compliance Committee, should be interpreted as also requiring the outcome of the public participation, including the comments received, to be addressed in the light of how they were taken into account.[133] This aspect was aptly captured by the IAIA international best practice principles, which included the necessity of 'reporting and [giving] feedback to stakeholders about the result of the PP [public participation] process, especially how their inputs have contributed to decision-making'.[134] This information is certainly important to the public in deciding whether or not to challenge the final decision, as well as serving as potential evidence in a review proceedings.

6.3.2.6 Periodic public participation

Simply ensuring early public participation in the decision-making process leading up to permission being granted for an activity to be effected should not be the end of public participation with respect to that activity. This is for the simple reason that subsequent changes relating to the activity earlier approved may have a different and, possibly, deleterious effect on the environment and human wellbeing. Therefore, as with the Bali Guidelines,[135] Article 6(10) of the Aarhus

129 See Guideline 11 and the Commentary on it.
130 *Lithuania* (n 25) para 81.
131 Ibid, paras 82 and 84; Aarhus Implementation Guide, 157.
132 Aarhus Implementation Guide, 157.
133 See *Spain* (n 77) paras 100–101; and Aarhus Implementation Guide, 157.
134 André et al. (n 3) 2.
135 Guideline 12.

Convention provides that states 'shall ensure that, when a public authority reconsiders or updates the operating conditions for an activity referred to in Paragraph 1, the provisions of Paragraphs 2 to 9 [on public participation] of this article are applied *mutatis mutandis*, and where appropriate'.

This provision is obviously a supplement to Paragraph 22 of Annex I, which triggers the obligations under Article 6(2) to (9) on the basis of physical change or extension of the activity in question, as it (i.e. Article 6(10)) distinctly triggers those obligations on the basis of subsequent administrative procedures that touch on the operating conditions of an activity.[136]

This provision was recently applied by the Aarhus Compliance Committee in a case relating to Armenia concerning the renewal of a mining licence; as the renewal effectively upgraded the licence to a special status that impacted the operating conditions of the mining activity, thereby ensuring a longer mining duration and providing for the possibility of a concession agreement and limited liability on environmental matters, the Compliance Committee held that the renewal fell under Article 6(10) and that public participation ought to have been ensured.[137]

Also, in a recent case concerning Slovakia in which the Compliance Committee held that Article 6(10) applied, the effect of the clause '*mutatis mutandis*, and where appropriate' as used in Article 6(10) was considered.[138] In that case, the Compliance Committee stressed that, whilst the clause gives the authorities 'some discretion . . . to determine where public participation is appropriate . . . [it] does not imply complete discretion'.[139] It went on to state that 'the clause 'where appropriate' introduces an objective criterion to be seen in the context of the goals of the Convention . . . Thus the clause does not preclude a review by the Committee [or indeed a court of law] on whether the Party concerned should have therefore provided for public participation.' [140]

6.4 Public participation in non-activity-specific decisions

This section will be broken down into two areas of public participation in environment-related decisions that are not on specific activities but border on broader issues. Whilst the first will deal with public participation as it concerns plans, programmes and policies (non-binding instruments) related to the environment, the second will consider public participation as it relates to the preparation of executive regulations and other legally binding instruments.

136 See Aarhus Implementation Guide, 158.
137 *Armenia* (n 65) para 58.
138 *Slovakia* (n 53).
139 Ibid, para 55. See Aarhus Implementation Guide, 159.
140 Ibid, para 56.

6.4.1 Public participation concerning plans, programmes and policies

Although public participation in the EIA project-specific process is a vital element in environmental law, this 'may come too late to result in major changes in proposed activities that can protect the environment' or adequately address the concerns of the public.[141] In view of the specific nature of the EIA process and others, it could also mean that the public has not been given a fair opportunity to participate, and that the value of public participation as a whole has not been maximised. These views, and more, underline the articulation by the European Commission at the 1992 Rio UNCED, of the need to broaden the reach of the EIA to the policy-making and planning (and programme) stages.[142] Such a procedure has come to be termed strategic environmental assessment (SEA).

SEA is intended to ensure early consideration of potential environmental impacts (at the higher levels) of plans, policies and programmes, which in turn shapes future development of specific projects.[143] It can help in early identification of possible problems and thus avoidance of resource wastage and future delays of actions owing to public opposition.[144] As a key principle, allowance for public participation is usually made in the SEA procedure,[145] especially as, for instance, it may be difficult or impossible to settle at the specific project level, matters which relate to the 'cumulative effects of other projects within the same or related programmes'.[146]

So where a public authority, for example, draws up a programme that involves the construction of several dumpsites, it will take a SEA procedure, which focuses on the programme and not simply on the individual projects, to appreciate fully the cumulative environmental impact of the proposed dumpsites, and appropriate alternatives to them (e.g. incinerators, recycling facilities etc.). This effectively makes SEA, where policies, plans and programmes are to be made, the first tier of assessment, and EIA the second.[147] Furthermore, flowing from the opportunity created by a SEA procedure to consider wider issues, it may also help to reduce disputes over the development of particular projects.[148]

141 Richardson and Razzaque (n 89) 180.

142 A Gilpin, *Environmental Impact Assessment: Cutting Edge for the Twenty-First Century* (Cambridge: Cambridge University Press, 1995) 76.

143 See R Therivel and MR Partidario (eds), *The Practice of Strategic Environmental Assessment* (London: Earthscan, 1996).

144 See TB Fisher, 'Benefits arising from SEA application: a comparative review of North West England, Noord-Holland, and Brandenburg-Berlin' (1999) 19 *Environmental Impact Assess Review* 143, 148.

145 HM Alshuwaikhat, 'Strategic environmental assessment can help solve environmental impact assessment failures in developing countries' (2005) 25 *Environmental Impact Assessment Review* 307, 311.

146 Gilpin (n 142) 172.

147 PGG Davies, *European Union Environmental Law: An Introduction to Key Selected Issues* (Aldershot: Ashgate, 2004) 179.

148 See M Poustie, 'Environmental justice in SEPA's environmental protection activities: a report for the Scottish Environment Protection Agency', 2004, 96, available at http://www.sepa.org.uk/system_pages/search.aspx?q=poustie (last accessed 15 February 2015).

Although generally weaker than the obligation under Article 6 of the Aarhus Convention, it is still commendable that Article 7 of the Convention obliges states, as a minimum, to 'make appropriate practical and/or other provisions' for public participation concerning plans, programmes and policies related to the environment and prepared by public authorities.[149] Similarly, the World Charter for Nature,[150] IAIA's international best practice principles,[151] the Bali Guidelines[152] and Agenda 21[153] all emphasise public participation as a core element in impact assessment at the stages of plan, policy and programme formulation and call on states to ensure public input at those levels. In addition, some specific international environmental treaties including, for example, the Desertification Convention, oblige parties such as Nigeria to ensure the public participates in SEA-related decision-making with respect to the focus of the regime.[154]

Although none of these regimes defines 'plans', 'programmes' and 'policies', a common-sense definition of the terms may suffice,[155] including that proffered by Wood and Djeddour: '[a] policy may . . . be considered as the inspiration and guidance for actions, a plan as a set of co-ordinated and timed objectives for the implementation of the policy, and a programme as a set of projects in a particular area.'[156]

This position seems to align with the view expressed in the Aarhus Implementation Guide that policies 'are typically less concrete than plans and programmes'[157] and with the definition of 'plan' and 'programme' in the EC Guide for Implementation of Directive 2001/42/EC on the Assessment of the Effect of Certain Plans and Programmes on the Environment,[158] where it was stated that a 'rigorous distinction between the two' is neither necessary nor possible. It has, however, been noted that in practice the sequence can vary, even though it is quite conclusive that they all lay the foundation and inform the development of specific projects.[159]

Furthermore, even though the above regimes do not expressly oblige states to undertake environmental assessment, a proper public participation procedure in the context of SEA is at the heart of its appropriate implementation.[160] Accordingly, the UNECE Protocol on SEA, whilst drawing inspiration from Principle 10 of the Rio Declaration and acknowledging the Aarhus Convention,[161]

149 See Aarhus Implementation Guide, 176.
150 Article 16.
151 André et al. (n 3) 1 and 3.
152 Guideline 13.
153 For example see ch 17, para 17.128, ch 18, paras 18.9 and 18.54, ch 21, para 21.40, ch 25, para 25.9(b), ch 26, para 26.3(b), ch 27, para 27.8, ch 29, para 29.5, and ch 36, para 36.10(a).
154 See ss 3(a) and 10(2)(f).
155 See Aarhus Implementation Guide, 180.
156 C Wood and M Djeddour, 'Strategic environmental assessment: EA of policies, plans and programmes' (1992) 10(1) *The Impact Assessment Bulletin* 3–22.
157 Aarhus Implementation Guide, 180.
158 Paragraph 3.3.
159 Therivel and Partidario (eds) (n 143) 5.
160 Aarhus Implementation Guide, 174.
161 Preamble.

stipulates that the relevant provisions of the Protocol (which includes public participation) will apply 'without prejudice' to the Aarhus Convention.[162]

As for who is entitled to participate in decisions-making on plans and programmes formulation, Article 7 of the Aarhus Convention does not provide a straightforward answer. The principal obligations expressed in its first sentence refer to 'the public'. The second sentence, however, goes on to provide that the public authority shall *identify* 'the public which may participate . . . taking into account the objectives of this Convention'. This expression introduces some confusion.[163]

However, in practice, if implemented in good faith, it is more likely to be interpreted as 'the public concerned' as defined in Article 2(5) of the Aarhus Convention; in support, this is the express position taken in UNECE's Protocol on SEA.[164] On the other hand, the obligation to provide for public participation under Article 7 may logically be said to rest on the shoulders of the 'public authority' (as defined in Article 2(2)), which was therein referred to, albeit indirectly.[165]

Also, with respect to plans and programmes, Article 7 expressly incorporates Article 6(3), (4), (8) and (2) (by virtue of its incorporation into Article 6(3)). However, contrary to the views expressed in the Aarhus Implementation Guide, which largely concedes that under Article 7 public authorities are not bound by any other provision in Article 6 since they were not expressly incorporated,[166] considering that Article 7 also stipulates that the participation be done 'within a transparent and fair framework', it is submitted that other relevant paragraphs of Article 6 are implied and indirectly incorporated into Article 7 *mutatis mutandis*. This is because it is arguably futile to argue that a participatory process that does not comply with Article 6(7), (9), and (10) is a *transparent* and *fair* process. In support, provisions similar to Article 6(7) and (9) of the Aarhus Convention are also part of the public participation procedure under the UNECE Protocol on SEA.[167]

With respect to policies, Article 7 separately provides that 'to the extent appropriate', states 'shall endeavour to provide opportunities for public participation in the preparation of policies relating to the environment'. This brief provision gives public authorities a good measure of flexibility in its implementation. Nonetheless, as a general rule, that flexibility must be exercised in provable good faith and in a manner compatible with the objectives of the Aarhus Convention. So, even though that provision does not expressly incorporate the provisions of Article 6, it is foreseeable that its successful implementation would necessitate the incorporation of some Article 6 paragraphs.

This position is buttressed by the UNECE Protocol on SEA, which is similarly brief on the issue of public participation in the formation of environment-related

162 Article 15.
163 See ibid, 118.
164 Article 8(3). See also arts 5(3), 6(3).
165 Cf Jendroska (n 20) 122–23.
166 Aarhus Implementation Guide, 179.
167 See arts 8(4) and 11(2).

policies, but provides that in implementing this obligation, appropriate principles and elements in other parts of the protocol should be considered.[168]

6.4.2 Public participation concerning executive regulations and other legally binding instruments

In international environmental law, there is the general recognition that the public has a role to play in the development of normative instruments which relate to the environment. In this light, the preamble to the Aarhus Convention recognises 'the desirability of transparency in all branches of government' and calls on 'legislative bodies to implement the principles of this Convention in their proceedings'. As with the Bali Guidelines,[169] the Aarhus Convention provides for a soft obligation on states, thus:

> Each Party shall strive to promote effective public participation at an appropriate stage, and while options are still open, during the preparation by public authorities of executive regulations and other generally applicable legally binding rules that may have a significant effect on the environment.[170]

For this obligation to be met, the Aarhus Convention further provides some steps that should be taken: '[t]ime-frames sufficient for effective participation should be fixed'; '[d]raft rules should be published or otherwise made publicly available'; '[t]he public should be given the opportunity to comment, directly or through representative consultative bodies'; and '[t]he result of the public participation shall be taken into account as far as possible'.[171]

6.5 Enforcing the right to participate in environmental decision-making

Effective and adequate enforcement mechanisms are required to strengthen and give teeth to legal provisions for public participation in environmental decision-making processes, and to help ensure their consistent and effective implementation.[172] Therefore, as entrenched in Principle 10 of the Rio Declaration, there is the widely recognised need to provide for '[e]ffective access to judicial and administrative proceedings, including redress and remedy' as it relates to provisions for participation in environmental decision-making.[173] In that light, Article 9(2) of the Aarhus Convention requires that, through national legislation:

168 Article 13.
169 Guideline 13. See also, Aarhus Implementation Guide, 181–85.
170 Article 8.
171 Ibid.
172 Aarhus Implementation Guide, 178.
173 See Popovic (n 122) 703.

> Members of the public concerned
>
> (a) Having a sufficient interest or, alternatively (b) Maintaining impairment of a right, where the administrative procedural law of a Party requires this as a precondition', have access to a review procedure before a court of law and/or another independent and impartial body established by law, to challenge the substantive and procedural legality of any decision, act or omission subject to the provision of Article 6 [on participation in activity specific decision-making] and, where so provided for under national law . . ., of other relevant provisions of this convention.

The reference to 'other relevant provisions of this convention' in the last line of the above quotation means that states may choose to make the implementation of Articles 7 and 8 reviewable. Under the same phrase, taken together with the general Article 9(3), which allows for review of alleged contraventions by public authorities of its 'national laws relating to the environment', states will have to ensure that the implementation of other provisions relating to participation in decision-making in Articles 3 and 5 are reviewable, considering in addition that they 'lay the groundwork for many of the obligations set out in Article 6 and are relevant to its implementation'.[174] Furthermore, expanding on the quoted section of Article 9(2) above:

> What constitutes a sufficient interest and impairment of a right shall be determined in accordance with the requirements of national law *and consistently with the objective of giving the public concerned wide access to justice within the objective of this Convention.* To this end, the interest of any non-governmental organisation meeting the requirements referred to in Article 2, Paragraph 5, shall be deemed sufficient for the purpose of subparagraph (a) above. Such organisation shall also be deemed to have rights capable of being impaired for the purpose of subparagraph (b) above.
>
> The provisions of this Paragraph 2 shall not exclude the possibility of a preliminary review procedure before an administrative authority and shall not affect the requirement of exhaustion of administrative review procedures prior to recourse to judicial review procedures, where such a requirement exists under national law.[175]

In addition, the above enforcement procedures, both as a general principle of law and as reflected in the Aarhus Convention and in the Bali Guidelines, must provide adequate and effective remedies, be fair and equitable, and be timely and not prohibitively expensive.[176] According to the Aarhus Convention and the

174 Aarhus Implementation Guide, 193.

175 Aarhus Convention, art 9(2), emphasis added.

176 See Aarhus Convention, art 9(4); and Bali Guidelines, 19–22. See generally A Andrusevych, T Alge and C Konrad (eds), *Case Law of the Aarhus Convention Compliance Committee (2004–2011)* (Lviv: Resource & Analysis Center 'Society and Environment', 2011) 81–88.

Bali Guidelines, states should 'consider the establishment of appropriate assistance mechanisms to remove or reduce financial and other barriers to access to justice';[177] in this regard, the Bali Guidelines propose 'the development and use of alternative dispute resolution mechanisms where these are appropriate'.[178]

6.6 Conclusion

The above analysis elucidates what may be considered as international best practice for laws and practices with respect to public participation in environmental decision-making processes. The elucidated best practice has the potential to contribute majorly to the delivery of the benefits of participatory environmental governance, whilst minimising the potential excesses that may follow from the process. The implementation of similar norms in Nigeria will contribute in ensuring for the public better and more meaningful access to, and participation in, environmental decision-making processes. In any event, if Nigeria is to comply with its international environmental law commitments in that regard, those are the norms to follow in designing its laws and guiding its practices. The extent to which this is the case with Nigeria, and recommendations for improvement where necessary, are dealt with in the next chapter.

Bibliography

Aarhus Convention Compliance Committee, *Report of the Compliance Committee to the 3rd Session of the Meeting of the Parties*, ECE/MP.PP/2008/5, 22 May 2008.

Alshuwaikhat HM, 'Strategic environmental assessment can help solve environmental impact assessment failures in developing countries' (2005) 25 *Environmental Impact Assessment Review* 307.

André P with Enserink B, Connor D and Croal P, *Public Participation: International Best Practice Principles* (Special Publication Series No 4, North Dakota: International Association for Impact Assessment, 2006).

Andrusevych, A Alge, T and Konrad C (eds), *Case Law of the Aarhus Convention Compliance Committee (2004–2011)* (Lviv: Resource & Analysis Center 'Society and Environment', 2011).

Appelstrand M, 'Participation and societal values: the challenge for lawmakers and policy practitioners' (2002) 4 *Forest Policy and Economics* 281.

Black's Law Dictionary (8th edn, 2004).

Davies P, 'Public participation, the Aarhus Convention, and the European Community', in Zillman DN, Lucas AR and Pring G (eds), *Human Rights in National Resource Development: Public Participation in the Sustainable Development of Mining and Energy Resource* (Oxford: Oxford University Press, 2002) 155.

Davies PGG, *European Union Environmental Law: An Introduction to Key Selected Issues* (Aldershot: Ashgate, 2004).

177 Aarhus Convention, 9(5); and Bali Guidelines, 20.
178 Guideline 26.

Dictionnaire de la culture juridique (2003).
Draft Commentary to the UNEP Guidelines for the Development of National Legislation on Information, Public Participation and Access to Justice in Environmental Matters, available at http://www.unep.org/civil-society/Portals/24105/documents/Guidelines/Commentary-to-the-guidelines-for-the-development-of-national-legislation.pdf (last accessed 2 February 2015).
Ebbesson J, Gaugitsch G, Jendroska J, Marshal F and Stec S, *The Aarhus Convention: An Implementation Guide* (2nd edn, New York and Geneva: UN, 2014).
Fisher TB, 'Benefits arising from SEA application: a comparative review of North West England, Noord-Holland, and Brandenburg-Berlin' (1999) 19 *Environmental Impact Assess Review* 143.
Gilpin A, *Environmental Impact Assessment: Cutting Edge for the Twenty-First Century* (Cambridge: Cambridge University Press, 1995).
Hesselink MW, 'The concept of good faith', in Hartkamp AS, Hesselink MW, Hondius E, Mak C and du Perron E, *Towards a European Civil Code* (4th edn, The Hague: Kluwer Law International, 2010) 619.
Jendroska J, 'Public participation in environmental decision-making: interactions between the convention and EU law and other key legal issues in its implementation in the light of the opinion of the Aarhus Convention Compliance Committee', in Pallemaerts M (ed), *The Aarhus Convention at Ten: Interactions and Tensions Between Conventional International Law and EU Environmental Law* (Groningen: Europa Law Publishing, 2011) 92.
Koester V, 'The Compliance Committee of the Aarhus Convention: an overview of procedures and jurisprudence' (2007) 37(2–3) *Environmental Policy and Law* 83.
Popovic NAF, 'The right to participate in decisions that affect the environment' (1993) 10 *Pace Environmental Law Review* 683.
Poustie M, 'Environmental justice in SEPA's environmental protection activities: a report for the Scottish Environment Protection Agency' 2004, 96, available at http://www.sepa.org.uk/system_pages/search.aspx?q=poustie (last accessed 15 February 2015).
Richardson BJ and Razzaque J, 'Public participation in environmental decision-making', in Richardson BJ and Wood S (eds), *Environmental Law for Sustainability* (Oxford: Hart Publishing, 2006) 165.
Sands P and Peel J, *Principles of International Environmental Law* (3rd edn, Cambridge: Cambridge University Press, 2012).
Therivel R and Partidario MR (eds), *The Practice of Strategic Environmental Assessment* (London: Earthscan, 1996).
Wood C and Djeddour M, *'Strategic Environmental Assessment: EA of Policies, Plans and Programmes'* (1992) 10(1) *The Impact Assessment Bulletin* 3.

7 Public participation in environmental decision-making: Nigerian law and practice in comparative perspective

7.1 Introduction

In view of the international best practice principles on public participation in environmental decision-making processes critically set out in the preceding chapter, this chapter seeks comparatively to analyse the Nigerian law and practice in that regard and, where necessary, to make recommendations for improvement in that light, considering some relevant non-legal realities of the country. From the Nigerian perspective, apart from a few other local instruments that will be referred to, the 1992 EIA Act will be at the heart of the (comparative) discussion in this chapter. This is because the EIA Act, apart from regulating the general EIA system in the country, is the flagship law for public participation in environmental decision-making in Nigeria; '[p]ublic participation is a fundamental component of the environmental impact assessment (EIA) process'[1] and 'EIA is not EIA without consultation and public participation.'[2] The analysis in this chapter will follow a similar progression as in the preceding chapter.

7.2 Public participation in activity-specific decisions

7.2.1 Issues on scope

In determining the scope, and hence partly the value to the public, of the Nigerian regime that enables public participation in environmental decision-making on specific activities vis-à-vis the best practice discussed earlier, the focus in this section will be on: (1) the issue of who can participate; (2) the body required to ensure participation; (3) the activities open for participation.

1 N Hartley and C Wood, 'Public participation in environmental impact assessment: implementing the Aarhus Convention' (2005) 25 *Environmental Impact Assessment Review* 319.

2 CM Wood, *Environmental Impact Assessment: A Comparative Review* (2nd edn, Harlow: Prentice-Hall, 2002) 275.

7.2.1.1 Who can participate?

As a minimum, 'the public concerned', which will include NGOs, is the response of best practice to this question. Similarly, the Nigerian law answers the question in section 7 of the EIA Act, which stipulates that 'government agencies, members of the public, experts in any relevant discipline and interested groups' must be given the opportunity to make comments on the EIA of a proposed activity before any final decisions can be taken by the responsible authority.[3] In addition, some later provisions of the EIA Act make reference to the fact that 'the public' and 'any person' must be given the opportunity to file a comment on EIA reports into the proposed activity.[4]

Apart from making comments on EIA reports, the relevant authority may, in line with the EIA Act, subsequently decide to refer the proposed project to mediation or a review panel for further assessment. If the project is referred to mediation, only 'parties who are directly affected by or have a direct interest in the project' may be allowed to participate in the mediation 'through representatives'.[5] By the same token, if the project is referred to a review panel, 'the public' must be offered the opportunity to participate.[6]

It is commendable that, with respect to those who can make comments on EIA reports and participate in the assessment by the review panel, the EIA Act generally does not fall below best practice. Although in those regards 'the public' essentially has the right to be involved in the decision-making process, as argued in the preceding chapter, it is mainly the 'the public concerned' that usually bothers to engage in the process.

It is also noteworthy that in these twin opportunities for public involvement in the decision-making process, the EIA Act gives NGOs and other groups reasonable opportunity to participate without restrictions. In addition, the reference to 'the public' and any interested group and experts, has the potential to include the public abroad, including foreign or international environmental NGOs, and the relevant Nigerian authorities are advised to be guided by the way the counterpart provision in the Aarhus Convention is being interpreted by the Aarhus Compliance Committee, as discussed in the preceding chapter. In addition, section 48 of the EIA Act – headed 'International environmental effect' – provides for the establishment of 'a review panel to conduct an assessment of the international environmental effects of the project' and for the notification of 'the government of any foreign State' that is likely to be affected as a result of the project in issue; this could be an opportunity for the actual foreign 'public concerned' to participate in the review panels assessment in line with the reasoning of the Aarhus Compliance Committee in the Ukrainian case discussed in the preceding chapter.

3 See s 8.
4 See ss 21(3) and 24(2).
5 EIA Act, s 30(a)(i).
6 Ibid, s 36(b).

However, it seems that in practice the relevant authorities sometimes employ a narrower scope with respect to those who participate in the decision-making process than that prescribed by the EIA Act. For example, Frederick Igere, a community representative in the Niger Delta, lamented recently that oil 'exploration activities affect many communities in Escravos but the oil companies [and government officials] only deal with the community that has the oil well',[7] making it unlikely that companies will know of and consider the impact of their activities on other communities.

Whilst this practice may be the result of ignorance as to the scope of the law in issue, or even an unhealthy desire for speedy development, it is also arguably a reflection of the historical culture of public exclusion from environmental governance by public authorities and some developers. In these cases, reorientation, public/NGO pressure and consistent public enforcement of the law in court are needed to ensure that those who are supposed to be included in the process are indeed included.

Furthermore, the scope of those who can participate in the mediation falls below best practice and does not aid effective public participation (probably because mediation by nature is not necessarily suitable for huge numbers of parties, but for a few). The reference to 'parties who are '*directly* affected by or have a *direct* interest in the project' (emphasis added) as those who can participate in the mediation, provides a much higher threshold than that reflected in best practice, which simply refers to 'effect' or 'likely effect' of the decision on the public, or only requires 'an interest' in the decision-making process for members of the public to be eligible to participate in it.

In effect, a significant proportion of the public who may be significantly affected or who have considerable, but not *direct*, interest in the proposed project, would be excluded. The same fate may also befall NGOs that may have relevant expertise and significant local experience that would be of benefit to the process, except those that may be chosen as the representatives of the directly affected/interested public.

So if after public comment on the EIA report, the proposed project is referred to mediation and not the review panel, the spectrum of those who can participate with reference to the public, would be severely limited, contrary to best practice. In addition, it is quite worrying that members of the public have no influence as to whether or not the referral should be made to mediation or the review panel, as the relevant government body has unfettered discretion over this matter. Therefore, in view of the fact that, in substance, the function of this mediation process as provided in the EIA Act is not different from that of the review panel,[8] and the agency that is to make the final decision is not bound by the final reports

7 B Obayanju and M Obaseki (eds), *Defending the Environment: The Role of Environmental Impact Assessment* (Benin City: Environmental Rights Act/Friends of the Earth, Nigeria, 2009) 58.

8 See ss 16, 33 and 36.

it produces,[9] it might be best to excise it (the mediation process) from the EIA Act. This would remove an opportunity for excessive limitation of those that can participate in the decision-making process.

7.2.1.2 The body required to ensure participation

The body required to ensure public participation under the EIA regime is similar to the Aarhus Convention's position. Under the EIA Act, the government 'agency', in conjunction with its 'council' in some cases, are responsible for administering the EIA Act and in consequence ensuring, to a large extent, that the public participates at the relevant stages of the EIA process. The agency is responsible for reaching a final decision on whether or not to permit an activity, and may be assisted by reports produced from mediation or a review panel, as decided on and constituted by the council in consultation with the agency, where appropriate.[10]

The EIA Act defines the 'agency' and the 'council' as the 'Nigerian [Federal] Environmental Protection Agency' (FEPA) and the 'Federal Environmental Protection Council' (FEPC),[11] respectively, as established by the Federal Environmental Protection Agency Act (FEPA Act).[12] However, the FEPA Act has been repealed (and replaced) by section 36 of the National Environmental Standards and Regulation Agency Act (NESREA Act).[13] In other words, FEPA and FEPC are no longer in existence as their functions have been taken over by NESREA (with zonal and state offices across Nigeria) and its council, which were established in their place by the NESREA Act.[14]

However, even though it can be implied, the EIA has not been amended to reflect this change despite the existence of a 2010 EIA (Amendment) Bill, which was placed before the Nigerian legislature (but did not receive the required attention) and which proposed, among other things, the amendment of section 61 of the EIA Act to reflect this current reality.[15] This amendment is here recommended as the present anomaly is not in line with Article 3(1) of the Aarhus Convention for frameworks enabling public participation to be 'clear, transparent and consistent'.

The agency is responsible for establishing and maintaining a public registry that holds all relevant information with respect to the environmental assessment of the project on which a decision is to be made, in order to facilitate public access to them.[16] Generally, under the EIA Act, the agency is also responsible for informing the public about the opportunity to examine and comment on EIA

9 See EIA Act, s 39.
10 See ibid, ss 29–39.
11 Section 61.
12 Cap F10, Laws of the Federation of Nigeria, 2004.
13 Federal Republic of Nigeria Official Gazette No 92, Vol 94 of 31 July 2007.
14 See NESREA Act, s 7.
15 Section 10.
16 See s 55.

reports;[17] receiving public comments;[18] taking due account of the outcome of the public participation in its decision;[19] and making available and/or publishing its decision on the proposed activity in a manner in which the public or the public interested shall be notified.[20]

However, the proposed activity may be referred by the council, in consultation with the agency, to mediation or to a review panel, depending on the nature of the potential environmental harm a proposed activity might engender or the significance of the public comments received with respect to its environmental effects, among other considerations.[21] These forums must provide an avenue for public participation; as provided, it is also expected that the input of the public at these forums should receive consideration and have an impact on their final reports (which should contain a summary of comments received from the public, in the case of a review panel) to be sent to the agency (and council) for further consideration before the final decision is made by the agency on the activity.[22]

In summary, the agency, the council and, where both government bodies deem fit in line with the relevant EIA Act provisions, the mediator(s) or the review panel, are the entities required to ensure public participation in project-specific environmental matters in Nigeria. This is generally in line with the contemplation of the Aarhus Convention and the exposition of the Aarhus Compliance Committee, apart from the anomaly caused by the outdated definition of agency and council in the EIA Act.

7.2.1.3 Activities in which public participation is required

The aspects of the EIA Act that provide for the types of activity that may require public participation, generally falls short of best practice. Similar to the Aarhus Convention, the EIA Act contains a schedule entitled 'Mandatory Study Activities', which contains a fairly broad list of activities with varying sizes and qualities. All activities, whether proposed by the public or private sector,[23] listed under this schedule are to be subjected to detailed EIA studies, which will provide an opportunity for the public to participate in deciding whether or not to permit the proposed activity or on what condition(s) it should be allowed to operate.[24]

The list broadly covers the following 19 activities (excluding their detailed specifications): agriculture, airport, drainage and irrigation, land reclamation, fisheries, housing, industry, infrastructure, ports, mining, petroleum, power generation and transmission, quarries, railways, transportation, resort and recreational

17 See ss 21(3) and 24.
18 See ss 7, 21(3), 24(2) and 36.
19 See ss 7, 8, 16(1)(c), 39.
20 Section 9.
21 See EIA Act, ss 29 and 30.
22 See ibid, ss 16(1)(c), 33(2) and 36.
23 See ibid, s 2(1) and (4). See also EE Okon, 'The legal framework of environmental impact assessment in Nigeria' (2001) 5(2) *Modern Practice Journal of Finance and Investment Law* 208, 220.
24 See ibid, ss 24 and 25.

development, waste treatment and disposal, and water supply. Considering these activities and those in Annex I of the Aarhus Convention listed in the preceding chapter (with their further specifications and nature), it can be posited, give or take, that the scope of the mandatory study list in the EIA Act is generally reflective of best practice.

Furthermore, similar to best practice, the EIA Act broadly makes provision for public participation in decision-making on activities, whether proposed by the public or private sector,[25] not listed as part of the mandatory study activities but of which 'the extent, nature or location of the proposed activity is such that it is likely to significantly affect the environment' (in which case, an EIA procedure, which generally requires public participation, would be undertaken).[26] The benefit of this flexible approach has been noted in the preceding chapter, and similar to the Annex I-listed activities in the Aarhus Convention, the mandatory study activities under the EIA Act might also serve as a guide in determining what is 'significant' with respect to non-listed activities.

Nevertheless, as with other provisions of the Act, the case of *Gbemre v Shell Petroleum Development Company Nigeria Ltd and Ors*[27] highlights the disappointing manner in which the above flexible approach is implemented by government authorities and developers. In that case, the first and second respondents failed to carry out an EIA in the applicants' community concerning the effects of their gas-flaring activities, despite the fact that this activity is well known for its significant negative impact on the environment and human wellbeing. It was nonetheless allowed to proceed without public participation. Although the court's judgment did not go far on this point, it was simply held to be a clear violation of Section 2(2) of the EIA Act.

This is the case with several other oil corporations in Nigeria where the relevant government agencies do not usually ensure that the potentially destructive activities of such corporations are subjected to adequate EIA and public participation processes and disallowed or significantly restricted if necessary, mostly as a result of the government's direct and huge economic interest in the oil industry. In this regard, the *Gbemre* case has not led to a noticeable change on the ground (especially considering several weaknesses in the EIA Act).

Furthermore, the EIA Act contains no identical provision to that in Annex I Paragraph 22 of the Aarhus Convention. However, it can arguably be posited that it does contemplate that physical change to or extension of existing activities that meets the criteria of any mandatory study activity, or is likely significantly to affect the environment, should equally be subject to public participation by being subject to EIA. However, with the absence of an *express* provision in this regard, public authorities and some developers who are used to the culture of public exclusion from environmental governance will hardly comply with an *implied* provision that puts a 'burden' on them.

25 See ibid, s 2(1) and (4).
26 See ss 2(1) and (2) and 7.
27 Unreported, Suit No FHC/B/CS/53/05, 14 November 2005.

Also, the absence of such an express provision can create an environment of uncertainty, which can serve to discourage members of the public who may wish to hold potentially erring companies and the government to account based on the significance of changes made to a project without public participation. So this may be a weakness in the EIA Act that needs to be strengthened with an express provision. These points, for example, may be validated by the complaint of Comrade Che, a community representative in the Niger Delta, that as 'a result of the *upgrading* of Elf facilities (independent power facility) in Egi, people have lost their farmlands'[28] (emphasis added), and from another, that the same project (seemingly executed without public participation), 'is tearing the people asunder'.[29]

What is more, the Act contains a provision that allows relevant projects to be excluded from undergoing EIA, and therefore public participation. The nature and implementation of that provision largely erodes the efficacy of the provisions of the EIA Act discussed above, which allows for public participation in certain activities, and is therefore contrary to best practice. That provision is Section 14(1) of the EIA Act, which provides that:

> (1) An environmental assessment of project shall not be required where –
>
> (a) [in the opinion of the Agency the project is in the list of projects which the President or the Council is of the opinion that the environmental effect of the project are likely to be minimal;
> (b) the project is to be carried out during national emergency for which temporary measures have been taken by the Government;
> (c) the project is to be carried out in response to circumstances that, in the opinion of the Agency, the project is in the interest of public health or safety.

Apart from exemption (b), exemptions (a) and (c), which are contrary to best practice and can be said to be relics of the military dictatorship that promulgated the EIA Act, should have no place in a democratic society as they potentially permit arbitrariness and should therefore be expunged from the EIA Act. In fact they have been used unjustifiably in this manner to exclude EIA and public participation in the establishment of major projects with significant environmental and human impact.[30] Omorogbe puts it best:

> It is difficult to see practical reasons for the first and third exclusions. Why should the fact that the President or the Council believe that there will be

28 Obayanju and Obaseki (n 7) 58.
29 Ibid, 55.
30 See ibid, 54–55 and 57; and Y Omorogbe, 'The legal framework for public participation in decision-making on mining and energy development in Nigeria: giving voices to the voiceless', in DN Zillman, AR Lucas and G Pring (eds), *Human Rights in National Resource Development: Public Participation in the Sustainable Development of Mining and Energy Resource* (Oxford: Oxford University Press, 2002) 549, 568.

> minimal environmental effects negate the need for an EIA? Why should a project in the interest of public health and safety not require EIA? A situation characterized as a national emergency presupposes that time is of the essence and, therefore, it is possible to comprehend that under such conditions, an EIA would not be feasible. The other categories suggested by section [14(2)] merely provide loopholes and lead one to believe that projects which are undertaken without EIAs in recent past, or which had reluctant participation by the private companies concerned, had probably been assured that they would not be required to comply with this Act.[31]

7.2.2 The public participation process

7.2.2.1 The duty to effectively inform the public concerned

With respect to informing the public about the environmental decision-making procedure and the opportunity to participate in it, the EIA Act, in line with best practice, contains general provisions which indicate that the public should receive such information; e.g. it severally obliges that the 'opportunity' to participate be given to the public as well as all information required to facilitate their participation.[32] Although such provisions in the Act are not detailed, the authorities responsible for their implementation can certainly be guided by the Aarhus Convention's detailed provision and the enunciation of the Aarhus Compliance Committee in this respect as discussed in the preceding chapter.

Even though the EIA Act makes no express reference to the fact that this information should be supplied in an 'adequate, timely and effectively manner', it is submitted that based on the principle of good faith discussed earlier, the responsible public authority can be held to account on those particular terms and must tailor its actions in accordance with them. This is in line with the reasoning of the Aarhus Compliance Committee earlier espoused.

As discussed in the preceding chapter, even though the Compliance Committee once held that failure to use those terms in an EIA law does not of itself amount to non-compliance, it did, however, note with concern that the lack of those express terms in an EIA regime may adversely affect compliance with them; and possibly, amongst other effects, it may give more room for the unhealthy exercise of discretion by authorities or heighten the possibility of relevant authorities overlooking the need for notifications to comply with those express standards where they are simply implied. In this light, the inclusion of those terms in the EIA Act is recommended, as a way of reinforcing them in the consciousness of the implementing bodies and preventing breaches and conflicts that may follow non-compliance with them.

Furthermore, in the Nigerian context, adequate and effective information would mean, for instance, that notifications should be made in English and in the

31 Omorogbe (n 30) 568.
32 See generally, EIA Act, ss 7, 21(3), 24, 33(1) and 36(b).

indigenous language(s) predominant in the area of the proposed project, especially where this is a rural area. It would also mean that the medium of notification should be informed by the likes of the mobility of the relevant local public and the technological and mass media infrastructure available to them, e.g. certain areas are mostly reliant on radio and have very limited access to TVs, and vice versa, as highlighted in Chapter 2.[33] Further connotations of what 'adequate, timely and effectively manner' entails, to serve as guide, have been discussed in the counterpart section of the preceding chapter.

In addition, the EIA Act further makes provision for public access to some information relating to the proposed activity itself. A primary source of information to which the public has a right to access under section 4 of the EIA Act is the EIA study/report which, similar to the Aarhus Convention's Article 6(6) list, must include the following minimum matters:

(a) a description of the proposed activities;
(b) a description of the potential[ly] affected environment, including specific information necessary to identify and assess the environmental effect of the proposed activities;
(c) a description of the practical activities, as appropriate;
(d) an assessment of the likely or potential environmental impacts of the proposed activity and the alternatives, including the direct or indirect cumulative, short-term and long-term effects;
(e) an identification and description of measures available to mitigate adverse environmental impacts of [the] proposed activity and assessment of those measures;
(f) an indication of gaps in knowledge and uncertainty which may be encountered in computing the required information;
(g) an indication of whether the environment of any other State or local government area or areas outside Nigeria is likely to be affected by the proposed activity or its alternatives;
(h) a brief and non-technical summary of the information provided under paragraphs (a) to (g) of this section.

Again, as with all matters where information has to be provided to the public in Nigeria, the issue of illiteracy and the fact that many members of the public concerned may not be able to understand English as effectively as they would their native language, must be considered in relation to the particular public being dealt with. Therefore, simplified explanations of complex issues (in the context of the mandatory 'brief and non-technical summary' of the report) and translation should be provided. There is hardly evidence that this is (properly) being done, and it raises questions as to the effectiveness of the provided information in the

33 The 2010 EIA (Amendment) Bill in s 7 broadly makes similar suggestions, and can be further improved.

context of many Nigerian societies. However, as noted in Chapter 5, if Nigeria commits more to improving literacy levels and public understanding of English, many of these complexities will disappear over time.

More generally, the EIA Act makes provision for the establishment of a 'public registry', which is to contain and allow public access *only* to information 'produced, collected or submitted' with respect to a specific activity that is subject to environmental assessment.[34] In other words, contrary to best practice, this extends neither to other environmental information related to the proposed activity nor to other information that may be relevant in ensuring an informed public participation.

Added to this, the Act provides for certain exemptions to information that should be contained in the public registry,[35] which exemptions are overly broad (and could aid arbitrariness), contain no proper 'public interest override', and so this provision critically falls below best practice. In fact, it has been noted that the establishment of such a public registry containing the stipulated information is hardly being implemented.[36] On the whole, this aspect of the EIA Act betrays its military and undemocratic history and is contrary to best practice, which ensures public access to a wide spectrum of information that is meant to make participation meaningful.

However, this gap in the EIA Act has been plugged, to some extent and subject to discussions in Chapter 5, by the 2011 FOI Act, which provides that: 'where the question whether any public record is to be made available, where that question arises under this Act, the question shall be determined in accordance with the provision stated herein.'[37] This provision only potentially expands the variety of information available to the public. It does not relieve the agency of its general duty under the EIA Act to ensure that the public has access to information on the *specific activity* being considered through an organised public registry, as the FOI Act provides that: '[t]his Act is intended to complement and not to replace the existing procedures for access to public records and information and is not intended to limit in any way access to those types of officials [sic] information that have been normally available to the public.'[38]

Nonetheless, it is advisable, for the purposes of improving the clarity and consistency in this aspect of the EIA Act in line with common sense and best practice, that provisions in the EIA Act on public access to information (e.g. Section 55(4)(c) and (6) on exemptions) that are not in line with the provisions of the FOI Act be improved and aligned with the latter. In this regard, issues such as the timeframe for accessing information under the FOI Act must be allowed to inform the timeframe set for the public to participate in the decision-making

34 Section 55(1)–(4).
35 See ss 55(4)(c) and (6).
36 ET Bristol-Alagbariya, *Participation in Petroleum Development: Towards Sustainable Community Development in Niger Delta* (Dundee: Centre for Energy, Petroleum and Mineral Law and Policy, 2009) 165.
37 FOI Act, s 30(2).
38 Section 30(1).

procedure, 'so as to facilitate informed public participation' as recommended under the draft Commentary to the Bali Guidelines.[39]

Finally, the practice of ensuring that the public has access to the relevant environmental studies is quite weak and needs to be strengthened. In the first place, there are cases where project proponents that are subject to the EIA procedure have 'bluntly refused' to carry out EIA studies (that will assist in informed participation in the decision-making process), and 'because government is bent on deriving revenues and meeting the project deadlines the safety of the environment and the people . . . [are usually] sacrificed on the altar of expediency'.[40] There are also cases where EIA reports are produced but the agency fails to publish/advertise them (to enable the public comment on them).[41]

Even when such environmental reports are produced and advertised, reviews by some independent experts suggest that the quality of many EIA reports is poor, containing inadequate and inaccurate information.[42] In fact, according to former Shell employee, J P Van Dassel, 'there is a major problem with most of the environmental studies carried out in the Niger Delta, as they are carried out by Nigerian universities or private consultancies which have generally low scientific level and little technical/industrial expertise'.[43] So, in such cases, even when members of the concerned public manage to gain access to this vital information, one cannot completely claim that they were enabled to participate in an *informed* manner in the decision-making process.

Therefore, to comply with the duty adequately to inform the public about the project in issue, apart from improving the law to support better practice, relevant project applicants must not only be made to carry out the required EIA studies, but must also be made to engage bodies with appropriate technical know-how to carry out the studies. This should be ensured by the relevant government agencies, and by public/NGO pressure and enforcement.

7.2.2.2 Early public participation

Article 6(4) of the Aarhus Convention, reflecting best practice as shown in the preceding chapter, provides that '[p]arties shall provide for early public participation, when all options are open and effective public participation can take place.' This is with the aim of addressing the shortcoming of traditional public participation procedures coming too late in the environmental decision-making process.

39 See Commentary to Guideline 8.

40 See N Bassey, 'Environmental impacts and the defence of communities', in Obayanju and Obaseki (eds) (n 7) 17, 20.

41 See R Ako, 'Resource exploitation and environmental justice: the Nigerian experience', in FN Botchway (ed), *Natural Resource Investment and Africa's Development* (Cheltenham: Edward Elgar Publishing, 2011) 72, 90. See generally Amnesty International, *Nigeria: Petroleum, Pollution and Poverty in the Niger Delta* (London: Amnesty International Publications, 2009) 51.

42 O Omokaro, 'Non-Implementation of environmental impact assessment and its impact on the environment and local livelihood', in Obayanju and Obaseki (eds) (n 7) 27, 34.

43 Quoted in ibid, 33.

In Nigeria, there is no equivalent provision as Article 6(4) under the EIA Act. The earliest opportunity the public has to participate in environmental decision-making under the Act is to make comments on completed EIA study reports just before the agency takes a decision based on such reports.[44] An EIA study report, according to the EIA Act, may be a 'screening report' (which is produced where a project is not described in the mandatory study list or any exclusion list)[45] or the 'mandatory study report' (which is produced where a project is described in the mandatory study list),[46] both of which are substantially the same in terms of the scope of environmental assessment that they evidence.[47] The agency's decision, based on an environmental assessment report and the public comments on it, may create a subsequent opportunity for (representatives of) the relevant public to participation in a mediation or public review panel.[48]

Whilst allowing for public comments on EIA study reports is welcomed, it arguably comes too late in the decision-making process, is contrary to best practice and is inimical to effective participation. Public input should be allowed to inform the actual environmental assessment and the report itself, rather than simply allowing for public comments on the finished EIA study report; '[u]nder the Nigerian EIA Act, it is not stipulated that public opinion should form a part of the report to be approved by the agency . . . There will be active PP [public participation] where the Act ensures local input in the EIA report itself rather than comments on the report.'[49]

In fact, the stipulated minimum content of an EIA report in Section 4 of the EIA Act does not include public input, meaning that the authorities and developers can carry out the environmental assessment without involving the public and still be in compliance with the Act. However, in practice, some form of public consultation *may* still be carried out during the actual EIA studies and report preparation stages, with the objective of identifying early, the concerns of the relevant public regarding the impact of the proposed project in order to address them during the actual study and reflect their views in the project's EIA report.[50] In some cases, public involvement at this stage has had to be actualised by forceful

44 See s 7.

45 See EIA Act, ss 15, 18, 21, and 2(1) and (2). See also N Echefu and E Akpofure, 'Environmental impact assessment in Nigeria: regulatory background and procedural framework', in M McCabe and B Sadler (eds), *Studies of EIA Practice in Developing Countries: A Supplement to the UNEP Training Resource Manual* (UNEP, 2003) 63, 69; and Omorogbe (n 30) 565.

46 See ibid, ss 22 and 25.

47 See ibid, s 15.

48 See ibid, s 21, 25, 33 and 36.

49 RT Ako, 'Ensuring public participation in environmental impact assessment of development projects in the Niger delta of Nigeria: a veritable tool for sustainable development' (2006) 3(1–2) *Envirotropica* 1, 11. See generally Amnesty International (n 41) 58.

50 O Ameyan, 'Environmental impact assessment: insight into the environmental impact regulatory process and implementation for qualifying projects', a paper presented at the seminar titled 'Preparing Business in Nigeria for Environmental Challenges and Opportunities' organised by Manufacturing Association of Nigeria, held in Lagos, Nigeria, on 4 November 2008, 6, at http://softwaresupermart.com/mangreencourses/papers/paper6b.pdf (last accessed 3 February 2015); Echefu and Akpofure (n 45) 69.

public insistence, which on occasion has led to the stalling or halting of some projects;[51] this highlights the need for public participation in EIA studies and report preparation to be made mandatory in line with best practice.

In addition, as it relates to 'scoping', the EIA Act does not provide the relevant public with the right or opportunity to participate in deciding the general scope of the EIA study, the information to be assessed and covered in the EIA report or the factors to be taken into consideration with reference to the EIA.[52] As discussed in the preceding chapter, public participation at this 'scoping' stage is welcomed by the Aarhus Compliance Committee. This further highlights the lateness of subsequently allowing for public comments. At this 'scoping' level, the relevant public, from local experience especially, could provide particular and vital information on issues to be assessed during an EIA that the project proponents and public authorities may not be aware of, or may deliberately be trying to avoid in order to have the project approved quickly or easily.

Perhaps, it is in this light that, in practice, the relevant government authority in Nigeria has a discretion to allow for some form of public participation during 'scoping' in selected cases.[53] However, the necessity of participation at this early stage warrants that it should be made a statutory requirement at the 'scoping' stage in general.

Similarly, there is no provision for public participation in the 'screening' of proposed projects to determine whether or not it should be subjected to the EIA procedure.[54] As stated in the preceding chapter, public participation at this stage is significant, considering that the decision that comes out of it determines whether or not the public will have a voice in the project implementation at all, and the fact that the local public especially will be helpful in identifying potential significant impacts that might elude public officials. In this light, even though it seemingly goes beyond best practice, it is recommended that 'screening' be subject to public participation under the EIA Act.

Furthermore, in the counterpart section of the preceding chapter, the point was made that in line with best practice, the grant of a permit or conclusion of any form of contract or agreement between public authorities and private entities relating to matter that will (subsequently) qualify for public participation and which actually limits the range of options available during public participation, goes against the notion of *early* public participation considering that the public had no input in the negotiation and formation of the contract, agreement or terms of the permit. This is another aspect in which Nigerian authorities have fallen short of best practice and would need to realise that *all* options must be open to influence by public participation at the appropriate time, and even before an EIA is carried out.

51 See R Adomokai and WR Sheate, 'Community participation and environmental decision-Making in the Niger delta' (2004) 24 *Environmental Impact Assessment Review* 495, 511; and Ako (n 49) 12.
52 See s 16(3).
53 See Ako (n 49) 12; and Bristol-Alagbariya (n 36) 160.
54 See EIA Act, s 15.

Such a misplaced practice is exemplified by the dealings between the Nigerian Government and bitumen companies with respect to preparations to commence extraction of huge bitumen deposits in the southern Nigerian states of Lagos, Ogun, Ondo and Edo; a process with a major potential negative impact on the environment and people's livelihood and which will fall under the mandatory study list of the EIA Act and should therefore be subject to public participation.[55] The following statements from some members in these bitumen communities capture the point in context:

> None of the companies *granted exploration rights* have visited us. They have not talked to us and we don't know what they are doing . . . The only official communication between the community and the Bitumen Implementation Committee on this issue was a letter to invite us to the 'ground breaking' ceremony performed by the president and another to thank us for attending the ceremony.[56] (High Chief Adesanya of Agbabu, Ondo state)
>
> There are sacred forests here where people don't hunt. Our ancestors have protected these forests for years. Government has now *granted license to companies to move in there*, even the burial grounds.[57] (Francis Ajuwa, Adviser to Alagbabu of Agbabu on Bitumen Matters)
>
> We have formed committees in this community to ensure that everybody is well represented in whatever we are doing concerning this project. There are youths, women and leaders from the 33 streets in Ode-Aye. We want to talk as a united people, we don't want dispute. So we are ready to talk to them [government and the company] but . . . [a]s at now we have not seen anybody from *the company that has been granted right to this area* . . . they have not called us for any formal meeting. We heard on radio that they want to begin operation and we think that is not good enough.[58] (His Highness Oba Oyenejo Eyinejofo, Oba of Ode-Aye, Okitipupa LGA, Ondo state)

So from the above, by granting exploration licences and rights to the various companies with respect to bitumen deposits without public participation, the Nigerian Government may be said to have foreclosed, for instance, the option of refusing to grant permission for the companies to carry out a project in relation to their licences when the outcome of subsequent EIA and public participation so dictates. In this case, public participation cannot be said to be *early* in line with best practice.

Also, the option of challenging the validity of such licences in view of the participation opportunity given to the concerned public under the EIA Act may not be an attractive one or even an effective solution to this problem, especially

55 GU Ojo and A Oluwafemi (eds), *Before the Earth Bleeds Again* (Benin City: Environmental Rights Action/Friends of the Earth, Nigeria, 2004) 71–87.

56 Ibid, 82 (emphasis added).

57 Ibid, 83 (emphasis added).

58 Ibid, 85–86 (emphasis added).

considering the many barriers to access to justice with respect to issues relating to the EIA Act in Nigeria, as will be discussed below. Even if a court rules against such pre-public participation licences, the government's action of disregarding public participation in issuing the licences already strongly suggests that they have made up their mind to ensure the establishment of the bitumen projects no matter what, and will easily take advantage of their extensive discretion under the EIA Act to achieve that end.

7.2.2.3 Reasonable timeframes between phases of public participation

Whilst *early* participation in the decision-making process as discussed above relates to *when* the public gets engaged in the process, this section deals with the pace of the participation that ensues. If the latter is not well managed, it could render the participation process ineffective and meaningless; and on this issue of pace, the best practice developed in the preceding chapter can serve as a useful guide to authorities in Nigeria as to what adequate pacing or reasonable timeframe between the various phases of participation entails, in order to ensure effective participation.

To start with, as it relates to making comments on an EIA report, the EIA Act does not specify a timeframe within which the public should make their comments. Generally, it permits the agency to set a deadline that gives the public the 'opportunity' to make their comments.[59] In furtherance of this duty, the agency usually gives the public 21 working days to file their comments with the agency from the day in which the EIA report is made publicly available and the public has been so notified.[60] This agency practice of allowing only 21 days for public comment arguably falls below best practice and does not help ensure effective and meaningful public participation.

Such a maximum timeframe of 21 days clearly does not take into account the varying nature, complexities and sizes of proposed activities, as well as other realities on the ground. Generally, that timeframe may not be sufficient for the public to seek other relevant information from public institutions, as well as to study and become familiar with it and the EIA report, before making their comments.

This is so, especially when one considers the relatively high level of illiteracy in Nigeria, particularly in the rural areas where many EIA-qualified projects are undertaken, where it is foreseeable that in many instances, if public involvement will be effective, more than 21 days would be required for the public to go through the formal processes involved, as well as the usually long and technical EIA report and other documents, and even put together and consult with their private specialist (this being a growing trend).[61] Without a doubt, the flexible minimum

59 See ibid, ss 7, 21(3) and 24.
60 See Echefu and Akpofure (n 45) 69; Adomokai and Sheate (n 51) 499; and Ameyan (n 50) 7.
61 See Adomokai and Sheate (n 51) 501.

timeframe explained in the preceding chapter, rather than the maximum timeframe of 21 days, is best for Nigeria and in tune with best practice and the goal of effective public participation.

Furthermore, after public comments on EIA reports are received, there will be another phase for public participation in a hearing if the relevant government agencies decide to refer the proposed activity to mediation or a review panel. Although the EIA Act, with respect to these forums, provides that all the information required for the mediation or assessment by the review panel be made available to the public and participants before the commencement of the mediation or the assessment by the review panel,[62] this stipulation does not clearly address the need for the public to be given sufficient time to become acquainted with the information made available and prepare to participate in the process.

In addition, even though the EIA Act, with respect to those forums, provides that the public be given the opportunity to participate in them,[63] this participation process will usually be in stages in line with the various issues to be addressed with respect to the proposed activity. Again, those provisions do not clearly do justice to the need to ensure that each stage of the process is effectively paced to ensure effective public participation. As the government agencies have the duty to 'fix the terms of reference' of the mediation and review panel,[64] it is recommended here that the timeframe provided in the terms of reference be such that addresses these twin issues raised in line with best practice on reasonable timeframes for the various stages of public participation.

7.2.2.4 The right of the public to contribute

Under the EIA Act, the opportunity for the public to make a contribution or participate in the decision-making process is generally different from what is reflected in best practice. First, when a proposed project is subjected to an environmental assessment, the agency is obliged to 'give opportunity to . . . members of the public, experts in any relevant disciple and interested groups to make comments on the environmental impact assessment [report] of the activity';[65] but '[t]his is the most violated provision of the Act assuming there is any part of it that is observed',[66] according to Chima Williams, a key official of Environmental Rights Action/Friends of the Earth, Nigeria.

A major issue here is that the EIA reports are usually displayed for 21 days (to enable public access and comment) at the headquarters of the local government (which mostly cover several villages/towns) hosting the project and other

62 Sections 33(1) and 36(a).
63 Sections 33(2) and 36(b).
64 EIA Act, ss 31(b) and 35(b).
65 Ibid, s 7.
66 PC Williams, 'The Environmental Impact Assessment Act and process as an environmental and livelihood advocacy tool', in B Obayanju and M Obaseki (eds), *Defending the Environment: The Role of Environmental Impact Assessment* (Benin City: Environmental Rights Act, 2009) 7, 12.

government offices, which may be relatively far from some of the affected communities; the result is that '[f]ew people are aware of this, and fewer still have the resources [and time] to visit local government offices to read these documents'.[67] For better dissemination of this information that will help mitigate these problems and improve access, soft copies of the EIA reports and other important documents must be made available online to facilitate access by ICT devices with internet connectivity. Importantly also, hard copies must be placed at a central location of the villages/towns, e.g. the palaces and offices of the traditional rulers or the town halls.

Furthermore, reasonably in line with best practice, the relevant provisions of the EIA Act indicate that comments are to be filed with the agency that has the responsibility of taking them into consideration and making the final decision, or other official body setup by the agency for onward transmission to it.[68] Upon consideration of the assessment reports and any comments filed, the agency, together with the council, shall refer the project to 'mediation' or a 'review panel' where they are of the 'opinion' that (1) 'the project is likely to cause significant adverse environmental effects that may not be mitigable; or (2) public concerns respecting the environmental effects of the project warrant it.[69]

Furthermore, the project is only referred to mediation if the Council is satisfied that: (1) those 'directly affected by or have a direct interest in the project have been identified and are willing to participate in the mediation through representatives; and (2) the mediation is likely to produce a result that is satisfactory to all of the parties'; or 'to a review panel, in any other case'.[70] According to the EIA Act, these two forums provide the only opportunity for the public to engage face-to-face with the project proponent.

It is argued that these participatory opportunities granted to the public in Nigeria are provided for in a manner that largely inhibits effective and adequate public participation. Whilst the initial provision for mandatory public comments on the environmental assessment report under the EIA Act seems generally in line with best practice, as there is no provision allowing these public comments to be informed by a face-to-face inquiry and dialogue process with the applicant and other parties, the quality of the comments made may leave much to be desired.

It is argued that any comment partly informed by face-to-face engagements with the project applicants and other interested parties that offers the public an opportunity to ask questions based on available information, confirms stated facts and clarify any ambiguity with the project, are likely to be more informed than comment made only after reading the documents provided to the public. At this level, the project applicant and other relevant parties can seek clarification from and better understand the concerned public, considering also that certain matters are better expressed in person than through writing.

67 Amnesty International (n 41)51. See generally Ameyan (n 50) 7.
68 See ss 7, 21(3), 24(2) and 35–36.
69 See EIA Act, ss 21(b), 25(a) and 26.
70 Ibid, s 30.

In addition, as alluded to above, the EIA Act makes no provision for a public right to a public hearing or inquiry with relevant project proponents and other interested parties. Although the review panel under the Act is obliged to 'hold hearing in a manner that offers the public an opportunity to participate in the assessment',[71] this is subject to the discretion of the agency/council as to whether or not a proposed project is referred to the review panel in the first place as stated above;[72] a discretion that can easily be exercised to exclude this participation processes in favour of speedy development at the expense of the environmental and public wellbeing.

The same applies to the mediation process that,[73] as noted above, overly restricts those entitled to participate in it, contrary to best practice. In fact, apart from the exercise of the agency's overly broad powers under the EIA Act to exempt and exclude projects from the EIA procedure entirely as noted earlier, the above discretionary powers would also seem to have been exercised relatively frequently to prevent participation, as the following experience from various community representatives at an NGO-organised EIA workshop shows: '[t]hey said that often host communities are not involved in the EIA processes or at best they are invited into a meeting where the corporation will tell them that they have done an EIA and that the projects had been approved for commencement.'[74]

Although, in limited cases, outwith the framework of the EIA Act, some project proponents may hold some form of consultation with the affected public,[75] this pales in comparison to the requirements for effective public participation in environmental matters reflected by best practice. It is important that a provision mandating public hearing or inquiry be made in the EIA Act, as encouraged by the best practice considered in the preceding chapter, especially considering the earlier noted substantial benefits of participation by face-to-face engagement. In this light, such a provision is also vital lest it become difficult to justify in many cases the fact that public participation was actually adequate and meaningful.

Also, the fact that some aspects of the EIA process may differ from country to country notwithstanding, Hunter, Salzman and Zaelke, in accordance with best practice, have posited that: '[o]ne of the primary reasons for conducting environmental assessments is to inform the public of proposed projects *and to engage them in a meaningful dialogue* about the potential benefits and environmental and social costs of a proposed activity' (emphasis added).[76] This engagement is also about ensuring that the public authority has an appropriate range of

71 Section 36(b).

72 See Okon (n 23) 228. See also Echefu and Akpofure (n 45) 69; and Ameyan (n 50) 6–7, for a discussion of the 'in-house review'.

73 Ibid.

74 Obayanju and Obaseki (eds) (n 7) 58.

75 See Bristol-Alagbariya (n 36)159–63.

76 D Hunter, J Salzman and D Zaelke, *International Environmental Law and Policy* (New York: Foundation Press, 1998) 369.

environmental information before it to make a good decision. These views are supported and elaborated on in IAIA's international best practice principles.[77]

Furthermore, it is regrettable that some ordinary members of the public may generally lack the ability to comment effectively, participate and question experts during the decision-making process owing to a lack of (basic) technical and legal knowledge or guidance, as well as knowledge of public inquiry procedures and financial resources, as empirical research has shown.[78] Nigeria is certainly not exempted from this potential state of affairs, especially in view of the relatively high levels of poverty and illiteracy, and the language limitation as, generally, many members of the public are not able to communicate effectively in Nigeria's official language – English – but only in their native languages.

Be that as it may, based on Article 3(2) of the Aarhus Convention, which obliges states to ensure that public authorities 'assist and provide guidance to the public . . . in facilitating participation in decision-making', which is arguably in line with the general principle of good faith, the Nigerian Government at all levels has the responsibility to take steps to ameliorate the fundamental disadvantages some members of the public may face in the process and enable them to participate more effectively. For example, the public authorities could ensure that an interpreter is available during the public hearing to help facilitate/improve communication between the parties, where necessary.

The establishment of a fund to aid financially challenged members of the public concerned to take advantage of the participation process effectively may also be a way of discharging this responsibility.[79] Such funding will, to an extent, help 'redress the financial imbalance among parties and support full and effective public participation'.[80] An IAIA international best practice principle headed 'Support to Participants' also refers to the point that there should be some 'financial assistance', as well as '[c]apacity-building' and general assistance for deficient groups;[81] similar to the draft Commentary to Bali Guideline 14.

However, NGOs that generally have a much better standing in all those potentially limiting areas could help give appropriate voice to the general interest of the public during the participation process.[82] NGOs may also provide alternative views in the few cases where, as empirical research shows, owing to the relatively high level of poverty and illiteracy in Nigeria (especially in the rural areas), (a section of) the concerned public may be more interested in bargaining for economic benefits in the course of the participatory process at the expense of securing their environment and related wellbeing, and some may not be keen to

77 P André with B Enserink, D Connor and P Croal, *Public Participation: International Best Practice Principles* (Special Publication Series No 4, North Dakota: International Association for Impact Assessment, 2006) 1–2.

78 See Hartley and Wood (n 1) 332.

79 See AR Lucas, 'Canadian participatory rights in mining and energy resource development: the bridges to empowerment?', in Zillman, Lucas and Pring (eds) (n 30) 305, 322.

80 Ibid.

81 André et al. (n 77) 2.

82 See generally K Raustiala, 'The "participatory revolution" in international environmental law' (1997) 21 *Harvard Environmental Law Review* 537, 558.

participate meaningfully in favour of whatever economic benefits come with hosting the proposed project.[83]

Nonetheless, as stressed in Chapter 3, such perceived weakness of an aspect of the public does not constitute a justifiable excuse to deny them the opportunity to participate in environmental decision-making processes, given that they arguably have 'the right to be wrong' on issues of this nature (and perhaps, will learn from their experiences over time), and the fact that such a process has its own educative value about environmental democratic norms.

NGOs can also play an oversight role over the participatory process that may make the process more effective.[84] For instance, through diligent observation and mobilising public pressure, they could ensure that powerful project proponents and colluding regulatory bodies do not use the weakness of the public against the latter, that laid down rules are followed by all parties involved and that the process is conducted in good faith. In addition, environmental and human rights NGOs generally have many years of experience in working with and protecting the rights and interests of local people and '[t]heir knowledge of local society and culture and the local reputation they have built up cannot be acquired instantly by outside entities that choose to get involved in that specific area.'[85]

In the process of working with local people, NGOs generally acquire 'a level of credibility among local people that neither government nor firms enjoy. This credibility [and experience] can be essential to the dialogue process . . . [also] NGOs will be more accurate than government in identifying stakeholders.'[86] So even though NGOs may not be considered public representatives in a democratic sense, in line with their aforementioned value, Nigerian authorities must do more to boost the legal and practical opportunities for them to participate effectively in decision-making processes, in line with the best practice requirement for NGOs to be supported and not sidelined.

It is by no means being argued here that all environment-related NGOs and interest groups are always representing the general interest of the public and amplifying their voices in reality. Whilst many may seek and serve to amplify the position of the general public in their involvement in the participatory process (and should be supported), there are others who may have their own separate agendas to push, which may be legitimate and invaluable to the process, so long as they are expressed and taken as one of the many other expressed views in the process, and not as that of the general public.[87]

83 See Adomokai and Sheate (n 51) 500, 510 and 514; and Omorogbe (n 30) 586.

84 See generally Raustiala (n 82) 560–63.

85 F Tanner, 'Conflict prevention and conflict resolution: limits of multilateralism' (2000) 82(839) *International Review of the Red Cross* 541, 554.

86 C Nwapi, 'A legislative proposal for public participation in oil and gas decision-making in Nigeria' (2010) 54(2) *Journal of African Law* 184, 210.

87 See M Lee and C Abbot, 'The usual suspects? Public participation under the Aarhus Convention' (2003) 66 *Modern Law Review* 80, 86–87; and OW Petersen, 'European environmental human rights and environmental rights: a long time coming?' (2008) 21(1) *Georgetown International Environmental Law Review* 73, 99.

However, other so-called environment-related NGOs and interest groups may simply not be interested in amplifying the voice of the general public or pushing a separate legitimate interest, having been established as a money-making venture for their 'proprietors' or as a front for their sponsors (usually, corporations and government entities), as one may find in Nigeria and other countries around the world.[88] It is in that light that an emerging trend in Nigeria must be welcomed and more local communities supported to implement it, especially as a useful complement to the participation of the public concerned and NGOs. This trend is aptly documented by Adomokai and Sheate:

> Communities, who may not have the knowledge or confidence to adequately represent themselves in such fora, find that they do not contribute much to the process. However, some communities who have individuals interested in the process and are educated ensure they participate in the process in order to ensure the interests of the community as a whole are incorporated in the EIA process . . . A few communities have taken this approach further by constituting committees who have environmental specialists, lawyers and consultants to act on their behalf. They are usually indigenes from the community who provide the service free of charge to the community. This signifies a new and promising trend in community participation in the Niger Delta and shows the ingenuity of communities in being proactive, thereby ensuring their interests, especially . . . in the decision-making process. Examples include Bonny town in Rivers State [Nigeria], where the Bonny Environmental Committee Consultants (BECC) is comprised of indigenous consultants – lawyers, environmentalists, etc. – who participate fully and are consulted when projects are planned for Bonny . . . They consult with the indigenes of Bonny and ensure their comments and concerns are included in the decision-making process. In Gbaran, Bayelsa State [Nigeria] the community set up a committee called Biosphere Monitors, who are indigenes and environmental experts. They monitor the impact of proposed company activities in their community especially as it relates to the oil and gas industry . . . Both of these examples, therefore, represent forms of what might be regarded as a 'qualified public'.[89]

This active introduction into the participatory process of these organised community-based experts and indigenes, who may also be armed with first-hand local knowledge and experience and are likely to be directly affected by the proposed activity, will be a plus to any participatory decision-making process. This will contribute to generally improving the level and quality of environmental public participation, and the resulting decisions, in Nigeria, especially if the other

88 See E Oshionebo, 'Transnational corporations, civil society organisations and social accountability in Nigeria's oil and gas industry' (2007) 15(1) *African Journal of International and Comparative Law* 107, 121–22; and Lee and Abbot (n 87) 87.

89 Adomokai and Sheate (n 51) 501.

elements of environmental public participation are adequately reflected in the EIA Act and implemented (in line with the general discussion in this chapter).

7.2.2.5 The duty to consider and communicate

The EIA Act also obliges the Agency, which is the authority responsible for making the final decision, to take due account of the outcome of the public participation. Section 8 of the Act provides that: '[t]he Agency shall not give a decision as to whether a proposed activity should be authorised or undertaken until the appropriate period has elapsed to consider comments pursuant to section 7 and 17 of this Act.'[90]

One writer has queried the use of the word 'appropriate' in that provision, stating that it 'will create problems of interpretation' and that a specific period for considering comments and taking a decision of say '30 days or 60 days [or] 90 days . . . could have been better'.[91] However, that view seems flawed as the circumstances surrounding every project differs just as the amount of public comments to be considered will also vary with each proposed project. So setting a specific timeframe for considering the public's comments could easily mean that in many instances the comments will not be appropriately and thoroughly considered.

Therefore, the Section 8 provision is in line with best practice as earlier discussed. What is left is for the agency to, on a case-by-case basis, utilise a *reasonably* 'appropriate period' – considering that a balance needs to be struck between efficiency in decision-making (which project proponents and the public are entitled to) and effective participation – in considering seriously the public's input before making a decision, as best practice requires. Whether or not the agency properly carries out this responsibility should be left to an administrative review panel and, if necessary, a court, to decide in view of the prevailing circumstances of the particular case.

Further, in line with best practice and ensuring that the public participation has an impact on the outcome of the process, one will also expect the agency to take account of the public's input adequately in its final decision, in accordance with the basic principles of natural justice and transparency upon which the English Lord Hewart CJ asserted that 'justice should not only be done, but should manifestly and undoubtedly be seen to be done'[92] – a principle that is now widely applied.

However, in practice, it appears that this is usually not the case in Nigeria,[93] and an express provision in the EIA Act requiring the inclusion of the public's input in the motivation of its final decision, would arguably be needed to alert the relevant authorities as to this obligation and contribute in informing better practice in

90 Whilst s 7 makes reference to public comment on EIAs, s 17 makes reference to s 39(1) of the EIA Act, which deals with the final decision of the agency in cases where there has been mediation or a review panel and their report has been submitted to it. See also ss 21(3) and 25.

91 Okon (n 23) 219.

92 *R v Sussex Justices, ex parte McCarthy* [1924] 1 KB 256 at 259.

93 For example see various final EIA approvals for projects by Shell Nigeria, and their EIAs, available at http://www.shell.com.ng/environment-society/environment-impact-assessments.html (last accessed 3 February 2014).

this regard. This improvement is needed considering that alarm has already been raised that 'there is no means for checking that . . . the public comments are considered in the agency's decision.'[94]

In addition, the EIA Act mandates that the decision of the agency 'be in writing' and 'state the reason therefor',[95] and that the same 'be made available to any interested person or group';[96] '[i]f no interested person or group requests for [sic] the report, it shall be the duty of the Agency to publish its decision in a manner by which the members of the public or persons interested in the activity shall be notified.'[97]

Although this provision is partly in compliance with best practice, it should be improved to align with it fully. In view of how that provision of the Act is couched, it seems that if a member of the public happens to be aware that a decision has been reached by the agency and that individual requests and receives a copy of the decision, this will free the agency from the responsibility to publicise the decision to other members of the public or inform them about its accessibility, many of whom would not be aware of the decision. This may negatively affect the public's ability to appeal the decision in view of legal time limits and the possibility of the subject matter being substantially altered. In addition, basing the duty to publicise the decision on the event that 'no interested person or group requests for' it, does suggest that sufficient consideration was not given to the need to inform the public 'promptly' about the decision.

Moreover, in accordance with the principle of good faith and best practice as argued in the preceding chapter, the relevant government agency is expected to include in its written decision, information about the opportunities available to the concerned public to appeal the final decision. This, however, does not appear be the practice in Nigeria, especially as the relevant government agency is not so mandated by the EIA Act. It is vital that such an obligation be included in the Act in order to contribute to informing better practice in this regard, especially when one considers the empirical study, which suggests that public 'ignorance of legal rights' is a major barrier to access to courts in the Nigeria.[98] This vacuum possibly contributes to the low level of litigation relating to compliance with the EIA Act, despite the frequent public complaints about its contravention by government bodies and developers.

7.2.2.6 Periodic public participation

Unfortunately, in Nigeria, there is no provision for, and usually no practice of, subsequent public participation in environmental decision-making that concerns

94 Ako (n 41) 90.
95 Section 9(1).
96 Section 9(2).
97 Section 9(3).
98 JG Frynas, 'Problems of access to courts in Nigeria: results of a survey of legal practitioners' (2001) 10(3) *Social and Legal Studies* 397, 408.

an activity for which permission has been granted. This is contrary to best practice. Although the EIA Act contemplates scenarios where the manner in which a proponent intends to carry out an approved project has 'subsequently changed' or 'where the proponent seeks the renewal of a licence, permit or approval', the decision-making at this subsequent stage is ostensibly left in the hands of the relevant government agency and the EIA Act is silent on public participation in the subsequent decision-making processes.[99]

This is a potentially dangerous gap in the Nigerian EIA Act, and one that might undermine the interest of the potential 'public concerned', as renewed permits and subsequent changes to such a project without public participation could easily be inimical to the environment and public wellbeing, and lead to a costly conflict between the public and project proponents.

Even though in practice final EIA approvals for projects may sometime be made subject to the condition that there 'shall be continuous consultations with the project's host communities throughout the life span of the project' as one of such approvals to Shell Nigeria shows,[100] this is only done in an ad hoc and discretionary manner, with no legal basis and therefore can hardly be enforced by the public. Apart from the fact that there is barely any evidence of the implementation of such a condition, it is doubtful whether the general public is even aware that such a provision is included in the EIA approval in order for them to be able to demand that it should be fulfilled. Therefore, it is recommended here that the element of public participation be clearly included in the EIA Act with respect to subsequent decision-making processes on initially approved projects.

7.3 Public participation in non-activity-specific decisions

As with the counterpart section of the preceding chapter, the analysis in this section will be broken down into two parts: whilst the first will deal with public participation as it concerns plans, programmes and policies (non-binding instruments) related to the environment, the second will consider public participation as it relates to the preparation of executive regulations and other legally binding instruments.

7.3.1 Public participation concerning plans, programmes and policies

Although generally weaker than provisions for public participation in project-specific decision-making, international best practice does make clear that states should put in place measures to ensure public participation in the preparation of plans, programmes and policies relating to the environment, along the lines

99 See ss 20 and 23.
100 Final EIA Approval for Afam Field Development Gas Supply Project (n 93).

of the principles discussed with respect to participation in project specific decision-making.

This aspect of public participation in environmental decision-making relating to plans, programmes and policies, is one in which the Nigerian legal system critically falls short, as there is no formal practical procedure or public right to participate at those levels of environmental decision-making. This is despite the fact that Nigeria's National Policy on the Environment calls for action to be taken to 'ensure public input in the definition of environmental policy objectives'.[101] Even in practice, the public is generally not given the opportunity to participate informally at those levels of decision-making in Nigeria,[102] which levels of environmental decision-making in the country do need (more) public input if their aims (especially towards the latter specific-activity stage) will ever be reasonably realised as research has suggested.[103]

So in view of the strategic importance of SEA as discussed in the preceding chapter, and the need to maximise the benefits of public participation in environmental decision-making in general, it is recommended that a formal SEA procedure that allows for wide public participation in line with best practice, is provided or legislated for in Nigeria.[104] Contemporarily speaking, in view of the fact that formal participatory culture is still finding its feet in Nigeria, it will be best if the SEA procedures were made law as a way of checking abuse of discretion by public authorities that will be foreseeably rampant if the SEA provisions do not have the binding force of law and are not enforceable by the public.

There is, however, the legitimate concern that the potential scale and broadness of the evaluation under SEA, in terms of jurisdictions and activities, will in many cases make targeting 'the public concerned' a very burdensome task, and the public participation process too complex an undertaking.[105] 'The cost in resources and time would probably not make the SEA cost-effective' if attempt is made to involve the full range of stakeholders in the process.[106] However, for now, this concern may be largely minimised by the fact that in reality, empirical research shows that there is generally low public will to participate in SEA procedures or comment on SEA decisions owing to the rather abstract character of plans,

101 Paragraph 6.6(a).

102 See Oshionebo (n 88) 123.

103 See MB Nuhu, 'Public land policy, new trends: challenges in Nigeria's institutional frameworks for state and public sector land management', a paper presented at the International Seminar on State and Public Sector Land Management, held in Verona, Italy, on 9–10 September 2008, 17–19; and AS Gbadegesin and FB Olorunfemi, 'Changing trends in water policy formulation in Nigeria: implications for sustainable water supply provision and management' (2009) 11(4) *Journal of Sustainable Development in Africa* 266, 270 and 283.

104 F Olokesusi, 'Legal and institutional framework of environmental impact assessment in Nigeria: an initial assessment' (1998) 18 *Environmental Impact Assessment Review* 159,172; and Bristol-Alagbariya (n 36) 154, have both made a similar call.

105 M Gauthier, L Simard and J Waaub, 'Public participation in strategic environmental assessment (SEA): critical review and the Quebec (Canada) approach' (2011) 31 *Environmental Impact Assessment Review* 48, 51.

106 H Abaza, R Bisset and B Sadler, *Environmental Impact Assessment and Strategic Impact Assessment: Towards an Integrated Approach* (Geneva: UNEP, 2004) 67–68.

programmes and policies and the fact that these strategic issues do not give rise to immediate concerns (as specific projects do) and have only an indirect impact on the public.[107]

The public is generally more enthusiastic about decision-making processes at the project stage, which will have a direct impact on them, their livelihoods and their properties; and Nigeria-based empirical research reflects this point quite well.[108] However, with more public enlightenment on the value of participating in SEA procedure, and as the practice of SEA becomes popularised over time, it is reasonable to foresee a general improvement in public interest in the process.

Yet, public input is vital in SEA and experience from countries where SEA is practised reveals that the position of the public is usually represented mainly by pressure groups and other representatives at this level of decision-making.[109] Similarly, 'selected "focus groups" of representatives of key stakeholders to provide public input on a continual basis' has also been proposed as way of ensuring a reasonable measure of public scrutiny and input in SEA and ensuring the sustainability and manageability of the process at the same time.[110] These measures for allowing public input in SEA could be adopted in Nigeria should a binding SEA procedure be put in place.

Finally, it is important to note that the success of public participation in a SEA procedure, and of the SEA itself, 'is heavily dependent upon the availability of environmental information that is easily accessible and on a nature and scale that is appropriate to the area being studied'; such will include information on the nature, scale and location of likely future development and those borne out of the ability to predict impacts on that large scale, in terms of time and space.[111]

Unfortunately, most information of this nature and scale does not always exist (especially in developing countries such as Nigeria), and unreliable data and indefinite predictions will likely undermine public support for SEA and the plans, programmes and policies that result from it.[112] So when a formal SEA procedure becomes a reality in Nigeria, this will surely necessitate capacity-building for the staff of the relevant public authorities and, possibly, partnership with other institutions with the required expertise to piece together such information properly, in order to ensure faithful compliance with their obligation under Section 2(1) of the FOI Act to record and keep all information related to their functions. This will consequently help to make public participation in SEA procedures in Nigeria effective, and the procedure itself, successful.

107 See Gauthier and others (n 105) 51–52.
108 See Adomokai and Sheate (n 51) 504.
109 Gauthier and others (n 105) 51.
110 Abaza et al. (n 106) 68.
111 See S Thompson, JR Treweek and DJ Thurking, 'The potential application of strategic environmental assessment (SEA) to the farming of Atlantic salmon (*Salmo salar* L)' (1995) 45 *Journal of Environment Management* 219, 228; and HM Alshuwaikhat, 'Strategic environmental assessment can help solve environmental impact assessment failures in developing countries' (2005) 25 *Environmental Impact Assessment Review* 307, 314.
112 Alshuwaikhat (n 111) 314.

7.3.2 Public participation concerning executive regulations and other legally binding instruments

For the many benefits it carries, Nigeria certainly needs to imbibe this widely recognised practice. Currently in Nigeria, the public has 'little or no opportunity to meaningfully partake in the design or formulation of regulatory law', including those relating to the environment.[113] This is despite the fact that public willingness to participate in law-making in Nigeria appears relatively higher than their interest to engage with the less popular and non-binding plans, policies and programmes. Little wonder why many Nigerian laws relating to the environment have enraged the public over the years, seeing that they did not benefit from adequate public input and so do not reflect, and in most cases, completely run counter to public values and wishes, especially as it relates to the environment.

An example of such an environment-related law that has continued to enrage the Nigerian public is the fundamental 1978 Land Use Act[114] (discussed in Chapter 2), which was promulgated undemocratically under military dictatorship and completely revolutionised land tenure system in Nigeria, vesting all lands in the state.[115] The generally weak character of the EIA Act, especially its public participation element, is, arguably, largely also a result of the dearth of public participation in its formation process, being a product of military dictatorship.

Very little has changed with respect to the level of public participation in (environmental) law-making in current democratic Nigeria, even though one may sometimes hear of a 'public hearing' being held with respect to the formation/revision of certain laws at the federal level, but hardly at the state/local levels of government. Seemingly admitting the dearth of public participation in the (environmental) law-making process in Nigeria and of the need for it, the deputy Senate president of Nigeria at a recent international conference on 'Law Reform and Law-making Process in Nigeria', conceded that:

> If we must get better laws, then we must first endeavour to get the law-making processes right and in tandem with *global best practices*. If we must also get our law-making processes right, then, we must necessarily . . . enrich interface between it [the legislature] and other critical stakeholders such as the . . . *civil society*, etc. . . . It serves the general interest of the polity if inputs are made into laws while they are in the making rather than practically ambushing them in the courts . . . If we must tag our laws as people's laws, it is only reasonable and moral for the process to be a [sic] truly people-driven.[116]

113 Oshionebo (n 88) 123.

114 Cap L5, Laws of the Federation of Nigeria, 2004.

115 See RT Ako, 'Nigeria's Land Use Act: an anti-thesis to environmental justice' (2009) 53(2) *Journal of African Law* 289–304; and KSA Ebeku, 'Oil and the Niger delta people: the injustice of the Land Use Act' (2002) 35(2) *Law and Politics in Africa, Asia and Latin America* 201–31.

116 I Ekweremadu, 'Opening Address', delivered at the International Conference on Law Reform and Law-making Process in Nigeria, held in Abuja, Nigeria, on 16 July 2012, available at http://www.nassnig.org/nass/news.php?id=366 (last accessed 3 February 2015). Emphasis added.

The deputy Senate president further stated that 'public hearing' should be taken as a 'critical law-making process' and not as a 'mere fulfilment of legislative ritual or "righteousness"'.[117] He particularly stressed 'the need to integrate the larger population of Nigerians residing in the rural areas into the law reform and law-making process'. Expressing concerns about the barriers of illiteracy, especially as it relates to the concept of statute law (reform) and the law-making process, as well as the mobility of rural dwellers, many of whom are economically disadvantaged, the deputy Senate president remarked thus: 'unless we find a way of properly integrating our rural populations as active participants in the process of making laws under which they are compelled to live, we would have short-changed the greater majority of Nigerians.'[118]

Being an acceptable one, the executive branch of government in Nigeria should also take heed of the deputy Senate president's views, as some statute laws in Nigeria give the executive arm of government the power to make subsidiary regulations within the ambits of the main statute law;[119] the prescriptions of best practice also covers such regulations. It is, however, hoped that those words by the deputy Senate president will translate into action in the near future at the federal, state and local levels of government, especially in respect of environmental law.

Also, in order to avoid a clumsy implementation of this intention it will be advisable, at least, to lay down a formal procedure that will help guide public participation in law-making processes. Furthermore, the public and NGOs are expected to be proactive in demand for this opportunity, seeing governments hardly create such without a level of sustained pressure from the people.

7.4 Enforcing the right to participate in environmental decision-making

This section mainly relates to public participation in environmental activity-specific decisions that best practice prescribes should be justiciable, as against participation in non-activity-specific decisions that have relatively weaker provisions, and for which Nigeria has no formal procedure. As noted above, access to judicial bodies and adequate remedies are needed to contribute to ensuring that provisions for public participation in environmental decision-making processes are taken seriously, properly implemented and not observed in the breach by the relevant authorities. In fact, a law (such as the EIA Act) that provides for environmental public participation is generally inadequate if it does not sufficiently provide for the justiciability of acts and omissions relating to the observance of its provisions.[120]

117 Ibid.
118 Ibid.
119 For example see EIA Act, s 59.
120 MR Anderson, 'Human rights approach to environmental protection: an overview', in A Boyle and MR Anderson, *Human Rights Approaches to Environmental Protection* (Oxford: Clarendon Press, 1996) 1, 16.

The EIA Act does not clearly provide for or elaborate on the right of aggrieved members of the public concerned to challenge the substantive and procedural legality of any decision, act or omission under the EIA Act judicially. The EIA Act merely provides in section 57 that: '[a]n application for judicial review in connection with any matter under this Act shall be refused where the sole ground for relief established on the application is a defect in form or a technical irregularity.' It would be difficult successfully to justify a complete denial of participation before a court on the basis that it was a technical irregularity or a defect in form.

Arguably, however, that provision largely bars members of the public concerned from subjecting to judicial review acts and omissions that negatively impact on their ability to participate effectively under the Act, or the procedural legality of the Agency's final decision. This is so, given that most of the elements of public participation that make the process effective and meaningful as discussed above (e.g. as it relates to the provision of environmental information and the timing – initiation and pace – of public participation) can easily be classed as 'forms' or 'technicalities',[121] and so any 'defect' or 'irregularity' as to how they are implemented will not be justiciable. This is clearly contrary to best practice and will need to be revised.

In addition, unlike the FOI Act, as the EIA Act does not specify those with the right to file an action under the Act, the issue then falls to the general standing rule in Nigeria. Unfortunately, the general standing rule in this regard is generally very restrictive,[122] as it is based on the controversial 'civil rights' test laid down by Bello JSC, in the case of *Adesanya v President of the Federal Republic of Nigeria*[123] thus: 'standing will only be accorded to a plaintiff who shows that his civil rights and obligations have been or are in danger of being violated or adversely affected by the act complained of.'[124] Those who can pass this 'civil rights' test and go on to file a suit are further narrowed down by extensive case law, which has questionably construed 'civil rights' in that test to mean 'private legal right'.[125]

Even the standing test of 'sufficient interest' in the application for judicial review procedures under the various rules of courts in the country,[126] which should ordinarily be interpreted in a more relaxed, liberal manner, must now meet the more restrictive requirements of the 'civil rights' test.[127] However,

121 The ordinary meaning of 'form'/'technicality' usually relates to procedural matters similar to those under discussion in this chapter. For example see *Black's Law Dictionary* (8th edn, 2004), 'Form'.

122 MT Ladan, 'Judicial approach to environmental litigation in Nigeria', a paper presented at the 4-Day Judicial Training Workshop on Environmental Law in Nigeria, in Abuja, Nigeria, on 5–9 February 2007, 16.

123 (1981) 1 All NLR 1.

124 Ibid, 39.

125 For example see *Attorney-General, Kaduna State v Hassan* (1985) 2 NWLR 483, 508D, 509A–B; *Amodu v Obayomi* (1992) 5 NWLR 503, 512F–513C; *Ejiwunmi v Costain (WA) Plc* (1998) 12 NWLR 149, 164H.

126 For example see Federal High Court (Civil Procedure) Rules, 2009, Ord 34, r 4.

127 TI Ogowewo, 'Wrecking the law: how Article III of the constitution of the United States led to the discovery of a law of standing to sue in Nigeria' (2000) 26 *Brooklyn Journal of International Law* 527.

unsettling the field, a few court decisions have deviated from the norm in favour of broader standing.[128] According to Ogowewo, 'the position now seems to be that the courts proceed on a case-by-case basis, intuitively deciding who should have standing.'[129] However, overall, to a large extent courts continue to follow the 'civil rights' test, which is restrictive and, at best, seemingly confused.[130]

According to Ogowewo, this standing rule has a 'court-closing' effect, and it 'immunizes from judicial review a substantial aspect of the [non-]exercise of governmental power'.[131] The rule's fixation with 'private legal rights' especially, will significantly prevent NGOs and many concerned individuals from seeking review of actions and omissions relating to the EIA Act and laying claim to the participatory opportunity provided thereunder, contrary to the wider rule of standing reflected by best practice.

Instructive here is the popular case of *Oronto Douglas v Shell Petroleum Development Company Nigeria Limited and Ors*,[132] where the plaintiff sued the defendants – the Nigerian federal government, the NNPC and several oil companies – which had together set up the multi-billion dollar Nigerian Liquefied Natural Gas project at Bonny, for non-compliance with the EIA Act. Claiming declaratory and injunctive reliefs, the plaintiff sought to restrain the defendants from commissioning and operating the project which fell under the EIA Act, until an EIA was carried out with active public participation from those to be affected.

The court struck out the case on the ground that the plaintiff had no standing to sue. Belgore CJ held that 'the plaintiff shows no *prima facie* evidence that his [private] right was affected nor any direct injury caused to him' by the non-compliance with the EIA Act.[133] This decision was reached despite the plaintiff's lawyer's argument that Douglas had both a private interest in the suit as a native of a village affected by the project, and a public interest as a well-known environmentalist.

Although the Court of Appeal (CtA) set aside that decision and remitted the case back to the Federal High Court (FHCt) for retrial on the grounds that the FHCt had breached a number of procedural rules, the retrial did not proceed because the project had been completed by the time the CtA delivered its judgment in December 1998.[134] Ogowewo has, however, argued that even if the retrial had taken place, the same result would still have been reached if the plaintiff failed to

128 For example see *Adediran v Interland Transport* (1991) 9 NWLR (pt 214) 155; and *Fawehmmi v Akilu* (1987) 4 NWLR 797.

129 TI Ogowewo, 'The problem of standing to sue in Nigeria' (1995) 39(1) *Journal of African Law* 1, 18.

130 See JG Frynas, *Oil in Nigeria: Conflict and Litigation between Oil Companies and Village Communities* (Hamburg, New Brunswick NJ and London: LIT/Transaction, 2000) 207; and Ladan (n 122).

131 Ogowewo (n 127) 542.

132 Unreported Suit No FHC/L/CS/573/96, 17 February 1997. The Court of Appeal's decision is reported in (1999) 2 NWLR 466.

133 Ibid (unreported judgment), 2.

134 RT Ako, 'The judicial recognition and enforcement of the right to environment: differing perspectives from Nigeria and India' (2010) 3 *NUJS Law Review* 423, 439.

show how his private legal right had been violated and that: '[i]t makes no difference that s. 7 of the [EIA] Act makes provision for public involvement in the decision-making function of the environmental agency, since this does not confer a civil right', at least going by the court's restrictive jurisprudence on the 'civil rights' test.[135]

However, an easy route for ensuring wide access to justice with respect to the issue of public participation in environmental decision-making is to avoid this restrictive and unsettled water of the general standing rule, and create a separate system under the EIA Act, just as the FOI Act does, which specifies those who can bring an action under the Act.

In addition, best practice requires that existing review procedures be fair and equitable, and provide adequate and effective remedies. In the light of the above discussion, one can hardly say that these criteria are being met in Nigeria with respect to public participation in environmental decision-making. Best practice also requires that existing review procedures be timely. Generally, this is another criterion that litigation under the EIA Act will be difficult to meet considering that 'delay in the disposal of cases', as identified by empirical research,[136] has been a major barrier to access to court in Nigeria, mainly as a result of congestion of cases in the courts. It is not uncommon to find a case lasting up to 10 years in court before final judgment is delivered. The provision for a summary procedure similar to that in the FOI Act discussed in Chapter 5 would help to improve the situation under the EIA Act.

Furthermore, such review procedures are not to be prohibitively expensive, according to best practice. Again, supported by empirical research,[137] litigation under the EIA Act may frequently fall short of this criterion considering the usual substantial court and lawyers' fees and the cost of expert witnesses, together with the potential for such cases to drag on in court, all viewed in the light of the relatively high level of poverty in the country. In addition, currently, Nigeria's legal aid scheme does not apply to the provisions of the EIA Act. In this light, in line with the best practice recommendation, it is reasonable for the EIA Act to go beyond its sole 'judicial review' provision, and provide also for the usually simpler, cheaper and faster administrative review procedure, as a way of tackling some of the challenges related with accessing courts in Nigeria, e.g. high costs, excessive delays in disposing of cases and complex court procedures.

Although a new independent and impartial administrative body could be created for the purpose of ensuring adequate enforcement of public participatory rights under the EIA Act, the capacity of the National Human Rights Commission (which is largely independent of government) to undertake the responsibility could certainly be explored and bolstered, if necessary, especially given the human rights nature of the right to participate in environmental decision-making processes.

135 Ogowewo (n 127) 541–43.
136 See Frynas (n 98) 410.
137 See ibid, 406–407, and 433–34.

Apart from the possible civil actions under the EIA Act, section 60 of the Act provides that:

> . . . [a]ny person who fails to comply with the provisions of this Act shall be guilty of an offence under this Act and liable on conviction in the case of an individual to ₦100,000 [£400] fine or to five years' imprisonment and in the case of a firm or corporation to a fine of not less than ₦50,000 [£200] and not more than ₦1,000,000 [£4000].

However, this provision is mainly a 'paper tiger', considering that none of the entities that have breached the EIA Act is known to have been held to account under it. This is because such criminal provisions are only enforceable by or with the permission of the government, which actually lacks the political will to do so against its own agencies and major corporations, particularly when considering the 'overwhelming influence' the latter have over government agencies.[138]

Apart from these, the meagre fines to be imposed for violating the Act, which have not been reviewed upwards in the 20-year history of the Act, is arguably a testament to the government's lack of will in ensuring adequate compliance with the Act and deterring potential defaulters. This further highlights the need for an effective private enforcement system under the Act. Given the above restrictions on public access to court as it relates to the EIA Act, little wonder environmental NGOs and concerned individuals hardly ever commit scarce resources to challenging non-compliance with the Act, especially in relation to the participation opportunities it provides. Therefore, as Ako stated, 'there is yet to emerge a legal decision that posits that public participation is legally enforceable in Nigeria.'[139]

Relevant government agencies and developers are by now aware of the difficulties that members of the public have with enforcing the EIA Act, and thus disregard its provisions when it suits them. In fact, in addition to the exposition made so far, according to an EIA expert who had worked with oil companies in Nigeria for decades: 'EIAs should be done at an early stage when decisions have not been taken and you can look at options. But in Nigeria the EIA is often done after the decisions have been taken. Sometimes the EIA is done after work has already started. I have visited one site where the work was completed before the EIA was done.'[140] However, the difficulties in accessing courts have contributed to the feeling of frustration among the populace, sometimes leading to the employment of extra-judicial means (such as sabotaging of oil installations and kidnapping of oil workers) in order to settle scores.[141] According to Chima Williams, the EIA Act must, amongst others, be brought

138 See Williams (n 66) 14.
139 Ako (n 49) 13.
140 Amnesty International (n 41) 57–58.
141 AA Adedeji and RT Ako, 'Hindrances to effective legal response to the problems of environmental degradation in the Niger delta' (2005) 5(1) *Unizik Law Journal* 415, 434.

up to speed with 'international best practice' so as to ensure the effectiveness of the regime.[142]

7.5 Conclusion

In summary, this analysis and comparison shows that the Nigerian regime on public participation in environmental decision-making processes, especially as it relates to specific projects, achieves some standards reflected by best practice. Nevertheless, the general discussion demonstrates that Nigerian law and practice on the subject critically falls short of best practice and needs to be radically improved in line with best practice, in consideration of the prevailing non-legal realities in the country.

The EIA Act was shown to be largely anachronistic and – given its undemocratic and military background – generally not in tandem with basic democratic norms of transparency, accountability and public participation. It urgently needs to be revised. In addition, the lack of adequate mechanisms for public participation in non-project specific environmental decision-making processes in Nigeria was highlighted, as well as the need for concrete steps to be taken to reverse the situation, considering the importance of public participation at such higher and strategic levels of decision-making.

Bibliography

Abaza H, Bisset R and Sadler B, *Environmental Impact Assessment and Strategic Impact Assessment: Towards an Integrated Approach* (Geneva: UNEP, 2004).

Adedeji AA and Ako RT, 'Hindrances to effective legal response to the problems of environmental degradation in the Niger delta' (2005) 5(1) *Unizik Law Journal* 415.

Adomokai R and Sheate WR, 'Community participation and environmental decision-making in the Niger delta' (2004) 24 *Environmental Impact Assessment Review* 495.

Ako RT, 'Ensuring public participation in environmental impact assessment of development projects in the Niger delta of Nigeria: a veritable tool for sustainable development' (2006) 3(1–2) *Envirotropica* 1.

Ako RT, 'Nigeria's Land Use Act: an anti-thesis to environmental justice' (2009) 53(2) *Journal of African Law* 289.

Ako RT, 'The judicial recognition and enforcement of the right to environment: differing perspectives from Nigeria and India' (2010) 3 *NUJS Law Review* 423.

Ako R, 'Resource exploitation and environmental justice: the Nigerian experience', in Botchway FN (ed), *Natural Resource Investment and Africa's Development* (Cheltenham: Edward Elgar Publishing, 2011) 72.

Alshuwaikhat HM, 'Strategic environmental assessment can help solve environmental impact assessment failures in developing countries' (2005) 25 *Environmental Impact Assessment Review* 307.

Ameyan O, 'Environmental impact assessment: insight into the environmental impact regulatory process and implementation for qualifying projects', a paper presented at the

142 Williams (n 66) 60.

seminar entitled 'Preparing business in Nigeria for environmental challenges and opportunities' organised by the Manufacturing Association of Nigeria, held in Lagos, Nigeria, on 4 November 2008, available at: http://softwaresupermart.com/mangreencourses/papers/paper6b.pdf (last accessed 3 February 2015).

Amnesty International, *Nigeria: Petroleum, Pollution and Poverty in the Niger Delta* (London: Amnesty International Publication, 2009).

Anderson MR, 'Human rights approach to environmental protection: an overview', in Boyle A and Anderson MR, *Human Rights Approaches to Environmental Protection* (Oxford: Clarendon Press, 1996) 1.

André P, Enserink B, Connor D and Croal P, *Public Participation: International Best Practice Principles* (Special Publication Series No 4, North Dakota: International Association for Impact Assessment, 2006).

Bassey N, 'Environmental impacts and the defence of communities', in Obayanju B and Obaseki M (eds), *Defending the Environment: The Role of Environmental Impact Assessment* (Benin City: Environmental Rights Act/Friends of the Earth, Nigeria, 2009) 17.

Black's Law Dictionary (8th edn, 2004).

Bristol-Alagbariya ET, *Participation in Petroleum Development: Towards Sustainable Community Development in Niger Delta* (Dundee: Centre for Energy, Petroleum and Mineral Law and Policy, 2009).

Ebeku KSA, 'Oil and the Niger delta people: the injustice of the Land Use Act' (2002) 35(2) *Law and Politics in Africa, Asia and Latin America* 201–31.

Echefu E and Akpofure E, 'Environmental impact assessment in Nigeria: regulatory background and procedural framework', in McCabe M and Sadler B (eds), *Studies of EIA Practice in Developing Countries: A Supplement to the UNEP Training Resource Manual* (UNEP, 2003) 63.

Ekweremadu I, 'Opening Address', delivered at the International Conference on Law Reform and Law-making Process in Nigeria, held in Abuja, Nigeria, on 16 July 2012, available at http://www.nassnig.org/nass/news.php?id=366 (last accessed 3 February 2015).

Frynas JG, *Oil in Nigeria: Conflict and Litigation between Oil Companies and Village Communities* (Hamburg, New Brunswick, NJ and London: LIT/Transaction, 2000).

Frynas JG, 'Problems of Access to Courts in Nigeria: results of a survey of legal practitioners' (2001) 10(3) *Social and Legal Studies* 397.

Gauthier M, Simard L and Waaub J, 'Public participation in strategic environmental Assessment (SEA): critical review and the Quebec (Canada) Approach' (2011) 31 *Environmental Impact Assessment Review* 48.

Gbadegesin AS and Olorunfemi FB, 'Changing trends in water policy formulation in Nigeria: implications for sustainable water supply provision and management' (2009) 11(4) *Journal of Sustainable Development in Africa* 266.

Hartley N and Wood C, 'Public participation in environmental impact assessment: implementing the Aarhus Convention' (2005) 25 *Environmental Impact Assessment Review* 319.

Hunter D, Salzman J and Zaelke D, *International Environmental Law and Policy* (New York: Foundation Press, 1998).

Ladan MT, 'Judicial Approach to environmental litigation in Nigeria', a paper presented at the 4-Day Judicial Training Workshop on Environmental Law in Nigeria, in Abuja, Nigeria, on 5–9 February 2007.

Lee M and Abbot C, 'The usual suspects? Public participation under the Aarhus Convention' (2003) 66 *Modern Law Review* 80.

Lucas AR, 'Canadian participatory rights in mining and energy resource development: the bridges to empowerment?', in Zillman DN, Lucas AR and Pring G (eds), *Human*

Rights in National Resource Development: Public Participation in the Sustainable Development of Mining and Energy Resource (Oxford: Oxford University Press, 2002) 305.

Nuhu MB, 'Public land policy, new trends: challenges in Nigeria's institutional frameworks for state and public sector land management', a paper presented at the International Seminar on State and Public Sector Land Management, held in Verona, Italy, on 9–10 September 2008.

Nwapi C, 'A legislative proposal for public participation in oil and gas decision-making in Nigeria' (2010) 54(2) *Journal of African Law* 184.

Obayanju B and Obaseki M (eds), *Defending the Environment: The Role of Environmental Impact Assessment* (Benin City: Environmental Rights Act/Friends of the Earth, Nigeria, 2009).

Ogowewo TI, 'The problem of standing to sue in Nigeria' (1995) 39(1) *Journal of African Law* 1.

Ogowewo TI, 'Wrecking the law: how Article III of the constitution of the United States led to the discovery of a law of standing to sue in Nigeria' (2000) 26 *Brooklyn Journal of International Law* 527.

Ojo GU and Oluwafemi A (eds), *Before the Earth Bleeds Again* (Benin City: Environmental Rights Action/Friends of the Earth, Nigeria, 2004).

Okon EE, *'The Legal Framework of Environmental Impact Assessment in Nigeria'* (2001) 5(2) *Modern Practice Journal of Finance and Investment Law* 208.

Olokesusi F, 'Legal and institutional framework of environmental impact assessment in Nigeria: an initial assessment' (1998) 18 *Environmental Impact Assessment Review* 159.

Omokaro O, 'Non-implementation of environmental impact assessment and its impact on the environment and local livelihood', in Obayanju B and Obaseki M (eds), *Defending the Environment: The Role of Environmental Impact Assessment* (Benin City: Environmental Rights Act/Friends of the Earth, Nigeria, 2009) 27.

Omorogbe Y, 'The legal framework for public participation in decision-making on mining and energy development in Nigeria: giving voices to the voiceless', in Zillman DN, Lucas AR and Pring G (eds), *Human Rights in National Resource Development: Public Participation in the Sustainable Development of Mining and Energy Resource* (Oxford: Oxford University Press, 2002) 549.

Oshionebo E, 'Transnational corporations, civil society organisations and social accountability in Nigeria's oil and gas industry' (2007) 15(1) *African Journal of International and Comparative Law* 107.

Petersen OW, 'European environmental human rights and environmental rights: a long time coming?' (2008) 21(1) *Georgetown International Environmental Law Review* 73.

Raustiala K, 'The "participatory revolution" in international environmental law' (1997) 21 *Harvard Environmental Law Review* 537.

Tanner F, 'Conflict prevention and conflict resolution: limits of multilateralism' (2000) 82(839) *International Review of the Red Cross* 541.

Thompson S, Treweek JR and Thurking DJ, 'The potential application of strategic environmental assessment (SEA) to the farming of Atlantic salmon (*Salmo salar L*)' (1995) 45 *Journal of Environment Management* 219.

Williams PC, 'The Environmental Impact Assessment Act and processes as an environmental and livelihood advocacy tool', in Obayanju B and Obaseki M (eds), *Defending the Environment: The Role of Environmental Impact Assessment* (Benin City: Environmental Rights Act, 2009) 7.

Wood CM, *Environmental Impact Assessment: A Comparative Review* (2nd edn, Harlow: Prentice-Hall, 2002).

8 Conclusion

This book proceeded from the standpoint that the drive for effective public participation, as it relates to public access to environmental information and participation in decision-making processes, is rooted in human nature and widespread in human culture; and that Nigerians and Nigeria were not exceptions. Little wonder why, as noted earlier in the book, the concept is an integral part of human rights law from which the environmental perspective discussed in this book generally sprouted and is based on. Given the potential positive influence of public participation in environmental matters on the environment and human wellbeing, numerous international environmental regimes have also sought to require or commit states to guarantee adequately the public right to access environmental information and decision-making processes. As highlighted, Nigeria is bound by or committed to many of these international environmental regimes, and is thus expected to develop laws and practices that ensure adequate public participation in environmental matters.

In addition, apart from this legal motivation, the relevance of public participation to proper and sustainable societal and environmental development in Nigeria as already discussed, are fundamental reasons for Nigeria to ensure that the twin elements of public access to environmental information and decision-making processes are effectively guaranteed in the laws and practices of the country.

Thus far, a valuable contribution of this book to the procedural environmental law field is the transnational comparative methodological approach it employs to assess and recommend improvements to laws and practices relating to public participation in environmental matters in Nigeria. The elaborate justification and use of the norms in the Aarhus Convention, blended with similar norms from other international environmental regimes, to develop a body of international best practice principles that is politically and legally relevant to Nigeria has fulfilled a dual function.

First, it has enabled an informed assessment of whether or not, or to what extent Nigeria's laws and practices are in compliance with its international procedural environmental obligations and commitments, as well as providing a basis for recommending remedial actions where gaps were revealed the better to enable Nigeria to meet those obligations and commitments. Second, in achieving the first, the approach has also helped to identify broadly why the laws and practices on environmental public participation in Nigeria may not be effective or may run into problems, and how such a situation may be addressed.

On the whole, the usefulness of the methodological approach is not limited to the Nigerian context but will arguably be useful for other countries, especially those that share similar international environmental law commitments with Nigeria. More than this, the approach of the book has also demonstrated in broad terms the usefulness of the Aarhus Convention; in this case, not as a binding document to be enforced vis-à-vis the parties to it but, arguably, as an authoritative reflection of a burgeoning set of general or customary rules of international (environmental) law, which can be used as a widely acclaimed and effective interpretative guide in non-treaty contexts.

Furthermore, public access to environmental information is one of the two major elements of environmental public participation dealt with in this book. The discussion basically exposed 'Nigeria's' history of relative openness in pre-colonial traditional governance, its century of official secrecy initiated during its colonisation, and how far the country has come in this regard since its return to democratic rule in 1999 and the enactment of the Nigerian 2011 FOI Act. In this regard, a thorough discussion and comparative analysis of Nigeria's recent FOI Act, together with the general state of its implementation thus far, was undertaken. The analysis found that considerable strides towards achieving standards reflected in international best practice were achieved with the enactment of the FOI Act.

The findings confirm that some core provisions of the FOI Act are essentially sound and in line with best practice; and, in a few instances, they even go beyond it. This has helped to engineer the gradually unfolding practice of ensuring public access to (environmental) information that would never have been released to the public prior to the enactment of the Act. However, the comparative discussion equally uncovers weaknesses and gaps in certain provisions of the Act (and access practices) and reveals that, arguably, the older and more entrenched traditions of official secrecy have partly been maintained via liberal exemption provisions. These findings led to recommendations for the improvement of the Act and its implementation in line with best practice, in order to ensure better public access.

The second major public participation element that forms the other part of the book is public participation in environmental decision-making processes. The analysis of this issue essentially unravelled Nigeria's history of relative participative pre-colonial traditional governance, the transformation to public exclusion from processes of governance for many decades as initiated in the wake of colonialism, and the progress the country has made in this regard since the promulgation of the 1992 EIA Act. However, unlike the case with access to environmental information, the comparative analysis and discussion in this regard has revealed that Nigeria would seem to have made very little progress in the aspect of ensuring public participation in environmental decision-making processes, despite the existence of the EIA Act to that effect for more than two decades now.

The EIA Act, which embodies the provisions on public participation in environmental decision-making on specific activities, was shown to be largely inadequate in achieving the latter. Cconsidering the interrelationship between the two elements of public participation as earlier above, it may be safe to conclude that the general lack of meaningful public participation in environmental decision-making processes, if at all, partly limits the usefulness of the recently acquired public right to access environmental information. This is so considering that members of the public may not be able fully to deploy relevant environmental information that they have accessed to influence some major environmental decision-making processes that affect their lives.

The provisions of the EIA Act, which are largely anachronistic and fall below international best practice, were also argued to have provided the enabling environment for government agencies and developers to exclude the public from environmental decision-making processes on a regular basis. This weakness of the EIA Act and its inability to engender better practices on public participation cannot be separated from its undemocratic and military background. In this light, the EIA Act was generally recommended for urgent comprehensive review in order for the practice of public participation in environmental matters to be enhanced and made effective in Nigeria, and for the country to come into compliance with its international obligations and commitments in this regard.

In addition, further discussion on this theme revealed the lack of an existing formal procedure for public participation in plans, programmes, policies and legislations/binding measures relating to the environment. In this regard, the point was made that, given the importance of public participation at these levels of decision-making which, if missed, could seriously and negatively complicate matters further down the road to development, there is the need for Nigeria to develop formal (binding) measures that would enable the voice of the public to be heard at those levels.

However, drawing on earlier discussions, it is clear that improvements to laws and practices on public access to environmental information and decision-making processes in Nigeria would have to take due account of the socio-political and economic realities of the country, including the issues of illiteracy, poverty, official corruption, language diversity etc. Recognition of these was seen to be crucial to the successful reform and implementation of any law concerning public participation. Also, the point was made that consideration must be given as to how the rapidly growing use of ICT in the country can be engaged to contribute further in enabling effective public participation in environmental matters among the relevant segment of the public.

In fact, to ensure sustainable environmental public participation, whilst taking these non-legal factors into consideration in the meantime, the Nigerian Government must sit up and radically tackle the problems of the elements that are crucial to effective environmental public participation; e.g. if poverty and illiteracy is drastically reduced, the public will be better armed to engage in participation in environmental governance, and if public understanding of the English language is improved, the need to spend resources on translation will be reduced.

In general, the analysis in this book has shown a significant level of government hesitation or weak political will to enforce and give effect to the available laws in the country relating to public access to environmental information and participation in decision-making processes. Obviously, this attitude must change if environmental public participation is to be enhanced in Nigeria and its benefits delivered to society, considering that public institutions are naturally well placed to play a significant role in fostering appropriate implementation and enforcement of environmental procedural rights in the polity.

For example, earlier discussion in this book generally highlighted the strategic responsibilities placed on public entities such as the Nigerian Attorney-General of the Federation and NESREA to implement and ensure compliance with the FOI Act and the EIA Act, respectively, how they have carried out some of their duties and the room for improvement. The discussion in this regard also touched on the key role public institutions can play in ensuring alternative non-judicial enforcement of environmental procedural rights as a way of helping aggrieved members of the public scale the barriers to accessing justice in Nigeria.

The Nigerian Government must engage in self-reorientation, and faithfully commit itself, not just to reworking the country's laws on public participation in environmental matters in line with best practice, but to serious and innovative implementation of their provisions, in a manner befitting the transition from an era of dictatorship to one of democracy. An important starting point for the reflection of this required political will to ensure a thriving system of environmental public participation would be the government's provision of adequate resources to realise the objectives of environmental public participation laws. Finally, the valuable role of consistent public pressure on public institutions to ensure adequate laws on environmental public participation and, importantly, their faithful and innovative implementation, cannot be over emphasised.

Index

For Product Safety Concerns and Information please contact our EU representative GPSR@taylorandfrancis.com Taylor & Francis Verlag GmbH, Kaufingerstraße 24, 80331 München, Germany

Batch number: 10725973

Printed by Printforce, the Netherlands